D1536762

The Delusion of Knowledge Transfer

The Impact of Foreign Aid Experts on Policy-making in South Africa and Tanzania

Susanne Koch &
Peter Weingart

A NOTE ABOUT THE PEER REVIEW PROCESS

This open access publication forms part of the African Minds peer reviewed, academic books list,the broad mission of which is to support the dissemination of African scholarship and to fosteraccess, openness and debate in the pursuit of growing and deepening the African knowledge base. *The Delusion of Knowledge Transfer* was reviewed by two external peers. Copies of the reviews are available from the publisher on request.

First published in 2016 by African Minds
4 Eccleston Place, Somerset West 7130, Cape Town, South Africa
info@africanminds.org.za
www.africanminds.org.za

ISBN: 978-1-928331-39-1
eBook edition: 978-1-928331-40-7
ePub edition: 978-1-928331-41-4

ORDERS:
African Minds
4 Eccleston Place, Somerset West 7130, Cape Town, South Africa
info@africanminds.org.za
www.africanminds.org.za

For orders from outside Africa:
African Books Collective
PO Box 721, Oxford OX1 9EN, UK
orders@africanbookscollective.com

Contents

List of Tables

List of Figures

List of Abbreviations

AfDB	African Development Bank
AIDS	Acquired Immune Deficiency Syndrome
ANC	African National Congress
ART	Antiretroviral Treatment
ARVs	Antiretroviral Drugs
AusAid	Australian Agency for International Development
BMZ	Bundesministerium für Wirtschaftliche Entwicklung und Zusammenarbeit (German Federal Ministry for Economic Cooperation and Development)
BTI	Bertelsmann Transformation Index
CAPE	Cape Action for People and the Environment
CBD	Convention on Biological Diversity
CEPF	Critical Ecosystem Partnership Fund
CFR	Cape Floristic Region
CHAI	Clinton HIV/AIDS Initiative
CIDA	Canadian International Development Agency
CPIA	Country Policy and Institutional Assessment
CSIR	Council for Scientific and Industrial Research
DAC	Development Assistance Committee
DANCED	Danish Cooperation for Environment and Development
Danida	Danish International Development Agency
DBE	Department of Basic Education
DEA	Department of Environmental Affairs
DEAT	Department of Environmental Affairs and Tourism
DEO	District Education Officer
DFID	Department for International Development
DHET	Department of Higher Education and Training
DoH	Department of Health
DPG	Development Partners Group
DPG-E	Development Partners Group on Environment
DPs	Development Partners
ED-DPG	Education Development Partners Group
EDP	Essential Drugs Programme

EMA	Environmental Management Act
EMA-ISP	Environmental Management Act Implementation Support Programme
EMIS	Education Management Information System
ESDC	Education Sector Development Committee
ESDP	Education Sector Development Programme
EU	European Union
GBS	General Budget Support
GEF	Global Environment Facility
GERD	Gross Domestic Expenditure on Research and Development
GFATM	Global Fund for AIDS, Tuberculosis and Malaria
GIZ	Gesellschaft für Internationale Zusammenarbeit (German Agency for International Cooperation)
GMOs	Genetically Modified Organisms
GDP	Gross Domestic Product
GNI	Gross National Income
GNP	Gross National Product
GPE	Global Partnership for Education
GTZ	Gesellschaft für Technische Zusammenarbeit (German Agency for Technical Cooperation)
HAART	Highly Active Antiretroviral Therapy
HCT	HIV Counselling and Testing
HEDP	Higher Education Development Programme
HIV	Human Immunodeficiency Virus
HR	Human Resources
HSRC	Human Sciences Research Council
ICAI	Independent Commission for Aid Impact
ICT	Information and Communication Technology
IDA	International Development Association
IDC	International Development Cooperation
IHI	Ifakara Health Institute
IIAG	Ibrahim Index of African Governance
IK	Indigenous Knowledge
ILFEMP	Institutional and Legal Framework for Environmental Management Project
IMF	International Monetary Fund
IPCC	Intergovernmental Panel on Climate Change
IPD	Institutional Profiles Database
IRA	Institute for Resource Assessment
JAST	Joint Assistance Strategy for Tanzania
JICA	Japan International Cooperation Agency

LEAT	Lawyers' Environmental Action Team
LGA	Local Government Authority
MAC	Ministerial Advisory Committee
MDGs	Millennium Development Goals
MKUKUTA	Mkakati wa Kukuza Uchumi na Kupunguza Umaskini Tanzania (Tanzania National Strategy for Growth and Reduction of Poverty)
MNRT	Ministry of Natural Resources and Tourism
MoEVT	Ministry of Education and Vocational Training
MoH	Ministry of Health
MoHSW	Ministry of Health and Social Welfare
MRC	Medical Research Council
MSDGC	Ministry for Social Development, Gender and Children
MUHAS	Muhimbili University of Health and Allied Sciences
NACOSA	National AIDS Committee of South Africa
NAP	National AIDS Plan
NBSAP	National Biodiversity Strategy and Action Plan
NCTP	National Care and Treatment Plan
NEMA	National Environmental Management Act
NEMC	National Environmental Management Council
NGO	Non-governmental Organisation
NHI	National Health Insurance
NIMR	National Institute for Medical Research
NSP	National Strategic Plan for HIV&AIDS and STIs
ODA	Official Development Assistance
OECD	Organisation for Economic Co-operation and Development
PAF	Performance Assessment Framework
PEDP	Primary Education Development Plan/Programme
PEPFAR	US President's Emergency Plan for AIDS Relief
PES	Payments for Environmental Services
PFM	Participatory Forest Management
PHC	Primary Health Care
PMO-RALG	Prime Minister's Office Regional Administration and Local Government
PMTCT	Prevention of Mother-to-Child Transmission
PRSP	Poverty Reduction Strategy Paper
PRC	People's Republic of China
PS	Permanent Secretary
RDP	Reconstruction and Development Programme
REDD	Reducing Emissions from Deforestation and Forest Degradation

SANAC	South African National AIDS Council
SANBI	South African National Biodiversity Institute
SANParks	South African National Parks
SARRAH	Strengthening South Africa's Revitalised Response to Aids and Health
SETAs	Sector Education and Training Authorities
Sida	Swedish International Development Cooperation Agency
STDs	Sexually Transmitted Diseases
STIs	Sexually Transmitted Infections
SUA	Sokoine University of Agriculture
SUBSTTA	Subsidiary Body on Scientific, Technical and Technological Advice
SWAp	Sector-wide Approach
TA	Technical Assistance
TACAIDS	Tanzania Commission for AIDS
TB	Tuberculosis
TC-SWAp	Technical Committee of the SWAp
TIE	Tanzania Institute of Education
T-MAP	Tanzania Multi-sectoral AIDS Programme
TWG	Technical Working Group
TWNSO	Third World Network of Scientific Organizations
TZ21	Tanzania 21st Century Basic Education Program
UK	United Kingdom
UN	United Nations
UNCCD	United Nations Convention to Combat Desertification
UNDP	United Nations Development Programme
UNEP	United Nations Environment Programme
UNESCO	United Nations Educational, Scientific and Cultural Organization
UNFCCC	United Nations Framework Convention on Climate Change
UNFPA	United Nations Population Fund (formerly United Nations Fund for Population Activities)
UNICEF	United Nations Children's Fund
UPE	Universal Primary Education
US	United States
USAID	United States Agency for International Development
VPO	Vice-President's Office
VPO-DoE	Vice-President's Office-Division of Environment
WB	World Bank
WGI	Worldwide Governance Indicators
WHO	World Health Organization
WWF	World Wildlife Fund

Acknowledgements

This book would have been impossible without the contribution and manifold support of a number of people. First and foremost, we want to thank all individuals in South Africa and Tanzania for their willingness to spend their precious time and to share experiences. It is their openness that facilitated this study. The more time we spent in Tanzania and South Africa the more we came to appreciate the intricacies of the relationship between local administrators, policy-makers and scholars on one side and the 'foreign experts' on the other. We very much hope that they profit somehow from this book.

Furthermore, we want to thank Johann Mouton and CREST at Stellenbosch University for their support and cooperation in establishing contacts, gathering data and carrying out interviews. Our gratitude also extends to the Stellenbosch Institute of Advanced Studies (STIAS) whose foundation first motivated the inception of this project. STIAS also hosted the feedback workshop in Stellenbosch: In October 2013, the preliminary findings of this study were presented to a group of previously interviewed experts, government members and academics. The delegates provided critical comments on the results of the research which were instructive for scrutinising the relevance and strength of arguments.

We also want to thank Oliver Schilling who played an important role in getting this project started in the first place, provided valuable input in its early stages and only had to leave it for personal reasons.

The project 'Scientific Experts in Developing Democracies' was funded by the German Research Foundation DFG (reference number WE 972/30-1).

For conducting interviews in Tanzania, the project team received research clearance from the Tanzania Commission for Science and Technology (COSTECH) (reference number RCA 2012/72).

Susanne Koch and Peter Weingart

PERPETUATING DEPENDENCE: EXPERT ADVICE AS TOOL OF FOREIGN AID

Foreign aid has been subject to critique continuously for quite some time, not least by individuals who have been involved in formulating and executing policies and programmes. William Easterly, a former World Bank economist and now professor at New York University, published a book with the provocative title *The Tyranny of Experts: Economists, Dictators, and the Forgotten Rights of the Poor*. Therein, he condemns aid agencies for maintaining the 'technocratic illusion' that expertise will solve the problems of the developing world; in his view, the advice of technocrats has helped to oppress people rather than to free them from poverty (Easterly 2013). While certainly taking one of the strongest positions, Easterly has not been the first critic of expert advice as a tool of development aid. Doubts about the impact of expert support were broached early on. Already in 1968, an economist at Washington State University published an article 'Why Overseas Technical Assistance is Ineffective' (Loomis 1968). In 1989, Richard Jolly, at that time Assistant Secretary-General of the United Nations, stated that "the vast bulk of technical experts and expertise at present provided by the UN and donor system has outlived their usefulness" (Jolly 1989: 21). A few years later, Edward VK Jaycox, the World Bank's former vice-president for Africa, described the use of expatriate advisors as "a systematic destructive force which is undermining the development of capacity in Africa" (Jaycox 1993).

The aid community has reacted to the persistent critique of one of its main devices by routinely commissioning studies on the impact of technical assistance under which expert advice is commonly subsumed.[1] Though varying in terms

---

1   See, for instance, Forss et al. (1988); Berg (1993); Royal Ministry of Foreign Affairs Norway & Asplan Analyse (1994); Williams et al. (2003); World Bank (2005a); DFID (2006); ECDPM & ACE Europe (2006); Land (2007); JICA (2008); OECD (2008); World Bank Independent Evaluation Group (2008); Morgan (2010).

of focus, scope and methodology, many of these evaluations yielded similar findings; to give just a few examples:

Looking at the 900 man years of assistance we must conclude that the institutional framework that should lead to a transfer of knowledge was non-existent or crippled. (Forss et al. 1988: ii)

Technical cooperation has not produced the national capacity necessary for self-reliance. (Royal Ministry of Foreign Affairs Norway & Asplan Analyse 1994: 9)

A significant proportion of current technical assistance is ineffective (…). (Greenhill 2006: 24)

It is only in a minority of the cases reviewed that a capacity development impact can be identified. (DFID 2006: xiv)

Almost without exception the reports share the same circular structure: the identification of obstacles which impeded 'capacity-building' is followed by recommendations on how to improve the practice of technical assistance in order to increase its 'effectiveness' in future.

We refrain from following this pattern considering the problems of aid to be merely flaws of implementation. Rather, we see them to be fundamental in nature, pertaining to the structural complexities of knowledge transfer to young democracies as such. They concern issues of legitimacy and sovereignty on the recipients' side, interacting with vested interests and domestic political dependencies on the donors' side. Despite all rhetoric of 'partnership', aid relations are subject to intrinsic constraints that thwart the claimed objective of foreign support, namely helping recipients to become self-reliant. Quite the contrary, the persistent interference by outside actors in our view undermines the development of young into strong democracies as it puts governments at risk of losing control over their own policy agendas.

Various scholars in political science, international relations and development studies have demonstrated that donors continue to exert significant influence on policy decisions in recipient states, even though aid 'conditionality' has formally been abandoned in the post-structural adjustment era.[2] The new emphasis on national 'leadership' and 'ownership', many argue, makes things worse since it overplays the agency of beneficiaries, while masking

---

2   See, for instance, Helleiner (2000); Gould & Ojanen (2003); Harrison (2004); Wangwe (2004); Dijkstra (2005); Holtom (2007); Pender (2007); Mkandawire (2010); Ear (2013).

the pervasive involvement of external funders. Focusing particularly on the World Bank's role in Africa, Harrison (2004: 88) has shown how the innovation of mechanisms such as Poverty Reduction Strategy Papers (PRSPs)[3] and Sector-wide Approaches (SWAps)[4] has legitimated "intense and routine donor involvement" in recipient countries' policy space. Dijkstra (2005: 462), analysing the formulation processes of PRSPs in Bolivia, Honduras and Nicaragua, found that these were "written because donors want them to be written", that the elected parliaments were barely involved, and that donor-organised 'dialogue' with civil society served as a 'cosmetic' element rather than being a serious effort to enhance participation. Holtom (2007) and Pender (2007) came to a similar conclusion for the PRSP process in Tanzania. The latter inferred that the new 'partnership' with donors "involves more, not less, domination" (Pender 2007: 117). In one of the most recent and comprehensive publications on contemporary aid and power relations, the authors examined to what extent aid-receiving governments in Africa have been able to retain control over their policy agendas, and why some have been more successful than others (Whitfield 2009b).[5] The economic, political, ideological and institutional conditions of states were deemed decisive in this regard since they heavily influenced governments' strategies for dealing with donors. While Whitfield and other authors investigated aid as a matter of negotiation, we look at it primarily as a problem of (imposed) expert advice which, as will be argued, invariably carries vested interests and perpetuates existing dependencies in donor-recipient relations.

---

3   In 1999, the International Monetary Fund and the World Bank made the formulation of Poverty Reduction Strategy Papers a requirement for multilateral debt relief under the Highly-Indebted Poor Countries (HIPC) initiative and for access to concessional lending. In many aid-receiving countries, PRSPs have replaced earlier national development plans and have become governments' overriding policy frameworks.

4   In international aid circles, the concept of SWAps came up in the late 1990s when the traditional project approach was increasingly criticised for being donor driven and leading to duplication and fragmentation. This should be avoided by adopting a SWAp under which the recipient government takes the lead and owns a sector-wide programme which external partners jointly support. The Inter-Agency Group on Sector-wide Approaches and Development Cooperation, which elaborated the concept, defined a SWAp in the following way: "All significant funding for the sector supports a single sector policy and expenditure programme, under government leadership, adopting common approaches across the sector, and progressing towards relying on government procedures to disburse and account for all funds" (Foster et al. 2000: 1).

5   The research referred to above was carried out under the auspices of the Negotiating Aid project (2005–2007) based at the Global Economic Governance Programme, University of Oxford. The country studies included Botswana, Ethiopia, Ghana, Mali, Mozambique, Rwanda, Tanzania and Zambia. Full findings have been published in Whitfield (2009b); central results are summarised in Whitfield and Fraser (2010).

Aim and structure of the book

This book sets out to reveal the complexities of expert advice in the aid context and to assess its impact on policy-making in young democracies. To do so we carried out empirical research in South Africa and Tanzania, two African countries which over the past decades have received lavish donor support for system reforms in almost all fields of governance.[6] The focus of this study is on the areas of education, health and environment on the grounds that (a) they are high on the development agendas of both countries; (b) they have been priority areas of external engagement; and (c) they rely on different types of expertise and 'evidence' for policy legitimation. By comparing different sectors in two different countries, both of which are comparatively young democracies but have very different economic strengths, we expected to find out (1) what are the complexities of knowledge transfer through foreign experts in general; and (2) what role structural conditions such as the political and administrative systems and economic wealth have in helping the recipients of outside aid in retaining control over their policy agendas.

The book is structured as follows: Chapter 1 presents the theoretical framework. Unlike other studies we consolidate considerations from the theory of democracy and from the sociology of science, providing us with a unique perspective on the problems implied in knowledge transfer from Western to Southern countries. In Chapter 2 we give the reader an introduction to South Africa and Tanzania as sites of investigation; in Chapter 3 we briefly describe our research methodology and in Chapter 4 the actors and their interests in the aid business.

Chapter 5 dwells on the obstructive preconditions of expert advice in development assistance: the linkage between aid and politics, it will be argued, makes advice volatile, conditional and supply-oriented insofar as it becomes driven by shifting fads, legitimation and accountability pressures. Moreover, the chapter will show that structural flaws pertaining to the employment of external experts by donor agencies hamper knowledge transfer and 'mutual' learning. Beyond that, unequal relationships between actors in aid are reinforced through knowledge hierarchies that de-valuate experts in recipient countries, and increase the discursive power of agents working for international organisations.

The various constraints outlined in Chapter 5 explain why expert advice in the context of aid largely fails to achieve its main objective, namely to increase the capacity of recipients to an extent which would make them independent

---

6   For a more detailed justification of South Africa and Tanzania as sites of empirical investigation, see Chapter 3.

from outside assistance. As a result, governments run the risk of ending up in a perpetual cycle of being advised by external experts who potentially (and illegitimately) gain significant influence in the policy space. Under which conditions recipients are able to defend their decision-making autonomy in such a setting will be analysed in Chapters 6 and 7.

Assessing South Africa's and Tanzania's relative strengths with respect to determining their own political agendas, we regard three factors decisive for dealing with external advice: financial resources, administrative capacity and the local knowledge base (i.e. scientific community). As outlined in Chapter 6, there are significant variations not only between the two countries, but also across the different sectors. Six case studies examine to what extent South Africa and Tanzania as recipients of aid have been able to retain their agenda-setting control in the respective areas (Chapter 7). Starting with a brief outline of sectoral challenges, governance structures and donor presence, each case study provides detailed reconstructions of past and present policy processes, with a particular focus on how external experts were involved therein and to what degree they were able to shape decisions. Chapter 7 concludes with a synthesis of findings drawn from the comparative view on the empirical accounts.

Chapter 8 summarises the main results. Instead of concluding with suggestions as to how to make expert advice in development assistance more 'effective', we offer some thoughts on what kind of support might better help young democracies to grow their own knowledge bases and, thus, to become truly independent from external expertise.

Normative assumptions and issues of terminology

Doing research and writing about aid means to enter a highly politicised terrain covered with ideological booby traps concerning terminology. Authors are easily pigeonholed not only on the basis of arguments, but also because of the wording they use.[7] This is why a few remarks concerning the terminology and the scholarly perspective adopted in this book are in place. Our argumentation implies some normative assumptions drawn from political science. In line with Bickerton et al. (2007), we take it to be a core aspect of sovereignty that

---

7   Easterly (2013: 12–13) pointed out the hazard of 'code words' for the perception of development writers by stating: "Mention *markets* and you are presumed to favor a world with zero government. Mention *liberty* too often and you are presumed to be in favor of some extreme right-wing ideology (…). If you mention *colonialism, racism,* or *imperialism* too often (…), you risk being seen as a leftist ideologue."

states govern themselves and define their own policies.[8] A loss of control over the agenda amounts to a loss of democratic legitimacy.[9] Therefore, we see the interference of external actors in the policy space of young democracies as highly problematic, irrespective of the intentions they may have.

As to issues of terminology: we are aware that speaking about 'local' and 'foreign' experts, or referring to 'donors' and 'recipients' implies a generalisation which in a way oversimplifies reality and disregards contextual differences. Post-structuralist scholars would further criticise, commenting that by using such notions we reproduce the hierarchical classifications and unequal power relations which are objects of our study, and would not be satisfied with the defence that this is far from our intention.[10] In fact, we agree with Ziai (2011: 2) that "it makes a fundamental difference whether we describe reality in one way or another". Being conscious about the significance of language, it is also true that language alone does not change political realities. If we deliberately draw on a rather conventional vocabulary in writing about aid, this is because the 'reality' we encountered was and still is characterised by asymmetries and boundaries. Replacing the conceptual pair of 'donors' and 'recipients' with alternative terms (as done, for instance, by Eriksson Baaz (2005) who substituted the latter with 'partners') would mask persisting dependencies instead of helping to reveal them. We also noted that although much wording in the written discourse on aid has changed, the actors affected on either side still resort to the 'old' terminology when giving account of their experiences. This is why we refrain from using alternative constructs which are seemingly more impartial but often remain vague and confusing. We hope to provide the reader with clear language, giving priority to precision over premature political correctness.

---

8   In our view, Brown's distinction between the sovereignty of a country and the control over its political agenda is splitting hairs. He argues that the loss of the latter, although not uncommon, does not entail loss of the former (Brown 2013). We disagree by regarding self-determination a fundamental device of sovereign states.

9   Speaking about public control over the agenda as a fundamental requisite of democracy, Robert Dahl in an interview for the *Annual Review of Political Science* rhetorically asked: "If somebody else is controlling the agenda, what's it all about?" (Dahl & Levi 2009: 5).

10 For reflections on the relevance of discourse for the construction of reality, see Ziai (2011).

Chapter 1

KNOWLEDGE TRANSFER TO YOUNG DEMOCRACIES: ISSUES OF LEGITIMACY, SOVEREIGNTY AND EFFICACY

The role of knowledge in democracy

Since the fathers of the American Constitution it has generally been accepted that knowledge, or rather education in general, is a safeguard for democracy. Education, and thus the acquisition of systematic knowledge, prevents (or is supposed to prevent) citizens from populist or ideological temptations and protects the political process from the irrationalities that come with them. The assumption underlying this model is that the citizens reach decisions and consensus through enlightened deliberation and, in the process, accommodate their respective interests with the factual possibilities (technical and material resources) to realise them. The counter model is the liberal pluralistic one. In this model decisions are reached among citizens whose interests are assumed to be fixed and which can only be accommodated by the search for compromise. These two different notions of democracy, if taken as the endpoints of a continuous spectrum, are to be found in a multitude of combinations.

One dimension of the role of knowledge in democratic regimes concerns the degree of participation of the citizenry in decision-making. Here the spectrum reaches from the 'mere' choice of leadership, which is the rationale of 'representative' parliamentary systems, to 'direct' participation. The federalists distrusted the wisdom of the electorate so much that they introduced an additional tier, the electoral college, that chooses the president and may, in the extreme case, contradict the popular vote. The Swiss democracy allows its citizens to decide 'directly' certain purportedly fundamental issues. At least in the European democracies one may recently observe a somewhat strengthened movement towards more direct participation in reaction to an alienation of the citizenry from the 'professionalised' political class (Crouch 2005). But this movement is met with the well-known and justified warnings of populist decisions implied in direct participation which can only be avoided by having a layer of 'representatives'. Central to these variants – although often implicit – is the role of knowledge, whether in terms of the general level of education and/or as the use of specialised technical advice by policy-makers. Given the quest for rational, informed decision-making, the latter has become a central tool of democratic rulers. The governance, administration and regulation of modern societies have become extremely complex; this has led to the discourse that policy-makers depend on academically trained specialists who provide expertise for the formulation and execution of policies.

What is generally overlooked in such diagnoses is that this increased reliance on specialised (scientific) knowledge on the part of governments, at least insofar as they are democratic regimes, amounts to a shift toward technocracy. The more intense the alleged dependency of governments on scientific knowledge, the more pronounced the conflict between politicians and experts becomes. This conflict reaches deep into the fabric of democratic societies because it emanates from contradicting types of legitimacy: politicians are legitimated by popular vote and are supposed to represent the interests and preferences of their respective voters. Scientific experts are legitimated by their specialised knowledge, which is supposed to provide answers to factual problems. In other words, the logics of politics and science do not coincide; they may diverge and even be contradictory.

All modern states have developed institutional arrangements to regulate the use of knowledge in the political process. These arrangements address, in various ways, the problem of the underlying conflict between governments' dependency on knowledge, that is, its instrumental function, on the one hand, and the potential loss of control over decision-making to technocratic experts, on the other:

> *Both variability and convergence can be seen as an expression of the potential threat that any advice poses to the legitimacy of governments and, likewise, that politicisation poses to the authority of scientists, i.e. the reciprocal interest to control the advisory process and outcome (…). All advisory bodies and their procedural rules are situated somewhere on a continuum whose endpoints are dominated by one or the other: dependence of the advisers and their politicisation on one hand, and independence or autonomy of the advisers and the technocratic shaping of politics on the other.* (Lentsch & Weingart 2011: 10)

The contradiction between expert knowledge and the political formation of opinion and decision-making has particular significance for 'young democracies' whose local science base is comparatively weak and in which, as a consequence, science-based policy advice is predominantly provided by foreign experts in the context of development aid. [11]

The role of knowledge in development aid

Expert advice in the form of 'technical assistance' has been an instrument of foreign aid since its inception in the late 1940s/early 1950s when the attached system of international organisations came into being. In the aftermath of the Second World War, the United Nations was established with the aim "to promote social progress and better standards of life in larger freedom", and, therefore, "to employ international machinery for the promotion of the economic and social advancement of all peoples" (United Nations 1945). The then President of the United States, Harry Truman, in his 1949 inaugural address emphasised the need to participate in that machinery and provide assistance to countries in need as follows:

> *[We] must embark on a bold new program for making the benefits of our scientific advances and industrial progress available for the improvement and growth of underdeveloped areas. More than half the people of the world are living in conditions approaching misery (…). For the first time in history, humanity possesses the knowledge and skill to relieve the suffering of these people.*
>
> *The United States is pre-eminent among nations in the development of industrial and scientific techniques (…). I believe that we should make available to peace-loving peoples the benefits of our store of technical knowledge in order to help them realize their aspirations for a better life. And, in cooperation with other nations, we should foster capital investment in areas needing development.*
>
> *We invite other countries to pool their technological resources in this undertaking. Their contributions will be warmly welcomed. This should be a cooperative*

---

11 We use the term 'young democracies' for countries that experience a process of democratic transformation, irrespective of the year in which they have formally adopted 'democracy' as a form of government. This allows us to also include countries such as Tanzania, which turned from an authoritarian, socialist 'one-party democracy' into a multi-party democracy in 1995 and, since then, has undergone significant reform processes in all fields of governance.

*enterprise in which all nations work together through the United Nations
and its specialized agencies whenever practicable.* (Truman 1949)

The fourth point of Truman's speech is cited in some length here since it points
to essential elements of the discourse that was to shape the first decades of
aid: on the one hand, a division of the world into 'developed' (i.e. prosperous,
scientifically and technologically leading) and 'underdeveloped' (i.e. deficient,
unprogressive) nations facing conditions of misery, whereby the latter were
depicted as unable to end the suffering of their people without the 'knowledge
and skills' of the former; on the other hand, the problem-solution, namely the
transfer of capital, science and technology. On the grounds of this narrative,
so-called 'technical assistance' became a major means of aid, complementing
large investment and infrastructure projects designed and carried out by
Western experts sent to the South to provide a 'tech-fix' to the 'problems' of
supposedly impotent, needy societies.

Although criticism of the technological and epistemic determinism
underlying this practice was raised early on even by influential voices from
within the system, the idea that donors would provide appropriate concepts and
tools to trigger economic growth and development in recipient countries was
upheld over decades (Cherlet 2014). During the 1980s, international financial
institutions started to impose neoliberal policy reforms on borrowing states; the
Washington Consensus of 1989 formally consolidated the hierarchical model
of 'donorship' (Faul 2016: 188) enacted in the era of structural adjustment.

The 1990s paved the way for a discursive turn. In light of the detrimental
effects of structural adjustment programmes on social and economic conditions
in 'beneficiary' countries, the critique of the "top-down, authoritarian
enterprise" (Ziai 2014: 9) of aid articulated in both development and academic
circles could no longer be disregarded. The idea that the North could solve
the problems of the South by exporting its expertise and technology seemed
increasingly obsolete. The 'knowledge for development' agenda emerging in
parallel to the upcoming partnership paradigm emphasised the need "to assess
and adapt relevant policy and technical knowledge to local situations" (World
Bank 1999c: 7), and to incorporate local knowledge into transformational
processes. The new narrative highlighted "that local conditions matter for the
success of programs, that people on the ground have the most knowledge
of local conditions, and that the challenge of knowledge for development is
to combine local knowledge with the wealth of experience from around the
world" (World Bank 1999c: 14).

The framing of aid relations and the role of knowledge therein has changed
significantly over the past decades. The dichotomic rhetoric of the 20th
century (developed versus underdeveloped, donors versus recipients) has

been replaced by a rhetoric of equality which pertains to decisional power and expertise alike. Hence, seminal documents such as the Busan Partnership Agreement endorsed in 2011 no longer speak of 'technical assistance' and knowledge transfer, but knowledge 'exchange' and 'mutual learning' (Fourth High Level Forum on Aid Effectiveness 2011). The 2030 Agenda for Sustainable Development adopted by world leaders in 2015 outlines a vision of 'partners' who aim to 'share knowledge, expertise, technology and financial resources' in a 'spirit of strengthened global solidarity, focused in particular on the needs of the poorest and most vulnerable and with the participation of all countries, all stakeholders and all people' (United Nations 2015).

The discursive shifts, however, have not (yet) substantially changed international cooperation – neither in terms of power relations nor with regard to the use of expertise. As Ziai (2014: 12) points out, aid agencies remain based on the assumption of "knowledge on social change which is universal in character and therefore applicable all over the world". Consequently, 'international' experts continue to play a key part in the aid business, as administrators, policy advisors or 'technical assistants'. While it is somehow assumed that they impart their knowledge and skills to local actors by their mere presence (see also Chapter 5), the reality of knowledge transfer, exchange, absorption and adaption is much more complicated than the World Bank's optimistic (or cynical?) declaration that "knowledge is like light" and "can easily travel the world" suggests (World Bank 1999c: 1). In this book, we examine expert advice as an instrument of foreign aid. By doing so, the arrangements of advisory processes at the science–politics interface best serve as the model because only they reveal the complexities of the transfer of knowledge. Before we dwell on these complexities, we briefly discuss what kind of knowledge is at stake in the discourse on 'development'.

Differentiating 'knowledges'

When in 1999 the World Bank issued its World Development Report and likewise UNESCO its 'Declaration on science and the use of scientific knowledge', both organisations addressed the inequality of knowledge between nations (UNESCO 1999; World Bank 1999c). The reference was primarily to scientific knowledge, even though the World Bank distinguished between scientific and technical knowledge, on the one hand, and knowledge about attributes, for example, the quality of goods, on the other. The assumption underlying these declarations is that scientific knowledge is a, if not the, crucial factor responsible for development identified with economic well-being (Weingart 2006: 164). This assumption, whether true or not, is in line with the rhetoric of the 'knowledge society' that has informed the science and innovation policies of Western countries, but has also been adopted by, for example, South Africa. One is tempted to conclude from the respective declarations that since the end of the last millennium the policies and programmes of donor countries toward 'developing' countries in general, and Africa in particular, would focus on (a) strengthening scientific knowledge production in these countries in order to attack the development problem at its roots instead of tampering with symptoms and (b) strengthening local knowledges and promoting constructive co-production of knowledge. Yet, the dominant approach used by aid agencies has been and continues to be to send advisors and consultants supposed to transfer and share their 'expert knowledge' with counterparts in recipient governments.

Just as the framing of aid relations has changed over the last decades so has the understanding of knowledge as part of it. The 'knowledge for development' agenda brought the differentiation between Western scientific and local knowledge to the fore. This distinction among many other possible ones is most pertinent to the issues of 'development' and 'knowledge transfer'.

The very term 'knowledge' is so vague as to allow many interpretations and associations of meanings and interests. If, as is here the case, the focus is on the relation between the North and the South, on development and aid, knowledge refers to Western scientific and technical knowledge, part of which – as alluded to in the World Bank statement – is economic and management knowledge. Given the global predominance of this type of knowledge, it is also associated with the supremacy of the West over the developing countries. At the same time, it is seen to be superior to the 'local' knowledge that is to be found in the 'developing countries', not least because by definition science is global and purportedly not specific to and dependent on particular cultural contexts (Agrawal 1995). But 'local knowledge' is an equally vague concept that has become associated with romantic idealisations and misguided expectations, although it has also given rise to concrete policies.[12] This crude picture has been replaced and refined in the course of the shift to the rhetoric of 'equality'. In particular, common assumptions about certain properties of scientific knowledge have been called into question, such as its epistemic superiority (power of prediction, certitude), its independence of (cultural) contexts and universal validity and, thus, its applicability. Parallel to this, 'local' knowledge has been invested with expectations regarding 'development' that most likely overstretch its actual potential (Agrawal 1995). Rather than following the various arguments invariably coloured by political and ideological convictions

---

12 Antweiler (1998: Table 1) gives a list of terms and connotations for 'local knowledge', pointing to it being both instrumentalised and romanticised.

reflecting allegiances to the respective development paradigm, the discussion here has to be limited to answer just a few questions:

- What kind of knowledge is at stake in aid relations?
- What kind of knowledge (scientific/global and/or local) is available; what is lacking in the countries concerned?
- What kind of knowledge can be/is being provided from 'outside' and under which circumstances?

Not all fields of knowledge, let alone scientific knowledge, are relevant in 'development'. Hornidge (2012: 25), in a review, lists five related discourses that pertain to knowledge: (a) the construction of 'information' and 'knowledge societies'; (b) the development agenda of international donor organisations, summarised under 'knowledge for development'; (c) bridging of 'the global digital divide' summarised under 'ICTs for development'; (d) current trends of 'innovations' and 'innovation systems'; and (e) the adaptive capacities of 'knowledge' for the living with change processes, ranging from climatic and environmental changes to socio-economic and political transformation processes. The delineation of these discourses is fuzzy and does not lead one to concrete fields of knowledge. In fact, they also reflect fads in development, such as the shift from engineering knowledge to soft social science issues such as 'good governance' as a precondition of development. The more concrete reference of the World Bank to 'knowledge about technology' and 'knowledge about attributes' (i.e. quality of goods and services), points to types of knowledge which clearly reside in Western knowledge systems. The same can be said about the "narrowing down of the former 'knowledge for development' to 'ICTs for development', a process possibly also nurturing the interests of the ICT industries of mainly developed countries, and thus supporting an 'expert knowledge'-focused approach in development cooperation" (Hornidge 2012: 33). The discourse on innovation and national innovation systems (NIS) represents another example of broadening the scope of the development agenda to institutional and social issues. The notion of NIS was taken up, for example, by South Africa which has formulated a national innovation systems policy, thereby following an international fad. However, the very term is controversial in academic discussions not least because it is trendy rather than providing political orientation. This is documented by the OECD's assessment that the "relatively strong" system under the apartheid regime has been re-shaped into "another strong" system since 1994, implying that SA had an NIS without it being called as such, thus documenting the vacuousness of the term itself (OECD 2007:10). Finally, the issue of processes of change, for example climate change mitigation and adaptation, points to the most concrete conflict between types of knowledge, since the climate models are developed by a high-tech instrument-intensive Western science, while in the 'developing' countries people rely mostly on local observations and long-term experience.

Much if not most of the knowledge negotiated in these discourses, assuming that they represent the foci of 'development strategies' over the last two or three decades, is organisational, management and economics oriented, and it is mostly Western based. The 'knowledge deficits' on the part of the recipient countries accrue in part from the 'development agendas' of the donor countries and from the international development paradigms. Knowledge on governance, finance and management, as well as quality management as it is either implied in or explicit in the World Bank's and other donor countries' development agendas, is very much a domain of Western business schools and political science departments at universities. It is also the kind of knowledge that is typically communicated by 'experts' from the West. The asymmetry with respect to knowledge is, in part, also determined by the knowledge base that exists in both donor and recipient countries. Some donor countries have selected aid programmes for which they have particular expertise, such as the Scandinavian countries' programme on forestry in Tanzania. For these they can draw on their own scientific resources. But their 'experts' meet with local people who have in-depth knowledge about and experience with their natural environment. In the case of South Africa, its science base with respect to bio-diversity and the protection of the specific flora of that country is so strong that administrators can take the attitude of equal partnership or even conditional acceptance of outside expert advice, as they are able to rely on renowned academics at the country's own universities.

In the examples given it is not clear which part of 'local knowledge' is also part of Western scientific knowledge, and which is 'local' in the sense of it being locally restricted and context-bound. The assumption that Western scientific knowledge and 'local knowledge' necessarily clash because they are epistemically incompatible is simplistic and mostly unjustified. There are many ways in which Western scientific and local knowledges can and factually do interact, ranging from dominance all the way to innovative adaptation and mixing (cf. Antweiler 1998: 482, Table 6). The problem of any transfer of knowledge resides in the degree to which the 'external' knowledge is abstract with respect to the 'local' issue to be solved and the knowledge held by 'local' recipients of 'external' advice. Simple standardised technical solutions to problems such as installing water pumps are much more easily transferred to a community with little technical knowledge than complex designs of, for example, an effective and just taxation system. The underlying economic and social knowledge for the latter is abstract, fraught with uncertainties and requires substantial input of 'local' knowledge about the socio-economic situation of the population, political loyalties among the citizenry, and pertinent provisions of the legal system etc., to be applicable and useful. In view of this, the very term 'knowledge transfer' suggests the superiority of the 'external' Western type of knowledge and disdain for the 'local' knowledges in question; this has consequently drawn a lot of criticism, resulting in the development discourse becoming more sensitive and egalitarian. The 'transfer' of supposedly universal and value-free knowledge is a highly complex matter in its own right. The knowledge in question, such as about financial and project management, regulation of markets, rules of 'good governance' and the like is far from certain. It is subject to fads such as 'new public management' and it comes with cultural contextualities. Even seemingly 'objective knowledge', for example the evidence of the HIV/Aids link, has been contested for political reasons. The attitude on the part of the donor organisations and of the experts they commission can make all the difference, and often enough corroborates the criticism, for example, if highly paid foreign experts are commissioned to advise local governments on a short-term basis with little or no time nor concern for the applicability of their knowledge to the local context. This is exacerbated by the fact that these experts appear to develop their own professional identity and pursue their own interests as an 'epistemic community', most notably the diffusion of concepts deemed valid by themselves and the agencies on behalf of which they operate (cf. below).

Thus, the paradigmatic shift towards an egalitarian approach in development, to equal partnership and to a recognition of local knowledge all point to a more sophisticated understanding of the communication of knowledge which would create conditions that allow for a process of co-creation of knowledge that is both scientifically sound and up to date, as well as adequately adapted to local circumstances. To what extent that ideal is realised is the object of this study.

Risks of aid-related expert advice for young democracies

The major threat to young democracies is that they lose control over setting their own political agenda. Obviously, the ability of a citizenry to elect their representatives into political office where they can design policies that reflect the electorate's wishes and interests and reach compromises with their opponents is the core element of any democratic system. It is the principle of self-determination. This principle is undermined if decision-making primarily follows the objectives of external agents instead of being responsive to those of the country's population. Young democracies are particularly vulnerable to this threat posed by donors in the form of aid programmes and expert advice because of their internal instability: their governments' legitimacy with their electorates is often tenuous, their institutions are still fragile, and their scientific communities (i.e. their knowledge bases) are usually comparatively small, isolated and underfunded, which makes the respective countries dependent on knowledge from outside. There is an obvious asymmetry between donor and recipient countries insofar as the latter do not match the Western democracies, be it in terms of institutional stability, sophistication of administrative infrastructure and staff, juridical and governance systems, higher education and research systems in terms of volume, level of education, research output and absorptive capacity. This is regardless of the vast differences between countries within Africa (see Chapter 6).

The consequence of such asymmetry is that governments of countries that are recipients or addressees of aid programmes respectively come under influence from outside to varying degrees. This may impede their ability to determine their own political agendas and thereby run the risk of losing legitimacy with their own citizenry. This risk has become an object of a broad debate especially between observers of international aid policy and analysts from the aid community itself.

Therefore, it is worth taking a closer look first at the nature of legitimacy as being threatened, then at those conditions that appear to be crucial for recipient control over political agenda-setting: financial strength, the quality of public administration, especially with respect to its ability to critically absorb knowledge provided by external experts (absorptive capacity), and the strength of the 'local' knowledge base.

Legitimacy

The acceptance of a political system by its citizenry and, thus, its legitimacy, depends on both the institutional arrangements on the input side and the actual effectiveness of governmental institutions, most obvious in the provision of socio-economic benefits, but also in the rule of law, on the output side. The concept of 'legitimacy' in theories of democracy has several meanings. A common distinction is that between 'input legitimacy' and 'output legitimacy' (Scharpf 2005). This suggests that legitimacy is constituted not only by the institutions which allow for the participation of the electorate, such as political parties, interest groups, NGOs and the media in framing political decisions, but also the institutions that guarantee the quality of the decisions and their implementation. The combination of 'input' and 'output' legitimacy is particularly pertinent for this study as it points to the various factors shaping the relationship between recipient and donor governments, and allows an assessment of the impact of knowledge transfer 'from outside'.

In young democracies, the most immediate threat to legitimacy from external experts, it can be hypothesised, will most likely come from a displacement of accountability of governments. This amounts to the open or implicit denial of 'voice' (i.e. participation) in shaping and making decisions, in particular about the political agenda. This is underscored by the exemplary and frequently quoted statement from President Paul Kagame of Rwanda:

> *To realize our development vision, we in Africa must substitute external conditionality – that is, what the donors tell us to do – with internal policy clarity – that is, knowing ourselves what we need to do and articulating this clearly and consistently to our people and our development partners (…). This requires that, among other things, we need to learn to 'say no' to donors whenever their priorities do not align with domestic objectives and agenda.* (Kagame 2007: 5)

In order to capture the potential threat to the legitimacy of recipient governments posed by donor engagement it has been suggested to look at the "aid negotiation process as including the full policy cycle: agenda-setting, policy formulation, implementation, evaluation, and revision" with special emphasis "on the agenda-setting and policy formulation stages because these stages involve the strongest forms of recipient government control over its national development strategy and policies" (Whitfield & Fraser 2009: 39–40). By assuming this analytical perspective, both partners in the negotiation process come into view and are taken seriously as having their own interests and strategies in this process. More than that, it points to the particular conditions under which each party enters the process, such as governments' dependence on aid.

When looking at young democracies and their particular sensitivity to knowledge transfer from outside the crucial point is that both donors and recipients are subject to legitimacy issues. Donors depend on public opinion 'back home', on the criteria and conditions of giving aid that are formulated by their parliaments, on the paradigms of the aid policy that may change with each new government. Likewise the recipient governments depend on the public consent of their respective citizenry to the various aid projects which add up to their aid policy. This dual orientation to each one's source of legitimacy makes the negotiation between the two parties very sensitive. Mkandawire also points to this dual accountability when he writes:

> *The more accountable a donor is to its own voters, the more onerous and invasive will be its intervention in the receiving economy and the more likely it is to undermine the recipient democratic government's accountability to its own voters.* (Mkandawire 2010: 1168)

In particular, it makes aid programmes that in many, if not most cases require time to show the desired effects, subject to frequent and sudden changes, thus putting an additional burden on governments' credibility with the public.

Financial strength

A fundamental condition of political sovereignty, it would appear, is financial independence. As Pender (2007: 112) writes, it is

> *the idea of material capacity to act which blurs the lines between sovereignty and economics. Power always depends on material strength, and sovereignty has always implied some degree of autonomy from, and control over, economic processes.*

Governments that have enough financial means to run their own affairs do not depend on financial aid from outside and consequently do not have to accept advice that potentially interferes with their own agenda-setting. This is so self-evident that it hardly needs to be discussed. The reverse argument is that governments in need of foreign funding have a weaker position in negotiating with donors over political objectives and priorities. In the extreme case the price they pay for securing aid is a loss of policy-making autonomy which threatens their legitimacy if decision-making becomes more responsive to external demands than to public preferences.

Yet, there are some considerations that suggest a more differentiated view on the effect of finances. Findings from recent studies indicate that there is no direct correlation between aid dependency, as measured in terms of foreign funding as a share of national budgets or gross national income, and the extent of external influence. Whitfield (2009a), for instance, has shown that countries such as Ethiopia and Rwanda show high degrees of control over their policy agendas in spite of being highly dependent on aid, as they are able to derive negotiating capital from favourable political and ideological conditions, amongst others.[13] This challenges the assumption that countries which suffer from lack of funds must accept donor interference. It also indicates that 'lack of funds' is a relative figure that has to be seen in reference to the economic

---

13 According to Whitfield (2009a: 333–341), the favourable political and ideological conditions in Ethiopia and Rwanda include their geostrategic importance for the West, the existence of clear development visions and a strong confidence of the governments in their authority relative to donors which they derive from their respective country histories. Ethiopia, for instance, had never been colonised as most other sub-Saharan states, and thus shows a strong sense of its own equality with donor countries; Rwanda is able to use the legacy of the genocide to de-legitimise external interference in domestic affairs.

18

power of the recipient country, but also to its political ambitions and objective needs. The onslaught of the HIV/Aids epidemic, for example, has imposed financial burdens on various African countries that were unanticipated and have threatened their economic well-being to different degrees.

It is more instructive therefore to look at the ratio outside funds constitute as a percentage of budgets available for certain policy fields. Then financial dependency becomes more concrete: political agenda-setting usually applies to sectors represented by line ministries. It is on that level that the range of political options is narrowed by advice from outside. Here interference with policy agendas is most direct and damaging to a government's authority and legitimacy.

Administrative capacity

Modern democracies rely heavily on efficient administration for both the preparation and implementation of political decisions taken by their legislatures. The administration of health care or education systems and the regulation of the labour market, to take just these examples, depend on systematic and reliable knowledge. The quality of bureaucracies has a strong influence on the quality of governments, their policies and their decision-making. With a constantly growing share of public administration being knowledge-based, bureaucracies have to have well-educated professional staffs which also connect them with their respective academic communities and allow them to gain some independence from the various lobby groups around them trying to gain influence over their actions. Control of the political agenda is thus an issue if bureaucracies are being confronted with expert advice they are not able to absorb properly, for lack of capable personnel or because – in the worst case – they are inefficient and corrupt. Then they are less likely to be competent parties in negotiations with donors than if they have a high level of professionalisation and well-trained staff. The perception that 'their' administrations are fit to deal with donors in a way that safeguards the local interests and guarantees performance that benefits their society will also gain a higher degree of trust from their constituency. Thus, the quality of bureaucracies in terms of their knowledge-related *absorptive capacity* is a crucial factor determining their 'strength' or 'weakness', respectively, and an important element of a government's output legitimacy. The significance of absorptive capacity, thus, lies in its function to enable governments of developing countries to retain the control over their own political agendas, and as this control is closely related to legitimacy in (new) democracies it is a very important political resource.

The precondition for strengthening the absorptive capacity and, thus, for gaining independence from and control over foreign experts lies obviously in an education system that provides the respective governments with well-educated manpower. Although most African states now have elaborate education programmes and policies in place, their actual implementation 'on the ground' is a recurrent topic of complaint.[14] Many lack the means and the competence to set up functioning education systems, although the quality varies greatly among them. Perhaps with the exception of South Africa, the education systems of many African states are not well developed and consequently the 'absorptive capacity' of these countries is comparatively low. As a result they are severely constrained in receiving the donors' experts with their own critical assessment of the information they are being given, and in doing their part of translating the expertise into their respective political, cultural and social contexts.

Local knowledge base

To a considerable extent the absorptive capacity of a country is also determined by the relative strength of its own science system. Although scientific knowledge is supposedly international and the scientific community is a global network of communication, the differences between countries, the North and the South in particular, are considerable. Compared to the leading 'scientific nations' such as the United States, the United Kingdom, Germany, France and since recently China, many African countries do not have the means to support a science system that can sustain internationally competitive research. Strictly speaking it is not necessary for a country to compete at the frontiers of research – and practically none can afford to do this in every field. But in order to tap that knowledge which is freely available and to adapt it to local conditions, a country needs a scientific community (and the requisite institutions) that is able to 'absorb' this knowledge. It is only then that knowledge can be converted to 'expertise' (i.e. knowledge) that is to be applied to solve practical problems. Only then will a roster of local experts be created, recruited from the national scientific community.

The difference between 'local' and 'foreign' expertise is an issue because the international community of experts has its own identity, its own culture, its own ideology and its own interests. The configurations of this community have been assigned different concepts over the last decades, from 'strategic groups' (Evers et al. 1988) to '(globalised) epistemic communities' (Haas 1992; Evers

---

14   See, for instance, Kisting (2012); Ayo (2013); Ndlovu (2013).

et al. 2009). These conceptualisations reflect to an extent the theoretical (and ideological) positions of their authors. But they also mirror the experience and the evidence gathered in numerous studies about the activities of foreign experts, their impact and their failures. The main point is that these groups or networks or communities of experts, even if they come from different disciplines and act on behalf of different governments or donor agencies, share a common set of qualities that Haas has characterised as being

> *(1) a shared set of normative and principled beliefs, which provide a value-based rationale for the social action of community members; (2) shared causal beliefs, which are derived from their analysis of practices leading or contributing to a central set of problems in their domain and which then serve as the basis for elucidating the multiple linkages between possible policy actions and desired outcomes; (3) shared notions of validity – that is, intersubjective, internally defined criteria for weighing and validating knowledge in the domain of their expertise; and (4) a common policy enterprise – that is, a set of common practices associated with a set of problems to which their professional competence is directed, presumably out of the conviction that human welfare will be enhanced as a consequence.* (Haas 1992: 3)

As vague as the delineation of these 'communities' is, the analytical significance of the concept is the thesis that they represent certain views which they successfully transfer into politics. The mechanism of influence, as Haas sees it, is such that members of these communities may identify interests for decision-makers or illuminate dimensions of an issue

> *from which the decision makers may then deduce their interests. The decision makers in one state may, in turn, influence the interests and behaviour of other states, thereby increasing the likelihood of convergent state behaviour and international policy coordination, informed by the causal beliefs and policy preferences of the epistemic community.* (Haas 1992: 4)

In other words, although on the surface one is made to believe that knowledge, scientific knowledge in particular, is universal and therefore neutral towards parochial interests and cultural contexts that assumption is naïve. The distinction between 'local' and 'foreign' expertise does make a difference.

Given the endemic weakness of the education and science systems of African countries, their governments are at the mercy of the international donor community – again with considerable differences between countries.

The realisation that this dependence is threatening their national and cultural identities, beyond posing a danger to their democratic institutions where they exist, has led to the appeal to 'indigenous knowledge'. The United Nations declared the period 1995–2004 as the 'International Decade of the World's Indigenous People' which was extended, as the second decade, to 2015. South Africa's National Research Fund established the interface of indigenous knowledge (IK) and Western science as a research focus. This emphasis on IK is clearly motivated by a quest for cultural and national identity; it implies a paradigm shift insofar as it places knowledge at the centre of development strategies, and recognises the importance of 'local' knowledge and participation (see Weingart 2006: 184).[15] Some authors have propagated IK as an alternative to Western science. That is the most concrete suggestion but it is also the least realistic option because it would isolate the countries that would follow this course from the global community, apart from the fact that the knowledge base would be far too small to allow full scale sustainable development. However, as Girvan (2007: 40) points out, the more realistic option to obtain a degree of independence is not to take the road into intellectual isolation but to set up local and regional knowledge centres in order to strengthen the respective science bases.

The real importance of 'local expertise' rests elsewhere. Experts who have been socialised and educated in the respective country at stake are representatives of the 'local' culture and the values that are being shared by its citizens, they speak the language. They have first-hand knowledge of the country's problems and needs and how to meet them. Educated both in the respective country and often also abroad as many of the local academic elite are, they are able to absorb knowledge (i.e. function as critical interpreters who scrutinise expertise with regard to its relevance, as well as underlying paradigms and implicit interests). All these qualities allow them to be equal partners in the negotiation of projects with 'foreign experts'. Finally, belonging to the recipient country's expert community is a crucial condition for having credibility with local policy-makers and the public at large because it is assumed that primary allegiance is to the own country.

'Capacity-building' and foreign experts

In response to the perceived weakness of the local knowledge bases in developing countries the concept of 'capacity-building' has been used to

---

15 In Tanzania, the significance of indigenous knowledge was already highlighted by the country's first post-colonial leader Julius K Nyerere in his 'education for self-reliance' policy (Nyerere 1967); for details, see Chapter 7.

circumscribe a prime objective of aid programmes. In fact, the notion of 'capacity-building' goes back to the end of the 1960s when it had become apparent that the transfer of knowledge embodied in technology required, apart from an economic infrastructure, an education base. Already then it had become clear that the copying of knowledge alone was not sufficient but that an 'absorptive capacity' had to be built, meaning an indigenous base of knowledge production. The UN Economic and Social Council stated already in its 1969 'World Plan':

> *It is difficult for a developing country without a science and technology capacity of its own, and particularly without the trained people involved, to know what useful technology exists elsewhere, to understand it, to select it, to adapt, to absorb, to repair and maintain, to operate.* (United Nations Economic and Social Council 1971: 102)

It thus considered it "a fundamental necessity to build up indigenous scientific capability in the developing countries" (United Nations Economic and Social Council 1971: 102).

If the problem of absorption is addressed here with reference to the transfer of technology, it has become even more acute as aid programmes have since shifted to more abstract issues: governance in general, administration and accounting procedures in particular, therefore involving not only natural science knowledge but also economic, social and political science knowledge. 'Capacity-building' as it is being used by the World Bank, for example, includes increasing the "effectiveness of the states in designing and managing public policies and programs; in implementing regulatory frameworks; in delivering public services; and in promoting accountability and transparency in economic, financial and administrative governance" (World Bank 2010a).[16] Thus, the term itself has become inflated and rather than addressing the issue of creating specifically a capacity for absorbing *knowledge* refers more generally to improving governance and financial management capabilities.

This is related to the kinds of experts who are engaged from 'outside'. Knack and Rahman (2007: 194) state that donors should be careful not to disturb the market for skilled labour by bringing in expensive expatriates (usually because they are well trained abroad) because not only may this "prevent valuable learning-by-doing on the part of local staff" but also "those same benefits could be obtained, without the negative consequences, from using the funds to increase salaries of underpaid civil servants, or through general

---

16 This is taken from a World Bank project information document related to its African Capacity Building Foundation (ACBF) Regional Capacity Building Project (Project ID P122478) running from 2011 to 2017.

budget support". The provision of advice as the dominant form of knowledge transfer is a process whose success hinges on mutual trust between advisor and his/her counterpart and on the ability of the latter to receive the advice with the competence to assess its value in the context of his/her problems and to apply and develop it further. Where these conditions are not met advice is inevitably the imposition of the advisor's interests and values on the recipient. The extensive use of experts from developed countries rests on the donors' perception that the administrations in developing countries are not meeting their standards. Their interest in obtaining visible results as fast as possible thus pushes them to rely on 'external' experts rather than to improve the competence of local ones. The legitimacy pressures on the donors override the need for legitimacy on the recipients' side.

The political intricacies of 'knowledge transfer'

As will be shown later in detail (see Chapter 5), donor organisations rarely have precise concepts about how to communicate knowledge in advisory processes, about the nature of the knowledge to be communicated (i.e. whether it is based on evidence or more loosely on experience), about what it entails on the recipients' side to actually absorb the knowledge offered and to build on it locally in a sustained fashion. Aid programmes are almost without exception targeted to operational problems such as the improvement of healthcare or the introduction of advanced accounting practices etc., but they do not reflect on the conditions of the transfer process itself. Providing aid is an activity that is ruled by criteria such as time constraints, efficiency and efficacy, it is oriented to achieving set objectives. In addition, the 'experts' that are being sent by the donor organisations or represent them act on their own and/or their organisation's behalf (see Chapter 4). Reflecting on the conditions of knowledge transfer is not one of their concerns, and even if it were, the realities of organisations prove to be dominating. In his analysis of knowledge management among the experts within the German GTZ (now GIZ) Hüsken (2006: 246) states that the "collection, evaluation and the exchange of knowledge between headquarter, country bureaus and projects is unsystematic, and it is subject to conflicts of interests and power" (translated by authors). Note that this does not even refer to the advisory process executed by GTZ experts to their counterparts in developing countries.

In addition, the aid programmes of the international donor community are subject to changing paradigms of aid:

> *Over the past three decades, Western aid policies towards Africa have been dominated by, in roughly chronological and cumulative sequence, economic conditionalities around structural adjustment programmes; political conditionalities around respect for human rights and governance; and 'partnership' policies involving intensive and extensive redesigning of policy formation and budgetary processes in recipient countries.* (Brown 2013: 263)

Several authors have argued that these programmes amount to "intrusions by outside agencies" (Plank 1993: 408). But regardless of whether analysts and critics believe that the actual control of nations over agenda-setting and outcomes may be threatened or if they regard modern aid programmes as a continuation of colonialism there can be little doubt that development experts as representatives of aid organisations and government officials of recipient countries enter a relationship which is characterised by potentially conflicting interests and inequality of control and discretionary powers. Even if the rhetoric of 'conditionality' has been abandoned, donors can and factually do determine which conditions the recipient has to meet in order to obtain aid. The power differential and, thus, the vulnerability of the young democracies' agenda-setting control remains and – contrary to the World Bank's assessment – is even more difficult to escape when the chief currency of aid is knowledge. Their legitimacy may be threatened even if that is no one's intention.

Chapter 2

ACCESSING THE WORLD OF DEVELOPMENT AID: STUDY DESIGN AND FIELDWORK

Questioning the 'knowledge is like light' assumption which prevails in international donor circles, this study set out to explain the intricacies of expert advice in the aid context by developing a generalised description of underlying mechanisms and conditions. Such an enterprise has to meet two requirements: first, the availability of "rich descriptions of empirical phenomena" that can be analysed, and second, a variance in data which "can be obtained by comparative case studies" (Gläser & Laudel 2013). The qualitative empirical study is based on 73 semi-structured expert interviews conducted in South Africa and Tanzania during four field trips in the years 2011, 2012 and 2013. A standardised background questionnaire distributed to informants and a comprehensive body of documents produced by government authorities and aid agencies were used to complement and contextualise the interview material.

As sociologists of knowledge have shown, results gained through academic research are always products of constructive processes rather than a detection of facts (Schütz 1953; Knorr-Cetina 1981; Knorr-Cetina 1984). In the following, we delineate the creative aspects of our empirical work and unfold experiences made 'in the field' which inevitably affected the interpretation of findings.

Tools of data generation: Expert interviews, questionnaires and document analysis

Since this study aimed to explore the impact of expert advice on policy processes in developing democracies, the focus of research was not on the technical content of policies as such, but rather on the processes through which they were developed. In order to reconstruct the latter, we approached the decisive actors involved therein, using expert interviews as the main method of investigation.[17]

What constitutes an individual as an 'expert' in the expert interview as a method of qualitative research is his or her exclusive knowledge on the researcher's object (Littig 2008).[18] It is particularly his or her knowledge and interpretation of the social situation – the process and interpretative dimension of expert knowledge – that is relevant for reconstructing social objects the researcher is not able to observe directly.[19] Applying this concept to this study, the 'expert status' has been ascribed to those who play a major role in policy-making in South Africa and Tanzania, and, given their direct participation therein, possess exclusive knowledge on how and to what extent decisions are influenced by external advice.

Suitable protagonists in this regard were found in government bodies, donor agencies, and partly in academia and civil society. The variety of their roles and functions required a flexible use of the interview guidelines that were designed to ensure comparability by focusing the interviews on specific major topics. We used the guidelines more as a memo than as a pre-fixed list of questions. A rather open interview approach was instructive insofar as it provided room for interviewees to "report cases of decision-making for reconstructing the supra-individual, field-specific patterns of expert knowledge" (Meuser & Nagel 2009: 31). Such reports and narratives about specific episodes, conflicts and problem solutions in the experts' professional activities are considered key points of reference for tapping "the tacit aspects of expert knowledge, which

---

17 A policy analysis based on documents might have had the potential to trace external influences to some extent, for example, by scrutinising national policy documents for their references to global conventions or normative guidelines of the international community. This approach, however, would have fallen short of revealing how external influences come into play, by whom they are enforced, and how they are dealt with. One could argue that participant observation would have allowed a more direct insight into negotiation processes between the different actors in the realm of policy-making. However, here this method would neither have been feasible nor would it have been the most appropriate one. Apart from the difficulty in getting direct access to policy negotiations and advisory situations as a researcher, the long-term character of policy processes would have been a major obstacle, given the time-frame of the study. It would also not have been possible to directly observe processes in three sectors and two countries, which would have meant that we lacked the variance of data required for comparison.

18 Littig (2008) provides an analysis of commonalities and differences regarding the discussion of expert and elite interviews in the German and English literature. The term 'expert' in this context is used as a relational concept decoupled from the professional roles or formal occupational status of interviewees (Meuser & Nagel 2009).

19 Bogner and Menz (2009) deconstruct expert knowledge into three dimensions: technical, process and interpretative knowledge. The first is closely related to the specialised knowledge the expert has accumulated in a particular technical area through formal qualification and training. Process knowledge, in contrast, is mainly gained through experience and relates to "sequences of actions, interaction routines, organizational constellations, and past or current events" (Bogner & Menz 2009: 52) in which the expert was involved through his/her practical activity. Interpretative knowledge as a third dimension includes "the expert's subjective orientations, rules, points of view and interpretations" (Bogner & Menz 2009: 52).

she or he is not fully aware of and which, on the contrary, become noticed only gradually in the course of the narration" (Meuser & Nagel 2009: 32). Narrative interview passages became particularly useful when interviewees seemed to provide more of an official answer rather than actual experience, hesitant to directly criticise prevailing practices or unwilling to disclose their expert knowledge for other reasons. Letting interviewees report about concrete cases often brought forward implicit patterns of social action and interpretations that were not explicitly formulated. It also helped to avoid socially desirable responses.[20] The perception of the interviewers' roles, competencies and assumed intentions may impact on the interviewee's way of responding.[21] For example, our nationality as Germans led a few interviewees to emphasise their 'good experiences' with German development cooperation. Hence, we explicitly informed the interviewees about the academic background of our research interests. Providing preliminary assumptions and hypotheses was particularly instructive to obtain experts' reactions and interpretations that pointed to underlying patterns and principles of acting in advisory situations.

In assessing "the meaning and significance" of interview statements, it is crucial to take into account the "institutional-organizational context within which the expert's position is embedded" (Meuser & Nagel 2009: 35). The standardised questionnaire was one tool which helped to define the different contexts of interviewees in the sample. It covered a maximum of 30 questions on the personal and professional background, the cooperation with partners, and the access to and management of knowledge. The questionnaire was distributed online prior to meeting the interviewees; however, the majority of them completed it after the interview was done, either online or using the paper version. Overall, we received a response rate of 82%.[22] It is important to emphasise, however, that the questionnaire was not designed to gain data which claim statistical significance. Instead, it has been used to describe our sample and to illustrate patterns with regard to qualifications, experiences and routine practices of the participants' professional activity. The data generated by the survey thus complement the qualitative findings taken from the interview material.

In order to contextualise the latter, an extensive corpus of documents related to relevant advisory and policy processes was gathered. The collection included a variety of text types such as project and programme reports disclosed by international organisations, job descriptions, evaluation studies, sector reviews, policy documents and official government publications. Juxtaposing

---

20 For a typology of interaction situations and interview strategies, see Bogner and Menz (2009).

21 See Meuser & Nagel 2009: 57.

22 60 out of 73 interviewees approached fully completed the questionnaire.

the interview statements with 'natural' text generated in the field of the interviewees' professional activity not only helped to embed narrations in a broader 'story', but also to compare, confirm or contrast representations of processes the interviewees were part of. Contradictions that emerge through this approach are not treated as irregularities or distortions of the findings; instead, they reveal different patterns of legitimation and thereby crucial aspects of the research objective.

The sample: Development experts, government officials, academics and activists

As outlined above, the aim of the expert interview is to access the exclusive knowledge of experts in order to be able to reconstruct social situations and processes in which they participated (Gläser & Laudel 2010). Thus, the main criteria for selecting potential interviewees in our study was their engagement in one of three policy areas we were interested in, namely health, education and environment.

In order to identify relevant actors on the donor side, we contacted country offices, embassies and 'development partner' secretariats in South Africa and Tanzania, and screened documents such as minutes of policy meetings, joint sector reviews, progress and evaluation reports of major projects and programmes which usually list participants or responsible staff. While the names of the current health specialist or an education advisor in a particular donor agency were found relatively easily (in some cases by mere online search), it was far more complicated to identify their 'counterparts' in government authorities (i.e. the Tanzanian or South African officials they interact with). Gaining contact details of policy-makers and technical staff from abroad proved challenging for a number of reasons. Compared to donor websites, the online presence of ministries and departments is often rudimentary and not up to date regarding office holders, phone numbers or email addresses. This appeared to be connected with a high staff turn-over in these organisations. Calling operators did not always help either. Lastly, being less familiar with formal organisational structures and informal power relations, it was difficult for us in the beginning to figure out the pivotal people within the bureaucracies who do have a say in policy decisions.

In this regard, recommendations of a few key actors with years of experience on government or donor side were extremely useful and often functioned as a door opener for arranging meetings with high-level role-players. To give just one example: a German health expert who had spent around eight years in Tanzania allowed us to refer to him when contacting his former partners. Doing so evoked a surprising turn-around of reaction in many cases. After hearing his name, Tanzanian officials, who were first hesitant to meet, now warm-heartedly invited us to visit them, sending best wishes to their 'colleague' and 'friend' – one even responded: "People in Tanzania will never forget what he has done for our country. You are most welcome!" This anecdote points to the great importance of personal relationships in the realm of development cooperation which we not only experienced during the research, but which also came up as a major issue in the interviews. The fact that we arrived at a point where we were given congruent recommendations of whom to meet from different people (referring us to the ones who had suggested them) hints at a marked feature of governance particularly in Tanzania, namely that policy-making power is held by a rather small group of protagonists.

During the second rounds of interviews in South Africa and Tanzania, we came to a point where we felt to have reached 'saturation' in the sense that interviews did not reveal new aspects or perspectives on the topic, but reconfirmed prior statements and legitimation patterns. Altogether, we conducted 73 interviews which took place in Dar es Salaam, Pretoria, Johannesburg and Berlin. The sample consists of a fairly heterogeneous group of interviewees who can broadly be grouped into three categories:

- *Experts working for bi- and multilateral organisations.* Experts working for bi- and multilateral organisations are deployed in the field in various different positions (see Chapter 4); hence the titles of our interviewees were manifold: amongst others, we spoke to senior (technical) advisors, programme managers, first secretaries, counsellors, team leaders, sector specialists, professional officers, attachés, and consultants. The variety of functions and relevance of positions result from the fact that donor and recipient countries organise the management of aid in very different ways.[23] The majority of interviewees from this group ranked themselves as being a senior staff member or at medium level in the hierarchy of their organisation.[24] One third of them had between 21 and 30 years of experience in development cooperation; roughly 50% between 11 and 20 years; and a smaller number less than ten years.[25]

---

23 For details on aid management structures in South Africa and Tanzania, see Chapter 3. For an overview of different organisational types on the donor side, see Chapter 4.

24 The allocation of questionnaire answers related to the level of seniority in detail: head of organisation/mission: 3.7%; high-ranking manager (e.g. vice-president, vice-chairperson, director): 3.7%; senior member of staff (e.g. head of department, team leader): 59.3%; medium level of seniority (e.g. attaché, advisor, project manager): 29.6%; other: 3.7% (= 100%).

25 The allocation of questionnaire answers related to the work experience of external experts in detail: 1–5 years: 7.4%; 6–10 years: 7.4%; 11–20 years: 51.9%; 21–30 years: 33.3%; 31 and more years: 0% (= 100%).

While 18 interviewees in this group were foreigners coming from Europe or North America, nine were 'local internationals' (i.e. Tanzanians and South Africans working for an international organisation). As many of them had prior experience in working for their governments and thus were knowledgeable of the problems and pressures on both the recipient and donor side, they had particularly interesting perspectives on the topic.

- *Government officials in recipient authorities.* The second critical group of interviewees in our sample is made up of those who constitute the main target group for external policy advice: the cadre of senior government officials who are the designated 'counterparts' of aid experts. Entering national ministries, departments and other government bodies, we spoke to permanent secretaries, deputy director-generals, heads of government agencies, and directors and programme officers who regularly interact with donor staff. Asked for the number of years of experience in development cooperation, answers ranged from two to 30 years. Among those with decades of experience, some were already retired from government service. Their statements based on years of dealing with donors were particularly fruitful for gaining a long-term perspective on developments both in the respective sector and the aid community. Having a more distant view on day-to-day politics, the senior interviewees provided valuable reflections on changing relationships, paradigm shifts and the overall impact of external advice on sector policies over time. While retired interviewees were able to speak frankly about conflicts and failures, government officials still in service seemed more cautious in their assessments, although we guaranteed anonymity with regard to the use of the material. Yet, we felt that most of them were quite honest in speaking about current policy processes and the involvement of external actors therein, with some being outspoken in their criticism and others communicating their messages between the lines.
- *Academics and civil society activists.* Academics and leading civil society activists make up the smallest group of interviewees in our study. Including them in the sample was instructive insofar as their experience of being or not being consulted by governments or donors was an important aspect of our research. Their assessment of who pulls the strings in policy-making complemented the picture painted by external experts and government officials with a third perspective. Moreover, they provided useful comments on preliminary hypotheses, argumentation lines and impressions that came up during the field trips.

31

On average, the interviews took around one hour. While some appointments were arranged in hotel lobbies or other venues suggested by interviewees, we usually met them at their workplace. It is worth making a side note on the experience these visits provided; in Tanzania, we got the impression that the status difference between donors and recipients is in the truest sense of the word cemented in the buildings of government authorities, country offices and embassies.

A note on interview locations

Scheduling meetings with aid experts in Dar es Salaam turned out to be relatively easy in the sense that except for the compound of the United States Embassy, a high security fort in the northern district, most foreign embassies and country offices of international organisations are located within a radius of three square kilometres in the city centre. Due to sophisticated registration and security check procedures, entering these buildings often took longer than expected. Once inside, we found ourselves in shining, air-conditioned entrance halls or foyers. After a fluent English-speaking (usually Tanzanian) receptionist had informed the interview partner about our arrival, we were picked up and guided to an office properly equipped with modern furniture and ICT, as it is standard in Western countries.

The contrast between the setting we found in donor edifices and the conditions in government buildings was striking. The facilities available for officials in ministries and departments are not comparable to the ones of foreigners working in the country in terms of both their outside appearance and the interior. Piles of paper stored on ledges and handwritten notes loosely stacked on desks were a common picture in Tanzanian offices, which often lacked not only technological equipment, but also basic office supplies such as shelves and files. The fact that it seemed easier to arrange appointments with government officials by phone (using private mobile numbers) than by email was not surprising, given the fragile power supply and network infrastructure at their workplace.

In South Africa, the contrast between donor and government buildings was certainly less extreme, but still apparent. With this anecdotal description of the field we encountered, we want to point out that local and foreign actors in the aid context obviously operate in two quite different worlds. Meeting our interviewees in their respective professional environments reinforced the impression of a rather unequal setting for cooperation between 'partners'.

Steps of analysis: Coding, interpretation and data consolidation

The findings of this study were produced through an iterative process of data collection and analysis.[26] After each phase of fieldwork, the respective interviews were transcribed and subjected to an inductive process of coding (i.e. indexing themes in the text in order to structure the material).[27] Deriving the codes from the empirical data, the coding system was constantly refined until a set of categories was developed that represented a first step of empirical generalisation. The information base constructed through the process helped us to selectively retrieve the text in search for patterns and causal explanations which were finally integrated into "a systematic, theoretically embedded explanation" (Gläser & Laudel 2013). Compiling the findings, we supplemented them with additional material taken from the collection of documents and the results of the questionnaire where suitable.

---

26   This is suggested by the grounded theory approach (Glaser & Strauss 1967).
27   For coding the interview material, we used the software Maxqda Version 11.

Chapter 3

SOUTH AFRICA AND TANZANIA: TWO DIFFERENT TYPES OF 'DONOR DARLINGS'

South Africa and Tanzania were selected as cases for a number of reasons. Both countries represent young African democracies which for the past 20 years have been undergoing profound transformation processes affecting basically all fields of governance.[28] The policy reforms carried out in this context have to significant extents been supported by the international community which, aside from money, has supplied expertise in the form of policy advice and technical assistance. The comparison between South Africa and Tanzania is of particular interest because both countries vary considerably in terms of general conditions and have adopted very different ways of dealing with and positioning themselves towards donors. In order to understand current aid relationships, it is instructive to take a look at the setting in which these have emerged. In this chapter, we thus briefly glance at the significance of aid for South Africa and Tanzania, and sketch out their history as recipients of official development assistance. This will elucidate why, despite all differentials, both have at times been 'donor darlings' in a distinct sense.

The significance of aid for South Africa and Tanzania

Comparing the significance of aid for national finances, the discrepancy between the two countries under investigation is striking: while in South Africa, aid amounts to less than 1% of the budget, it accounts for around

---

28 We call South Africa and Tanzania 'young democracies' on the grounds that they formally introduced this form of governance only about 20 years ago. South Africa's first non-racial election which marked the end of the apartheid regime took place in 1994 (see, for instance, Johnson & Schlemmer 1996); Tanzania held its first multi-party general elections which officially terminated the era of the single-party hegemony under the socialist leader Nyerere in 1995 (see Van Cranenburgh 1996).

40% in Tanzania (Economic and Social Research Foundation 2010; WYG International Limited 2011). To give an idea of the dimension of aid volumes, we provide some absolute numbers: in 2012, Tanzania received USD 2 832 million net official development assistance (ODA) (equivalent to USD 59 per capita), of which USD 205 million were used for technical cooperation; South Africa's volume of ODA comprised USD 1 066 million (equivalent to USD 20 per capita), including 179 million for technical cooperation (World Bank 2016b).[29]

As illustrated by Figure 1, aid flows to Tanzania in the period 1992–2012 were not only constantly higher than in South Africa, but also more erratic. In a low-income country for which aid is a pivotal element of the budget, such fluctuations have a noticeable impact on the government's scope of action.

Figure 1: Aid flows to Tanzania and South Africa 1992–2012

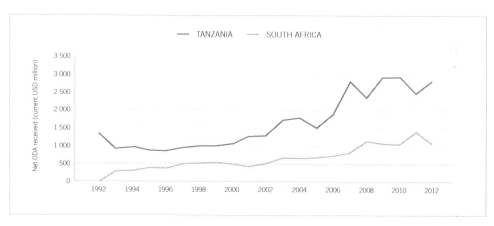

Source: World Development Indicators (World Bank 2016b).

For South Africa as a relatively resource-rich middle-income country, in contrast, ODA is not essential in financial terms, although some line departments and provincial authorities consider it an important source of additional income.[30] Instead, as will be shown later, its value lies in its leveraging effect as a tool of foreign policy, and particularly in the knowledge capital which comes with aid.

---

29 The data are taken from the World Development Indicators database of the World Bank which provides the following definition: "Net official development assistance (ODA) consists of disbursements of loans made on concessional terms (net of repayments of principal) and grants by official agencies of the members of the Development Assistance Committee (DAC), by multilateral institutions, and by non-DAC countries to promote economic development and welfare in countries and territories in the DAC list of ODA recipients. It includes loans with a grant element of at least 25 percent (calculated at a rate of discount of 10 percent). Data are in current U.S. dollars" (World Bank 2016b).

30 This point will further be elucidated in Chapter 6 and, in particular the case studies in that chapter.

Evolving aid relations in Tanzania

Tanzania has been receiving aid since its independence in 1961. The country's first post-colonial leader, Julius K Nyerere, successfully promoted his vision of African socialism based on the principles of self-reliance and familyhood (*'Ujamaa'*), and established close relations particularly with the Scandinavian states, Canada, West Germany and even the World Bank whose 'growth with equity' policy was concordant with Tanzania's economic strategy (Wangwe 2004). From the outset, donors provided not only loans and grants for investment projects, but also supplied technical assistance in order to "fill vacant posts until Tanzanians had been trained to take over" (Economic and Social Research Foundation 2010: 51).[31]

While the enormous amounts of aid flowing into the country during the 1960s and 1970s helped the government to realise key elements of its policies especially in social sectors (e.g. free primary education), it became more and more dependent on this source of foreign finance. From 1964 to 1980, the share of aid in central government expenditures rose from about 22% to 46% (Tanzania budget figures and World Development Indicators, as cited in Radetzki 1973: 172 and Bigsten & Danielson 2001: 25, respectively). The risk the reliance on aid implied became evident when the economic crisis emerging in the mid-1970s got many Northern countries to reduce their funding volumes and induced a change in the climate of giving. Hitherto, Tanzania's supporters had pretty much refrained from interfering in policy decisions; now, donor countries led by conservative, market-oriented governments, most notably the US, the UK and West Germany, started to push for the adoption of extensive neo-liberal reforms as recommended by the Bretton Woods institutions (Wangwe 2004). After years of resistance by Nyerere, the Tanzanian government under the new President Ali Hassan Mwinyi in 1986 eventually bowed to pressure and accepted the Economic Recovery Programme prescribed by the International Monetary Fund (IMF) and the World Bank. This step and the following structural adjustment of macroeconomic and social policies leveraged immense resource flows from the aid community. Tanzanian leaders, however, soon realised that they had lost their policy autonomy to external actors which now directed decision-making.

Relations deteriorated when donors in the early 1990s became increasingly upset about deficient counterpart commitment and irregularities regarding the use of funds (Wangwe 2004). The tense situation escalated when in 1994

---

31 During the 1960s, the Tanzanian government interestingly carried out the procurement process of technical assistants itself via international advertisement and a recruitment office in the UK; with increasing aid volumes, donors started to bring in experts from abroad according to their own regulations (Economic and Social Research Foundation 2010).

a massive scandal of financial mismanagement involving the minister of finance became public and led to an aid freeze (Harrison & Mulley 2009). To overcome this crisis, Denmark commissioned an independent group of local and international experts to assess the crisis in aid relations and to propose strategies to restore mutual confidence. The review which became known as the 'Helleiner Report' (named after the team's chairman, the Canadian Professor Gerald Helleiner) faulted the weak guidance exercised by the government, but also sharply criticised the high degree of donor interference which had eroded local 'ownership' (Helleiner et al. 1995).

Based on the report's recommendations, the Tanzanian government and donors formulated a set of 'agreed notes' which sketched out fundamentals of future cooperation (Government of Tanzania 2002). Emphasising country leadership, transparency, mutual accountability and efficiency in aid delivery, it pre-empted the principles of the Paris Declaration endorsed at the High Level Forum on Aid Effectiveness in 2005 and taken up in the Joint Assistance Strategy for Tanzania (JAST) of 2006 (OECD 2005; United Republic of Tanzania 2006b).[32] The national policy framework for aid management embraced the upcoming rhetoric of 'development partnership', provided for the establishment of joint policy dialogue and promoted general budget support (GBS) as the government's preferred channel of support. For the international donor community, Tanzania became a role model of its partnership paradigm, and "a forerunner in and major laboratory for experimentation with new modalities" (Gould & Ojanen 2003: 41).

While the new forms of cooperation aimed at restoring the government's leading role in the policy space, they at the same time institutionalised donor engagement therein. The terms for general budget support and basket funding agreed upon included regular interaction between high-level officials and aid experts through working groups and coordination forums at various levels. Donors were now expected to participate in policy discussions and advise the government on issues related to the implementation of Tanzania's National Strategy for Growth and Reduction of Poverty (popularly known as MKUKUTA), as well as on sectoral reforms. Instead of 'micro-managing' projects, they should provide their views in a coherent manner through the 'Development Partners Group' which had been formed to increase collaboration

---

32 The principles include: strengthening national ownership, aligning external support to government priorities and systems, harmonising government and donor processes, focusing on measurable results and ensuring mutual accountability of government and development partners (United Republic of Tanzania 2006a).

and thereby "to improve effectiveness and quality of development assistance" (Development Partners Group Tanzania 2010b: 2).[33]

Since the new arrangements have been put in place, the international community presents Tanzania as "as a prime example of 'ownership'" (Harrison & Mulley 2009: 283). Critical scholars, however, early on raised doubts about the validity of this claim (see, for instance, Gould & Ojanen 2005; Pender 2007; Harrison & Mulley 2009). In 2010, an evaluation conducted by the Independent Monitoring Group, which since 1994 has regularly assessed aid relations in Tanzania, found "signs of slippage in ownership" (Joint Assistance Strategy for Tanzania Working Group & Independent Monitoring Group 2010: 8) and come to the conclusion that trust, confidence and the quality of dialogue between the government and 'development partners' has considerably decreased. After years in which Tanzania served as the "poster child of the new partnership model of aid" (Harrison & Mulley 2009: 271), it seems as if relations have changed again.

Evolving aid relations in South Africa

As mentioned at the beginning of this chapter, South Africa – in contrast to Tanzania and many other African states – has never been dependent on external finances; given its relatively solid state budget and comparatively strong administration, it has always been a somewhat "paradoxical recipient" of official development assistance (WYG International Limited 2011: 6). Nonetheless, aid has played "a rather special role" (WYG International Limited 2011: 9) in the country's recent history, especially during the years of democratic transition.

Foreign aid already began to flow into South Africa in the 1980s when donors from all over the world backed the anti-apartheid movement in its fight against the ruling regime. While the National Party government was diplomatically isolated by the international community, civil society organisations received a considerable amount of assistance in the form of funding, but also in the form of scholarships and programmes set up to provide the oppressed population with opportunities of education and intellectual exchange. Major institutions which thereby served as conduits for channelling aid included the South

---

33   The Development Partners Group was formally established in 2004; as of 2014, it comprised 17 bilateral and 5 multilateral (UN counted as one) aid agencies engaged in Tanzania (Development Partners Group Tanzania 2014c). Members commit themselves to respect the agreed division of labour and "to represent a common DPG position once agreed (unless inability to be part of the consensus was made clear at the time of decision) (…)" (Development Partners Group Tanzania 2010b: 2).

African Council of Churches, the Kagiso Trust, and the United Democratic Front; the state, in contrast, was mostly bypassed (Bratton & Landsberg 2000).

However, in the early 1990s when there were clear signs of commitment to political change, funding streams began to shift. Following the first post-apartheid elections in 1994 (for which donors, amongst others, sponsored an independent commission and electoral observers), the new Government of National Unity led by the charismatic President Mandela became the major recipient of ODA. The international community rewarded South Africa generously for its peaceful transition, pledging more than USD 6 billion for the first five-year period of democracy (Bratton & Landsberg 2000). The willingness to give financial and technical assistance to a middle-income country which did not qualify for aid at all can be explained in terms of the strategic interests on the donor side. Not only were they eager to associate themselves with the new-born 'rainbow nation' and its unique success story of abolishing a system of racial oppression by means of negotiation, they also saw their chance to shape the fabric of the young democracy which promised to become the political and economic powerhouse on the African continent.

The new South African leaders, however, encountered the aid community with a strong sense of preserving agenda-setting autonomy. From the outset, they made it plain that donors were expected to support the priorities of the national Reconstruction and Development Programme (RDP).[34] Many of those who had newly moved into government departments were "well aware that elsewhere in Africa and the developing world, the policy conditionality of aid had proved extremely controversial", and were thus "anxious to ensure that the policy development process remained firmly in South African hands" (King 1999: 262). Hence, while external assistance was principally welcomed, not all offers were accepted. Concessional loans were widely rejected since the government took "the view that it does not need to give up its freedom, and mortgage its future to embrace potentially debilitating debt dressed up as development aid" (Soni 2000: 133).

South African actors were not only fairly clear about what type of aid they favoured, but also how it should be managed. Until 1996, all in-flows were centrally channelled through the RDP fund and the respective office was made the focal point for donors; later on, the responsibility for coordinating aid was shifted to the International Development Cooperation Unit (IDC) unit in the National Treasury. While all agreements needed to pass through this unit, the authority to negotiate aid remained with the respective implementing agencies, that is, national departments, and provincial and local authorities, which

---

34 A former government member who worked for the RDP office at that time stated in this regard: "Everybody wanted to throw money at us. And the big issue was: Yes, you can throw money at us, but against *our* agenda, not *your* agenda" (Interview 24).

were given a high degree of autonomy in soliciting support (see International Development Cooperation Unit 2003).

Faced with a recipient who seemed reluctant to be imposed with external rules and preferences, donors largely responded to South Africa's requests, directing assistance especially to the priority areas of education, democracy and governance, agriculture, business development, health and housing (Bratton & Landsberg 2000: 276). Initially, large parts of aid in these areas focused on the reformulation of policies and legislative frameworks, and the creation of new institutional arrangements and governance structures (Soni 2000: 50); post 1999, the focus gradually shifted to strengthening systems for implementation and service delivery. While aid helped to accelerate the pace of reforms insofar as it leveraged funding, the money as such was not substantial for their realisation. The main surplus of ODA for South Africa was the access to knowledge resources it facilitated. Putting in place new policies and legislation in basically all fields of governance was a huge challenge for an administration which had not only been re-structured, but was also staffed with new, often inexperienced (though committed) personnel (Bird 2001). Many line departments thus extensively drew on advisors and consultants provided by the aid community to assist in elaborating the technicalities of reforms.

For donors, South Africa appeared as a perfect case in which to present themselves as 'knowledge partners' rather than 'money-givers'. In its 1999 country assistance strategy for South Africa, the World Bank declared:

> *Since the 1994 elections, South Africa has provided the Bank with a unique opportunity to pilot our evolving role as a 'knowledge bank'. For South Africa, gaining access to international expertise and knowledge is at least as important as providing financial capital, and the Bank has operated as a clearinghouse and sounding board for international experts and best practice (…). In the future, we will continue to emphasize the Bank Group's role in contributing knowledge to development issues in South Africa.* (World Bank 1999b)

The majority of donors have adopted a similar approach in their engagement with South Africa, focusing assistance on the provision of expertise, 'up-stream' policy advice and the facilitation of knowledge exchange.

In contrast to Tanzania, the modes of cooperation in South Africa have hardly changed over the years; although the volume of sector budget support has increased (see WYG International Limited 2011), projects still constitute the predominant aid modality.[35] While in recent years mechanisms such as an annual Development Partners' Consultative Forum have been set up to improve coordination and coherence, South Africa has not established dialogue structures as found in Tanzania and other countries. Aside from the absence of general budget support which usually requires such arrangements, it seems that the government has also deliberately refrained from creating joint forums for more 'harmonised' assistance. The preference to interact with partners on a one-to-one basis partly results from the conviction that negotiating aid individually provides recipients with a greater leeway for manoeuvring than dealing with a "united donor front" (Harrison & Mulley 2009: 275). Broadly speaking, South Africa condones problems of aid fragmentation for the benefit of keeping control over development cooperation.

In recent years, aid relations have undergone a major change as several donors (e.g. Norway, Sweden and Denmark) have started to scale down or have completely phased out official development assistance (see Tjønneland et al. 2008). In 2013, DFID, hitherto a key partner particularly in the fields of health and business development, announced it would terminate its aid programme by 2015 with the intention to base the relationship "on sharing skills and knowledge, not on development funding, in recognition of the progress South Africa has made over the last two decades" (DFID 2013).[36, 37] The fact that South Africa is currently in the process of establishing its own development agency (see Besharati 2013) is certainly seen as a sign that the country's role in the international arena is shifting. Yet, this does not mean that donors are generally preparing themselves to close their Pretoria offices. Quite the contrary, several have begun to increasingly use them as a focal point for regional programmes and triangular cooperation agreements.[38] Hence, while traditional aid is currently declining, new arrangements with a focus on

---

35 A 2011 country evaluation of aid to South Africa found: "As of late 2009, there were at least 33 different development agencies implementing or preparing around 100 projects – this has escalated quite significantly with, for example, about twenty-five of some eighty EU 'Green Economy' commitments beginning in 2010" (WYG International Limited 2011: 55).

36 DFID's decision to end its aid programme for South Africa evoked harsh criticism both by UK MPs who blamed DFID for political expediency and disregard of recommended review procedures (Tran 2014) and on the part of the South African government which declared that the "unilateral announcement no doubt will affect how our bilateral relations going forward will be conducted" (Smith 2013).

37 A DFID advisor placed in the South African Department of Health commented on this decision as follows: "If things go as we hope they would go and the government is beginning to do the right things, our support is about catalysing change, it's not about telling government to do the right thing – they know what to do, it's making change happen quickly. Now once that started, they won't need DFID to help do that, and so we have a clear line by our current government that in four to five years' time, we will be starting to exit from this sort of work". (Interview 1)

38 Germany, for instance, together with the National Treasury and other government departments, has set up a Trilateral Cooperation Fund with the aim to carry out regional activities and foster South–South cooperation (GIZ 2007).

institutional and economic cooperation are on the rise. For the international community, South Africa remains an attractive counterpart: it represents both a strategic gateway to the continent and a prime example of a knowledge partnership which has yielded best practice and innovation.

Concluding remarks

The two countries which serve as the empirical cases of this study had different points of departure as recipients of aid and thus have adopted different approaches in dealing with donors. For the purpose of our research, the dissimilarity between South Africa and Tanzania is a crucial asset, allowing us to identify general intricacies of expert advice which are intrinsic to the aid context and exist irrespective of the particular country setting (see Chapter 5). At the same time, the dissimilarities enable us to investigate how different conditions delimit the extent to which recipients are able to absorb and use external expertise to advance their own development visions (see Chapters 6 and 7). Before we do so, however, we first present the actors involved in aid and dwell on their multiple interests related to development assistance (see Chapter 4).

MULTIPLE ACTORS, COLLIDING INTERESTS: THE MAIN PLAYERS OF THE AID GAME

We, Heads of State, Ministers and representatives of developing and developed countries, heads of multilateral and bilateral institutions, representatives of different types of public, civil society, private, parliamentary, local and regional organisations meeting here in Busan, Republic of Korea, recognise that we are united by a new partnership that is broader and more inclusive than ever before, founded on shared principles, common goals and differential commitments for effective international development.
(Fourth High Level Forum on Aid Effectiveness 2011: 1)

In December 2011, about 3 000 delegates from governments, aid agencies, civil society and private sector institutions met at the Fourth High Level Forum on Aid Effectiveness in South Korea to assess the current state of aid relations, and to define a future agenda. The event culminated in the signing of the Busan Partnership agreement whose introductory statement proclaims a "new partnership that is broader and more inclusive than ever before" based on "shared principles" and "common goals" (Fourth High Level Forum on Aid Effectiveness 2011: 1, see quotation above).

The partnership rhetoric prevailing in the contemporary aid discourse usually disguises the fact that aid is an arena of multiple, often competing interests. Figure 2 schematically displays major interests on the donor and recipient side at the level of governments, organisations and individual actors.

Figure 2 represents a simplifying abstraction of the respective interests of donor and recipient governments, their respective administrative authorities and individual actors.[39] Although incomplete, it indicates that

---

39 It does not claim to capture all particular interests existing at the different levels and excludes other players such as non-governmental organisations, foundations, lobby groups, academia and elites. For an attempt to illustrate the multiplicity of interests in German aid, see Nuscheler (2005).

Figure 2: Actors and interests in aid

DONOR SIDE		RECIPIENT SIDE
Donor governments: Increasing political influence Profiting from the aid market Fostering export and trade	Political/ economic interests	Recipient governments: Increasing financial resources and the capacity to act Strengthening foreign relations
Bureaucracies/aid agencies: Increasing budget volumes Increasing authority Maintaining relevance	Organisational interests	Ministries/public agencies: Increasing financial resources Increasing the scope of action
Donor staff/development experts: Increasing/maintaining authority, influence and status	Individual interests	Political actors/government officials: Increasing public popularity Accessing individual rewards

Source: Authors' own illustration.

the web of interests comprises political and economic objectives of nation states, organisational concerns of donor and recipient bureaucracies, and individual incentives of government members and development experts. In the following section, a closer look first focuses on the recipient side, then shifts to the donors. Finally, the spotlight is put on a group of actors who are part of the donor system, but who pursue distinct goals as knowledge brokers, namely the epistemic community of development experts. Summarising the observations of this section will be an understanding of the linkage of aid and interests that forms the complex setting for the advisory processes at the core of aid practices.

Recipient governments and bureaucracies

While attracting additional resources is a primary purpose of recipient governments under pressure to cope with underfinanced budgets, they do pursue other interests in receiving assistance. Development projects potentially increase the public popularity of government heads, and bring along material rewards for the officials in charge. Moreover, aid is a strategic tool used in foreign relations, even by countries dependent on external support.

Financial resources

Financial shortages are the chief motive for entering aid negotiations on the side of recipient governments. In low-income countries, external funding makes up a substantial share of the budget, in some cases up to 50%. It is a crucial amount for development expenses used for expanding road infrastructure, improving water supply or building schools and hospitals, amongst others.[40] Given that governments of developing nations often spend a large proportion of their budget on recurrent costs, many investment projects can only be realised with donor funding, even in relatively resource-rich countries such as South Africa (Bond 2001). Authorities in areas such as environment, which receive a lower share of domestic resources, especially depend on external financing to carry out programmes.[41] In countries such as Tanzania where even priority sectors are underfinanced, donor money critically extends line ministries' scope of action.

Public popularity

Opening a new construction site, inaugurating a day care centre or taking a power plant into operation are opportune events for policy-makers to demonstrate their efforts and achievements to the public. Aside from expanding the financial scope of governments, aid contributes to increasing the popularity of political actors. In Tanzania, pulling off aid is framed as a commendable merit. Government websites proudly advertise new international aid agreements, with pictures showing ministerial leaders shaking hands with donor representatives. Development cooperation activities are omnipresent in the media. Rarely a day goes by without at least one newspaper article covering a donor-funded project implemented by the government. The tenor of reports is usually very positive; negative effects of aid are seldom addressed. Policy-makers in Tanzania thus have an incentive to keep the status quo in terms of using foreign funding, although the government officially seeks to reduce its budgetary dependence (Tanzania Ministry of Finance 2013). As a retired government official commented about politicians in his country:

> *They don't want to cut aid. We are all afraid of loosing the polls. And that is something which is going to hurt us in the long run.* (Interview 64)

---

40 In contrast to the development budget, the recurrent budget is absorbed by operational expenses including salaries and wages for civil servants, the purchases of goods and services, and payments on national debts (Ministry of Finance 2012: 7).

41 The Cape Action for People and the Environment (CAPE) initiative in South Africa's Cape Floristic Region, for instance, very much gained from GEF funding which at times amounted to half of the overall budget (Global Environment Facility Evaluation Office 2008). For details, see Chapter 7.

Individual rewards

Not only high-level politicians, but also staff in ministries and agencies benefit individually from aid. Particularly among senior government cadres, donor-funded activities are considered as "potentially lucrative and status enhancing" (Chêne 2009: 6) since they make available tangible rewards to the functionaries in charge. As a Tanzanian civil society actor pointed out, monetary and non-monetary benefits constitute primary incentives for government members to engage with donor representatives:

> *I sit and talk with you because I think, maybe I'll get a study tool for capacity-building and I'll get my allowances or, you know, maybe through you I'll get a scholarship for my daughter to go to university or there's a tender to order something and I will get my commission. That's what it becomes, it becomes an opportunity for rent seeking.* (Interview 70)

Extra payments for government officials involved in aid activities are common practice in most recipient countries. Donors have co-created "per diem and allowance regime[s]" (Chêne 2009: 5) which are well entrenched, particularly in countries where the public service is severely underpaid.[42] In many African states, government wages have been declining as a result of fiscal adjustment policies, with the consequence that salaries not only at lower levels hardly suffice to make a living. Receiving extra pay in the form of per diems and allowances has become "one of the most popular coping strategies for compensating for low public sector wages in the developing world" (Chêne 2009: 4). According to a survey among public servants in Tanzania and Uganda, the large majority of them (77%) considered allowances as equally important as their basic salary, some (13%) assessed extra pay as even more important than the latter (Therkildsen & Tidemand 2007). While allowances were actually introduced to reimburse officials for real expenses (e.g. travel reimbursement), they have become a second pillar of their income. The fact that they are relatively high compared to basic wages makes them even more attractive. A study conducted by the Tanzanian Policy Forum made the following calculation with data from the year 2009: a middle-level officer could earn about a third of his monthly salary (TSh 384 850, government scale TGS D) within three days by attending a workshop outside Dar es Salaam for which he receives a per diem of TSh 35 000 (Policy Forum 2009). As rates for foreign travels are even higher, "a civil servant going on a 5-day trip abroad easily doubles his or her salary,

---

42 In Tanzania, donors fund around ten different types of allowances, such as per diems, honoraria or extra-duty top-ups. For an overview and details on what these allowances cover, see Rubin (2012).

even if this is the highest paid civil servant around" (Policy Forum 2009: 6). Thus, participating in events outside their offices pays off for government staff. Donor-funded workshops, trainings or conferences have become coveted extraordinary duties.

Competing for key public officials, aid agencies in some cases even offer "attractive international daily rates" (Chêne 2009: 5) to bring them to their events. For the agencies, the per diem system helps to meet their own targets insofar as the number of participants is commonly used as a performance indicator (Hepworth 2009, as cited in Policy Forum 2009; Søreide et al. 2012). While paying allowances ensures attendance, salary top-ups paid to ministry officials concerned with donor projects aims to secure commitment on the counterpart side. As anecdotal evidence shows, this can make up to 40% increase in salary for the civil servants in charge (Rubin 2012).

In Tanzania, cash incentives have become a decisive element in the interaction between donors and government officials. A World Bank expert who at the time of the interview was relatively new in the country commented:

> *In Tanzania, if you have a meeting, you're expected to pay people to show up and if you don't pay them to show up, if they don't care about it – which usually they don't, cause usually it's something that's cared about by someone else, imposed upon them – then they don't show up. So (...) everybody lines up at the back of these meetings to get little brown envelopes and it's shocking to me to see that happen – shocking.* (Interview 46)

The institutionalisation of this practice has profound consequences not only for development cooperation, but also for the organisational culture in developing countries' bureaucracies. Several studies have pointed out how the allowance regime creates room for fraud and corruption (Smith 2003; Ridde 2010; Vian et al. 2013), encouraging "opportunistic behaviour 'to get a piece of the cake'" (Søreide et al. 2012: xiv).[43] The individual benefits affiliated with aid activities lead government members to accept unnecessary support, to attend trainings irrespective of their 'capacity-building' use and to prolong processes in order to get projects extended (Chêne 2009; Vian et al. 2013).[44] A natural resources

---

43 In 2013, donors in Tanzania withdrew their support to the Local Government Reform Programme after an audit revealed the misuse of funds, amongst others for "excessive and unjustified per diem allowances and fees" (Mosoba & Mugarula 2013).

44 The misuse of allowances particularly in the context of capacity-building activities has been documented several times. A study on donor support for water resource management in East Africa found that "during a two year period of working alongside East African practitioners it became apparent that there were numerous discrete training and workshop based capacity building initiatives run by donors and external support agencies covering the same or similar material. An example is provided by an agency of an East African government who over a period of two years were engaged in three separate residential training courses which covered the same topics, were

expert working for a Nordic donor in Tanzania explained the delays in her programme on the counterpart side as follows:

> *I think it's deliberate that they were only able to use half of the money that we were giving them for two years – they used it in three and a half years. And you know, somehow in my mind is the idea that if it lasts for six, seven years, it's easier to get more daily allowances, all these per diems, discussion workshops organised and so on. So it kind of dilutes the whole thing.* (Interview 36)

Although donors have repeatedly claimed to tackle the self-made incentive problem by setting an end to extraordinary payments, the latter are still common practice and sometimes just termed differently. A study on donor compensations in Tanzania, Malawi and Ethiopia cites a senior staff member of a UN organisation saying:

> *UN organisations are now using all kinds of words to avoid the term 'sitting allowance' while in reality, they continue the practice. Very often, a cash payment of around TZS 80,000 is offered on top of 'the meeting package' – which includes accommodation and meals. In addition, they get a transport allowance – and this is an arrangement that can easily be manipulated. If they don't get paid well they just leave – even if they have arrived at a hotel and have shown interest in the topic.* (Søreide et al. 2012: 35)

The policies and practices related to allowances certainly vary among aid agencies and across countries. While in Tanzania, individual rewards constitute a strong incentive on the recipient side to engage with donors, the situation is different in South Africa where public sector wages are comparably high, and allowances are not an issue affecting donor–recipient cooperation.

Foreign relations

In countries in which the financial assets of aid play less of a role for both a government's budget and for actors involved, its non-monetary value as a strategic element of politics comes to the fore. This has particularly been emphasised by South African government officials; a director in the Department of Health stated in this regard:

---

attended largely by the same people, each workshop being organised and funded, with per diems and expenses, by a different source from within the donor community" (Hepworth 2009, as cited in Policy Forum 2009: 7).

ODA [official development cooperation] is all about what? It is all about foreign policy issues. It is all about strengthening our international relations. (Interview 18)

South Africa has never been financially dependent on foreign aid (see Chapters 3 and 6). A strong motivation of the government for becoming a recipient of official development assistance in 1994 was to re-build relationships after years of isolation by the international community. Obtaining financial and technical assistance was seen as a tool which would not only help economic development, but also foster political bonds and international trade.[45] Even today, development cooperation is considered a central element of bi- and multilateral relations. Strengthening relationships with strategic partners is a main interest underlying aid which manifests in the fact that decisions on entering agreements for support are guided by directives from the Department of Foreign Affairs, as a senior official in the health department explained:

They prioritize those governments and their relationships. So for example, if an interest is around, just an example, China, (...) whatever that they will provide or that they will give, whether we have resources on it or not, we have to make sure that we negotiate as to how we want to work together in the health sector. (Interview 18)

The acceptance of aid is thus not solely dependent on actual needs; strategic considerations related to foreign policy priorities, trade or other interests play a role. This is not only the case in a resource-rich country such as South Africa, although it may have a more comfortable bargaining position than others. Even poorer African states, for example Benin, Kenya and Zimbabwe consider foreign policy interests when deciding whom to approach for assistance and whose offers to accept (Wright 1999). A recent study reports that Ethiopia "treats different donors in different ways and adapts its language and strategy accordingly" (Greenhill et al. 2013: 28). The fact that the Ethiopian government utilises aid relations in a very deliberate way is also corroborated by foreign policy documents and statements which emphasise the close linkage between development cooperation and diplomacy (Federal Democratic Republic of Ethiopia 2002; Ministry of Foreign Affairs 2013). The case of Ethiopia illustrates that even highly aid-dependent countries adopt a strategic approach in securing assistance, taking its significance for foreign relations into account.

---

45 This is outlined in an influential article published in 1993 under Nelson Mandela's name which set out the direction of South Africa's foreign policy under an ANC-led government (Mandela 1993).

Donor countries and aid organisations

Donor governments provide aid not out of altruism or generosity. They engage in development cooperation not (only) for the sake of development, but because it serves themselves for multiple purposes (Easterly 2002; Browne 2006; Shikwati 2006; Lancaster 2007). While the extent to which aid is tied to such purposes varies, the general pattern is that political, economic and organisational interests are shaping donors' aid policies.

Political and economic interests of donor governments

If aid was given with the aim to help those in greatest need, the poorest countries would receive the bulk of assistance. As statistics show, this is not the case. Among the top ten recipients of aid between 1980 and 2011 were states such as India, Iraq and China, as ranked in Table 1:

Table 1: Top ten recipients of aid worldwide based on net ODA received 1980–2014

Rank	Recipient country	Net ODA received 1960–2014 in USD million
1	India	86 974
2	Egypt	86 000
3	Iraq	71 545
4	Pakistan	62 013
5	Afghanistan	61 301
6	Bangladesh	57 613
7	Vietnam	56 487
8	Ethiopia	53 166
9	Tanzania	52 870
10	China	49 433

Source: World Development Indicators (World Bank 2016b).[46]

Despite the international community's claim to focus on poverty reduction, an OECD survey of 2012 found a significant shift in aid allocations from least developed countries towards middle-income countries in the Far East and South and Central Asia (OECD 2013b). Various scholars, notably in the field of development economics, have shown that historical, economic and political ties decisively shape the direction of aid flows: former colonial powers such as the United Kingdom or France still provide substantial amounts of aid to their

---

46 The indicator "Net official development assistance received (current USD)" includes loans and grants disbursed by DAC and non-DAC countries and multilateral institutions. Data were retrieved on 4 August 2016.

ex-colonies, irrespective of the ruling regime or economic systems (Alesina & Dollar 2000; Berthélemy & Tichit 2004; Nunnenkamp & Thiele 2006).[47, 48] Trade linkages have a significant impact on aid allocation, with donors targeting assistance preferably to their most important trading partners in the developing world (Berthélemy & Tichit 2004; Berthélemy 2006; Nunnenkamp & Thiele 2006; Younas 2008; Hoeffler & Outram 2011). The significance of political allegiance for aid is reflected by UN voting patterns: donor countries tend to give more aid to countries who vote in line with them (Alesina & Dollar 2000; Neumayer 2003; Dreher et al. 2009; Hoeffler & Outram 2011; Pincin 2012). All these findings indicate that donor governments select recipients not primarily on the basis of poverty rankings, but out of strategic considerations.[49]

When official development assistance emerged after the Second World War, it was primarily legitimated with political interests. In the United States, President Truman in 1947 justified his request for economic and military aid to Greece and Turkey with the motivation that without assistance, both countries would fall under the influence of the Soviet Union. He introduced his speech to the Congress stating that "the foreign policy and the national security of this country [the United States] are involved" (Truman 1947). During the Cold War era, aid was widely used as a diplomatic instrument in order to win and keep allies, and thereby influence the geopolitical balance of power (Adamson 2006). Other countries such as Japan and Germany began to provide aid as a means of export promotion (Lancaster 2007). Development as a declared priority of aid came of age only during the decades of the 1970s and 1980s, shifting the focus on economic growth and (at a later stage) poverty reduction in the developing world (Lancaster 2007).

Comparing legitimation patterns prevailing today, governments can broadly be divided into two groups: the first frames development cooperation as an instrument for safeguarding foreign policy and economic interests; the second acknowledges general interests, but emphasises the obligation of giving aid as

---

47 In the period 1980–2004, 71% of UK aid and 51% of aid provided by France went to their respective former colonies (Hoeffler & Outram 2008: 23). Alesina and Dollar (2000: 55) found that "a non-democratic former colony gets about twice as much aid as a democratic non-colony".

48 In our study, interviewees in both South Africa and Tanzania highlighted the fact that donors preferably channel aid to regions in which they have historic ties. A South African official engaged in the education sector told us that when donors entered the country at the dawn of democracy, "they knew exactly where and who they want to support, where their missionaries were before, and now they were closely related to those geographic areas" (Interview 21).

49 While development economists' calculations generate evidence in the form of measurable results often presented as 'hard facts', we are cautious of some interpretations drawn from these findings insofar as they tend to include causal explanations which cannot be derived from the statistics produced. From our view, for instance, using only the correlation of UN voting patterns and aid flows as evidence for political interests in aid allocation is deficient insofar as it does not distinguish cause and effect.

an act of solidarity and shared responsibility. Exemplary justifications of aid in policy documents and statements of major donors are compiled in Table 2:

Table 2: Rationales legitimating aid in donor policies

Political and economic interests	Solidarity/responsibility
United States, Presidential Policy Directive on Global Development (22 September 2010): "The directive recognizes that development is vital to U.S. national security and is a strategic, economic, and moral imperative for the United States. It calls for the elevation of development as a core pillar of American power and charts a course for development, diplomacy and defense to mutually reinforce and complement one another in an integrated comprehensive approach to national security."	Norway, White Paper on Development Policy (Report No. 13, 2008–2009, to the Storting): "The central aim of our foreign policy is to safeguard Norwegian interests. In development policy, the focus is on poor countries' interests (...). An approach that includes an emphasis on common interests can further enhance understanding of and support for an active foreign and development policy, and can open up opportunities for new forms of cooperation. (...) However, the focus on safeguarding common interests and seeking to strengthen global public goods does not mean that the Government wishes to use development policy to further Norwegian economic interests or any other form of Norwegian self-interest. The objective of Norway's development policy is to reduce poverty and to promote human rights."
The Netherlands, Letter to the House of Representatives outlining development cooperation policy (2010): "The Netherlands has a direct interest in international stability and security, energy and resource security, a well-functioning international legal order and a level playing field, with all the necessary rules. Development cooperation is therefore an integral part of a broad foreign policy."	
	Sweden, Global Challenges – Our Responsibility: Communication on Sweden's policy for global development (2008): "The fight against poverty in its various forms not only remains the overriding goal of Swedish development cooperation but is also a central point of departure for the Government's overall development policy. Although the primary responsibility for poverty reduction and development lies with the governments of the developing countries, Sweden can and will contribute to equitable and sustainable global development. We must do so out of a sense of solidarity and because we share a responsibility for the future of the world. Assuming that responsibility, moreover, is in our own interests."
Germany, Coalition Agreement (2009): "In pursuing our objectives in development policy our values and interests are on par (...) Foreign trade and development co-operation must build upon each other and be integrated in a seamless fashion. Development policy decisions must take sufficient account of the interests of German economy, particularly the needs of small and medium-sized companies."	

Source: Ministry for Foreign Affairs (2008a: 6–7); CDU et al. (2009: 64); Norwegian Ministry of Foreign Affairs (2009: 10); Netherlands Ministry of Foreign Affairs (2010: 1); The White House (2010).

Table 2 displays contrasting rationales used by donors to legitimate aid, with one side referring primarily to self-interests and the other to humanitarian motives. This division is in a way stylised since, as will be shown later, even in countries which emphasise the primacy of development in giving aid, other interests come into play. Yet, as Van der Veen (2011: 5) points out, the "frames" governments use to justify aid "shape the overall organization and quality of aid programmes" and "affect specific features, such as the total size of the aid budget, or the geographical allocation of aid".[50] Donors who foreground self-interests are likely to select recipients for their strategic importance and to design programmes from which they potentially profit.

The crucial role of political and economic interests in giving aid is manifest in the case of South Africa. When the country turned into a democracy in 1994, a plethora of donors stood in a queue offering assistance although "by the usual criteria South Africa was too wealthy to qualify for much support" (Barber 2004: 149). Nevertheless, with USD 5 billion pledged from 1994 to 1999, donors offered "an enormous sum compared to other (more desperate) African countries" (Bond 2001: 25). The main rationale of the funders, with the European Union, the United States and Japan at the fore, was to re-build relations with the most powerful country and economic hub of the African continent. The new 'rainbow nation' became an attractive recipient, and "everybody wanted to be seen as 'we are assisting South Africa to rebuild itself'" (Interview 22). The fact that the supporters presumed political rewards from their new partner became obvious in situations in which South Africa acted against their expectations. The Taiwanese government, for instance, faced such a conflict. Aiming at retaining South African official recognition of Taiwan instead of the People's Republic of China (PRC), it presented itself as a generous friend to the ANC already prior to the first elections (Bond 2001). When in 1996, South Africa reversed its position by recognising the PRC, "the furious Taiwanese foreign minister John Chang suspended grants to South Africa worth [US]\$ 80 million and loans worth [US]\$ 50 million" (Bond 2001: 28).

While Taiwan failed to 'buy' South Africa's solidarity with aid, the United States secured itself more influence. In 1997, President Clinton's warning to withdraw all aid to South Africa as a reaction to the South African Cabinet's approval of arms sales to Syria – viewed as a 'terrorist state' by the US – showed the desirable effect (Barber 2004: 104):

> *Although Mandela replied in March 1997 that it was immoral to abandon countries that had supported the ANC in the anti-apartheid fight 'on the advice of countries that were friends of the apartheid regime' (i.e. the US), Defence Minister Joe Modise confirmed that a marketing permit was issued for the arms but that, in the wake of the US warning, 'We did not tender, as no documentation was received from Syria'.* (Bond 2001: 29)

---

50 Van der Veen (2011) uses the concept of 'frames' to classify ideas about goals and purposes of aid. Drawing on legislative debates from 1950 to 2000, he provides an in-depth analysis of frames and their impact on aid programmes in four European countries, namely Belgium, Norway, the Netherlands and Italy. His findings show how prevailing ideas shape aid policy and practices of donor countries.

There are plenty of similar incidents across the developing world where aid (or the suspension of aid) has been used to influence decisions related to both foreign and domestic politics in recipient countries. In recent years, donors threatened to cut aid to Uganda and Malawi as a reaction to the governments' homophobic positions; subsequently, Malawi repealed its anti-gay law (BBC News 2012), and Uganda put its harsh Anti-Homosexuality Bill temporarily on hold (Ndinda 2010). In Rwanda, major development partners suspended aid in 2012 following accusations from a UN report that the country supported rebels fighting in the Eastern Congo (Rwamucyo 2012). At first glance, these examples prompt that by withdrawing aid, the international community sanctions human rights violations and external intervention. A second look, however, reveals that criteria seem different for different countries, dependent on their strategic importance for the donors. Despite evidence of severe human rights abuses and political oppression, the Ethiopian government receives around USD 3 billion in aid every year (Stickler & Barr 2011). The generous donations of its major funders, namely the US, the EU and the UK, can be explained by the fact that they see President Meles Zenawi as a stable partner at the Horn of Africa who supports their fight against terrorism (Hagmann 2012).

The significance of security interests in connection with aid has strongly increased with the 'war on terror' proclaimed by the Western world after the September 11, 2001 attacks in the United States. While security issues have always been part of aid considerations, scholars argue that post 2001 they have taken precedence over poverty or human rights concerns (Woods 2005; Aning 2010). The "securitisation of development policy and practice (…) is manifest in aid rhetoric, policy discourse, institutional convergence and programming" (Howell & Lind 2009a: 1279; see also Howell & Lind 2009b). Articulating a causal linkage of poverty and terrorism, major donor governments have reframed the purposes and determinants of aid as an instrument serving security interests (Howell & Lind 2009a; Thede 2013).[51] The Director-General of AusAid, Bruce Davis, expressed the paradigm shift in Australian aid as follows:

---

51 Thede (2013: 795–796) provides an impressive list of major donors who reformulated their missions and priorities: "In 2002 the Canadian International Development Agency's mandate was revised to include supporting 'efforts to reduce threats to Canadian security'. In 2003 the Australian government cited poverty reduction as secondary to security considerations in its aid programme. In 2003 as well Japan modified its ODA charter, adding national security as a purpose of aid and including the prevention of terrorism as one of its principles. In 2004 Denmark added the fight against terrorism to the priorities of its aid programme, and has made aid allocations dependent on recipient country involvement in the 'war' on terror. In the USA the 2004 *White Paper* by USAID presents aid as an element of security strategies in the global war on terror. In addition, the EU has included cooperation in counter-terrorism by recipient countries as a prerequisite for EU development aid."

It was not too long ago that aid and development lay firmly on the periphery of serious considerations of Australia's security and strategic interests. Aid was often regarded as a somewhat ill-defined process of 'doing-good', a process which had little tangible impact on the strategic environment faced by Australia and its policy makers. These times are now over. (Davis in a speech on 27 October 2005, cited in Howell & Lind 2009a: 1283)

The new "security-first paradigm" (Aning 2010: 8) has not only brought about intensified collaboration and institutional tying of development and defence units, but has also affected the direction of funding flows, with 'fragile states' becoming prominent recipients (Howell & Lind 2009a). Various scholars have traced significant changes in aid allocations of Western donors, particularly the United States (Aning 2010; Fleck & Kilby 2010). Comparing USAID bilateral aid flows in the periods 1998–2001 and 2002–2005, Moss et al. (2005: 8) found that "Iraq and Afghanistan went from receiving virtually zero aid before the GWOT [Global War on Terror] to receiving two of the largest per capita allocations following 9/11. Jordan, already a major recipient, more than doubled its aid per capita from USAID". While shifts in allocation patterns may be most obvious (and most frequently researched) in the case of the US, they are also found in a range of other donor countries (Howell & Lind 2009a). This suggests that the status of a country in the 'war on terror' has become a decisive variable for Western donors' assistance decisions (Aning 2010).

Political influence and security, however, are not the only non-developmental objectives of aid. Economic interests are bluntly articulated by some donor governments and reflected in their aid agendas. In 2013, The Netherlands adopted a new policy titled 'What the world deserves: A new agenda for aid, trade and investment' which directly links aid and foreign trade (Government of the Netherlands 2013). In its coalition agreement of 2009, the liberal-conservative German government emphasised that "development policy decisions must take sufficient account of the interests of the German economy, particularly the needs of small and medium-sized companies" (CDU et al. 2009: 64).

Development cooperation is a conduit for business. Aid projects entail tenders for all kinds of goods and services, ranging from vehicles, medical drugs and equipment to construction and advisory services in various fields. Until a decade ago, it was common practice that such contracts were exclusively awarded to companies or service providers from the respective donor country. For recipients, such kind of conditionality not only took away any choice, but raised the price of aid products by 15% to 30% and had distorting effects on local markets (Jepma 1991; Browne 2006; Petermann 2013). In order to "reduce the high transaction costs" and "improve country ownership and alignment", DAC member states committed themselves in the Paris Declaration to "make progress" on untying aid (OECD 2005: 5). Subsequently, the share of tied bilateral aid decreased from 54% in 1999–2001 to 24% in 2007 (Clay et al. 2009: viii). These data, however, are to be taken with caution. First, since donors voluntarily report the tying status of their aid to the OECD system, data are incomplete and inconsistent; second, they are skewed since two strongly tied types of aid are not covered, namely food aid and technical cooperation. In a country such as South Africa, which receives aid mainly in the form of technical assistance, the proportion of tied aid is hardly measurable due to a lack of donor information. Qualitative data, however, provide "evidence of *de facto* tying, with source country consultants or companies brought in to do work that could potentially be done domestically" (Ramkolowan & Stern 2011: x, italics in original; see also Fölscher et al. 2010).

The fact that donors continue to use aid to feed their own industries with contracts is corroborated by plain numbers: in 2012, USAID awarded only 4% of contracts to firms outside the United States (Piccio 2013); 18 of the top 20 private consultancy partners used from October 2010 to March 2011 were based in the US (Villarino 2011). Numbers for DFID are similar: *The Guardian* revealed that only 9 out of 117 major contracts and procurement agreements awarded in 2011/2012 were given to non-UK firms, with the large majority going to well-established British consultancy companies such as Adam Smith International or the Mott McDonald Group (Provost & Hughes 2012). Considering that UK aid has officially been untied since 2001, the on-going dominance of domestic firms is striking. The list could be continued with data from various other agencies which show that large amounts of aid flow back to the respective donor countries' industries (for AusAid, see Parmanand 2013; for GIZ, see Buss et al. 2012). Various interviewees in our study broached the obvious relevance of business interests in development cooperation, with one stating:

> *If you're running a project and you want a project to get an extension, extended financial support, you have to ensure that there is provision for positions for foreign experts. Then you're guaranteed of getting a continuation of that support. But I think it's one way of job creation. Nothing else.* (Interview 69)

Apart from the direct gains derived from aid-related export of goods and services, aid brings along indirect benefits as it tends to trigger trade between donor and recipient countries also outside the field of development cooperation (Johansson & Pettersson 2005). The return of aid is thus potentially higher than the contract volume for donor companies arising out of aid activities.

A study which tried to measure both the direct and indirect effects of aid on export levels estimates that "aid is associated with an increase in exports of goods amounting to 133% of the aid" (Wagner 2003: 153), with exports of services not included.[52] Economic gains have always been used to legitimate development assistance in the domestic political debate of donor countries. When in 1995, the Republican Party in the United States threatened to cut aid, Andrew Young as former US representative to the United Nations argued:

> *We get a five to one return on investment in Africa, through our trade, investment, finance and aid. Don't you see? We're not aiding Africa by sending them aid, Africa's aiding us.* (Andrew Young as cited in Bond 2001: 28)

Despite the significance of aid as foreign policy tool and door-opener for business, it would be superficial to lump donors all together and to deny that some give primacy to other, less selfish objectives. There are indeed countries which seem more guided by recipient needs than by political or economic interests, notably some Nordic states (Alesina & Dollar 2000). Sweden, for instance, has repeatedly been commended as a role model of the donor community with "development at the heart of its foreign policy" (OECD 2013a: 16), as an OECD report put it. In 2012, Sweden's official development assistance amounted to almost 1% of its gross national income which exceeds the international target of 0.7% set by the UN. Allocating the major share of its aid flows to least developing countries, mostly in sub-Sahara Africa, the country adheres to its policy which emphasises poverty reduction as the primary goal of Swedish development cooperation (OECD 2013a). Yet, although Sweden underlines "solidarity with poor and vulnerable people in other countries" (Ministry for Foreign Affairs 2003: 18) as main rationale for support, it does factor in other interests.[53] In its 2008 policy for Africa, the government outlines a comprehensive approach to development which integrates security, aid and trade issues, stating:

---

52 Wagner (2003: 171) estimates "that 35 cents out of every dollar of aid comes directly back to the donor for exports of goods related to the aid-financed project and that another 98 cents finds its way back to the donor for exports of goods not directly linked to aid projects. These measurements exclude exports of services, which surely comprise a significant part of donors' exports to recipients."

53 The Swedish government is also increasingly pushed to consider non-developmental interests by domestic players which potentially gain from aid. In 2006, a consortium of Swedish exporters (including Volvo, Ericsson and Tetra Pak, amongst others) sent a letter to the minister for trade and industry in which they called for a closer involvement of the Swedish private sector in foreign aid, arguing that industry's engagement would create "many qualified job prospects in Sweden" (Greenhill 2006: 34).

> *Economic ties in the form of trade and investment benefit African as well as Swedish commercial interests, a potential that should be exploited more extensively. The Government intends to collaborate with the private sector so as to protect and promote Swedish business relations with Africa. Closer political contacts, cooperation in the international arena and cultural exchange can be stimulated by and contribute to stronger and deeper economic relations.* (Ministry for Foreign Affairs 2008b: 21)

Clearly, aid must be seen as a policy instrument which serves multiple interests at the same time, ranging from global development, poverty reduction and wealth creation to political influence, security and trade. While in every donor county, all of these interests to some extent play a role in giving aid, governments prioritise them in different orders. The ranking of priorities sets the agenda for those who deliver development assistance, namely the respective aid bureaucracies and organisations. In order to understand how these bodies operate, it is instructive to take a closer look at the organisational structures of bi- and multilateral aid providers.

Organisational structures of bi- and multilateral aid providers

Donor countries have established a range of different set-ups for development cooperation. Bilateral aid organisations vary particularly with regard to their affiliation with foreign affairs and their presence 'in the field' (OECD 2009a). Considering these features, we can broadly differentiate three organisational models.

In the first one, development cooperation units are directly affiliated with the ministry of foreign affairs or are even an integral part of it. Denmark, for instance, has fully shifted the responsibility for planning, implementing and monitoring official development assistance to the Ministry of Foreign Affairs. Its representations abroad, namely the Danish embassies and missions, manage aid in the respective recipient countries (Ministry of Foreign Affairs of Denmark 2014).

While similar structures are also found in Norway, Finland and the Netherlands, other countries have institutionally separated development cooperation and foreign affairs. The United Kingdom, for instance, has established the Department for International Development (DFID) as a standalone authority independent from the Foreign and Commonwealth Office. Led by a secretary of state who is member of the cabinet, DFID has a very strong standing of its own and "enjoys an unambiguous relationship with other ministries, which allows it to influence cross government thinking on development policy" (OECD 2009a: 16). While DFID offices in recipient countries are often housed in British embassies' venues, they are not subordinate to them. Similarly autonomous are the Canadian International Development Agency (CIDA) and, until 2013, the Australian Agency for International Development.[54]

Finally, there is a third model of managing aid adopted by a range of donor countries in which a superior authority is responsible for policy and decision-making, but a separate agency exists for the delivery of aid.[55] In Germany, for instance, the Ministry for Economic Cooperation and Development (BMZ) commissions the German development agency GIZ to implement aid activities. As a federal enterprise, GIZ has its own offices in recipient countries and operates as the executing arm of the BMZ in the field. Likewise, USAID, Swedish International Development Cooperation Agency (Sida) and Japan International Cooperation Agency (JICA) function as implementing agencies for the governments of the United States, Sweden and Japan, respectively (OECD 2009a: 33).

In addition to bilateral channels, donors use multilateral organisations and global funding mechanisms for allocating aid which usually have a three-tier system comprising headquarters, regional and country offices. In the period 2001–2011, "multilateral ODA has risen from [USD] 27 billion to [USD] 38 billion, accounting for close to one-third of gross ODA" (OECD 2012a: 11). For donor governments, multilateral agencies offer economies of scale and scope, a global outreach, and the potential to influence the international agenda in the respective field of specialisation, amongst others (see Martens 2008). Also, intergovernmental bodies are usually regarded as "more objective aid-givers who tend to allocate aid according to need and the potential effectiveness of aid allocations" (Schneider & Tobin 2010: 2) rather than to individual donor priorities. In fact, by pooling their funds, governments to some extent lose control over their money as "key decisions on what, where and how it is actually delivered are taken at supranational level" (OECD 2011a: 9). The perceived neutrality of multilateral aid, however, is misleading. The fact that governments try to influence aid policies of the multilateral agency according to their own priorities is reflected in strategic documents. The US administration under President Obama, for instance, emphasised the importance of multilateral aid in two seminal documents in 2010, namely the Presidential Policy Directive on Global Development and the Quadrennial Diplomacy and Development Review. While the former states that the US will "redouble our efforts to

---

54 On 1 November 2013, AusAid ceased to exist as an independent agency when it was merged into the Australian Department of Foreign Affairs and Trade; at the time of writing, the re-structuring process was still on-going (Australian Government 2013).

55 The superior authority can either be related to foreign affairs or be an independent development cooperation entity.

support, reform, and modernize multilateral development organizations most critical to our interests" (White House 2010), the latter outlines how such organisations should be used to foster the US agenda:

> *Multilateral diplomacy is a specialized skill set that allows us to advance American interests across a wide range of multilateral organizations. We must expand the ranks of diplomats skilled in multilateral diplomacy and improve the links between our multilateral and bilateral diplomacy, especially with respect to our engagement with the United Nations. Multilateral diplomats must both maintain relationships with international organizations themselves and mobilize member-states to support our priorities in those organizations.* (Department of State & USAID 2010: 55)

The extent to which individual governments are able to foster strategic interests through multilateral organisations strongly depends on the allocation of power within the respective institutions. In United Nations agencies, the presence of countries in decision-making bodies is usually based on inclusion and rotation mechanisms established to ensure that the interests and needs of all member states are equally taken into account, irrespective of their political or financial strength.[56] The World Bank as a multilateral financing institution, in contrast, has established a system in which countries' economic performance and financial contribution to the Bank are determinants of decision-making authority (Stumm 2011).[57] The majority of voting power lies in the hands of high-income countries, with the five main contributors alone holding 37% of all votes (International Bank for Reconstruction and Development 2013). The US as the largest shareholder with over 15% effectively has a veto on fundamental changes in the Bank. Consequently, the World Bank's overall

---

56 The World Health Organization, for instance, is governed by the World Health Assembly, the Executive Board and the Secretariat (World Health Organization 1946: 4). The Assembly as the supreme decision-making body is formed by delegates from all 194 member states. Taking into account an equitable geographical distribution, the Assembly elects 34 members entitled to designate a technically qualified person to serve on the Executive Board over a period of three years (World Health Organization 1946). In 2013, the Board was composed of seven delegates from the African continent, six from the Americas, three from South-East Asia, eight from Europe, five from the Eastern Mediterranean countries, and five from the Western Pacific region (World Health Organization 2013).

57 This applies to the allocation of the influential Executive Director positions and voting power: Five of the 25 Executive Director positions are given to the largest shareholders of the Bank – currently France, the United States, Germany, Japan and the United Kingdom (International Bank for Reconstruction and Development et al. 2013). All member states receive votes consisting of basic votes plus additional votes according to their share of the Bank's capital stock held (World Bank 2012c), which leads to appalling power imbalances between developing and developed countries (Vestergaard 2011).

agenda is strongly driven by the strategic interests of the most powerful Western countries, while member states from the developing world have little say.

To what extent headquarters of bi- and multilateral organisations shape aid on the ground strongly depends on the decision-making autonomy of the respective agents in the field.[58] The degree of authority delegated to staff in country offices varies considerably, both with regard to funding and programmatic issues. While some enjoy full financial authority over their country budget, others are not allowed to take any decisions on disbursements (OECD 2009b: 5–6).[59] Similar differences exist when it comes to decision-making on priorities and modalities of support. DFID's country offices, as well as the embassies of Norway and Denmark, for instance, enjoy a high degree of autonomy in terms of formulating country strategies, designing programmes and implementing activities. While the superior authority at the central level has the final say in approvals, country-based staff has a broad leeway to tailor cooperation to the demands of local counterparts. In Tanzania, the Dutch are well known for their responsiveness in this regard, as stated in an assessment of the Netherlands' programme:

> *In the health sector, the Tanzanian government appreciated Dutch flexibility to re-direct support to fill crucial gaps based on what was needed in Tanzania, rather than what was in vogue at home.* (OECD 2011d: 20–21)

The WHO adopts a similarly flexible approach. Although country strategies based on the global agenda and regional directions provide the broad framework for technical support, concrete activities are negotiated at the country-level between WHO staff and the local actors within the ministries and departments.[60]

---

58 Donors differ widely with regard to the allocation of staff between headquarters and 'the field'. The assumption that a higher share of staff in the field goes along with a higher degree of flexibility and responsiveness, however, does not hold true. The decisive factor in this regard is the degree of decision-making authority in the field, as elucidated above.

59 According to a study conducted by the OECD in 2009, nine of 19 DAC donors do not allow their field staff to make any financial commitments. In contrast, "DFID field offices can commit up to USD 15 million, and the Netherlands and Norway can delegate full commitment authority to the field within budget limits" (OECD 2009b: 5).

60 Globally, the WHO is guided by its "Eleventh General Programme of Work 2006–2015" (World Health Organization 2006) and the "Medium-Term Strategic Plan 2008–2013" (World Health Organization 2008). Further, there are regional policy documents, as, for example, the "Strategic directions for WHO 2010–2015" in the African region (World Health Organization 2010). Yet, WHO country strategies emphasise that technical assistance is solely provided upon the request of governments and fully guided by their respective priorities (World Health Organization 2009b; World Health Organization 2009c).

Contrary to these examples, there are organisations which maintain highly centralised decision-making structures. World Bank headquarters exert significant influence on the country assistance strategies that determine the Bank's scope of support. Each single project has to be submitted to the Bank's board of executive directors for consideration and approval (World Bank 2012b). Some bilateral donors, particularly those that use executing agencies, have similar centralised set-ups. USAID, for instance, is to a large extent driven by directives from Washington where the global agenda is set.[61] Changes of priorities at the central level immediately affect activities on the ground. When the agency released its new education strategy 'Opportunity through learning' in 2011, country offices world-wide had to align the fit of their on-going activities with the new directive. With goal one being "improved reading skills for 100 million children in primary grades by 2015" (USAID 2011), "every USAID office around the globe has to show outcomes in readings" (Interview 42), an education specialist at USAID in Tanzania reported. Consequently, he had to justify before his superiors in Washington programmatic elements dealing with math and science which in light of the new strategy were perceived as "out of alignment" (Interview 42).

Categorising aid organisations by the extent of their decision-making autonomy at the country-level, we can differentiate two types: the first one with little autonomy functions as a service-provider implementing the directives of its superior authority. There is a clear-cut institutional separation between decision-making and the delivery of aid. The second type is more than just an executing arm of respective headquarters. It is the sub-agent of the donor country on the ground, responsible not only for implementing activities, but also authorised to take financial and programmatic decisions. Although the superior authority gives overall guidance, representatives in the field have a relatively broad room for manoeuvre in prioritising their support.

Legitimating and organising aid: Donor typology

We can draw the following conclusions from the above: first, bi- and multilateral aid is to a varying extent driven by strategic interests of donor governments which use different rationales for providing assistance. While some frame aid as an instrument to foster their own political and economic interests, others justify it as a humanitarian act and a matter of responsibility. Second, the extent to which the donor's domestic agenda determines aid activities very

---

61 As an example, the global strategy "PEPFAR Blueprint: Creating an AIDS-free generation" (United States of America, Department of State 2012) released by the US State Department on World AIDS Day 2012 became the guiding document for the US AIDS response world-wide and heavily influenced second-generation PEPFAR programmes at country-level.

much depends on the degree of authority delegated to the agents in the field (i.e. staff in country offices or embassies).

Both features, legitimation patterns and organisational structures, determine the extent to which aid is tied to a certain donor agenda or responsive to recipients' priorities. Combining the two variables, four different types of donors emerge as displayed in Figure 3: Type I represents donors that subject aid to strategic self-interests and strongly direct the delivery of aid from a central level, making sure it adheres to the headquarters' agenda. Type II donors set an agenda led by vested interests, but concede a high degree of decision-making autonomy to staff in the field which allows for greater responsiveness to counterpart demands. Type III donors delegate less authority to country offices and representations, but are led by the principle of placing recipient needs over self-interests. Type IV is the antipode to the first one: guided by solidarity as political rationale for aid, donors of this type refrain from (strongly) tying aid to self-interests and delegate the responsibility for aid mainly to the field.

Figure 3: Donor typology based on aid rationales and decision-making structures

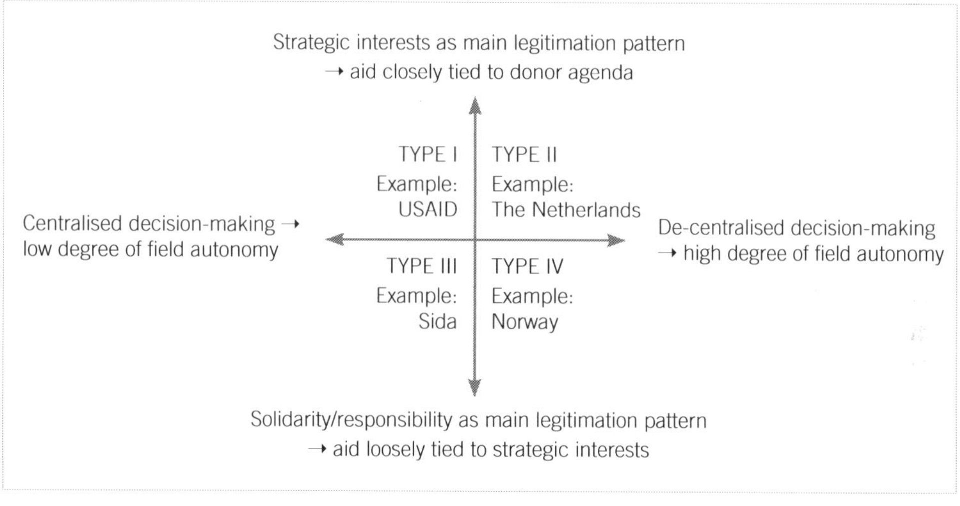

Source: Authors' own illustration.

Organisational interests of aid agencies

Donor governments use different conduits for channelling aid, ranging from different types of bilateral agencies to multilateral organisations. While these bodies vary in terms of mandates, missions and structures, they share one decisive feature: their primary organisational goal is 'moving money' (Easterly 2002: 22; Gould 2005a: 150). The legitimacy of aid organisations is based on aid delivery. Given the difficulty in assessing the quality of delivered aid in terms of actual change achieved in recipient countries, performance is measured against the volume of money disbursed. Although in recent years more emphasis has been put on observable outcomes of support (e.g. more children in schools), aid organisations still justify their work in terms of input, that is, money spent (Easterly 2002: 21): The World Bank on its country website for Tanzania mainly displays lending commitments and informs that "since 1995 the Bank has provided more than USD 6 billion to Tanzania in credits and grants" (World Bank 2013b). In the GIZ 2012 Annual Report, the state secretary of the German Federal Ministry for Economic Cooperation and Development in his function as chairman of the GIZ supervisory board declared that "GIZ made excellent progress by doing business worth over EUR 2 billion, and gaining an even firmer foothold on the international cooperation market for sustainable development" (GIZ 2013a: 5). The Danish Ministry of Foreign Affairs, presenting its performance against the strategic goal of tackling poverty and global inequality, noted that in 2012, "development assistance was increased by DKK 234 million and this amount will increase by a further DKK 366 million in 2013" (Ministry of Foreign Affairs of Denmark 2013: 16).

The fact that aid providers "redefine inputs to development as outputs" (Easterly 2002: 21) yields the logic that the more they spend the better. This equally holds true for creditor institutions that work towards higher lending volumes, for aid agencies that aim at increasing business volumes and for bureaucracies that seek to expand their budgets.[62, 63] In the case of the latter, the disbursement imperative is exacerbated by the risk that "parliaments will react forcefully if approved allocations are not disbursed" (Gould & Ojanen 2005: 22), that is, cut the ministry's budget.

The spending pressure pervading aid organisations has significant effects on the ground. First, it leads to donor-financed activities which lack any need on the recipient's side, being solely organised for the sake of shifting money. A former GIZ programme manager told us:

> *We had situations where (…) we received the directive to disburse around twelve thousand Euro within the next six weeks. Twelve thousand Euros are a hell of a lot of money to spend in a Tanzanian district. So what to do? I conduct a workshop as this is the fastest way to ditch money.*
> (Interview 73, translated by authors)

---

62 The conception of the German aid agency GIZ as a company pursuing entrepreneurial goals has been underlined by GIZ staff interviewed, with one stating: "We are an enterprise and this has been pushed a lot in recent years, with our current chairman of the supervisory board being one of the drivers of this development. (…) GIZ is clearly drilled on business, we deliver by order." (Interview 4, translated by authors)

63 For the budget-maximising goals of bureaucracies, see Niskanen (1971, repr. 2007).

Second, donor staff tend to refrain from withholding funds even if interventions fail to materialise or irregularities emerge. The organisational target to deliver what has been agreed tends to precede concerns about the usage of aid. An interviewee working at GIZ commented in this regard:

> *There were and there are cases of corruption in Tanzania where one wonders why certain donors did not suspend payments and instead just said, 'we continue to transfer money.' There you think there should be other interests on donor side.* (Interview 72, translated by authors)

The "disbursement anxiety" dominating the donor community is not only related to "concerns of institutional survival" (Gould & Ojanen 2005: 22). It also drives donor staff at an individual level since professional careers depend on the volume of project or programme budgets and the timeliness of delivery (Gould 2005a: 139–140; Mummert 2013: 59). Thus, neither aid organisations nor their functionaries have an incentive to make themselves redundant by reducing aid flows and the need for assistance. If they succeeded in solving the problems of developing countries, their very existence would be at stake. The Kenyan economist James Shikwati, an outspoken opponent of foreign aid, thus states that "it is not in the interest of the aid industry to promote African homegrown solutions, because it feeds on the African problem" (Shikwati 2006: 4).

The epistemic community of development experts

The aid industry provides employment opportunities for a broad range of professionals, ranging from bureaucrats to drivers. Its core cadre, however, is formed by experts who sell their knowledge and act as brokers in the field of development cooperation.[64] Operating on the ground, they serve as intermediaries between donor and recipient governments. Experts' brokerage facilitates the transfer of monetary and non-monetary resources from one side to the other, putting them in a crucial middle position in the aid arena where they constitute a 'strategic group' with distinct interests (Bierschenk 1988; Evers 2005). In the triad of aid relations, this group takes on the role of the *'tertius gaudens'* (Simmel 1950: 154 et seq.) that benefits from the opportunity to make profits and increase its own status, to accumulate power and expand

---

64 We draw here on brokerage as a mechanism enabling disconnected groups to politically, economically or socially interact via a third party which helps resources (e.g. goods, money, information, opportunities) to flow across the gap. For details on the concept, see Stovel and Shaw (2012).

its scope of influence. In the following chapter, development experts are described as a transnational epistemic community with a particular stock of shared knowledge whose roles and activities help to explain their impact in recipient countries.

Development experts: An epistemic community with knowledge as strategic resource

The rise of the 'knowledge for development paradigm' brought about the emergence of a global network of professionals who have become increasingly powerful: development experts in various roles and positions whose dominance is based on their ascribed expert knowledge on 'development' and all fields supposedly related to it. Haas (1992) defines such a "network of professionals with recognized expertise and competence in a particular domain and an authoritative claim to policy-relevant knowledge within that domain or issue-area" an "epistemic community". Although members may come from different disciplines and backgrounds, they share a set of normative and causal beliefs, notions of validity and a common policy enterprise, "that is, a set of common practices associated with a set of problems to which their professional competence is directed" (Haas 1992: 3). Their authority to diffuse their specific truth is based on the superior status of their knowledge which is both claimed by themselves and acknowledged by a given society and its elite (Haas 1992: 17).

In the realm of aid, these features apply to the epistemic community of development experts. Consisting of professionals from a great variety of disciplines, its members share basic concepts and ideas that construct a reality in which goals and strategies increasingly converge (Evers 2005: 11).[65] Their power to define 'development' and development problems, and their legitimacy in providing suitable solutions rests on the expert knowledge they claim to possess and the accepted authority of their expertise. This knowledge has five distinct characteristics: (1) a claim to authority borrowed from science; (2) a high degree of self-referentiality; (3) being permeated with economic and managerial knowledge; (4) a claim to universal applicability; and (5) the potential to transnationally diffuse a distinct set of norms and values.

What makes an expert an expert: Qualification criteria and professional backgrounds

In order to identify epistemic characteristics of development experts' knowledge and the sources of their expertise, it is a useful starting point to look at formal

---

65 The Millenium Development Goals proclaimed at the Millenium Summit in the year 2000 and agreed by 23 international organisations and 192 countries impressively illustrate the homogenisation tendency in the global development discourse.

qualification criteria and career backgrounds. They may indicate 'what makes an expert an expert'.

Comparing eligibility criteria for advisory-related positions, the most obvious pattern is the requirement for an advanced university degree even at the lowest levels. To enter the so-called "Professional and Technical career path" at the World Bank, for instance, "advanced academic achievements and/ or technical professional credentials such as Masters or PhD" (World Bank 2012d) are obligatory. In fact, a PhD is seen as essential for high-level advisory positions and promotion within the organisation (Dietrich 2006). In our sample, all interviewees working for an international organisation at least had a masters degree, one out of three a PhD.

A noticeable aspect related to the experts' academic background is *where* they have received their professional training. Among the foreign experts (i.e. experts who are not South African or Tanzanian nationals), 89% have acquired their highest level of education either in North America (US or Canada) or in Europe, the remaining 11% in both a developing and a developed country. Among the South African or Tanzanian nationals working for a donor organisation, two out of three have earned a degree in the West; only one out of three received their education solely in South Africa or Tanzania. This supports the observation that the expert community in the development arena is dominated by graduates whose expertise is certified with academic credentials achieved at Anglo-American or European universities.[66] In the case of the World Bank, many of them pass through the same schools, especially those of the US Ivy league and British elite universities such as the London School of Economics (Dietrich 2006: 33).[67]

The range of subjects studied by staff in international organisations is broad. In the sample interviewed, the majority is related to health sciences, educational sciences and natural/environmental sciences which corresponds to the policy fields of the study; the remainder can be categorised into economics and financial management, international relations/development studies and other social sciences. Many respondents specified more than one discipline. In many educational profiles, sector-specific studies were combined with additional training in public administration or development, for instance, "Sustainable Development and Environmental Studies, Public Financial Management,

---

66 Given that our study focused on traditional donors and did not include agencies from emerging donors such as Brazil or India, one may criticise that the results presented are geographically biased. However, as European, North American and multilateral agencies still are the dominant organisations in aid, we argue that our sample, which includes experts working for 13 different agencies, provides a valid basis for our conclusion.

67 In her study on World Bank careers, Dietrich (2006: 33) cites a staff member saying: "A colleague of mine told me that there are more than 70 different nationalities working for the Bank, but they all come from ten different graduate schools."

International Studies", "Public Health and International Development" or "Environment and Society and MBA". The variety and the cross-disciplinary nature of educational backgrounds is a common pattern identified in the aid community which is the result of a shift towards multi-sectoral approaches and 'cross-cutting' issues (e.g. 'good governance') requiring "good team players who can work across sector boundaries", as a World Bank report put it (World Bank 2005a: 34).

In all fields of development aid, management and administrative skills have increasingly gained importance. Several interviewees on both the recipient and donor side noticed a remarkable shift in employment practices in the sense that sector specialists in country offices have been replaced by administrators, accountants and economists. A South African government official responsible for international relations delineated this development as follows:

> *Now what you then have in the period 1995 to let's just say 2000 if I had to mark it (…) is that foreign governments would place in development cooperation offices experts and people who had great interest in the transformation agenda in South Africa. And these were experts in their fields. Now what happens after that period is that you find administrators coming in, who have a very different interest and approach to development issues. So that's I think a very critical issue.* (Interview 21)

The changing composition of advisory cadres is closely related to the changing nature of advisory positions and responsibilities. A study on DFID's use of advisors confirms this shift:

> *There has been a move towards promoting interdisciplinarity, cross-sector working, and therefore multi-sector posts. This trend can be seen in the emergence of 'results advisers', 'poverty advisers', MDG advisers etc. (…). As DFID has placed more emphasis on defining core competencies and on ensuring they align with corporate strategy this has led to a stronger emphasis on management skills and experience.* (Mendizabal et al. 2012: x)

Aside from the shift related to educational backgrounds and the respective expertise of advisors, a second aspect of qualification is in flux, namely the scope and nature of development experts' work experience. In this regard, the DFID study states that

> *whereas a decade ago DFID advisers had substantial professional background and experience, recruited mid-career and of an older age,*

advisers are being recruited earlier in their careers with less experience, and are unable to offer advice with the same depth. (Mendizabal et al. 2012: 11)

Similarly, a World Bank report finds that in some regions,

the number of team leaders with less than three years experience in the Bank is relatively significant. For example, in the Africa Region the staff profile is becoming less experienced at a time when the operational challenges call for more experience, knowledge of what works and how to do it, and capability to help enhance country capacity. (World Bank 2005a: 37)

Many experts enter international organisations relatively soon after finishing their studies with little work experience in their profession outside the development domain. This tendency is supported by an increasing number of programmes for young professionals designed to bridge the time span between graduation and advisory positions, and provide a stepping stone for a straight-forward career in the aid community.[68]

International experience, preferably in the development world, is a crucial asset for this career. Once in the business, advisors accumulate assignments in a remarkable list of developing countries, staying at one place on average for two to four years.[69] The professional profiles indicate a high degree of international mobility, with experts shifting from one developing country to the next or commuting between headquarters and the 'field'.[70] Interestingly, language skills and cultural knowledge seem to be of minor importance for the secondment to a host country. In our sample, 83% of the foreign experts

---

68 Examples are the Junior Professional Officer Programme of the United Nations agencies (UNDP 2013a), the World Bank's Young Professional Programme (World Bank 2012f) or the Development Cooperation Trainee Programme offered by GIZ (GIZ 2013b). All of these programmes require a university degree at the masters level, around two years of practical experience (preferably in a developing country), and set the age limit for applicants between 30 and 32 years.

69 In our sample, 72% of the foreign experts indicated they would stay in South Africa and Tanzania, respectively, for 2 to 4 years (11% between 5 and 7 years, 16.6% permanently). Nationals working for development organisations, in contrast, show a different pattern in this regard: many have a permanent contract for working in the respective country office. In our sample, six out of seven 'national' experts who gave details about the duration of their stay are deployed on a permanent basis (answer "unlimited").

70 The internal regulations with regard to rotation differ. While some organisations do not set strict rules, others apply specific rotation principles and limit the duration of stay in overseas offices to a certain time span after which staff has to go back to headquarters for a while. The justification for this practice mentioned in interviews is to ensure that experts keep up with headquarters' policies and professional knowledge, and avoid 'going native' in the field.

did not have basic knowledge of Kiswahili or Afrikaans, respectively.[71] Both in South Africa and Tanzania, the working language between advisors and their counterparts is English, the primary global language used within the expert community.

The brief glance at professional backgrounds and careers allows a first characterisation of the epistemic group of development experts: they share a common belief in 'development' and interest in providing knowledge-based concepts for the same. The formal criteria qualifying members for their professional activity is first of all technical knowledge acquired through high-level academic training. This specialised knowledge is combined with managerial skills and merged with practical experience gained primarily within the professional field of development cooperation.

Implications for the nature of development knowledge

Based on these patterns, the knowledge shared by the epistemic community of development experts shows five distinct characteristics. First, development experts' expertise derives its credibility from the reference to scientific knowledge and the adoption of scientific styles of presentation. Expert knowledge is certified by academic degrees usually acquired in developed countries of the North. Although aid experts are not part of the science community, nor do they (regularly) participate in the scientific discourse, the authority of their advice is to a significant extent based on the claimed scientific grounding; it is an authority borrowed from the truth claim of science.[72]

Secondly, the expertise aid experts provide is neither based solely on scientific nor on professional knowledge outside the development domain. The working experience of advisors remains restricted, given the direct entry into the aid business. The generation of practical knowledge is thus primarily taking place within the realm of development cooperation. Consequently, a specific type of 'development knowledge' emerges that is highly self-referential.[73]

---

71 Among the foreign experts interviewed, only three had attended a language course before coming into the country. In general, preparatory training before going into the field does not seem to be standard: two out of three experts in the sample had not received any technical, cultural or language training courses prior to their arrival in the country. The fact that only a small number of organisations – in our sample Norway, Sweden, GIZ and USAID – provide preparatory courses is remarkable as one third of the interviewees in the study perceive cultural differences as problematic or even extremely problematic. More than half of the sample (54%) assesses different styles of communication as a major obstacle for cooperation.

72 Text (studies, evaluations, reports etc.) produced in the context of development cooperation resembles scientific publications in terms of formal characteristics such as the style of writing and referencing.

73 The self-referential nature of development knowledge is displayed in texts produced in the context of development projects, which primarily refer to publications produced within the aid community.

Thirdly, while the stock of knowledge on development comprises a variety of specialist knowledge, it is increasingly permeated with economics and managerial thinking. This is evidenced by a rising demand for specialised economists (such as health or environmental economists) and an increasing number of generalists and administrators filling expert positions. The changing composition of expertise impacts on advisory processes insofar as it leads to a primacy of procedural and finance-related aspects within cooperation (see also Chapter 5).

Fourthly, the mobility of experts and the establishment of global knowledge networks suggest that the epistemic community regards its specific development knowledge as locally unbound and transferable. The practice of adopting and testing ideas and concepts in different countries around the globe implies a validity claim of universal application (Evers et al. 2009).

Such a claim ignores the contextual nature of knowledge (i.e. that knowledge is infused with norms and values).[74] As Haas (1992: 4) points out, an epistemic community's advice "is informed by its own broader worldview". In the aid context, expert knowledge transmits a distinct perspective on development and democratic governance as constructed by the donor community. The potential to transnationally diffuse norms and values affiliated with these concepts is the fifth significant characteristic of the knowledge promulgated by the epistemic community of development experts. As will be shown in the pursuant case studies, the specific nature of development knowledge has distinct implications for advisory processes and the impact of expertise.

Representatives, advisors, and consultants: Typology of experts in the field

While sharing a transnational epistemic culture and using knowledge as a 'strategic resource' (Evers et al. 1988; Evers 2005), development experts take on different roles and operate at various levels in recipient countries. The positions they hold differ in terms of employment conditions, authority and functions, particularly with regard to the linkage of administrative, programmatic and advisory responsibilities. Taking these aspects into account, one can broadly differentiate three types of experts in the field: representatives, advisors and (short-term) consultants.

With job titles ranging from senior policy advisor, programme director or counsellor to first secretary for a specific sector, experts which we categorise as *representatives* are assigned to fulfil a combination of administrative, programmatic and advisory functions, and are usually deployed for a period

---

74 For the context specificity and constructiveness of knowledge, see Berger and Luckmann (1966); Knorr-Cetina (1981); Knorr-Cetina (1984).

of three to four years. Placed in the country office of an organisation or in the embassy of a donor country, they administrate a sector portfolio or programme, being responsible for both overseeing funding flows and progress. Acting as official representatives of their organisation, they also participate in high-level meetings in which priorities and scope of support are negotiated. At the same time, they are regularly engaged in policy discussions and closely interact with senior government officials and policy-makers. An exemplary job description of UNDP for the position of a "Programme Specialist Energy and Climate Change" in Tanzania illustrates the broad range of responsibilities, listing 36 points of duties which comprise "substantive support to national counterparts in policy planning and advocacy", "participation and leadership in the joint identification of programmatic and policy issues to be addressed and formulation of joint programme strategies" and "oversight of planning, budgeting, implementing and monitoring of designated UNDP projects, and monitoring the use of financial resources in accordance with UNDP rules and regulations" (UNDP 2012).

Experts in such a multifunctional position are not necessarily sector specialists in the sense that they have a training background in the field they are concerned with. For the UNDP job above, the educational requirement was a masters degree or higher in the field of science, engineering, economics, development or a related field. A DFID education advisor in our sample was trained in geographic information science. A CIDA education team leader with a background in international affairs and development studies explained:

> I'm a generalist, basically, and that's fairly typical for who CIDA puts in positions like mine. (...) Our expertise is more in how to work with governments, and how to work with our headquarters, and how to get projects approved, and through the process and so on, and then how to manage resources as needed. (Interview 30)

The tendency to employ generalists instead of specialists is supported by the increasing number of hybrid posts covering more than one sector. DFID in Tanzania, for example, in 2004 had established an advisory position responsible for education, water and health (Mendizabal et al. 2012).[75] As will be discussed later (see Chapter 5), the move away from sector specialists has significant implications for advisory processes as it changes the expertise provided in policy discussions.

---

75 While the establishment of a hybrid advisor reduced staff costs in the Tanzanian country office, it also led to a decreased influence of DFID, particularly in health. An evaluation concluded that hybrid advisors are not suited to influence policies in multiple sectors simultaneously, with advisors struggling to provide substantial input at a technical level (Mendizabal et al. 2012).

Compared to representatives, the work of the second type of experts categorised here as *advisors* is less concerned with representational and administrative tasks and more focused on providing technical expertise. Advisors are usually trained as specialists in the area they are involved in and deployed to assist in a specific process over a period of on average one to four years. They are often physically placed in the government ministry or department in order to closely interact with their counterparts who are usually senior government officials in the highest ranks of the technical cadre. A typical example is the Health Policy, Planning and Management Advisor of Danida's health sector support (2009–2014) who was embedded in the Ministry of Health and Social Welfare in Tanzania and supposed to closely liaise with the director of policy and planning and the chief medical officer (Ministry of Foreign Affairs of Denmark & Government of Tanzania 2009). Similarly, DFID seconded a senior health advisor to the South African Department of Health who in the context of a comprehensive programme directly advised the director-general on on-going reform processes (DFID South Africa 2013). Advisors thus operate within the inner circle of governments. Their deployment is justified in terms of 'capacity gaps' in recipient authorities which they are expected to fill and at the same time to transfer knowledge and skills to their counterparts.[76]

The third type of expert is the consultant hired by development organisations and/or recipient institutions for the delivery of expertise in the form of specific products, such as appraisal and feasibility studies, mid-term and final evaluations, expenditure tracking surveys, guidelines, etc. The time frame for short-term consultancies is usually far less than a year, on average ranging from a few weeks to six months. In many cases consultancies are solely based on the analysis of records and written documents. The interaction with ministerial staff is mostly limited to gaining information and access to data sources from the local institution. To what extent recipients take up reports and recommendations is out of the consultant's responsibility and control, as a Finnish specialist acknowledged:

> *Doing consultancy is much like you do short term things and then you write a report and even if you manage to communicate very well about it to the people with whom you've worked, then you don't know if something is done, if your recommendations are really being implemented or what happens after that.* (Interview 36)

In aid-receiving countries donor experts of all three types "work in a routinised fashion at the centre of policy making" (Harrison 2004: 90). Comparing their potential influence, the short-term consultant is at the lower end. Several

---

76 The intricacies of this task will be discussed in Chapter 5.

interviewees assessed the impact of consultancies as marginal. As a GIZ advisor in South Africa put it:

> *Arriving as a short-term consultant, you hand in your analysis, here is the report, these are the recommendations. They say, 'Yes, thank you' – and put it in the shelf.* (Interview 4, translated by authors)

The other two types of experts, in contrast, have a broader scope of impact. Advisors seconded to counterpart ministries interact with senior officials on a daily basis, operating at the highest technical level of government. Representatives may less directly take a hand in particular issues, but instead shape the strategic direction of sector discussions. Investigating the impact of external experts in South Africa and Tanzania, it is thus crucial to consider their different roles and levels of influence in the realm of policy-making.

Advisory activities of development experts

The omnipresence of development experts in the respective government agencies of aid-receiving countries provokes a simple question: what do these experts actually do, that is, what kind of support do they provide? The common answer given to this question, namely providing technical assistance or advice, is rather vague. In the donor community, the term is used as a placeholder for a variety of advisory activities which address different elements of policy-making and governance. Table 3 displays a categorisation of advice provided in the South African and Tanzanian ministries and departments included in this study:

Table 3: Advisory activities, types of support and impact levels

Advisory activity	Type of support	Impact level
Technical advice	Provision of technical expertise	Content of policies
Provision of international experience	Bringing in experience and evidence from other countries	Content of policies
Process facilitation	Facilitating dialogue and supporting the policy process	Policy processes
Managerial advice	Introduction and transfer of managerial methodologies	Governance practice
Organisational development	Assistance in setting up or re-structuring government bodies	Governance systems

Source: Authors' own compilation based on empirical material.[77]

---

77   Table 3 only includes expert activities related to advice; it does not comprise administrative tasks or programmatic responsibilities.

In Table 3 technical advice is defined in a narrow sense as the provision of expertise for problems which require specialist knowledge. Experts in our sample, for instance, prepared guidelines for the initiation of antiretroviral treatment on HIV patients, analysed data for environmental resource assessments or provided input in the process of revising policies, in some cases even drafted the final policy document.

Less directly, experts shape policy content by providing international experience, namely, presenting approaches adopted in other countries for similar problems. A South African government official described the advisory service of an expert seconded to his department in the following way:

> *He [the advisor] will go out and research what is it that we are trying to do and find out very good learning experiences from other places (…). So he would be able to say, 'Look, I know this what you are trying but in this other places, this is how they approach this issue and it seems as if you have got these options, these are consequences.' And where he could not come up with a clear recommendation, he will phone other people that he was working with to search for the solutions that were used in their countries and what were some of the problems.* (Interview 22)

Here, the strategic resource experts draw on is less specialised knowledge, but rather their access to a global network in which experiences are stored and shared. This network also enables them to source internal and external expertise which governments are struggling to obtain. The mobilisation of knowledge is a typical activity classified under the broader rubric of 'facilitation' or 'catalytic work'. While in Tanzania, a large proportion of advice is still focused on the provision of technical expertise, many experts in South Africa saw themselves as facilitators rather than as knowledge providers. A typical response in this regard was given by an advisor placed in the South African Department of Health who stated:

> *A lot of the work that we're doing is like facilitating groups, getting together, making sure due process is adhered to so if you're going to do a consultation, make sure all the right groups are there, it's that sort of thing. More facilitation and doing catalytic work, not so much the technical content of policies because that on the whole is here, that's not where the gap is.* (Interview 1)

In practice, this means that advisors support the policy process by setting up meetings, preparing agendas, distributing information, drafting the minutes and monitoring follow-up actions. While this may seem as standard bureaucratic work, it does affect policy processes in a significant way. By providing administrative assistance, experts impact the pace, procedures and priorities of policy negotiations. As brokers between stakeholder groups, they also to some extent influence who is given a voice in the dialogue. Finding civil society members or representatives of the private sector in policy discussions is often the result of donor persuasion. As a World Bank expert in Tanzania put it:

> *A significant portion on the Bank's value added is that you force all these people in a room together to talk about things, you know. They would say we're a 'convening power'.* (Interview 46)

This 'convening power' becomes manifest in meetings and events which are not likely to take place without external facilitation. A study tour on climate change financed and organised by the World Bank in the year 2012 serves as a case in point in this regard. In cooperation with DFID and the UNDP, the Bank brought a range of high-ranking Tanzanian government officials and civil society actors to Namibia for a week of workshops and discussions with 'knowledge providers' from Mexico, South Africa, Zambia and the host country. The aim of this 'Learning Week', as the World Bank termed it, "was for Tanzanian decision makers and advocates to learn from successful approaches to climate change planning in different economic and regional contexts and apply these lessons to their own context" (World Bank 2012g). The impact of this sort of facilitating work is hard to measure directly. Yet, through organising discourse behind the scenes, experts are able to push certain topics (such as climate change in the example above), to channel who is doing the talk and to accelerate the pace of policy-making concerning the respective matter.

A direct impact of expert engagement which is more easily observable concerns the practice of governance: managerial advice to recipient bureaucracies has fundamentally changed their ways of working. Since the rise of new public management, experts have introduced "new methodologies of governance based on corporate plans, surveys and closer budgeting/ monitoring techniques" (Harrison 2004: 90). Asked what kind of expertise World Bank and UNDP experts provided to his organisation in the context of a joint environmental project, a South African official explained:

> *I think they did bring with them a lot of project management skills which was useful, also evaluation mechanisms, you know, to evaluate your effectivity on the ground, your project effectivity, your cost effectivity, and so on. I think what also came out of this process very nicely was [that] it gives you the opportunity to stand back and evaluate objectively what*

*you're doing and why you are doing it, to question on a regular basis
that what you do is in fact aimed at a proper goal and a proper objective.*
(Interview 13)

The adoption of project management tools and evaluation mechanisms has
far-reaching implications for government ministries and departments. It not
only changes the language and format of their policies and plans which now
commonly entail 'strategic objectives' and 'logframe tables', but also basic
principles ('efficiency and effectiveness') and practices of governance.

The last type of support in this categorisation of advisory activities is
organisational development. Our study provides various examples in which
external experts assisted in restructuring government bodies (e.g. the South
African National AIDS Council) or establishing new units or offices (e.g. the
South African Office of Health Standards Compliance), and thus engaged in
shaping governance systems of aid-receiving countries.

Addressing policy content and processes, as well as governance systems and
practice, development experts deal with core issues of democratic governance.
As Gould (2005b: 9) observes, they interact with a "growing assertiveness" in
the political arena of recipient countries. Given their intimate involvement
therein, it is striking that experts tend to dissociate themselves from the
political processes in their host countries (Gould & Ojanen 2003).[78] Reflecting
on their professional role, several experts in our sample rejected any political
influence.[79] Similar to others, a GIZ advisor said:

> *Whether I adopt a health financing system based on a social insurance
> model as we have in Germany, or a private one as in the US, or the NHS
> [National Health Service] in the UK, is a political decision. These decisions
> are made and must then be implemented by technical experts. We do not
> take part in political decision-making, we advise and recommend, but the
> decisions have to be taken at a different level.* (Interview 4, translated
> by authors)

Only two senior experts, one of them retired, explicitly acknowledged having
shaped political decisions in their host countries to a significant extent. The
majority of donor representatives interviewed rather downplayed their role in

---

78 Gould and Ojanen (2003: 15) observed the "dissociation from political processes" as a "defining
characteristic" of the transnational expert elite, with donors "commonly avoid[ing] the appearance
of engaging in 'politics'".

79 Interestingly, when asked for an assessment of their organisation's impact on policy processes in
South Africa and Tanzania, almost two out of three donor interviewees (65.4%) in our sample
ranked their organisation as being "amongst the most influential key players" (7.7% "most
influential key player"; 23.1% "middle-range impact"; 3.8% "low impact").

policy-making. Framing advice as a technocratic exercise, however, not only disguises the impact of external experts on policy-making and governance in young democracies; it also makes it impossible to hold them to account for consequences of their advice, despite their considerable discursive power in the political realm.

Summing up this chapter on actors and interests in aid, it has become clear that development assistance is used as a strategic tool by all players involved. While donor governments aim at maintaining geopolitical influence, as well as fostering export and trade, recipient governments seek to increase their budgets and thus their capacity to act, but also to strengthen relations with partners on their diplomatic priority list. Hence, aid is an instrument of foreign and domestic politics on both sides, albeit used from different angles.

Looking at the level of organisations, the logic 'the more aid, the better' equally applies to bureaucracies that receive and to those which deliver it. Underfinanced ministries and departments in developing countries are usually keen to access as much additional funding as possible which often results in struggles between treasuries, line ministries and authorities at lower levels competing for donor money. As 'moving money' is the primary objective and source of legitimacy of aid bureaucracies, they share their partners' interest in high spending volumes and on-going disbursements. Continued need for external support legitimates their existence.

This also holds true for the individual employees of aid organisations who have tangible incentives to 'keep aid rolling' since their careers depend on it. Development cooperation has created a profitable market for professionals from various branches who are attracted by material and non-material rewards: with salaries matching donor countries' pay scales, aid experts commonly enjoy a relatively high living standard in their host countries. Their (ascribed) expert knowledge grants them access to the highest government levels. Naturally, individuals work towards keeping that status. New aid projects and programmes, however, not only advance the careers of donor staff. They also promise benefits for officials in recipient institutions who can personally profit from extra payments commonly connected with donor-funded activities.

In this summary, we paint a very 'selfish' picture of the agents involved in development cooperation. That calls for a qualification: it is not to be doubted that there are good intentions in aid, that is, that donor governments provide assistance out of a political culture which emphasises solidarity; that recipient institutions secure aid in order to fix health systems or improve education etc.; or that experts and government officials cooperate in aid projects with the goal of making a change for the people. The purpose of this chapter, however, was to shed light on the web of interrelated interests playing a role in development cooperation. The fact that aid is driven by actors with multiple motives and agendas which sometimes correlate, but often collide, provides a complicated setting for advisory processes. The intricacies of expert advice that result from the linkage of aid and politics and other structural flaws in the context of aid are spelled out in more detail in the following chapter.

Chapter 5

INTRICACIES OF EXPERT ADVICE IN THE AID CONTEXT

Expert advice provided in the context of aid takes place in a setting characterised by colliding interests, political pressures and asymmetric power relations. Such preconditions are obstructive to advisory processes in several regards. First, the linkage of aid and politics makes advice volatile, conditional and supply-oriented in that it is driven by shifting fads and legitimation pressures. Second, advisory processes are hampered by structural flaws related to conceptual deficiencies and employment practices on the part of donor organisations which impede knowledge transfer and learning. Third, advisory relations in the context of aid are structured along a knowledge hierarchy that reinforces power imbalances and marginalises rather than strengthens local expert communities. The various constraints which will be outlined in this chapter explain the failure of expert advice as a means of development assistance. This manifests itself in the persistent dependency on external expertise after decades of 'capacity-building' interventions.

The linkage between aid and politics

Aid provided by states to states is inherently political insofar as it is an outcome of political negotiation, and carried out in the realm of politics. The current knowledge paradigm which legitimates external assistance as primarily capacity building tends to mask the intrinsically political nature of aid. The prevailing "economic-centric, technocratic approach to development" (Carothers & De Gramont 2013: 3) is preferred by the international donor community for good reasons:

> While economics appears as a rational, scientific domain, politics seem to imply inevitable entanglement with the irrational side of human affairs – with ideological fervor, nationalistic impulses, and other volatile passions.

Economics emphasizes consensual ideas, like the universal appeal of prosperity and the tragedy of poverty. In contrast, politics is all about conflicting visions and objectives. Economics deals in definite goals, with easily measurable signs of improvement. Politics is about subjective values, with signs of progress hard to agree on, let alone measure. (Carothers & De Gramont 2013: 3–4)

This chapter aims to highlight the linkage between aid and politics and its implications for expert advice provided in the context of development cooperation: first by showing how advisory processes are affected by shifting fads regarding aid priorities and modes of operation which are driven by global and domestic politics on the donor side. Attention will then be turned to the legitimation and accountability pressure in aid which, translated into extensive reporting practices, substantially impacts on advisory relations and bureaucracies in recipient countries. Finally, it is elucidated how the linkage between aid and politics causes a twofold mismatch of supply and demand for expertise: the first pertains to advisory subjects and derives from conflicting agendas on both the donor and recipient side; the second concerns a general discrepancy between advice provided and requested which emanates from the fact that it serves donors as a means of influence and control.

Shifting themes and modes of operation

Due to its dependency on politics, the aid community is "very fickle" (Interview 27), as a South African civil society leader stated. This equally holds true for priority areas of support and favourite modes of operation. They shift with global trends and domestic developments in donor states. A retired government official in Tanzania commented in this regard:

Sometimes priorities change. Sometimes an initiative begins well – and then there are things called elections [laughing]. They just happened in France the other day, and you have a change of government – this change of government comes with different policies saying now we are getting out of environment, now I think we are looking at gender, you know. Those kinds of things can actually happen. (Interview 66)

Fluctuating trends in aid topics and modalities
The fluctuation of topics in aid can be traced both across and within sectors. Figure 4 displays aid flows to selected areas in the period 1990–2012, drawing on aggregate ODA data from all donors captured in the OECD/DAC reporting

system. The sharp increase of aid to 'Government & Civil Society', a cluster summarising assistance for issues such as public management, institution-building, and fiscal policy and planning, is eye-catching. Aid spent on these areas more than doubled from USD 3 373 million in 1999 to USD 7 236 million in 2000 and went up to USD 21 325 million in 2011 which reflects the career of 'good governance' as an aid topic over the last decade. In the same period, HIV/Aids began to receive significant attention from the international community. The steep rise in allocations for health can mainly be ascribed to HIV/Aids-related funding which was pushed through the establishment of the Global Fund and PEPFAR around 2002/2003. With the advent of governance and HIV as donor priorities, the previously strong emphasis on education diminished. While in the early 1990s, education was among the sectors absorbing the bulk of aid resources, it was gradually superseded by other topics in the first years of the new millennium. Despite global campaigns such as the 'Education for All' initiative, spending relatively stagnated: whereas the total sum of ODA from 1990 to 2012 increased by 62%,[80] the volume of aid to education only increased by 14%. Similarly, aid allocated for water supply and sanitation did not keep up with other sectors that came onto the agenda, as, for instance, environment which has emerged as an issue in recent years. The volume of aid spent on general environmental protection quintupled from 1995 (the first year in which it was captured as a separate category in the OECD database) to 2012. Since as a cross-cutting theme, environment is also targeted by activities in other sectors (e.g. a forest management programme in the forestry sector), the total amount of environment-related aid can be assumed to be much higher than the graph in Figure 4 indicates (OECD 2012b).[81]

The composition of aid not only shifted across but also within sectors. In education, the once prominent field of vocational education and training faded from the spotlight when at the 1990 World Conference on Education for All in Jomtien basic education came to the fore. Although the concept was originally "associated with the fulfilment of basic learning needs related to learning and life skills for every person – child, youth, and adult" (Buchert 1995: 19), many donors narrowed their focus on (early) childhood development, shifting resources to primary education at the expense of other areas. This new emphasis was reaffirmed by the Millennium Development Goals which set universal primary education by 2015 as a global target. Yet, even prior to 2015, spending figures indicated a sharp downturn in support to basic education

---

80 According to OECD data extracted on 16 January 2013 from OECD.Stat, total ODA amounted to USD 203 221 million in 1990 and to USD 328 339 million in 2012.

81 In 2009–2010, the sum of only bilateral aid which scored environmental sustainability as 'principal' or 'significant objective' exceeded USD 25 billion, "representing a quarter of bilateral sector allocable ODA" (OECD 2012b: 57).

Figure 4: Aid to selected sectors 1990–2012

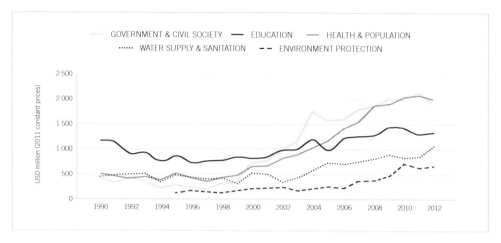

Source: OECD.Stat (2014a).[83]

particularly in low-income countries, with some donors completely pulling out of the area (Global Campaign For Education 2013). Instead, 'old' priorities come back into the picture, as an expert working in the Swedish Embassy in Dar es Salaam observed:

> We've been (…) focusing on basic education for the last [years], but before that during the 1990s we were very much into vocational training and before that we were also into folk education quite a lot. The Swedish government and Sida Stockholm decided to phase out the vocational training – but now we are moving back as many others. (Interview 40)

In health, the most significant change was caused by the rise of HIV/Aids as an aid priority. The share of HIV-related funding grew rapidly from around 3%–5% of total health assistance during the 1990s to 24% in 2010, which constituted the largest portion allocated to one specific health area. Moreover, in line with the increasing attention to governance in the first decade of the millennium, 'health systems strengthening' came onto the agenda. While still a minor area, its share sharply rose from only 0.2% in 1990 to 4.2% in 2010. A topic which lost its previous significance is maternal, new-born and child health. Although spending in absolute numbers grew at a stable pace between

---

82 Data were extracted on 16 January 2013 from OECD.Stat for the following codes: Government & Civil Society (150), Education (110), Health (120) which was added up with Population Policies/ Programmes and Reproductive Health (including HIV-related funding) (130), Water and Sanitation (140) and General Environmental Protection (410). For a detailed itemisation of topics in the DAC Creditor Reporting System system, see OECD (2012c).

1990 and 2010, its portion of total health-related aid diminished slightly over time. The variation of spending patterns is illustrated by Figure 5 which covers development assistance for health by focus areas from 1990 to 2010 (Institute for Health Metrics and Evaluation 2012b: 70–71):

Figure 5: Spending patterns in health-related aid 1990–2010

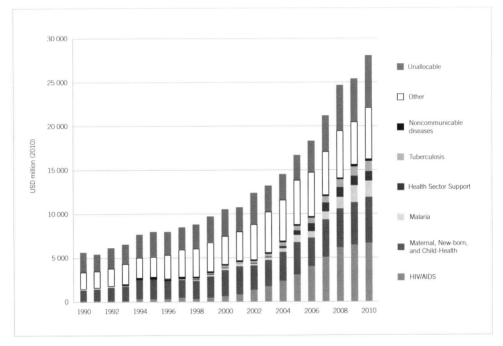

Source: Institute for Health Metrics and Evaluation (2012b: 70–71).[83]

For a certain time span, HIV/Aids was the most dominant theme of the international community but by 2013, it seems that it had lost this prominence as an aid priority. Various interviewees pointed out that donors have now shifted their attention to climate change as a new topic of global concern. The following statements were made by an HIV/Aids activist in South Africa,

---

83 The table draws on data published by the Institute for Health Metrics and Evaluation (IHME) in its 2012 report on global health financing. Tracking development assistance for health at a global level, the IHME extracts data from the OECD/DAC Creditor Reporting System, but additionally uses other channels such as audited financial statements and annual reports from public and private organisations. Given the divergent approaches used for capturing aid flows, the total spending figure for health in Figure 5 slightly deviates from Figure 4 which is based on the OECD dataset. Due to donor reporting, a significant proportion of aid to health could not be disaggregated by focus areas and was thus classified as 'unallocable'. Expenditures which were tied to distinct health targets, but did not fit into one of the six defined focus areas, were summarised in 'Other'. For details on methodology and data sources, see Institute for Health Metrics and Evaluation (2012a), (2012b: 25, 70).

by the leader of an education NGO and by a senior officer at the National Environmental Management Council in Tanzania, respectively:

There's the fact that other issues have arisen, so you know, they're putting money into climate change rather than into health, and we have to persuade them or try to persuade them that HIV is not gone away. (Interview 27)

The discourse of climate in development, you do it because that's the new HIV/Aids, that's the new agenda, you have to check that box. (Interview 70)

Every donor now is running with climate change. Even now here in Tanzania there are other things – we have a lot of problems here. Like the desertification, we have land degradation, we have a lot of erosion, but [those issues] are not receiving attention. You've got these conventions, we have the CBD, we have the UNFCCC, we have the other one on desertification, but when you relatively compare these three sister conventions, it's climate change now on top of the agenda. (Interview 59)

The observation that climate change is the current 'order of the day', as a Tanzanian environmental expert put it, is confirmed by spending figures. Since 1998, the OECD/DAC has tracked aid related to global environmental objectives by using the so-called 'Rio markers' which help to identify assistance in implementing the UN Convention on Biological Diversity (UNCBD), the UN Framework Convention on Climate Change (UNFCCC) and the UN Convention to Combat Desertification (UNCCD) (OECD 2012b: 60). Figure 6, which covers activiti cipal objective', indicates the rapid growth of climate change-related aid. Despite a drop following its peak in 2010, spending on climate change mitigation is still on the rise, while funding for combating desertification has stagnated and aid for biodiversity has declined.

Aid changes its composition not only with regard to sectors and priority areas. We also find shifting fads with respect to modes of operation. Here one can witness almost a cyclical movement: while during the first decade of the millennium the use of harmonised approaches such as sector and general budget support increased, there is now a reverse trend back from joint arrangements to individual assistance in the form of projects.[84] In Tanzania, various donors pull out from budgetary support although it is still the government's preferred aid modality (Economic and Social Research Foundation 2010: 9–10). DFID, for

---

84 For details on the emergence of budget support and sector-wide approaches, see Foster (2000) and Haan and Everest-Phillips (2010).

Figure 6: Aid targeting global environmental objectives 2002–2012

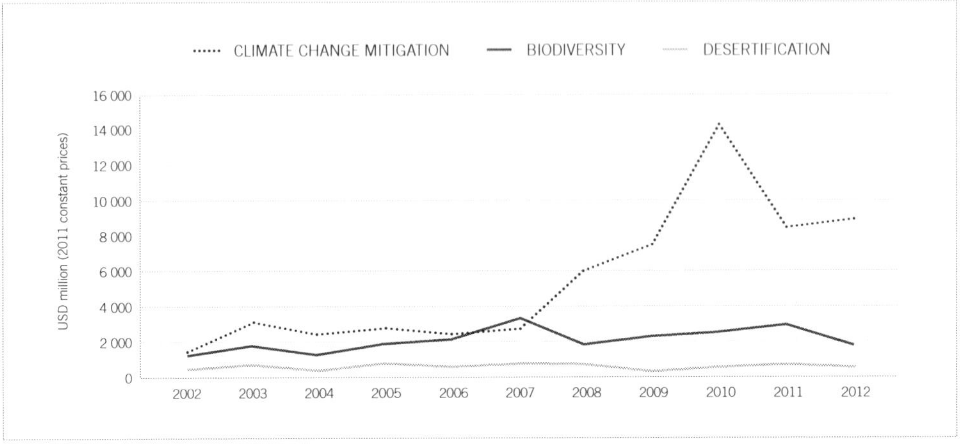

Source: OECD.Stat (2014b).[86]

instance, in its operational plan for Tanzania 2011–2015 announced a reduction in general budget support, arguing that according to an evaluation it "was not the most effective way to deliver results in the current circumstances" (DFID Tanzania 2011: 3). At the time of the interviews, Sweden critically discussed whether to continue with general budget support; Canada reconsidered its sector budget support for education. Germany, once a driving force in the establishment of a sector-wide approach in health and one of the largest contributors to the health basket fund, indicated its intention to pull out of the basket and to redirect the focus of assistance towards a system-strengthening approach with emphasis on results-based financing and targeted interventions (GIZ Tanzanian German Programme to Support Health 2011: 6).[86]

Global and domestic politics as causes of aid volatility
The volatility of aid priorities and modes of operation derives from both changing global ideological fads and domestic political developments in donor countries. International agreements reflect the shifting paradigms and principles: the Paris Declaration (2005) placed 'ownership' in the centre of aid relations, fostering harmonised approaches, the use of country systems and mutual accountability (OECD 2005). The Busan Partnership Document

---

85 Data were extracted from OECD Stat on 21 January 2014 using the Rio markers 'Biodiversity', 'Desertification' and 'Climate Change Mitigation' and counting only activities scoring one of the global environmental objectives as 'principal objectives'. Data were available since 2002. As the marker 'Climate Change Adaption' was only created in 2010, it was not included.

86 A retired expert who had worked for GIZ for decades annotated the shifts in German assistance as follows: "This is what happens in development cooperation, it goes back and forth and back again" (Interview 73).

(2011), in contrast, features a focus on results and "the participation of the private sector in the design and implementation of development policies and strategies to foster sustainable growth and poverty reduction" (OECD 2011b: 10). Although the agreement reiterates the principles of Paris, it implies a different message, prioritising issues such as 'value for money' and 'aid for trade'. As a Swedish expert in Tanzania put it:

> *The message nowadays after Busan – we have forgotten everything about ownership, alignment, harmonisation, and what we are talking about in the government is 'get in the private sector and everything will be solved more or less' and 'find new modalities'. Now of course [I'm] exaggerating, but it's going into that direction.* (Interview 40)

The reorientation towards the private sector and trade has been pushed by two parallel developments, namely the recession of the global economy in 2008–2009 and a liberal conservative shift of politics in aid-giving countries. As a result of the global financial crisis, many donor governments were under pressure to tighten their budgets and thus cut aid; in 2011, ODA from OECD countries decreased for the first time since 1997 (OECD 2012b). Selling a reduction of ODA to recipients, however, is easier if framed as a deliberate decision derived from the discovery that "with trade and specifically with my country, we will solve many more problems now" (Interview 38), as one interviewee commented. The argument is indeed brought forward in this tone: in its Annual Report 2012, the OECD emphasises the "need to engage the private sector much more", arguing that "the rewards will be substantial: new markets, new productive partnerships, new innovative technologies for developing countries, and more income and jobs" (OECD 2012b: 28). DFID even announced that its new focus on the private sector would "help private enterprise work its miracles as the engine of development" (DFID 2011: 4).[87]

This legitimation fits well with the market-oriented thinking spreading across Western governments where liberal-conservative parties have come to power which justify aid with economic interests and revamp development assistance accordingly.[88] When in 2009 a member of the Liberal Party became minister for economic cooperation and development in Germany, he not only advanced an institutional reform process, but also promoted the involvement

---

87 The sudden turn to the private sector as new addressee and theme of aid programmes has provoked stark criticism even within donor countries. The Independent Commission for Aid Impact, a watchdog institution of UK aid reporting to the British parliament, stated in a recent report that "DFID needs to recognise that the private sector is not a developmental panacea", finding that objectives of private sector work are "excessively ambitious and fail to reflect what is possible, given the complexity of the challenge" (ICAI 2014: 9/33).

88 For the prevailing rationales used by governments to legitimate aid, see Chapter 4.

of the private sector through public-private partnerships and business-oriented alliances (CDU et al. 2009; Riedel 2010; BMZ 2011). The Netherlands followed this trend shortly after: in 2010, the newly elected government led by the liberal Prime Minister Mark Rutte presented a major overhaul of Dutch development policy. He moved away from social to economic sectors, aligned aid with trade and placed Dutch self-interests in front (Netherlands Ministry of Foreign Affairs 2010, 2011). In Sweden, general budget support came under scrutiny when a liberal politician – herself originally trained as an auditor – took over the post of the development minister and started an intense debate on accountability and control mechanisms, arguing for results-based approaches (Carlsson 2012).[89]

These examples indicate that domestic politics have a significant impact on policies of giving aid (Lancaster 2007). As political actors within donor governments change, this often results in a redirection of priorities and modes of operation. 'Cash on delivery' and other forms of results-based aid are the prevailing mode of thinking among politicians concerned about the traceability of aid. Promising transparency and performance, the new modalities are based on a governance logic which is currently in vogue:

> *It is basically an iteration of the recent fashion in rich countries to place targets on everything from hospital waiting lists to grades in secondary school. Achieve the target, and you get paid a bonus; fail to achieve it, and you don't.* (Glennie 2011)[90]

Developed by think tanks and innovation units in aid bureaucracies, the new approaches have been embraced by researchers, practitioners and politicians who are optimistic about making aid more 'effective'. This is not surprising, given that introducing new modalities as soon as (or even before) the current ones show signs of failure, is an intrinsic reflex of the aid community. With reference to alleged innovations donors promise that aid will have more impact in the future than in the past (Lancaster 2007). For recipient countries, however, the frequent changes of political philosophies underpinning development strategies and ways of working attached to them are detrimental. A Tanzanian education specialist engaged in the education sector for more than forty years on both government and donor side described her experience as follows:

---

89 Gunilla Carlsson, a member of the liberal conservative Moderate Party, served as Minister for International Development Cooperation in Sweden from 2006–2013.
90 For details on 'cash on delivery' and other forms of results-based financing, see Birdsall et al. (2011) and Pearson (2011).

Sometimes these new internationally processed concepts and styles and approaches have a much bigger impact than we think of. Of course for us scholars, it is a way of experimenting and innovation. An idea worked in Ethiopia, maybe it will work in Tanzania. So, perpetually, these countries are experimental. That sustainability and maintaining the system is not really going to happen unless we reach a point of saying, 'Enough is enough!' We cannot move with what is workable. Let's not just introduce new ideas, let's move on.

Because what I'm hearing constantly now that people of my age, a bit older, say, 'But we did it in the old days. We had good teachers, children were learning in class, what was happening then that's not happening today?' It's the changes, the approaches. So every time the government is in a learning curve. Sometimes I pity them, because the changes are coming so quickly – before you learn this other one, (…) you are already changing. (Interview 31)

The volatility of aid emanating from its dependency on global and domestic politics has adverse effects on government systems and programmes in recipient countries. It impairs understaffed bureaucracies with ever-changing procedures and requirements, and makes support unpredictable. Government officials interviewed for this study reported various examples of projects and initiatives which had reached deadlock when donor interests changed. A retired doctor in Tanzania who had worked for the government in the field of public health remembered:

There was a school health program in the 1980s and the donor decided 'that's the end', without consultation, all of a sudden it was stopped (…). Locked the doors, no money, no facilities, nothing. Then they come back after some time to continue with that project, they continued, finished, off they go. That was a bad one. (Interview 65)

Similarly, a senior environment management officer working for the National Environmental Management Council in Tanzania reported:

We had another project from the Swedish – way back in the 1990s. And I don't know what happened, but they withdrew their support. So everything what we had planned within the council also ceased to be implemented. (…) So once [donors] shift their priorities, you have a problem. You find that whatever you planned, you fail to implement. (Interview 59)

In South Africa, a high-ranking official engaged in the education sector reported on a donor government which, when joining the war in Iraq, unilaterally cut aid to schooling initiatives in Limpopo and the Eastern Cape, two provinces in dire need of educational support – "that was a dear lesson for us about commitments" (Interview 21), he commented.

Currently, governments in developing countries are concerned about the drastic decline of international HIV/Aids funding, primarily due to cutbacks in PEPFAR and the Global Fund (see, for instance, IRIN News 2012, 2013a; Collins 2013; IRIN News 2013b).[91] Given that many government-run programmes are highly dependent on external financing, the reductions put national treatment, care and prevention programmes at risk. In South Africa, PEPFAR funding cuts particularly threaten NGO-run HIV services and specialised clinics which the government struggles to take over (Kahn 2012).[92] Tanzania currently tries to lessen the effects of diminished external support by setting up an AIDS Trust Fund (Lamtey 2012), in order "to prepare ourselves to continue keeping it as a priority regardless of who else keeps it as a priority" (Interview 63), as a high-ranking member of TACAIDS put it.

The detrimental effects of shifting fads on advisory processes
The "fickleness of aid" (Browne 2006: 7) not only has detrimental effects on budgets and programmes, but also on advice which is above all impeded by discontinuity. Several interviewees in both South Africa and Tanzania under-lined that advisory processes require a long-term focus and duration, particularly when they aim at bringing about systemic changes and strengthening capacity. Similar to other respondents, a South African academic stated:

> I think that it's about being willing to focus on a few things and do it well over long periods of time. I think stability and continuity are absolutely key (...) – iterative processes of learning, focusing on systems and some stability in the policy thinking and ideas. (Interview 28)

Advisory support which met these conditions often had a substantial impact. A South African interviewee, for instance, highlighted the contribution of GIZ experts in the field of local governance, a permanent focus area of German development assistance since 1994:

---

91 In November 2011, the Global Fund which accounts for around a quarter of international financing to fight HIV and AIDS announced it would provide no new grants until 2014 due to substantial budget reductions in some donor countries (Boseley 2011; Kelland 2011). In 2013, the US administration under Obama resolved on a continued drop in PEPFAR funding in its budget for the fiscal year 2014 (Aziz 2013).

92 In March 2013, around one thousand South Africans protested against US funding cuts which had led to the closure of a specialised AIDS clinic in Durban (AIDS Healthcare Foundation 2013).

These guys had a massive impact in the way in which local government takes place in South Africa. Until today, the whole idea of having integrated development plans was done with the help of GTZ (…). They were there through thick and thin. Refined the thing, made it work, and it's working until today. (Interview 8)

Similarly, South African government officials emphasised the value of German assistance in the area of skills development which profited from the long-term relationship of key actors involved and the fact that it was continued for over a decade (for details, see Chapter 7). One explanation for the relatively stable phase of German development cooperation is that it was headed by the same minister from 1998 to 2009. Eleven years of ministerial leadership, however, is rather an exception to the rule, given the four- to five-year election cycles in many Western countries. Cabinet reshuffles on both the donor and recipient side often come with far-reaching changes in agreements and relationships which directly bear on aid activities in recipient countries.[93] Advice is affected by such changes with respect to its form and substance: the ways of how advice is delivered shift along with preferred modalities of newly constituted donor governments; previously promoted policy approaches are replaced by new concepts, resulting in a "mad pace of new ideas" (Interview 28) recipients are confronted with. The 'fickleness' of politics thus collides with the necessity for advisory persistence, which is particularly essential in developing countries where governance is usually more fragile than in established democracies.

Legitimation and accountability pressures

Foreign aid is financed by taxpayers' money. Decision-makers in donor countries thus have to justify aid before citizens, and they need to ensure it is responsibly used for the intended purposes. Accountability is required at all levels of administration involved in aid, from ministries in donor capitals to implementing units in recipient countries. Donor governments are put under pressure to legitimate the expenditure of public funds and account for their use. This strongly affects their advisory activities and has profound implications for administrations in developing democracies.

---

93 A high-ranking government official in South Africa mentioned that from his experience, political changes have most significant consequences in the case of the United States: "If a particular party loses, the whole top management must go. So even the agreements that were signed, some of them, people don't know about them. So it becomes very difficult to pursue those agreements. So that is why some of those agreements were very short-term, I mean, if you look at the Bush administration – when the political party did not win subsequent elections, it was very difficult" (Interview 22).

Results as means of legitimation

While impact and accountability have always been issues in the public debate around aid, they have gained centre stage in the aftermath of the global financial crisis arising in 2008. In times of shrinking budgets, expenditures for development assistance need to be justified even more than before and be completely traceable – "we need to be careful with every nickel" (Interview 30), a Canadian Embassy official remarked. Bilateral donor organisations are particularly obliged to explain what they are doing and with which results. In the UK, for instance, DFID activities are under close scrutiny; a staff member in the Tanzanian country office reported:

> *Regularly, we have to give responses to parliamentary questions from MPs, and they would relate to programmes of DFID. [For] Tanzania, specifically with regard to education, I usually have to give some sort of direct response to MPs from constituencies. There's a parliamentary account committee which has done reports on how DFID spends money and their value for money, the effectiveness of the support. And under the current government, the liberal democrat conservative coalition which came into power in 2010, they established a new agency called ICAI which is an Independent Commission for Aid Impact, and they are also now doing country or sector thematic studies. They did one on three East African Countries, Tanzania, Rwanda and Ethiopia a year ago, and they also came to these conclusions, you know. Typically you're putting too much on budget support, we need to focus more on results and accountability.* (Interview 35)

ICAI evaluations and DFID management responses are disclosed online; the findings are critically discussed by the British parliament and widely reported in the media (see, for instance, Chorley 2013; Express 2013; Provost 2013).

Voices slashing development assistance and questioning if it helps at all have become louder, not only in the UK. For aid organisations, this has increased the pressure to give evidence of their impact. They do so primarily by presenting numbers, as the following statements extracted from donor websites illustrate in exemplary fashion:

> *USAID in Tanzania, HIV/Aids:*
> *By March 2013, 90 918 individuals were receiving antiretroviral treatment through USAID-supported facilities while 129 206 were benefiting from clinical care and 99 498 from community care. During the same period, USAID provided support to 181 092 vulnerable children, and 1 303 individuals with TB received integrated TB/HIV care and treatment.* (USAID 2013)

World Bank in South Africa, Biodiversity Conservation and Sustainable Development Project:
The total number of hectares under formal conservation agreements (…) almost doubled from 1,054,033 ha to 1,953,246 ha by 2011, exceeding the target of 1,454,033 hectares. (World Bank 2013a)

Sida in Tanzania, education and learning:
The Swedish budget support has contributed to sharply increasing public investment in education. One concrete result from the support in 2012 is the construction of 130 new classrooms for around 4 000 students on the island of Zanzibar. (Sida 2013a)

The need to produce 'visible' results strongly affects the form and substance of assistance. Various interviewees emphasised that donors tend to prefer project interventions whose impact is directly measurable, at best in geographical areas easy to reach for delegations.[94] Donors refrain from joint support modalities, arguing they are not able to trace their individual contribution. In the field of HIV/Aids, the treatment focus of external support can partially be explained by the fact that it is simple to count patients provided with antiretroviral drugs, but not the number of lives saved through awareness campaigns – "from care you get results today, you don't get results today from prevention" (Interview 62), a Tanzanian interviewee remarked.

The accounting imperative in aid

Demonstrating results has become the survival strategy of aid agencies. Monitoring and evaluation practices – often abbreviated as M&E – are their means of legitimation. Performance and audit reports serve as proof of accountability, a notion which in the context of aid tends to be reduced to its technocratic dimension (Mkandawire 2010). Accountability is translated into auditable accounting, as Rottenburg (2000) points out. In practice, this means that all kinds of aid activities, irrespective of their form and substance, are somehow made measurable, compressed into log-frames displaying baseline indicators, inputs, milestones and targets against which they are regularly assessed.

The current practice of generating factuality in the form of quantitative parameters through which the impact of aid is traced is problematic in several

---

94 A retired Tanzanian government official commented in this regard: "If you leave them *[donors]* on their own, they would always start projects in places close to Dar es Salaam or close to Arusha, or where they can be reached quickly, like Mwanza, like Iringa. They won't go to places like Goma, where you can have sometimes no flights the whole week. So when their bosses come around, they can't take them there that easily. So they want to do it around Dar es Salaam, so that when their bosses come, they can show the results" (Interview 64).

aspects. First of all, presenting the social world as "an assembly of facts which can be counted, aggregated and audited uses a rhetoric of de-politicization and absolute objectivity" (Rottenburg 2000: 148) which disguises the creational element of accounting. Figures used in appraisal reports, programme documents and evaluations inevitably are a result of method and choice since, put simply, "there are always several means of counting things" (Rottenburg 2000: 147). Hence, numbers are always a product of deliberate decisions for certain ways of calculation and representation. The HIV/Aids situation of countries or regions, for instance, looks different if one draws on prevalence rates as a measure for the extent of the epidemic or incidence rates which indicate the dynamic of HIV transmission.[95] Likewise, assessments on the status of education vary depending on the indicators used; the perennial debate around how to measure the quality of education hints at the constructed character of figures.[96] Nonetheless, they have become the primary reference for proving impact and legitimating decisions in development cooperation. The continuation of general budget support, for instance, depends on the recipient government's progress against criteria outlined in 'Performance Assessment Frameworks' (PAF) (Driscoll et al. 2005). In Tanzania, the 2013 PAF matrix entailed 38 outcome indicators covering issues such as Standard IV exam pass rates, the number of village land forest reserves or the proportion of births at health facilities (Development Partners Group Tanzania 2012). Given that despite some positive achievements, targets in key areas were not achieved, the Swedish ambassador, speaking on behalf of development partners, announced at the annual review meeting that "the 2014 commitments and disbursements from DPs will be affected, as the performance tranches cannot be released in full" (Hjelmåker 2013).

Similar mechanisms have been established at the sector level where progress is assessed in the course of joint annual reviews. Findings generated through that process strongly affect future support – "you cannot go back to Canada, seek more money when Form Four results are getting worse" (Interview 31), an education advisor working for CIDA in Tanzania commented. Failures in meeting the agreed targets thus put all players involved under pressure. Government representatives need to explain why they were unable to bring

---

95 This argument was brought forward by a high-level officer of TACAIDS who strongly argued for using incidence as an indicator for the epidemic (Interview 62). Prevalence rates describe the percentage of a certain population or group infected at a particular point in time, whereas incidence rates display the percentage of newly infected people over a certain time span. High prevalence can occur with low incidence and vice versa. Due to data availability, AIDS authorities, international organisations and media mostly use prevalence as an indicator for the epidemic. Incidence, however, is a better measure for reflecting dynamics in the spread of HIV. For details on prevalence and incidence rates, see Mattheyse (2007) and Puren (2011).

96 For details on the debate around quality indicators in education, see, for instance, Barrett et al. (2006) and Alexander (2008).

about the expected changes despite external assistance; donor staff in country offices struggle to justify the quest for further support to their headquarters.

The significance of figures in legitimating aid explains the frictions around defining indicators and interpreting results reported by various interviewees in both South Africa and Tanzania. In 2013, the performance review in the Tanzanian education sector caused a serious dispute between the actors involved. From the donor's perspective, the government tried to finagle continued financial support by meeting the minimum percentage of outcomes required with minimum effort, whilst neglecting central issues. An education specialist at the World Bank in Dar es Salaam vigorously complained about the strategy he assumed to be behind the government's behaviour:

> *The government develops milestones which fit in the routine nature of activities. Then at the end of the day it will report: this done, this done, this done (...). When you sum up you find they have made 70%. But sometimes you find that those items which they didn't do, they are the most important ones to make the effect, the really intended results in that particular milestone or activity.* (Interview 45)

Similarly, a DFID education advisor reported:

> *Even jointly agreed indicators [have] come up with some friction, because I think there's quite a complicated matrix that has got all the process-like indicators. Just saying that you have a process review and the like, whilst increasing the indicators about examining past results, the distribution of teachers in the country, are the pupil-to-teacher ratios equivalent to the remoter parts as to the urban parts of the country, and that's proved difficult to get in place. In this year, from the exam results of the last year, end of primary and end of secondary, we've seen very major drops. But those indicators are things that in theory will trigger performance tranche payments to the government. Those aren't likely to be met.* (Interview 35)

The government explained its failure with major constraints in implementation, namely "inadequate budget allocations and late receipt of funds; large number of specific actions, which lead into partial implementation of milestones; agreed milestones are not necessarily the same as the Government's priorities; and, some milestones or specific actions are not clearly worded or well understood by all parties" (United Republic of Tanzania 2012b: 3). Although some of the crucial targets were not achieved, the government's final 'score' in the 2012 education sector assessment was 62%, which according to the underlying scale implies a 'satisfactory performance' – an assessment which sounds very moderate in light of the education crisis exclaimed by civil society activists, media and parents who blisteringly criticised the government for the deteriorating situation (Nkosi 2012; Tambwe 2013; Twaweza 2013). For donors, however, the public articulation of social change is not pivotal in decision-making. Instead, they legitimate actions on the grounds of the 'reality' as constructed in written documentation based on parameters generated through techniques of standardisation and calculation (Rottenburg 2009).

Complexities of data generation in developing countries

Drawing on reports and accounts in countries which struggle to produce the data required for numerical representations of the social world poses a problem. A high-ranking government official engaged in the education sector described the situation in Tanzania as follows:

> *This country is very big. You cannot compare [it] with Germany (…). Infrastructure development is not the same. If you have to go from Berlin to Bonn, in a few hours you are already there. You can use email, because power, electricity supply is everywhere. People have got computers, and I'm told nowadays, normally people don't even write much. They use laptops, desktops and the like, now iPads.*

> *In our context, that information someone has to scribble and then from the school that report is taken to the district. The district has several schools, they have to be typed, some people have to analyse what is contained in the reports and then that report is taken to region, that region is processed and then it's taken to the centre. It can take more than the time allocated in the MoU [Memorandum of Understanding] because the MoU is saying you must be reporting every quarter. In some areas that information reaches the school when the quarter has elapsed (…). Now because you didn't get the report timely, you are disbursed less.* (Interview 60)

In addition to the difficulty of delivering data on time in a country made up of 169 districts which lack a proper road network and basic technological infrastructure, the interviewee pointed to another problem related to reporting, namely the low level of training among actors involved in the compilation of educational figures:

> *What is basic education in UK, for example? I'm told generally there are very few – unless immigrants – who don't go for secondary education. The majority goes up to college. But here, the majority remains at grade seven. This is purely primary. So don't expect the quality of a thing prepared by*

someone with grade seven can be as good as from a graduate of university. So we say sometimes, 'Please, you need to understand and bear with us.'

So there's that departure – expectations vis-à-vis the reality on the ground. We over-expect. Based on the current reality, you shouldn't over-expect that much the competence and the capacity of those providing those reports (…). The teachers have never been taught records management. Why should we blame them? (Interview 60)

From the view of the government official interviewed, donors blend out the environment in which recipient governments operate and lose sight of what is happening on the ground. Given the focus on written evidence in aid activities, newly acquired chairs in classrooms do not 'count' without formal documentation – "but the reality is that the chairs are there, being used by the kids" (Interview 60). The accounting imperative of the aid community encumbers recipients with reporting requirements which – even in a country such as South Africa which has a comparatively strong administration – overstretches their capacities.

Overstrained recipient bureaucracies

The detrimental impact of aid on recipient institutions has been thematised by various scholars who point to the weakening of already overstrained bureaucracies through project proliferation and donor fragmentation (see, for instance, Morss 1984; Bräutigam & Botchwey 1999; Knack 2001; Bräutigam & Knack 2004; Knack & Rahman 2007; Moss et al. 2008). In response to this criticism, donors proclaimed the principles of 'harmonisation' and 'alignment' in the Paris Declaration. But their rhetorical commitment has been little translated into practice (Wood et al. 2011). Instead of coordinating procedures and using country systems, agencies continue to impose their own standards of managing and monitoring aid. Several interviewees of this study reported on the pressure related to meeting donors' demands. An official in the South African department commented in this regard:

The German government might say, 'I am giving you money to deal with STIs [sexually transmitted infections] but I would like you to report on one, two, three, four, five indicators just to tell me, show me what you are doing with my money.' And when you look at the existing systems, it doesn't really accommodate what the Germans want. What do we do? We need to go back to our systems and change them to accommodate those or we create another system just for them to show our accountability. (Interview 17)

The complexity of dealing with donor requirements increases further when multiple players are involved. Even organisations agreeing on 'joint' interventions insist on adherence to their respective rules and procedures. A case in point is the 'CAPE Biodiversity Conservation and Sustainable Development Project' carried out from 2004 to 2010 in the South African Cape Floristic Region.[97] While it was praised as the first GEF-funded project jointly implemented by UNDP and the World Bank, the persons in charge of coordinating the cooperation at the South African National Biodiversity Institute faced serious administrative challenges. A key actor involved told us:

> *Interviewee: There are lots and lots of different forms that you have to fill in. You're doing quarterly reports, we had to do financial reports and financial management reports, one for the World Bank, one for the UNDP, and the formats were completely different ... It was very interesting working with both of them because they loved it and it seems to have been one of the very first projects where those agencies have worked together on the ground. And we can see how valuable it was for them and because of that we're happy to have done it. But for us, it caused a huge amount of extra work behind the scenes, because even though they promised to align reports and would sort of align supervision missions, so they would come at the same time. But out of those supervision missions would still come one thing for the UNDP, one thing for the World Bank (…).*
>
> *Interviewer: And did you find over time that those processes were more closely aligned or did they stay kind of divergent?*
>
> *Interviewee: No, I don't think that they became aligned. I think that they got their own sort of monsters to feed back on.* (Interview 25)

The compulsion of complying with standards designed to ensure accountability in many cases causes severe tensions, delays and deadlocks in cooperation. A high-ranking official involved in the initial stages of the primary education sector reform programme in Tanzania remembered the tedious negotiations between the government and donors on a common reporting format:

> *We have the government system of reporting. Donors wanted different systems and it was very unfortunate that different donors had different formats. Now which one would you take? The one of GIZ, would you take*

---

97 Details on the project are outlined in the case study on the South African environment sector (see Chapter 7).

the DFID, would you take that of Sida Sweden? So it was very difficult. It took us more than six months to agree on the format. And during that discussion nothing was going on because we haven't agreed on a format. And someone was saying now, 'Which kind of format do you people need?' And eventually they employed [name], he was in Rwanda, was just completing his Masters and he joined for a year, then he provided a good format over there. They said, 'Wow, this is it.' And we handled that format for just a year – then they said, 'Oh no, the format is very complicated, we must go back'. (Interview 60)

The struggle described above took place in the early years of the new millennium when the first Primary Education Development Plan was prepared. At the time of our interviews, more than ten years later, it was still a contentious issue in donor-government cooperation. The subject of deficient quality and timeliness of reports has become particularly sensitive due to the deteriorating situation in the education sector, with donor representatives struggling to justify the quest for further support to their headquarters. The fact that annual reports are not delivered as agreed poses a serious problem for field staff. A Tanzanian education specialist working for CIDA expressed her distress as follows:

The reports don't show results. I mean they are writing the way they write (…). We have sat together, we have developed the template. And that template, we are saying ideally this is what we should see in your report, (…) this is how it should look like so we see the results and blah, blah, blah. But then, there are times when we are questioning – this chapter on financing is not actually telling us anything. (Interview 31)

The original idea behind designing a common reporting format for the education sector programme was that it would be used both by the government and donors in order to avoid a duplication of bureaucratic efforts. Yet, there are still parallel reporting procedures in place:

In order to get funding from treasury, they have their own quarterly reports in which case the accounting officer in that ministry being the parliament secretary, sits down and says, 'This is what was done' and the accounting officer, 'You gave me this much, this is what we did, these are the shortfalls or whatever', however they are writing it. So quarterly he writes that, he gets money, he continues to implement his activities – and we are sitting here, waiting for an annual report. (Interview 31)

The significance of those annual reports as a means of legitimation and decision-making on the donor side leads to the paradoxical situation that experts in the field themselves take over drawing up 'government' reports:

> *We were caught up for some years in actually helping to shape those reports. Why? Because you sit down, you write your project document, in the end of it you say you are going to get this annual report ... Now you also have a duty to fulfil this side, you know. So that report has to come through in a way, you are pushing. But there are times when you are actually – even though we say, we read and we provide input, it is not quite just an issue of reading and providing input – sometimes you are actually writing the sentences.* (Interview 31)

This behaviour and the various frictions on reporting issues sketched above indicate the extent to which the reality of development aid is based on presentational practices of documentation (Rottenburg 2009). The reference frame for actors in the aid arena derives from reports and accounts, against which they are assessed.

The fabrication of facts to legitimate advice

The accounting imperative not only puts pressure on recipients to demonstrate 'development' in the form of figures. It also coerces donor experts to substantiate the impact of their activities in numbers, which is particularly difficult when it comes to advice. First, its impact on policy processes and governance is neither quantifiable nor directly traceable. Second, it usually does not bring about visible change within the narrow time frames of aid interventions. Experts help themselves by generating 'far-fetched facts' (Rottenburg 2009) which link advisory support and sector developments in spite of knowing that such causalities are fictitious. The dilemma is evident: either the virtual impossibility to account for demonstrable effects of advice is acknowledged at the cost of negative effects on their missions or the 'effects' have to be somehow constructed in order to please their clients.

A health specialist illustrated this dilemma using the example of the so-called 'Multi-sector HIV and AIDS Prevention Programme' implemented by GIZ in South Africa on behalf of the German Ministry for Economic Cooperation and Development (BMZ). A substantial element of the programme was the delivery of long-term as well as short-term advice which aimed at strengthening national, provincial and local AIDS councils and improving their coordination and dialogue. Given that these councils were to a great extent dysfunctional at the time the programme was conceptualised, capacity and organisational development were indicated as main components of support by GIZ.[98] Such a programme proposal, however, is difficult to sell to the ministry in Germany:

> *The difficulty with this proposal was that we are convinced that it is necessary to strengthen intermediary structures. With three million Euros over three years, it would be crazy to expect making a difference at target group level, so we decided to focus on intermediary structures. But then BMZ [the ministry] says, 'No, we want to see the change at target group level.' Then you say, 'Well, it will eventually occur somewhere.' 'No, but we insist on that.' Basically, the ministry would preferably see us using the three million and proving that as a result of our intervention, the HIV testing rate among adolescents has increased about 50% in this or that district. This is just not possible. But they do not want to hear that.* (Interview 5)

Nonetheless, the proposal in the version on hand did include target indicators such as "the knowledge of the population in supported provinces about the prevention of HIV transmission has increased to at least 80%", with 'baseline' data ranging from 14% to 41% in different provinces.[99]

The pressure to demonstrate measurable impact at target-group level – which in donor rhetoric is ultimately the population in recipient countries – was also articulated by interviewees in other sectors. A senior manager working on skills development for GIZ in South Africa confirmed being obliged to indicate direct effects in programme concepts, preferably in the form of quantitative data:

> *BMZ doesn't like qualitative indicators. BMZ prefers concrete indicators and we rack our brains how to get them through quantifiable assessment methods. That is a balancing act.* (Interview 3)

In the 'Skills Development for Green Jobs' programme the interviewee was concerned with, one articulated goal was that "70 per cent of graduates from the various green occupations requiring initial or continuing vocational education and training should find suitable employment in the green economy" (GIZ 2013c). As in the HIV awareness example above, it is questionable to what extent the achievements of such targets are attributable to one specific donor intervention, given the multiplicity of efforts and players in the field. The fact that aid agencies nonetheless claim credit for positive changes exclusively

---

98 This information, as well as the following details, was obtained from an internal GIZ programme document which was given to the authors of the study.

99 The programme document extracted the baseline data from a 2008 survey conducted by the Human Sciences Research Council on HIV knowledge and prejudices in the South African population.

for themselves causes annoyance on the recipient's side. A retired high-level official at TACAIDS remembered an incident when the wife of the then US President George W Bush came to Tanzania, praising the success of US assistance in tackling HIV:

> *Laura Bush came to the country some time and she was speaking in one of the different centres and she was saying, 'Through PEPFAR, so many hundreds of patients were on treatment.' And we were saying, 'That's lies, those are lies!' These were the national figures and there's the Global Fund and other people who have actually contributed that. That has brought problems.* (Interview 65)

Hypothetic causalities are a prevalent feature of donor legitimation, although experts are fully aware of their fabricated nature. As a Swedish education specialist in Dar es Salaam stated:

> *I don't really believe that it's that easy to say that there are either a lot of results or no results, it's not causal – we cannot find these relationships between our interventions or our support. It's more complex.* (Interview 40)

In addition to the difficulty of constructing causality, experts face the problem of conflicting temporalities of aid interventions in developing countries. The time frames set by their organisations do not allow to "wait for results" (Interview 53). Several interviewees working for different donors pointed to the impossibility in delivering the results expected by their headquarters at the end of a three- or four-year programme. A counsellor in the Norwegian Embassy in Dar es Salaam, for instance, commented:

> *For 12 years we have been supporting re-forestation and sustainable forest management in Shinyanga area. And it took ten years before we actually had a forest there, before we had the success story and we are saying, yes, it is re-forested. The local communities are harvesting, improved livelihoods there. They have funds now to send their children to schools, they have milk that they can sell at the market, and all these things. So I think that is also a challenge for us working here, that we have to sell these stories. You can't have, you won't have results in three years or four years. You have to have ten, 12 years at least before you can really have results.* (Interview 39)

Advice targeting policy and governance issues does not bring about change – howsoever measured – within the short lifespan of donor projects and programmes. Nonetheless, donor staff need to outline targets in spite of knowing they are not achievable. A Tanzanian environment specialist working for UNDP in Dar es Salaam admitted:

> *Sometimes I feel embarrassed when you say 'I will develop a strategy within two years.' And two years come, you still have stakeholders who are not buying into the strategy you are going to develop. It takes a lot of time.* (Interview 41)

The fact that superior authorities on the donor side nonetheless insist on the formulation of concrete advisory outcomes reflects the accountability pressure which dominates the aid community, and which is transmitted from development ministries to their implementing agencies, from headquarters to country offices, and finally from field staff to their recipient counterparts. This becomes manifest in the exemplary experience reported by a professor at the University of Dar es Salaam who was decisively involved in the Norwegian–Tanzanian cooperation on REDD (Reducing Emissions from Deforestation and Degradation). When we visited him for the interview in his office, he had just returned from a meeting with his Norwegian partners which had brought about a serious discussion:

> *The reason why I was at the Norwegian Embassy: I think a minister for foreign affairs will be coming down to Tanzania from Norway. Then, of course, the Embassy wants some of the activities to be accomplished by the time the minister is here. So that at least they can impress upon him or her and say, 'These are things we have done'. But some of these achievements depend on – they have to go through the government system. And each and every government has a bureaucracy, has the procedures to adopt things, to approve things. So you cannot just say, 'I am the donor, I want xyz to be accomplished tomorrow.' It doesn't work that way. So you find more of a mismatch on the understanding. And for me who is actually responsible for the REDD initiative in this country, I am caught in between because the Embassy wants some things to be concluded at a given time frame. But the government has stipulated bureaucratic procedures in approving things. And there is no way you can bypass that procedure.* (Interview 69)

External pressure to fast-track aid-related issues and push processes is also experienced in South Africa. A government official working for the Department of Environmental Affairs commented on the impatience of donors:

They use the rationale that they're investing in South Africa and we need to react immediately. And with our processes within the government, we can't react immediately. So, sometimes there is that pressure, especially with the GEF funded projects. (Interview 15)

The implication of donors referring to their financial investments to legitimate their demand for prompt government response is evident: their need of accountability potentially undermines state–citizen accountability in aid receiving countries.

The erosion of internal accountability as a result of aid
The deteriorating effect of foreign aid on internal accountability in developing democracies has been thematised by several scholars sharing one argument: when policy-makers are obliged to defend their actions and decisions first and foremost towards external financiers before turning to domestic constituencies, a key democratic mechanism, namely the fiscal–social contract based on taxation, is annulled (Bräutigam 1992, 2000; Therkildsen 2002; Gould 2005a; Glennie 2008; Moss et al. 2008; Mkandawire 2010).

> *If donors are providing the majority of public finance and governments are primarily accountable to those external agencies, then it may simply not be possible to expect a credible social contract to develop between the state and its citizens. Using the current terminology, aid may undercut the very principles the aid industry intends to promote: ownership, accountability, and participation.* (Moss et al. 2008: 269)

The observation that aid erodes public consultation and oversight has been made particularly in countries which receive large parts of their budget from outside (see, for instance, Mwenda (2006) on Uganda). But even in South Africa where aid accounts for less than 1% of government resources, concerns about the political accountability and control of official development assistance are raised. In the National Treasury's Development Cooperation Review 2010, the authors point out:

> *Currently the main central mechanism is the annual report on the RDP [Reconstruction and Development Programme] Fund, which only covers RDP fund ODA programmes and concerns the management of the fund (deposits, disbursements and balance) but not the onward management of resources. There is therefore no mechanism that provides Cabinet, parliament and the public with an overview of ODA of all kinds into South Africa on an annual basis.* (Fölscher et al. 2010: 16)

Comprehensive and disaggregated data on aid flows and their use are not even accessible to the receiving executive, given donors' restrictive disclosure policies. Government officials from both South Africa and Tanzania reported on their struggles to obtain accurate information on donor activities in their respective sectors. Not only are there specific expenses, such as the amount spent on expert advice, which is usually not reported to recipient institutions. Moreover, donors bypass government systems which exacerbates the deterioration of democratic control. In Tanzania, only 28% of external contributions for HIV/Aids interventions are captured in budget books (TACAIDS 2011). PEPFAR funding provided by the US, which makes up 72% of the HIV/Aids aid budget, is channelled directly to NGOs without going through government structures. A financing officer at TACAIDS criticised this practice in that it divests democratic institutions of their oversight function:

> *If the money does not pass through the government machinery, it means it is not being reflected in the books of parliament. And parliament passes the budget though the money is outside, and therefore they cannot follow how it was worked on and how it is accounted.* (Interview 61)

Given that various donors sideline authorities in recipient countries, which deprives their governments of fiduciary control, their commitment to 'mutual accountability' emphasised in the Paris Declaration appears hypocritical. Various interviewees in our study from both government ministries and aid agencies stated that accountability in aid relations is still unidirectional and asymmetric: while recipients are constantly pressured to be accountable to their financiers, namely taxpayers in the donor countries, they have no means to hold aid agents liable for their interventions and unintended consequences (Rottenburg 2000).

In sum, aid being given by democratic donor countries to democratic recipient countries results in a paradoxical outcome:

> *As things stand, the more accountable a donor is to its own voters, the more onerous and invasive will be its intervention in the receiving economy and the more likely it is to undermine the recipient democratic government's accountability to its own voters.* (Mkandawire 2010: 1168)

This logic holds for advice as one distinct form of aid as well: the more accountable a donor is to its own voters, the more its advisory activities are directed by its own agenda and interests rather than those of the recipient. That this is indeed the case will be shown in the following section.

Mismatch of supply and demand for expertise

For more than 20 years, a plethora of studies have criticised advice in the form of technical assistance as being "driven by donors rather than provided in response to aid-recipient priorities" (Forss et al. 1988; Jolly 1989; Berg 1993; Royal Ministry of Foreign Affairs Norway & Asplan Analyse 1994; Williams et al. 2003: iii; Land 2007; European Commission 2008; World Bank Independent Evaluation Group 2008). Authors consistently find that "this basic and pervasive factor – the donor-driven character of so much technical cooperation – is a root cause of the ineffectiveness of this form of aid" (Berg 1993: 95). In response to the critique, donors acknowledged the importance of 'local ownership' and announced that recipients would be allowed more participation in the procurement and management of experts. Shifting administrative responsibilities, however, does not tackle the actual problem which is grounded in the linkage of aid and politics: donors leverage aid to foster issues of their own agenda and use advice as a means of influence and control. The political interests related to aid and the accountability pressures in donor countries explain the frequently diagnosed mismatch of supply and demand of technical assistance.

This is corroborated by our own findings. Ministry officials from both Tanzania and South Africa perceived the donor community as little responsive to their own respective priorities. A member of the South African National Treasury summarised his experience as follows:

> *Interviewee: If you look at the general development partner relationships, there are only a handful of partners who would come in and say, 'We are prepared to support what you would want from us.'*

> *Interviewer: Who would that be?*

> *Interviewee: That would be, well, it used to be Sweden. I'm not very attached to the Swedish approach anymore. The Swiss are very much doing the same thing now. The Dutch used to do that, they don't do that anymore. In fact they have got their own attitude about it. The Norwegians have a similar kind of approach currently. The Danes had it, but they have literally withdrawn. The [European] Commission has very much moved in that direction. The Canadians are very strong in supporting us like that. So primarily, that is the core group that will provide support to us in that way.*

The rest of them pretty much come with agendas that are more than you and I could collectively work out. You know, it's just an incredible amount of agenda (…). So you can see that, you know, we sign all of these grand accords in Paris and elsewhere, and everybody is part of it – and nobody, they just pay lip-service to it. (Interview 38)

Despite the emphasis on 'demand-driven' support in international agreements, donors tend to give primacy to their own political agendas in giving aid, irrespective of whether they are in line with the recipients' priorities or not. As a senior official in the Tanzanian health ministry commented:

Some countries, their people are a little bit more flexible, they can discuss. But some, they are too rigid. For me, I see they all have an agenda and sometimes your agenda and their agenda just collide by coincidence. (Interview 54)

The precedence of donor priorities in development cooperation becomes manifest when agendas do not collide. In our study, several cases provided evidence for frictions which emerged from competing priorities on donor and recipient sides. A comparison of these incidents revealed three different patterns of incongruence.

First, donors intervened in the domestic political domain of recipient countries by pushing certain topics which had not genuinely been prioritised by the government. ICT for basic education, for instance, was driven forward in Tanzania by US assistance; the policy documents developed were mainly a product of donor-funded advisors.

Second, governments explicitly requested external support for a problem identified, but donors refused to assist as the topic was not part of their agenda. A typical example is the common disinterest of donors in higher education. Both the South African and Tanzanian government struggled to secure support for this area. At the time of our interviews, Tanzania's Higher Education Development Programme was shelved due to a lack of funding required for implementation.

Third and most notably, we found cases of colliding priorities which caused either open or covert conflicts between donors and recipients. The treatment versus prevention controversy in the field of HIV/Aids, which created tensions between the US government and various developing countries, is a blatant case in point.

All of the examples mentioned above are discussed in-depth in the case studies below (see Chapter 7). What should be illustrated at this point is that donors' political agendas play a decisive role in giving aid. This has significant implications for advice in the context of development cooperation: experts are used to leverage certain subjects on behalf of their funding governments which do not necessarily match the primary problems articulated by the recipients.

If advice, however, does not take the concerns of policy-makers into account, it fails to meet a crucial criterion of quality: expert knowledge provided by advisors must not only be technically (or scientifically) sound, but also "politically useful and acceptable. In short, it must be epistemically *and* politically robust" (Lentsch & Weingart 2009a: 7–8, italics in original).[100] In the realm of aid, one finds various examples of advice which does not meet the second requirement as it is driven by the preferences of the supplier (i.e. the funder) rather than responsive to the priorities of the recipients.

While this mismatch concerns the political layer of advice, vested interests related to aid also create a discrepancy between expertise provided and expertise required or requested. Evaluation reports repeatedly criticise insufficient needs analysis as a major reason for the failure of technical assistance, with donors paying little attention to organisational capacities on the recipient side (Forss et al. 1988; Berg 1993; Royal Ministry of Foreign Affairs Norway & Asplan Analyse 1994; DFID 2006; ECDPM & ACE Europe 2006; Land 2007; European Commission 2008). While such studies usually suggest a more systematic diagnosis of needs as a solution, we argue that improving methodologies will not solve the issue. The core problem consists in the use of capacity assessments as a tool for justifying advice which serves donors as a means of influence and control.

In aid-receiving countries, capacity gaps in state bureaucracies are predominantly defined by external actors. It is usually donor-funded consultants who compile sector analyses which commonly find 'severe capacity constraints at various levels'. Such assessments, however, are invariably biased: they are financed by donor governments who seek to get involved in the policy field under investigation. They are commissioned by aid agencies intrinsically interested in providing assistance. And they are written by professionals whose primary goal as individual consultants is to satisfy their clients in order to get follow-up assignments. While we do not insinuate that the authors of such studies consciously generate skewed results, we argue that they inevitably adopt the perspective of their principals. For the latter, assessment reports fulfil the function of justifying the deployment of experts in that they provide 'evidence' for the need on the recipient side. A lack of 'capacity' as stated in

---

100 At length, Lentsch and Weingart (2009a: 8) define political robustness of expertise as follows: "Political robustness of knowledge refers to the acceptability and the feasibility to implement recommendations based on it. An advice is robust if it can be politically implemented and meets the needs of the policymakers. Political robustness normally implies that the knowledge and the preferences of those who can be considered stakeholders are taken into account."

such documents thus serves as "a generalized (and depoliticized) means of legitimizing external intervention" (Gould & Ojanen 2005: 45).

Given its legitimating implication, 'capacity' has become a sensitive notion in the aid arena. An expert working for the Canadian Embassy in Tanzania told us:

> *It is actually whenever we mention that word 'capacity' to the government, it says, 'Who do you think you are?' And the question is, what do you mean by 'capacity'? So this is also now being taken as a badge, you know, 'Why are you wishing us that? We are ok'.* (Interview 31)

Several interviewees on the donor side expressed the sentiment that the government did not acknowledge capacity gaps and, as a matter of principle, rejected any advice offered despite – in the view of donors – being in need of assistance.

Interviews with government representatives revealed a different narrative. In their perception, donors come with a "mentality that there's nothing on the ground" (Interview 17), disregarding the local capacity available. Leading officials both in South Africa and Tanzania find themselves under constant pressure to repel the glut of advisors donors try to embed into their systems – "there is always the attempt of 'let me bring some people'", a Tanzanian interviewee commented (Interview 63). As an example, she told us an anecdote about tedious negotiations with the government of Japan which had proposed a project with a plethora of advisors attached to it:

> *That proposal for support of maternal and child health had everything, including people working for the mortuary. I think that is abuse! Because the starting point should be what are the needs? So we negotiated, we negotiated, we negotiated and negotiated. Finally, after something like just over a year and a half of negotiations, we ended getting a laboratory – which was not the starting point. But it was like extracting a normal tooth – a long painful process. So why does one come to negotiate with the assumption that everybody is asleep and the only people who are awake are coming from Japan? It's wrong.* (Interview 63)

While this particular incident happened in the Tanzanian health sector a while ago, it is still a prevailing pattern that donors seek to place advisors into recipient countries' institutions, irrespective of articulated capacity needs. A WHO officer in Tanzania frankly stated that he sees the majority of external experts in the health ministry as 'supply-induced':

We [the development partners] ask the ministry: How many can we bring to you? They don't request it from us. They don't request from us, they don't request in terms of numbers, and in what areas. And sometimes we generate demand for them. (Interview 44)

The observation that development partners 'generate demand' indicates that they pursue other interests in providing experts, aside from supporting recipients. In some cases, it is pretty obvious that donor agents bargain for technical assistance in order to care for the careers of their colleagues in the aid market. The following experience, which illustrates such an attempt at job creation, was reported by a leading functionary at TACAIDS:

There's one particular donor who – we agreed they will give us a technical assistant for a period of one-year negotiable and we said one and we agreed one. Six months down the line, he dares come to me and say, 'We have an excellent person, his contract has ended at ministry X, I think he could be very useful to help you in one, two, three.' I said, 'Well, how do you know? You don't work here. I work here and I've not identified that need, sorry.' And it was like he couldn't believe it, he went on and on for four months. Finally, I just decided 'Look here, if you come here one more time for this, I'm going to the ambassador because it's not right what you're doing.' (Interview 63)

While in this case, the recipient representative refused to accept the unrequested offer for expert assistance, decisions become more difficult when advice comes as an explicit or implicit condition for funding. Although the donor community officially agreed to untie financial from technical support (see United Republic of Tanzania 2006b), it is still common that organisations come with a "package [which] includes bringing in technical assistance" (Interview 69).

Experts placed in ministries and departments grant access to the inner sphere of government and control over resources.[101] This explains why donors insist on posting advisors to recipient units irrespective of capacity needs. The linkage of advice and money was picked out as a central theme by several interviewees; donor staff strongly criticised the prevailing practice of deploying experts for organisational self-interests. A World Bank specialist in Dar es Salaam sharply criticised the aid community for this kind of 'imposed' assistance:

---

101 The merging of advisory, administrative and supervising tasks in technical assistance assignments has significant implications for the relationship between advisors and counterparts which will be discussed in Chapter 5.

Because you are supporting a programme, because you are bringing money, then you would like to bring anybody to provide the technical assistance – irrespective of whether they need it, whether this guy has actually better capacity and there is no transparency in terms of how you get this guy from the mother country, whoever the supporting country is. (Interview 47)

The question whether there is a genuine demand for expertise becomes difficult to answer when money is tied to it, even more so when governments are highly dependent on external funding. As an expert working for the Netherland's Embassy in Dar es Salaam said:

If a [donor] country would really come with a package: 'We want to invest in the water sector over the next five years (…), but we definitely, we insist we want you to get two TAs because it's really needed' – I think that, if it's good or bad, Tanzania would not refuse that. (Interview 38)

The assumption that policy-makers in Tanzania are not likely to reject support although it entails "prescribed technical assistance" (Interview 47) is proved true by the experience of interviewees. An example is given by a Tanzanian health expert who remembered Danida placing nine advisors in the ministry of health as a condition for money and material:

We asked our bosses, 'But how do you agree on this?' They said, 'No, without them we could have not got the EDP [essential drugs programme] drug kits.' It was a condition that if you want EDP drug kits and this programme to run, you have to have these advisors. So you are aware, your people don't have drugs – please bring them. (Interview 44)

A government committed to improve the 'quality of life and social well-being' of its citizens (United Republic of Tanzania 2010) would face a moral dilemma if it waived the provision of essential drugs for its population (which it cannot afford to procure by itself) on the ground that it does not want to have experts sitting in its ministries. While there certainly are exceptions, decision-makers in Tanzania tend to accept external advice as it increases their scope of action rather than decline support due to its conditionality.

This equally applies to the institutionalised interaction with donor experts in the context of joint funding mechanisms such as general budget support, sector budget support or baskets. Policy dialogue is an obligatory condition of these modalities which have brought about "intense and routine donor involvement"

(Harrison 2004: 88) in government decision-making.[102] In technical working groups, SWAp meetings or annual reviews, donor representatives regularly meet with policy-makers and senior officials to discuss policy issues. From the recipient perspective, however, the starting point for this kind of interaction is the government's shortage of financial resources and its interest in increasing the budget with external funding. Since consulting donors is a procedural conditionality for disbursements, policy-makers have little other choice than to accept being advised. A director in the Tanzanian education ministry pragmatically stated:

> *They're the funders. They're the ones who support you, so you have to go into negotiation.* (Interview 49)

In Tanzania, a lot of advice provided either through dialogue structures or technical assistance is pushed through by donors without an explicit request by the government. This can bring about situations where advisors end up placed in offices "with nothing to advise" (Interview 44). As will be shown in the case studies (see Chapter 7), it also leads to overt and covert resistance against external interference in the form of enforced advice which manifests in frictions between external experts and their counterparts.

In South Africa, we found a very different picture. Neither is the government compelled to constantly interact with donors in dialogue forums, nor are departments 'invaded' by foreign advisors. The government tends to be selective in whose support to accept or reject. A director in the National Treasury delineated the country's strategic approach towards expert advice as follows:

> *There are some things we choose to bring in and some things we don't (…). And we say that this is the type of expertise we need. So we already start directing it from that point of view. And we try to control this process so far that we don't have experts coming in to redirect our policy space.* (Interview 23)

The government's leeway in selecting assistance is, amongst others, grounded on its relative independence from external financing. Donors cannot use money as a lever to place experts in authorities against an explicit demand. South Africa is an exceptional case in terms of its strong standing against donors, however. The bigger the financial and political power imbalances

---

102 For agreements which outline the conditions of joint funding mechanisms in Tanzania, see United Republic of Tanzania (2008a, 2008b, 2011).

between donors and recipients, the more the latter are struggling to defend themselves against 'imposed advice' in the form of institutionalised dialogue or technical assistance which does not match their needs.

Structural flaws pertaining to expert employment

Expert advice in the context of development aid is not only negatively affected by its linkage with politics. It is also impeded by several structural flaws related to conceptual deficiencies and employment practices on the donor side. First, aid agencies lack clear concepts of knowledge transfer and capacity-building without which expert advice becomes a black-box process with respect to its impact. Second, as a result of changing recruitment patterns in aid agencies, experts often lack adequate expertise, experience and competencies to provide valuable advice to recipients. Third, current employment practices obstruct the building of trust and interpersonal relationships which constitute crucial preconditions for knowledge sharing and learning processes. These obstacles at the micro-level of advice explain why external experts so often fail to achieve their proclaimed primary objective, namely to make themselves obsolete by capacitating counterparts in recipient bureaucracies.

Vague concepts of knowledge transfer and 'capacity-building'

'Capacity-building', 'capacity development' or 'capacity enhancement' are terms that are nowadays found in almost every donor document (Easterly 2002).[103] Yet, the aid community does not have a commonly shared understanding of what these terms mean. Some agencies have not even defined capacity-building internally and lack any kind of strategic vision of how it is supposed to take place. An OECD report compiled in 2009 found that out of 21 DAC members, only ten had "some form of overall capacity development guidance document – either in final or draft version" (OECD/DAC Capacity Development Team 2009: 4). The vagueness of the term also becomes evident in the interviews of this study. Talking about capacity-building, some respondents referred to concrete activities such as professional training courses, while others used it as an umbrella term and framed it as an overall goal of donor support, stating that "all of it is capacity-building in a way" (Interview 1). Considering the ambiguous meaning and use of the term, it is not surprising that the role of

---

103 As Easterly (2002: 53) points out, "capacity building has been a theme of donor recommendations since forever, although it continues to exert its fascination in the latest reports". Easterly made this comment in 2002, but his statement would still be valid today, almost a decade and a half later.

experts in that context is similarly vague. Aid agencies lack precise concepts of advice and its transformational impact on the recipient side.

A plethora of studies have identified the absence of knowledge transfer concepts as a major shortfall of technical assistance.[104] In practice, the prevailing assumption among actors in advisory functions is that the interaction between external experts and their counterparts implies a learning process on the part of the latter. This is reflected by a statement of a Tanzanian policy-maker who commented:

> *Transfer of knowledge is there because you take a report to the donor, they analyse the report, and they provide comments. On the basis of those comments you can improve your report. And you meet, you discuss, you get challenges through questions, you respond. In a way, there is an implied building of capacity.* (Interview 60)

This implicit process of capacity-building is somehow expected, but not ex ante articulated. Terms of reference for advisory positions and consultancies entail detailed lists of duties (e.g. participation in policy reviews, development of guidelines, conducting analyses etc.), but do not dwell on how knowledge transfer is meant to take place through these activities. The absence of a clear operationalisation makes external experts follow a "strategy of hope" (World Bank 2005a: 5) when interacting with their counterparts. An expert in the Finnish Embassy in Dar es Salaam admitted:

> *Sometimes it's difficult to know, of course, what is it that you or the other person picks up from this collaboration, what are the things? Is it the way of working or is it the way of expressing yourself or a way of seeing things? Maybe you understand only later on how it happens.* (Interview 36)

The performance of external experts is measured against the input they provided, not against their impact on the recipient side.[105] Given that knowledge transfer is not "factored within the agreement" (Interview 47), as

---

104 See, for instance, Forss et al. (1988); Berg (1993); World Bank (2005a); DFID (2006); ECDPM & ACE Europe (2006); Land (2007); JICA (2008).

105 A study on DFID-funded technical cooperation, for instance, states that "a significant problem in the assessment of capacity development impact is that the activities reviewed in general did not involve exercises to benchmark capacity and capacity targets were not set. As a result, monitoring of capacity impact was either not built into the project monitoring and evaluation system or was not done so using a consistent analytical framework (for instance one that distinguished the wider institutional setting, the elements of organisational capacity, or individual staff capacities). The absence of such a systematic framework or focus on capacity development limits significantly the quality of the information on which judgements about capacity development impact can be based" (DFID 2006: xiv et seq.).

a Tanzanian World Bank expert put it, it receives less attention by advisors who are under pressure to fulfil the tasks agreed in their contract. Delivering products, meeting reporting requirements and carrying out projects on time often gains primacy over sharing knowledge with counterparts, which takes time and requires commitment on both sides. As a result, experts end up as 'doers' instead of being 'mentors', with the risk that "when the advisor leaves, you are back to square one because the capacity was not transferred to the team" (Interview 33).

Cases of 'gap-filling' experts in government units who create a "vacuum" (Interview 23) after they leave have been reported many times. Interviewees of this study provided several examples from both South Africa and Tanzania where authorities faced serious setbacks when technical assistance ended, but no local staff had been capacitated to use a newly established software system or to conduct a follow-up analysis without external support. The absence of knowledge transfer as an explicit element in contracts and assessment frameworks for advisors is seen as a fundamental flaw in the design and management of technical assistance. The problem that experts thus lack incentives to train or mentor their counterparts (instead of taking over their work) is exacerbated by the fact that they have an interest in keeping their status: simply put, an advisor or consultant is not necessarily keen on making his or her service obsolete by sharing knowledge (for which he or she is hired) with others. As a high-level official in Tanzania commented:

> *The thing I have noted with consultants, they don't want to give you everything. They just give you very little because they want them to be unique, to be calling them every year. Now if they give you everything, you do it yourself, will they continue to have jobs? No. Consultants will always come, do a study, but also create a room for a second follow-up study.* (Interview 60)

The "competitive and money-based" (Interview 8) nature of the consultancy industry in particular creates the perverse incentive to keep knowledge exclusive instead of sharing it. That being the case, the assumption that knowledge transfer implicitly takes place through the interaction between experts and government officials is, to say the least, simplistic. If an expert activity is meant to have any transformational impact in terms of capacity-building, it would be a necessity to explicitly articulate how this is to be brought about and to make it a – if not *the* – decisive criterion for performance assessment. This is not yet common practice in the aid community, given the absence of clear concepts of advice and its linkage to capacity-building. Knowledge transfer is thus at best a contingent by-product of advisory processes whose quality is dependent on the commitment and relationship of the individual actors involved.

Insufficient fit of expertise, experience and advisory competencies

The composition of expert cadres is changing (see Chapter 4). Sector-specialists are increasingly being replaced by 'hybrid advisors' and generalists with a background in economics and administration. Work experience is becoming less important as a qualification criterion than high-level academic qualification and international mobility. These shifts in recruitment have significant effects on advisory processes insofar as experts often lack adequate expertise, experience and relevant competencies to provide valuable advice to their counterparts. The insufficient fit of expert backgrounds and the resulting weak quality of advice has repeatedly been criticised in evaluation reports (Forss et al. 1988; Jolly 1989; Williams et al. 2003; World Bank 2005a; DFID 2006; European Commission 2008; World Bank Independent Evaluation Group 2008). In our study, the problem of inadequate expertise was broached as an issue by interviewees on both the donor and recipient side, particularly in the fields of health and education in Tanzania. Many expressed the sentiment that the dialogue in technical working groups has been negatively affected by the changing composition of donor representatives. Generalists and administrators have little to contribute when it comes to sector-specific problems which require specialist knowledge and a deeper understanding of the matters at stake. Since their expertise, instead, increasingly lies in areas such as project management, auditing and accounting rather than on technical issues, it has become increasingly difficult to "talk the same language" (Interview 44) in policy discussions, as an interviewee put it. A Tanzanian health expert with many years of experience participating in donor-government dialogue explained the frictions which emerge from this mismatch:

> You have Rik in the Netherlands [a foreign advisor with a biomedical background], he can understand why you are talking this. But others do not understand because they look at the money, not at the product and they do not know the challenges that are in the country (...). They will stick to these audit reports etc., but they will not see the performance on immunisation coverage and cases like that. (Interview 44)

Similarly, a Tanzanian academic engaged in the education sector told us:

> Many of these development partners, they are not experts in education. But they are supposed to be coordinators or chairs for education and they

interact with the Ministry of Education. I have been with them, I have been to those meetings. It's very different from a university professor of education talking to the Ministry that 'this is how things can be done, this is how to change the mind set of science students, this is how laboratory work can be made interesting.' It's very, very different. Those people, the development partners, are interested in their money: 'Has the next tranche been paid, have you received the letter for the next tranche?' (…) That's their main interest. (Interview 71)

The managerial knowledge many aid experts nowadays hold helps to administrate programmes and to keep track of funding flows. It is, however, not the type of expertise suitable to fulfil the main objective of the dialogue, namely to provide 'sound advice' for tackling sectoral challenges in the respective areas (see, for example, Development Partners Group Tanzania 2007, 2010a).

In addition to the often inadequate expertise of advisors, interviewees expressed concerns about the tendency of donors to send young experts who might be highly qualified with respect to their academic credentials, but lack experience in dealing with complex policy issues. The fact that advisors increasingly become younger is a result of accelerated career paths in international organisations which attract graduates with a low starting age and fast-track promotion (see Chapter 4). While advisory assignments in developing countries push the careers of young professionals, the counterparts on government side often perceive their placement as little helpful if not burdensome. A Tanzanian health expert stated in this regard:

You bring a person who has never worked in the government, who has read his or her books well and then has got a master just like the other one who needs to be advised. And you are now coming to advise. Then instead of advising, you ask too many questions. How does this work out? (Interview 44)

A third aspect related to the aptitude of experts that turned out to be a central theme both in South Africa and Tanzania was what interviewees framed as 'personality'. Whether recommendations are perceived as advice, constructive or destructive criticism or even interference is deemed heavily dependent on the way they are brought forward; several officials reported of tensions which evolved when external experts appeared overly assertive and dominant.

Attitudes and behavioural patterns seem to play a decisive role in advisory contexts. Various reports confirm the significance of a certain set of competencies (often termed 'interpersonal skills') for the impact of advice, such as listening, communicative sensitivity, an ability to empathise and a commitment to assist rather than to prescribe (World Bank 2005a; DFID 2006).[106] In contrast to expertise and experience, however, such competencies are systematically neglected in the recruitment and assessment of experts.[107] Even though this may result from the fact that it is more difficult to capture them as qualification criteria, it is nonetheless a structural shortfall which in many cases impairs the quality of advisory relations.

The importance of adequate expertise, experience and advisory competencies on the side of advisors was repeatedly emphasised by interviewees of this study and illustrated not only by negative experiences, but also by examples of experts who were perceived as having the right 'fit' and were thus highly appreciated by recipients. A case in point mentioned by different officials was a health specialist working for GTZ (later GIZ) in Tanzania. Although at the time of the interviews, he had already left the country a couple of years earlier, his former counterparts still praised his support in the field of health and HIV. With a high level of specialist knowledge about public health systems and broad experience in other African countries, his advice was considered highly valuable. Officials of the Ministry of Health and TACAIDS described him as an outspoken, but respectful person who had shown sensitivity and commitment in engaging with his Tanzanian colleagues – "he truly believed in partnership as partnership" (Interview 63), a high-level decision-maker stated.

Apart from the individual attributes recipients ascribed to this individual, they highlighted the strong bonds he had built from a long-term cooperation. Staying in Tanzania for eight years, the health expert had an exceptionally long period of assignment in the country. His case illustrates that building advisory relationships requires not only the right mix of expertise, experience and competencies, but also conducive employment conditions; the latter, however, are usually missing in the aid context.

Lack of trust and social ties

A central theme throughout the interviews of this study was the lack of trust and continuity in advisory relationships resulting from employment practices

---

106 A World Bank study suggests 'listening', 'curiosity', 'patience', 'humility', 'flexibility', 'empathy' and 'building trust' as core competencies for advisory processes (World Bank 2005a: xiii). While we would argue that 'building trust' is more a result of behaviour which is also dependent on other factors (e.g. time), the remainder are similar to the essential competencies that can be identified in this study.

107 The World Bank report, for instance, finds that behavioural competencies are "hardly covered" in the bank's Overall Performance Assessment framework used for assessing staff (World Bank 2005a: 35).

on the donor side.[108] The theoretical and empirical insights of organisational studies of firms are instructive for analysing conditions at the micro-level of expert advice in aid. While organisational determinants vary, the basic constellation at the individual level is similar: actors encounter each other as potential knowledge sources and potential recipients. The crucial question is which factors determine whether their interaction is a successful learning process that results in knowledge transfer. A major finding in this regard is the significance of social ties, trust and shared visions as manifestations of social capital (Nahapiet & Ghoshal 1998).[109]

Social ties as a structural feature and interpersonal trust as a relational characteristic have proven to be two crucial elements for knowledge transfer which are closely interlinked (Tsai & Ghoshal 1998; Hansen 1999; Levin et al. 2003; Inkpen & Tsang 2005; Becerra et al. 2008). Several scholars have shown that a close working relationship, in which actors frequently interact, functions as a strong tie that stimulates trust; trust, in turn, enhances the potential of knowledge transfer, as actors are not only "more willing to give useful knowledge", but also "to listen to and absorb others' knowledge" (Levin & Cross 2004: 1478). Both elements, social ties and interpersonal trust, share two characteristic traits. First, they are actor-bound in the sense that ties or trusting relationships cannot easily be traded or passed from one person to others. Second, they depend on a "history of interactions" (Nahapiet & Ghoshal 1998: 244), making time and continuity key determinants for their emergence (Preisendörfer 1995; Nahapiet & Ghoshal 1998; Adler & Kwon 2002; Inkpen & Tsang 2005).

Looking at advisory relationships in the context of development aid, we find several conditions impeding the development of strong ties and trust between advisors and advised. A major obstacle in this regard is the high turnover of staff in donor organisations. Experts deployed as advisors spend around two to

---

108 Interpersonal relationships have not yet received much attention in the literature on expert advice. In evaluation reports, they are, if at all, mentioned as a side note, but are not further investigated. In organisational theories and management sciences, however, the impact of interpersonal relations and trust in knowledge transfer processes within and across organisations have become key objects of research. See, for instance, Nahapiet & Ghoshal (1998); Zaheer et al. (1998); Hansen (1999); Argote & Ingram (2000); Szulanski (2000); Levin et al. (2003); Levin & Cross (2004); Inkpen & Tsang (2005); Becerra et al. (2008); Hajidimitriou et al. (2012); Alexopoulos & Buckley (2013).

109 Social capital as a concept of social science is used in a wide range of theories and filled with different meanings. Adler and Kwon (2002) provide an overview of definitions across various disciplines. We follow Nahapiet and Ghoshal (1998) who defined social capital as the "sum of the actual and potential resources embedded within, available through and derived from the network of relationships possessed by an individual or social unit" (243), and differentiated three dimensions: a structural dimension which refers to the "overall pattern of connection between actors" (244); a relational dimension which focuses on the relationship between actors; and a cognitive dimension which includes "shared representations, interpretations, and systems of meaning" (244). The components of all three dimensions have been shown to significantly affect the outcome of knowledge transfer efforts within organisational contexts (Nahapiet 2011).

three years in a country; consultants often only a couple of months.[110] Similar to many other interviewees, a retired Tanzanian government member assessed the average stay of external experts as too short for building a fruitful advisory relationship:

> *I think it needs a much longer period of time of interaction between the local and external experts in working together for a common goal (...). When it's two years and an expert comes and goes, you don't really have much, much impact.* (Interview 65)

The impact of advice is seen as heavily dependent on the relationship between experts and their counterparts. The establishment of social ties through regular and continuing interaction between actors, however, is hampered by the "temporariness of interlocutors" (Interview 71), as an interviewee put it. Building up relationships and trust that constitute essential preconditions for advice requires a time span which exceeds the employment cycles prevailing in the aid community. As a World Bank expert commented:

> *By the time you get even on a personal level to understand the guy, then there's a new advisor coming in.* (Interview 47)

The development of trust is not only hampered by discontinuity but also by the double role of experts as advisors and administrators. In many cases experts not only have the function to provide advice to government officials, but also to monitor the progress of programmes, the adherence to agreements and the proper use of funds. Particularly in the case of technical assistants embedded in ministries or departments, the merger of advising and controlling responsibilities causes accountability conflicts and distrust. The perception among many recipients is that experts placed in state authorities primarily serve as donor agents. A Tanzanian professor expressed the sentiment he observed among government officials in ministries:

> *Why do you want them to be in our offices? They will just be here as spies and looking at what we are doing.* (Interview 71)

The practice of linking advisory and supervisory tasks reduces the trustworthiness of advice, as the intentions behind expert engagement get blurred. Recipients who are doubtful of the motivation of advice are less likely to be receptive to it. The fact that experts are perceived as working in the interest of donors

---

110 Details on employment conditions are outlined in Chapter 4.

and that they appear to benefit from their intermediary position, which grants them control over resources and access to decision makers, complicates the emergence of a trustful relationship.[111] Various statements of interviewees point to a mutual distrust on both donor and government side about the respective others' purposes within cooperation.

The perceived discrepancy of intentions and lack of common goals is also confirmed by questionnaire results of this study. Asked about their experience in working with their counterparts, many respondents assessed 'sharing similar interests in reaching targets' and 'sharing a common vision and similar motivation' as highly problematic issues within cooperation.[112] A shared vision constitutes a major cognitive element in relationships and is proven to have a considerable effect on the emergence of trust in knowledge transfer processes (Tsai & Ghoshal 1998; Levin et al. 2003).

In sum, developing a trustful relationship in a setting characterised by a discontinuity of actors, short time frames and non-transparent interests becomes an inherently difficult endeavour. While individual actors may still be able to build such relationships, the prevailing employment conditions of experts are not conducive to a "waxing process" (Interview 71) at the interpersonal level, thus impeding knowledge transfer processes in the context of aid.

Unequal relationships

With the rise of the 'knowledge for development' paradigm, 'local knowledge' and its importance for transformational processes have become a central theme in the international discourse on development.[113] The debate affected the aid

---

111 Delineating conflicting imperatives of the broker's role in the political sphere, Stovel and Shaw (2012: 151) state that "acting as a middleman between these two spheres frequently engenders severe distrust from actors on both sides of the divide". According to the authors, brokers face a constant dual-agency dilemma stemming from the tension between the personal ties essential for brokerage processes and the potential individual gains of their role: "Given that a broker – due to her greater access to information, control over resources, or structural power – has a clear opportunity to gain at the expense of either or both of the groups for whom she is brokering, how does she maintain the trust necessary to continue brokering between them?" (Stovel & Shaw 2012: 154).

112 The distribution of answers in detail (missings not calculated in the percentage): 'Sharing similar interests in reaching targets': 10.9% extremely problematic; 36.4% problematic; 40% rather unproblematic; 12.7% definitely unproblematic. 'Sharing a common vision and similar motivation': 14.5% extremely problematic; 41.8% problematic; 30.9% rather unproblematic; 12.7% definitely unproblematic.

113 See Warren et al. (1995); Odora Hoppers (2002); Santos (2007). The term 'local knowledge' needs some clarification as it lacks a common definition. Post-development/post-modernism scholars often use it interchangeably with 'traditional' or 'indigenous' knowledge developed and used by a society, as opposed to scientific knowledge. In the context of development cooperation, 'local knowledge' usually refers to the knowledge generated in developing countries in contrast to

community insofar as it questioned the prevailing approach of knowledge transfer and shed light on the ignorance of scientific and non-scientific knowledge produced by developing countries (Torres 2001; King 2004). In response to the critique, donor organisations have come up with new policies and strategies which emphasise the commitment to recognise, use and thereby strengthen recipient countries' knowledge base. Advice should no longer be a one-way street, but become a mutual learning process; experts should no longer *only* be sent from abroad, but *also* recruited within the 'partner country'.

Regulations on expert employment reflect this new approach. The World Bank in its guidelines for the selection and employment of consultants, for instance, highlights its "interest in encouraging the development and use of national consultants in its developing member countries" (World Bank 2011a: 2). Similarly, Danida's guidelines for technical assistance instruct preference to be given to national experts over external ones:

> *The first possibility to consider for any TA needs is whether the required expertise is available nationally. If **national expertise** is available and most suitable for the TA input required, it would in most cases be preferable if the partner organisation recruits this expertise directly, and under national rules. Using national consultants and institutions for technical assistance can be considered part of capacity development of the human resources base of a country.* (Ministry of Foreign Affairs of Denmark 2009: 16, bold in original).[114]

Although the emphasis on local knowledge has become a key element of the rhetoric of aid agencies, development cooperation is still characterised by a predominance of external experts and an asymmetric flow of knowledge from the North to the global South. The unequal setting in which donors and recipients operate is reinforced through the creation of "knowledge hierarchies" (Girvan 2007: 16) which marginalise experts in developing countries, and increase the discursive power of the transnational expert community working for international organisations. Procurement practices and employment conditions of these organisations consolidate the hierarchical classification of expertise in the context of development aid.

Western knowledge. In this study, we use the term to differentiate knowledge which is locally available in a given society (both scientific and non-scientific) from knowledge provided by external (foreign) experts.

114 After arguing that the use of national experts would strengthen the local knowledge base in the recipient country, the text continues: "National consultants are generally better attuned to government officials and departmental cultures, as well as to the private sector in the country – and, using national consultants may be a cost-effective solution" (Ministry of Foreign Affairs of Denmark 2009: 16).

The creation of knowledge hierarchies

The procurement of experts turns out to be a sensitive issue in the cooperation between donor organisations and recipient institutions. The frictions that arise in the context of procurement point to power struggles underlying the process of assessing expert qualification in which donors – despite all claims of 'local ownership' – still hold the authority to set formal and informal rules. In some cases, the gap between donor policies and practice is appalling. According to the World Bank policy for the selection of consultants, for instance, the responsibility of procurement lies with the borrower (World Bank 2011a); a Tanzanian expert working for the World Bank in Dar es Salaam, however, told us:

> *The participation of the ministry or the government is usually very minimal. I see in some areas they do participate in terms of selection, hiring and so on, but it's just face value.* (Interview 47)

The cases in which recipients are potentially involved in procurement are limited. Experts for representative positions such as sector specialists or first secretaries are internally recruited by the employing organisation and, in the case of bilateral agencies, often require citizenship in the donor country and respective language skills.[115] Consequently, while there may be some exceptions, representative positions are usually filled by foreign experts. This may not come as a surprise, but one has to bear in mind that experts in such positions are higher up the hierarchy and – at least in a country such as Tanzania – have the widest scope of influence in the sector they are concerned with.

When it comes to procuring advisors and consultants, the extent to which recipients have a say in the process varies from agency to agency. Generally, Nordic countries and UN agencies are perceived as less prescriptive than other bi- and multilateral agencies such as GIZ or the World Bank which set

---

115 Although English is used as a standard official language in the aid community, many of the bilateral organisations require advanced skills of their respective country's language for leading advisory positions. The Swedish development agency Sida, for instance, states on its website that "most positions require good knowledge of Swedish (written and spoken), and also Swedish citizenship or a residence permit" (Sida 2013b). In our interviews, this was justified by the need to be able to report to and communicate with headquarters in the respective language. Interestingly, online adverts for job vacancies are often distributed only in the official language of the donor country and not translated into English or French or the language of the country of assignment. At the time of research, Sida published vacancies on its website only in Swedish. Similarly, many job descriptions of GIZ are only published in German (although posted on the English website), making it difficult for experts from abroad to identify potential job opportunities.

strict conditions and requirements. Consistent with many other interviewees in recipient institutions, a senior officer working for the Tanzanian National Environmental Management Council summarised his experience in the following way:

> *Interviewee: In case it is a credit from the World Bank, they have a range of conditionalities that these kinds of projects must be internationally advertised and experts compete.*
>
> *Interviewer: And do they, have they got any influence on which experts you choose?*
>
> *(...)*
>
> *Interviewee: Yes, they have the final say. Because you have a number of experts, you conduct the evaluation, the evaluation has to be submitted to the World Bank, then they are the one who say that 'okay, this is the kind of expert we would like to work with based on the qualifications' (…). You don't have the final say as a country or as a project. Everything, whatever you raise, must have no objection from the World Bank. In fact, there is a little flexibility. Whenever we work with international organisations like the UNDP – they don't attach strict conditions like the other one. Because at least there is the flexibility. If we work with the UNDP, they can bring money, then we will do everything in terms of advertisement, sourcing the experts and everything.* (Interview 59)

While aid agencies differ in terms of setting procurement regulations and conditions, they share the practice of differentiating between "national" and "international" experts. National advisory positions are open only for nationals of the respective country. International posts, in contrast, are internationally advertised. The scope of recruitment, however, is not the only difference. Across all aid agencies, international experts tend to have superior positions in comparison to national experts. The hierarchy between the two becomes manifest in inequalities with regard to remuneration, authority and ascribed credibility of expertise. Prevailing procurement and employment practices create a market which structurally discriminates experts from developing countries.

Finding an answer to the question of how the distinction between national and international experts emerged and how it is legitimated is not easy. The categorisation is commonly used in human resources policies and staff management documents of donor organisations; it is, however, never thoroughly explained on which justification it is based and which demarcation criteria are used. Asked what decides whether a job is tendered as a national or international position, interviewees provided two answers. The first referred to the assumed availability of domestic expertise: the donor and the recipient jointly decide if experts are likely to be found locally, and if not, they would advertise for an international expert. This approach would be in line with the principles set out in policies of recipient countries, for example, the Joint Assistance Strategy for Tanzania which states that "procurement of TA will use national rather than foreign expertise or supplies whenever these are able to meet VFM [value for money] and capacity development requirements" (United Republic of Tanzania 2006b: 11–12).

The second answer justified the practice in terms of compliance with market rules: advisory jobs or consultancies that exceed a specific financial threshold require an international bidding process. In fact, aid agencies within the European Union which serve as public sector authorities are subject to EU directives and thus need to tender consultancy contracts amounting to EUR 200 000 and more in all EU member states (GIZ n.d.; European Union 2012). Similarly, the World Bank has set monetary thresholds for each borrowing country which determine whether short lists for consultancies may be limited to national consultants or must include foreign candidates. In both South Africa and Tanzania, this ceiling is currently set at USD 300 000 (World Bank 2016: 5). These regulations are justified with the aim to foster competition and ensure the best 'value for money'.

The differentiation between national and international experts in the context of development aid is so common that it is rarely questioned. Yet, it demarcates expertise, drawing a line between experts in recipient countries and experts from abroad. A Tanzanian government official in the Ministry of Natural Resources and Tourism remembered an occasion at which the differentiation of national and international experts was challenged:

> *Actually at one time, we had a very strong debate at the steering committee meeting. We just wanted to hire an international expert and someone from the university actually asked the chair, 'at least make a definition of an international expert. Who would be an international expert?' And the consensus actually came that someone might be a Tanzanian, but also have an international qualification.* (Interview 55)

Similarly, a permanent secretary in Tanzania argued:

> *Our professors learnt in universities from abroad, maybe similar universities. For example, at the University of Dar es Salaam, some of my*

good professors there studied at Harvard. Some are better, they got their PhD there. So they have got good expertise and they are also used by some international organisations like UNICEF and they present papers abroad, outside there. So this connotation of international and local is not good.
(Interview 60)

Many interviewees expressed the sentiment that the differentiation between national and international expertise implicitly downgrades the expertise and experience of experts in recipient countries. The perception of a hierarchical classification is, indeed, formalised in prevailing employment conditions. National and international advisory positions differ greatly with regard to remuneration and assigned authority. It is common practice in the donor community to use different payment scales for the two categories: the international expert is paid according to the organisation's headquarter's salary scale, while national experts get a 'local pay' (see, for example, World Bank 2010b; GIZ 2011; United Nations 2013b). Although the latter is normally adjusted to the highest level of payment for similar work in the local market,[116] the salary of an international expert usually exceeds the rate of a national one by far. This applies to both longer-term advisory jobs and short-term consultancies. A Tanzanian professor with an international reputation sharply criticised the huge inequalities in remuneration he experienced in the context of aid projects:

The international consultant being paid maybe EUR 1 500 per day, the local consultant, no matter how skilled you are, full professor, and you are told your rate is EUR 300; I think that's even on the high side. But actually at the end of the day, you are the one to do the work because (...) those foreign experts, they don't know the local environment, where to source the materials. They end up doing the editing of the document that you have done (...). And if you are lucky, you'll be acknowledged in the final document. If you are unlucky, even the name will not appear.
(Interview 69)

---

116 The United Nations agencies, for instance, pay locally recruited National Professional Officers and General Service staff members according to the principle that "staff should be compensated in accordance with the best prevailing conditions of service in the locality; consequently, they are paid not on the basis of a single global salary scale, but according to local salary scales established on the basis of salary surveys" (International Civil Service Commission 2013: 14). Similarly, the GIZ policy for national personnel states that remuneration should be "in line with usual market conditions", specifying that "remuneration is comparable with that provided by private sector and international companies and other DC organisations competing with GIZ in the country" (GIZ 2011: 2).

The huge discrepancy in remuneration was not only confirmed by several interviewees of our sample, but has also been documented by studies on the use of advisors and consultants in the aid context. A comprehensive report on technical assistance in the context of Global Fund grants, for instance, states:

> *While precise details are not available, the studies showed clearly that local consultants in all the study countries receive far less than their international counterparts: local consultant rates were in the range of [USD] 100–350 per day, whereas international rates ranged from [USD] 250–650 per day, with Ethiopia reporting international rates of up to [USD] 1000 per day. Although there is insufficient evidence with regard to cost effectiveness to draw any solid conclusions, it should be noted that in some countries local consultants are deemed to provide more effective support, in part because of their ability to understand and work within the local context.*
> (Coordinating AIDS Technical Support Group 2009: 8–9)

The difficulty in presenting concrete, comparable data results from the fact that most donor organisations do not disclose salary scales or rates for advisors – oftentimes, not even recipient institutions are informed how much international advisors get paid. Other organisations are not able to provide an official payment scale for the simple reason that they do not have one. A study on the use of consultants in the United Nations system found that UN agencies either used outdated or imprecise remuneration guidelines or did not have any internal policies or guidelines at all, resulting in "significant discrepancies and inconsistencies in remuneration across the system and within each organization" (Terzi 2012: 31). On its website, the UN provides indicative rates not for consultants, but for professional staff. In 2013, an internationally recruited senior advisor seconded to Dar es Salaam was offered a total annual salary between USD 142 614–183 934 (United Nations 2013a).[117] A National Officer employed as senior programme officer received between USD 53 988–88 537 (United Nations 2012).[118] Although the two positions differ in terms of the scope of responsibilities and thus the salary data do not allow a direct comparison, the numbers shed light on remuneration levels for national and international senior positions.

The unequal and opaque pricing of expertise in the context of development cooperation causes tensions and strained relationships, particularly when

---

117 This is the salary band indicated for internationally recruited professional staff at the senior level, that is, senior experts hired as advisors or programme directors.

118 This is the salary band indicated for experts categorised as national staff and employed as senior programme or senior administrative officers (total net remuneration: TSh 88 661–145 397 thousand).

experts from within the country and from outside are paired and supposed to deliver as a team. A high-ranking senior official in Tanzania remembered a programme in which two senior professors complained about being paid less than their team leader, a relatively young consultant from the UK:

> *The professor was saying: 'We have almost the same job, we know this country, we travel a lot, we almost do everything. This fellow is just coordinating our efforts and is paid very highly and we are paid lower. We are professors; he is just a PhD holder. I have my professorship for the past 20 years; this is just a doctor for seven years back.' The professors were not happy.* (Interview 60)

This case points to the second aspect of hierarchy to be found in employment conditions, namely the practice of putting international experts into a higher position than their national collaborators. Irrespective of academic degrees or work experience, "the lead will be the external, then the national consultant will do kind of support" (Interview 68). Job descriptions advertised by aid agencies confirm this pattern. While international experts are delegated leading tasks, national ones are employed to assist.[119]

Although donors vary, the status of international experts is usually higher than that of national staff in country offices.[120] The discrepancy is a pattern found across the aid community and documented by workforce data. In 2011, 49% of DFID's total staff held senior posts as civil servants or advisers, whereas only 18% of the national staff in overseas offices (so-called "staff appointed in-country") was employed at that top level (National Audit Office 2012). A similar picture is found at GIZ: national personnel in recipient countries made up nearly 70% of GIZ's total workforce in 2012. While this is a high share of locally recruited staff, only 11% of this group were employed as leading or

---

119 To give just one example of what these arrangements look like: a procurement notice published by UNDP announced a tender for one international and two national consultancy positions to support the implementation of the National Mine Action Programme in Vietnam. The roles and responsibilities were assigned in the following way: as the team leader, the international consultant should manage the team, design the scope and methodology of the study, and draft and finalise the report. The two national consultants, classified as team members, were given the tasks to collect and review documents, participate in the design of the study and its implementation, contribute and assist in the production of the required deliverables, and translate the reports into Vietnamese, amongst others (UNDP 2013b). This example reflects the prevailing division of labour when consultants are 'paired', as it is called in the aid community.

120 Generalising our observations, the discrepancies between international and national staff are greater in bilateral agencies and less pronounced in multilateral organisations. In UN agencies, for instance, national experts have a solid standing, forming the core technical cadre in country offices. In the World Bank country office in Dar es Salaam, key positions for certain sectors such as the senior health or education specialist were filled with Tanzanian experts at the time of our research. One level up the hierarchy, however, the posts of task team leaders in health and education were held by international experts, namely, foreigners.

senior professionals (GIZ 2013a).[121] Aid organisations tend to boast about the use of national staff in their 'partner countries'; however, as the data above show, this does not necessarily mean that they put local experts at equal level with experts sent from abroad.

The internal divide of staff is, however weakly, noticeable in donor organisations. A South African expert who had worked for a foreign embassy in her country for over ten years told us that she had constantly been aware of the status difference between herself and foreign colleagues who were consciously or unconsciously suggestive of knowing 'a little bit better'.[122] Such kind of implicit downgrading of local expertise was broached as an issue by national experts and government officials in both countries of the study, particularly in Tanzania. Repeatedly one comes across the sentiment that donors consider foreign expertise as more 'credible'. A Tanzanian health expert with years of experience working for the government reported:

> *There could be six-month consultancies which you can recruit from domestic market or you can recruit from abroad. Now you need to look at where do I get these professionals? You might have somebody in the domestic market with experience and he has done similar work – then we have the problem of credibility of the report he will be writing. Because the credibility, (if you are with) GIZ or Danida, you are more credible (…). When local, national experts are reporting, you get a lot of criticism. We have experience here. We were developing the health financing strategy with Professors from the University of Dar es Salam. I tell you, that strategy has never ended. In fact, it ended up them saying 'no, we cannot accept this document'.* (Interview 44)

The term 'credible' in this context implies both a high quality of expertise in a technical sense and 'objectivity' or 'independence'. The tendency to perceive international expertise as more neutral and local expertise as potentially biased is even reflected in official donor documents, in which the "lack of distance to the partner organisation" (Ministry of Foreign Affairs of Denmark 2009: 15) is mentioned as a potential risk of recruiting national consultants. Being aware of the subliminal disregard of local expertise on the donor side, decision-makers in government ministries and departments tend to adopt a very pragmatic strategy. A permanent secretary in Tanzania stated in this regard:

---

121 The remaining national personnel were categorised as professionals (29%), junior professionals (10%), assistants (20%) and support staff (30%). The shares were calculated using data taken from the company's 2012 Annual Report (GIZ 2013a: 55).

122 This statement was made during a feedback workshop in the context of the study. To preserve the anonymity of the person, no further details are provided.

For us, we argue that even the local ones have got expertise (…). But when they [the donors] say 'if you insist on the local, we don't provide money' and you want this thing to be done in order for you to make progress, so you agree. (Interview 60)

The unequal assessment of expertise leads to the paradoxical situation that experts in recipient countries come "behind the umbrella of the foreign companies" (Interview 59), as an interviewee put it. Local experts team up with consultancy firms abroad, creating a win-win situation for both: while the former increase their degree of credibility, the latter can claim to provide experts for the country of assignment, which increases their chance to win the bidding process. An officer in the Tanzanian National Environmental Management Council remembered such a case in the context of the World Bank/GEF 'Lake Victoria Environmental Management Project':

There was an assignment which was given to a Netherlands company, a consultancy firm. But you find most of the activities were being done by the Tanzanians. But the company which was engaged came from the Netherlands. They were just coming for about two or three weeks and went back, but all the fieldwork, data collection, everything was being done by professors from the University of Dar es Salaam. But as professors, they could not have that assignment (…). (Interview 59)

Local experts are not necessarily excluded from an international bidding process. Depending on the financing agency's procurement rules, they are in some cases also eligible to apply for international posts.[123] The rules of the game in that competition, however, put them in a rather inferior position in contrast to applicants from abroad. The process of selecting experts in the aid market is guided by standards set by donor organisations. Expertise is rated against qualification criteria such as university degrees, publications and previous assignments, and the quality of technical proposals. Applying such assessment

---

123 Unfortunately, it was difficult to obtain clear answers to the – at first glance – simple question whether experts from recipient countries are eligible to apply for internationally tendered advisory positions in their own countries. We were not able to obtain relevant information from documents publicly disclosed by donor organisations. Hence, we tried to clarify this issue by contacting some agencies directly by email (emails sent on 05 November 2013). DFID's press office did not reply at all. Two contacts at GIZ could not provide a definite answer, adding that this was a 'complicated question'; one of them explained that he had never worked with a national holding an international position, but he had heard from colleagues that there are exceptional cases. Only an agency commissioned by Danida for administering bilateral positions made a clear statement: "All bilateral Danida adviser positions are available to all nationalities, meaning that also experts in recipient countries are eligible to apply for the advertised positions" (Email of Mercuri Urval Denmark, received 05 November 2013).

factors tends to marginalise experts from developing countries, as they are not able to keep up with experts from the North, as the NEMC officer pointed out:

> *They [foreign experts] come with big CVs, so it is difficult to compete (...).*
> *In fact, in most cases – in my opinion – I think you find that whenever they*
> *submit their financial or technical proposals, probably they are quite good*
> *compared to our national experts. And you find that in most cases they*
> *have a track record. They have done quite similar kind of studies in other*
> *countries. So when it comes to competition, in most cases you find that they*
> *just win.* (Interview 59)

This experience of a Tanzanian natural scientist points to a couple of structural obstacles which diminish the competitiveness of local experts, irrespective of their actual individual expertise. First of all, given the constraints of science systems in developing countries,[124] the academic records local experts are able to provide are usually less comprehensive and, again, less recognised. In this context, two points were raised which concern local experts working as scientists and likewise as consultants, namely the problems of unequal credit distribution and a hierarchical classification of research output. An internationally well-respected Tanzanian scientist touched on both issues, reflecting what has been said in other interviews:

> *There is this misconception that there is this categorisation of the*
> *publications. Something published in Africa is 'grey literature'. Something*
> *published in the West, in America, that's top class literature. So even in the*
> *IPCC [Intergovernmental Panel on Climate Change], in the beginning we*
> *were told you have to handle 'grey literature' with care because it doesn't*
> *merit scientific credibility. Those kind of insulting sort of statements – and*
> *sometimes you get annoyed.*

And further:

> *Actually, if you find most of this good piece of work which has been done*
> *in Africa, much of it has been done by Africans, but they don't feature*
> *them in the documents. Mostly, scientists from the West take the credits.*
> (Interview 69)

---

124 For a comprehensive analysis of the state of public science in countries of southern Africa, see Mouton et al. (2008).

The problem of unequal credit distribution was reported for both scientific articles and consultancy reports. As the majority of publications are financed from outside, experts in developing countries frequently experience 'disappearance' when it comes to authorship, making it difficult for them to document research or consultancy experience.

The fact that funding usually comes from Europe or North America limits the employment opportunities of experts from developing countries, as there is a clear tendency of financiers to select advisors from their own region. A Tanzanian policy-maker summarised his experience in the following way:

> *EU member states, if they give your government money to recruit foreign consultants, if you take one from outside the EU member states, I can tell you even the report may be rejected. I don't know why. May I ask you because you come from the EU member states – do you have an implied policy that money from your state should be financing consultants from same countries?* (Interview 60)

The pattern that European or US financiers prefer experts from their own countries or regions was confirmed by various interviewees and mentioned as a major obstacle hindering the development of an African consultancy industry. Although international organisations increasingly emphasise the importance of South-South exchanges and make some sporadic attempts to create regional consulting pools,[125] there is still a funding gap and a lack of institutional backing for experts from developing nations. That, in turn, makes them less competitive in the international market. They are disadvantaged as they are less able to provide a comprehensive track record of previous assignments as advisors in other countries. Due to the lack of experience and institutional support, they may also be less conversant with the codes of the consultancy industry. As one interviewee put it, "a consultant is not here to create new things. He's here to package them well" (Interview 68). This packaging requires the use of certain terminologies, formats and methodologies developed and certified by international organisations. As Evers and Menkhoff (2002: 21) point out, "choosing the right language and the appropriate concepts is an essential prerequisite for success" in the market. To demonstrate such consultancy skills in applications and technical proposals is often a challenge for experts in developing countries with little experience in the market. The competitive edge they could claim over foreigners, namely profound knowledge of their countries with regard to political structures, societal and cultural issues, and

---

125 An example is the PEPFAR-funded Grant Management Solutions project which employed consultants from Africa, Asia, Latin America and the Caribbean to advise governments receiving Global Fund grants (Anderson 2008).

local language skills, is usually given less weight in the selection process than formal qualification criteria and certified technical competencies. Comparing adverts for international advisory positions, it is noticeable that in most cases previous experience in the country and/or basic skills of the local language in the country of assignment is – if at all – mentioned as an asset, but not as a decisive requirement.

In sum: with the authoritative power to define expertise, donors have created a market which ranks "international (that is, Northern) knowledge at the top and so-called local (that is, Southern) knowledge at the bottom" (Girvan 2007: 16). Procurement practices and employment conditions in that market reinforce the hierarchy between external and local expertise, and thus marginalise expert communities in recipient countries instead of strengthening them. The donor community thereby preserves the prevailing epistemic hegemony of the North which sets specific conditions for knowledge transfer between external and local actors.

Hierarchical relations between advisors and counterparts

The hierarchy between international and national knowledge characterises not only the expert market, but also the relationship between external experts and their local counterparts in their practical operations. Commenting on the manifest status difference between the two parties, a Tanzanian advisor working for a foreign embassy stated:

> *Once you are a recipient, the relationship cannot be equal. That cannot be.*
> (Interview 31)

Donor organisations frame advice as a process of mutual learning, but in reality the actors involved still perceive it as a one-directional transfer of knowledge, with foreigners imparting their knowledge to local officials. Many interviewees expressed the sentiment that external experts are generally ascribed superior expertise and competency. Even in cases where advisors and counterparts have a similar training background and scope of work experience, there is an implicit asymmetry in authority, as a Tanzanian professor pointed out:

> *We have been to school together, we know each other, we know our capacities. But of course, when they're here, they're treated as people who can give you instructions.* (Interview 69)

From the recipient perspective, donors often come with the attitude that local counterparts are not capable to perform without their assistance. This becomes evident in reactions on policies, plans and programmes which, if prepared without external support, are sharply criticised by the aid community. This leaves senior officials in government ministries and departments under the impression that donors generally downgrade local capacity in order to legitimate the placement of external experts within their organisations.

The fact that foreign experts, coming with expertise and money, often have regular access to high-level decision-makers exacerbates the status difference perceived by government staff. South African and Tanzanian officials interviewed for this study expressed their frustration about how foreigners work themselves into powerful positions and claim to interact only with the leading figures of recipient authorities. A director in the South African Department of Health said:

> *Sometimes they come here – which is a big, big, big problem – they come here and they prefer to work with people at the highest, highest level. For example, the head of the department or the deputy of the head of the department. And then they don't want to work with us. And we are the people that are more skilled and we are the people that have more information on this (…). I'm knowledgeable about these policies and frameworks. So their preference of wanting to meet with the highest level makes frustration.* (Interview 18)

Another factor that creates discrepancy and inequality in what is supposed to be a 'partnership' between local officials and external advisers is the obvious differences in living standards and salary. In the questionnaire sample, every second respondent assessed this as a problematic or extremely problematic issue within cooperation.[126] Again, it is difficult to provide data on donor and government pay which allow a sound comparison.

Table 4 provides only exemplary figures to give an impression of the existing salary differentials.

In extreme cases, consultants earn more in one day than what government officials get paid in a month.[127] Salary differentials of that extent create resentment among government staff towards experts from outside. Though not an openly addressed issue, the stark discrepancy implicitly affects the cooperation, as a Tanzanian World Bank officer pointed out:

---

126 Incidentally, a similar impression is also expressed by Tanzanian programme officers in the study Eriksson Baaz (2005: 94). The distribution of questionnaire answers in detail (missings not calculated in the percentage): 13.2% extremely problematic; 37.7% problematic; 39.6% rather unproblematic; 9.4% definitely unproblematic.

127 A study conducted by ActionAid International provided concrete numbers for Cambodia where "adviser fees of $17,000 per month are several hundred times higher than the salary of a typical government employee, at only $40 per month" (Greenhill 2006: 34).

Table 4: Monthly salary bands of advisors, consultants and government staff

Rank	Recipient country	USD min.	USD max.
TZ, PMO-RALG	Senior forest officer (government scale TGS F)	–	727
TZ, PMO-RALG	Principal economist Policy and Planning Division (government scale TGS H)	–	1 365
SA, DHET	Deputy director, Academic planning, monitoring and evaluation	–	4 867
DFID	Senior advisors (band A2)	7 036	10 145
DFID	National health advisor in Tanzania	2 539	3 754
United Nations	Senior level professionals in Dar es Salaam	11 885	15 328
United Nations	Senior level professionals in Pretoria	11 280	14 549
AusAid	Long-term advisor (discipline group c, job level 4, e.g. senior advisor on biodiversity)	13 017	19 525
AusAid	Short-term advisor (discipline group c, job level 4, e.g. senior advisor on biodiversity)	708 (daily rate)	1 063 (daily rate)

Source: DFID (2007: 224); Crown Management Consultants (2009: 72); AusAid (2012: 14); Best Jobs Tanzania Blog (2013); Department of Higher Education and Training (2013b); United Nations (2013b).[128]

Here is a foreign and here is a guy, local, and they're all experts according to their level. One, of course, is remunerated by his own government – very high, his living conditions and everything. This [other] poor guy is on a very rudimentary salary, a miserable salary, and they are supposed to be equal. That would also bring in some kind of tension (…). Now they are supposed to work at that level with somebody who definitely is different. I mean, they are equal but different. You see what I mean. (...) Although it's not straight outspoken, but you see that kind of element.

[The local guy] probably would just continue doing business as usual. Not really then having willingness to learn, readiness to learn from this guy – he will know it won't make any difference to me. But who would like to make a difference to the system, you see. So that commitment is a problem. (...) Basically you are bringing in advisors to try to strengthen a system which is a de-motivated system (…). At the end of the day, you just go back home and nothing has changed. That's my own experience, how I see it. (Interview 47)

All the different aspects delineated above – knowledge, influence, living standards – demarcate a boundary between external and local actors, and

---

128 To provide a sound comparison, salary data in this table have been converted into USD and inflation-adjusted.

rank them in an order in which the former is higher than the latter. The extent to which that hierarchy is pronounced certainly varies. In both South Africa and Tanzania, however, policy advice in the context of aid takes place in an unequal setting in which "knowledge serves the function of justifying hierarchical relations" (Girvan 2007: 6).

The intricacies of expert advice in the context of aid highlighted in this chapter can be summarised as follows: policy advice within development cooperation takes place in a setting permeated with conflicting interests and power inequalities between donor and recipient countries, with the latter being in a weaker position due to their dependency on external support. Given the strong linkage of aid and politics, advisory processes are affected by shifting fads in terms of topics and modes of operation, legitimation and accountability pressures, and a potential mismatch of donor interests and recipient needs. At the micro-level, structural flaws in expert employment and hierarchical relations create conditions that obstruct the knowledge transfer between advisors and their counterparts. As a result, expert advice largely fails to achieve its main objective, namely to increase the capacity of recipients in a way that ultimately makes them independent from outside assistance.

Consequently, governments in developing democracies find themselves caught in a perpetual cycle of being advised by external experts who circulate in core government institutions and are involved in all stages of policy-making. Considering that these experts share a certain epistemic culture and are primarily accountable to their financiers, that is, the donor community, the expertise they communicate to their client governments is not neutral, disinterested expert knowledge, but is shaped – often implicitly – by particular paradigms and interests. Expert advice in the context of aid thus becomes a conduit for external influence under the guise of knowledge transfer. This raises the question how this affects especially young democracies such as South Africa and Tanzania, as these are particularly vulnerable to the loss of decision-making autonomy and, thus, legitimacy. To what extent are they threatened by knowledge transfer as it was characterised and under which conditions are they still able to defend their decision-making autonomy in the political realm?

Chapter 6

RETAINING AUTONOMY OF AGENDA-SETTING IN DEALING WITH ADVICE: STRUCTURAL CONDITIONS

A key characteristic of a democracy is the continuing responsiveness of the government to the preferences of its citizens, considered as political equals.
(Dahl 1971: 1)

A core idea of democracy is that the rulers in power are responsive to the state's citizenry, whereby 'responsive' implies that they take the will of the governed into account (Dahl 1971). Thus, a central dimension of quality in democratic governance is the degree to which decision-making is guided by the needs and demands of the voters. Ideally, government policies reflect the majority preference of the people. This is, of course, a normative stance. A perfect congruence between what the citizens want and what the government does is utopian in any real world democracy, where unpopular decisions – for example, an increase in taxation – also need to be made. Yet, the legitimacy of democratic governments is based on the premise that they consider the demands of their constituencies "at least in broad outlines over the long run" (Gilens 2005: 779).

In aid-receiving democracies, the question whose interests are taken up in policy processes is often difficult to answer. Given the dependencies pervading aid and the omnipresence of donor-funded experts in the power centres of recipient countries, one can assume that a plethora of decisions are imposed from outside, reflecting the preferences of donors rather than those of domestic publics, that constitute the electorate. We want to explore the extent to which policy-making in South Africa and Tanzania is shaped by external experts acting on behalf of the aid community, focusing on education, health and environment as fields of investigation. These areas are particularly relevant for three reasons: first, they are high on the development agendas of both states; secondly, they have been target areas of foreign support; and thirdly, expertise and 'evidence' are deemed crucial for legitimating policy decisions in these fields. Aside from the policy *content,* which is different in each sector, we pay particular attention to the *process* of policy development, the *actors* involved therein as individuals and members of groups, and the *context* which provides the 'setting' for their interaction (Walt & Gilson 1994). Adopting a political economy perspective, this approach starts from a number of assumptions, namely that (a) structural conditions decisively impact on the outcomes of policy negotiation; (b) contemporary processes and relations are affected by past experiences which requires a historical perspective; and (c) conflicts of interest between local and foreign actors may well be grounded on legitimate political differences (Whitfield 2009b).[129] To what extent aid recipients in South Africa and Tanzania have been able to defend their views and set their own agenda against outside advice, and what accounts for their strengths or weaknesses in doing so, are the guiding questions of the six case studies that follow.

The extent to which developing democracies are able to defend their decision-making autonomy in the political realm primarily depends on three structural conditions: financial strength, administrative capacity, and the local knowledge base they can draw on. We explicate the relevance of these factors for aid-related advisory processes and look at South Africa's and Tanzania's status with regard to corresponding indicators in the fields of health, environment and education.

Financial strength

> *Let me tell the truth: If our relationship is also influenced by donating, do*
> *you think you have much power if you are a recipient?* (Interview 60)

This statement by a permanent secretary in Tanzania hints at a pervasive experience of aid recipients, namely that due to their dependency on donor resources, they are invariably the inferior party in negotiations. We assume that the degree of asymmetry in donor–recipient relations notably depends on the financial strength of the soliciting country. Hence the first hypothesis: the higher the financial dependency, the weaker is the recipient's position in defending the local agenda against external pressure.

---

129 See also Whitfield & Fraser 2009.

Governments in need of donor money are inevitably forced to accept that they have to enter some sort of negotiation with potential financiers and may need to compromise on the terms and conditions of assistance (Nissanke 2010); "...conditionality is the price the recipient pays in order to get access to transfers in case of nonaligned preferences" (Martens 2008: 289). Previous studies indicate that one factor determining the bargaining discretion of the beneficiary is the degree of dependency on aid as an essential source of finance (Gould 2005a: 143). When aid is constitutive of the overall performance of the domestic economy and a government's capacity to act, recipients are likely to accept external interference in policy-making for the sake of keeping their economy and state apparatus running. In extreme cases, the dependency on donor funding erodes governments' agenda-setting function since "priorities turn to whatever brings in the most money" (Polidano 2000: 812).

Among the various definitions and variables of aid dependency the indicator commonly used at present is the share of aid to the recipient country's gross national income (GNI).[130] Figure 7 displays the ratio of official development assistance and GNI in Tanzania, South Africa and sub-Saharan Africa from 1993 (the first year in which data for South Africa are available) until 2011. Most notably, it shows that the percentage of aid to South Africa's GNI ranging from the lowest value of 0.21% in 1993 to the highest of 0.47% in 2002 remained basically insignificant. Tanzania, in contrast, has very high ratio levels, both compared to South Africa and to sub-Saharan Africa as a region. Although the proportion of ODA to the country's GNI declined by more than half from 23.07% in 1993 to 10.32% in 2011, it is still significant, implying the high impact of aid on the Tanzanian economy.

Relating aid volumes to the gross national income (or the gross national product previously used as denominator) points to the significance of external finances to recipient economies and invites assumptions about the consequential influence of external financiers in spending decisions (Bräutigam 1992).[131] For our purposes, however, such measures have two flaws. First, they describe aid dependency of recipient economies rather than governments; and second, they are not useful for a sectoral analysis.[132]

An indicator which may be disaggregated by sectors is the ratio of aid as a percentage of government expenditure. The underlying argument: when

---

130 Glennie & Prizzon (2012); see also Lesink & White (1999); Bräutigam (2000); Knack (2001).

131 In an early article on the interdependencies of governance, economy and foreign aid, Bräutigam (1992: 11) stated that "when aid transfers reach ten percent or more of total GNP (as they did for at least 24 countries in 1989) and exceed total current revenue from other sources, those with the loudest single voice on revenue and expenditure issues are international lending agencies".

132 This equally applies for other commonly used indicators such as 'Net ODA received per capita' or 'Net ODA received as % of imports of goods, services and primary income' which cannot be disaggregated by different sectors.

Figure 7: Aid as share of GNI in South Africa, Tanzania and sub-Saharan Africa

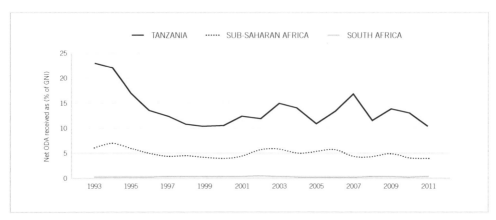

Source: World Bank database (World Bank 2014a).

donors fund a substantial share of sector budgets, they are likely to have a say in defining the priorities for which their money is spent. If a line ministry is highly dependent on external financing for implementing a national programme, its leaders can hardly reject support, even if it comes with conditions. These conditions may not even be explicitly written down in agreements, but conveyed in policy forums where donor experts and government officials interact. The latitude of decision-makers to take decisions against advice is severely restricted when their capacity to deliver basic services depends on donor money.

While the share of external contributions in government expenditures constitutes a suitable indicator for (sectoral) aid dependency, it has some crucial constraints pertaining to the accessibility and accuracy of data. As several scholars have pointed out, figures for this measure are scarce and not necessarily consistent, which makes it difficult to carry out time-series analyses and cross-country comparisons (Knack 2001; Glennie & Prizzon 2012). In the WDI database, the indicator "Net ODA received (% of central government expense)" lacks information for 15 out of 48 states in sub-Saharan Africa, including Tanzania; for the remaining ones, data are at best erratic. In addition to the limited availability of data on recipient government expenses, donor statistics pose a major problem. Aid agencies apply different definitions and standards in reporting which are not always clearly spelled out; for instance, many do not disclose which amount of a certain programme budget is actually transferred to the recipient or used for advisors and administration.[133] In many

---

133 In interviews and during a feedback workshop held in Stellenbosch in 2013, government officials from both South Africa and Tanzania strongly complained about donors not disclosing disaggregated data on financial disbursements and technical assistance, pointing particularly to the

cases, one finds appalling discrepancies between aid commitments and actual disbursements (Bulíř & Hamann 2008; Celasun & Walliser 2008). Moreover, donor figures are often different from those reported by recipient governments (Wood et al. 2011).[134] This is exacerbated by huge amounts of off-budget funding channelled outside government systems. Hence, information on aid flows varies depending on the sources selected.

In light of such constraints on availability of reliable data, any numbers related to aid have to be taken with caution. The data we present in Table 5 on donor funding as a share of total expenditures in different policy fields, thus need to be considered as indicative rather than accurate. Extracted from annual reports and expenditure reviews of government ministries and departments, they are based on different systems which are not methodologically congruent since the way external funding is accounted in South Africa and Tanzania varies. A common feature in financial statements of ministries and departments, however, is the indication of actual expenditures and the amount of aid thereof. Juxtaposing the calculated shares based on these figures may help to get an impression of the financial impact of donors in different policy areas:

Table 5: Aid as share of government expenditures in 2010/2011 (%)

	Total	Education	Health	HIV/Aids	Environment
South Africa	1.0	1.3	0.8	16.4	1.1
Tanzania	28.2	8.5	38.4	97.5	n/a

Source: Fölscher et al. (2010: 1); Policy Forum (2010b: 1); Department of Basic Education (2011: 21); Department of Health (2011a: 150); Education Sector Development Committee (2011: 115); Department of Environmental Affairs (2012a: 71); Ministry of Health and Social Welfare (2012: 14); Republic of South Africa (2012: 67); TACAIDS (2012: I). Our own percentage calculations.

Table 5 provides a snapshot of the impact of donor contributions on line ministries' and departments' spending for the fiscal year 2010/2011. A salient contrast is the generally low level of external funding amounting to around 1% (except for HIV/Aids) in South Africa, while in Tanzania aid is a substantial part of both total and sector expenditures. The extreme is represented in the field of HIV/Aids where donor funds made up 97.5%. Yet, to draw the conclusion that South Africa can do without aid would be too simple, since plain numbers never paint a whole picture. We therefore contextualise the

---

non-transparent practice of USAID which poses a severe problem for government planning and budgeting.

134 In a report on the second phase of implementing the Paris Declaration, the authors comment on the 'statistical obstacles' observed as follows: "It is not clear to what extent these reported problems result from poor or late reporting (at the international or national levels), to unsynchronised cycles and/or to actual discrepancies in commitments and/or disbursements. In any case they perpetuate uncertainty and do not encourage trust" (Wood et al. 2011: 13).

figures presented above with additional material in order to further delineate dimensions of aid dependency in the different areas.

South Africa's financial strength by sectors

A case in point that illustrates the limited informative value of numbers refers to the impact of donor funding in the South African environment sector. At the national level, the Department of Environmental Affairs (DEA) is the most important government organisation in charge. With 1.1%, aid made up only a small share of DEA's expenditures in 2010/2011, implying a very limited role of external funding.[135] Although the significance of aid for DEA has declined considerably over the last decade, it remains an essential source of income for other public entities and nature conservation agencies that are severely underfunded. The South African National Biodiversity Institute (SANBI), a national statutory body responsible for monitoring the state of biodiversity and providing research and policy advice on biodiversity matters, is heavily dependent on external funding in key areas of its mandate (Parliamentary Monitoring Group 2012). In 2011 and 2012, around half of the resources required for generating science-based evidence to inform decision-making related to biodiversity management and climate change were obtained from donors. In its strategic plan for 2013–2018, SANBI warns that "certain deliverables are at risk if the nature or extent of the external funding changes during the five-year planning period" (SANBI 2013: 20). Provincial conservation authorities such as CapeNature in the Western Cape face similar challenges. In recent years, grants from domestic and international donors have amounted to half of the organisation's total budget (Hamman 2009: 1), making the implementation of programmes and services contingent on external financiers. Given such resource constraints of key agents in the field of environment, the sector is to some extent dependent on donor money, although it appears marginal from a national perspective.

In education, aid is an issue of historical importance, but rather negligible in financial terms. During the apartheid era, various countries from Europe, the US and from other world regions provided overseas scholarships and extensive funding for educational initiatives in order to support the oppressed non-white population, bypassing the isolated government (King 1999).[136] When in 1994 the new democratic Government of National Unity came into

---

135 This is down from 20% in 1999/2000 and around 4.5% in 2004/2005 (Department of Environmental Affairs and Tourism 2006: 72). In 1999/2000, the department was still named "Department of Environmental Affairs and Tourism" (DEAT).

136 Details on the historical background of donor support to education in South Africa will be outlined in the respective case study (see Chapter 7).

power, the international community was ready to shift its assistance from civil society to the Department of Education and its envisaged reform activities. In the early years of the new state, "requests for educational collaboration were arriving virtually on a daily basis from prospective partners as large as the Russian Federation and as small as Croatia" (King 1999: 260). While an enormous number of bi- and multilateral agencies contributed to the subsequent transformation process, the financial volume of aid in relation to government spending remained marginal, making it "almost impossible to identify individual contributions of donors" (Ngeleza et al. 2000: 29).

This is still the case today. As in Tanzania, the education sector in South Africa receives the largest part of the government's budget. In recent years, its share gradually increased from 18.2% in 2010/2011 (ZAR 165.1 billion) to 20.2% in 2013/2014 (ZAR 232.5 billion). The resources are primarily allocated to the Department of Basic Education and the Department of Higher Education and Training responsible at the national level, and to the nine provincial Education Departments.[137] The figure on aid assistance as a percentage of expenditures indicated in Table 5 pertains to the Department of Basic Education in fiscal year 2010/11; with 1.3%, the share of foreign funding was negligible. In subsequent years, it remained at a similarly low level, increasing only slightly to 2% in 2012/13.[138] External contribution in expenditures of the newly established Department of Higher Education and Training consistently made up less than 1% in its initial years of operation.[139]

Given such small numbers, it is evident that the role of foreign money in the South African education system is marginal. Yet, various government officials interviewed emphasised the value of aid as a means for co-financing pilot projects and 'niche areas' such as inclusive education, for which the regular budget provides only limited resources. In 2010/11, donor funds were used for the development of the Human Resources Management Information System in education and for teacher training in special schools, amongst others (Department of Basic Education 2011: 128). For such initiatives, ODA provides an 'added-value' in education. Largely, however, the sector can be assessed as financially independent from donor assistance.

---

137 In 2009, the former Department of Education was split into two ministries. While the Department of Basic Education is now in charge of early childhood development, and primary and secondary education, the Department of Higher Education and Training covers tertiary education up to the doctorate level, adult basic education, and technical and vocational training (skills development) which was previously managed by the Department of Labour. Details on educational governance structures are provided in the respective case study (see Chapter 7).

138 The percentages are calculated from data on aid assistance in actual expenditures as indicated in the financial statements of the department's annual reports: Department of Basic Education (2011: 144), (2012: 128), (2013: 242).

139 This is drawn from financial statements in DHET's annual reports: Department of Higher Education and Training (2011: 146), (2012a: 160), (2013a: 209).

In health, we find a similar situation if looking at the sector in general. Although gradually increasing, external resources for health make up a very small percentage of total health expenditure in South Africa, as shown in Table 6:

Table 6: External resources as share of total health expenditure in South Africa

Year	96	97	98	99	00	01	02	03	04	05	06	07	08	09	10	11
%	0.1	0.1	0.2	0.1	0.3	0.2	0.4	0.4	0.5	0.5	0.7	0.8	1.2	1.9	2.2	2.1

Source: WHO Global Health Expenditure Database (WHO 2014).[140]

Budgetary figures of the Department of Health confirm the financial strength of the South African government. Aid assistance accounted for only 0.8% (of the department's actual expenditures in fiscal year 2010/2011, see Table 5. Department of Health 2011a: 150), equivalent to previous years. Such numbers suggest that foreign money is insignificant for public health financing. While this holds true in principle, there is one important exception: in HIV/Aids, the focus area of donor engagement, external funding plays a critical role.

Although the South African government "is the primary investor in its own national and provincial response to the HIV/AIDS and TB epidemic" (Republic of South Africa 2012: 92), donors substantially contribute to financing interventions. In 2009/2010, external sources amounted to ZAR 2 126 million (equivalent to USD 265 million), which made up 16.4% of all HIV/Aids and TB spending in South Africa (Republic of South Africa 2012: 67). Compared to other African countries where over 80% of HIV programmes are funded from outside (Venter 2013), this figure may still seem moderate. Yet, the significance of assistance recently became manifest when the two largest external financiers, that is, the United States through PEPFAR and the Global Fund to Fight AIDS, Tuberculosis and Malaria (GFATM), cut their contributions.[141] Since 2004, the PEPFAR programme has channelled nearly USD 4 billion to South Africa (Kavanagh 2014). The bulk of resources were allocated to NGOs offering direct services for patients in need of antiretroviral drugs. Now that the US has ceased funding in the course of the PEPFAR 'transition', many specialised HIV treatment centres have been forced to close (Katz et al. 2013); the South African government has struggled to absorb patients and staff into

---

140 The figures presented in Table 6 relate to all channels of health spending (i.e. government, private sector and NGOs). Data were extracted on 20 February 2014 (WHO 2014).

141 Over the period 2008–2010, ZAR 2 500 million were channelled through the PEPFAR programme and ZAR 680 million through the Global Fund, which together amounted to 58.3% of external aid for tackling HIV/Aids (Republic of South Africa 2012: 92/95).

an overstretched public health system (Kavanagh 2014).[142] Thus, aid funding has some relevance in South Africa's HIV/Aids response, despite its limited volume in relation to domestic resources.

Tanzania's financial strength by sectors

Assessing Tanzania's financial strength in the environment sector is challenging since it is handled as a cross-cutting issue for which various ministries share responsibility. In contrast to HIV/Aids (which is also termed cross-cutting), environment is not captured in a separate 'code' in budget books. Hence, as other authors have pointed out, it is impossible to give accurate figures or percentages of government and donor spending in this policy area.[143] In order to nonetheless delineate the impact of external funding on environment, it is instructive to look at the budgetary situation of major players involved.[144] The Division of Environment in the Vice-President's Office (VPO-DoE) and the Forestry and Beekeeping Division in the Ministry of Natural Resources and Tourism (MNRT) are primarily concerned with the matter. Table 7 displays actual spending of these units as indicated in the government's budget books, that is, disaggregated into recurrent and development expenditures. While the former cover operational expenses (e.g. for salaries and wages, purchases of goods and services), the latter are used for development projects and investment activities. Two issues stand out: first, development expenditures are almost entirely financed from foreign sources (except for VOP-DoE in 2009/2010); and second, external contributions are notably volatile in terms of their financial volume.

Table 7: Environment-related expenditures (TSh million)

Vice-President's Office, Division of Environment							
Fiscal Year	Development expenditure			Recurrent expenditure	Total expenditure	Foreign as % of dev. total	Foreign as % of total
	local	foreign	dev. total				
2009/10	957	0	957	6 316	7 274	0.0	0.0
2010/11	0	481	481	3 682	4 163	100.0	11.6
2011/12	168	3 713	3 881	4 548	8 429	95.7	44.1

142 In 2012, the US announced it would gradually reduce PEPFAR funding to South Africa from USD 484 million in 2012 to USD 250 million in 2017 (Kavanagh 2014: 9).

143 See Luttrell & Pantaleo (2008); Kulindwa et al. (2010). Trying to compile an overview on the environment budget in Tanzania, Kulindwa et al. (2010) itemised allocations to environment-related programmes carried out by 13 different ministries; the contribution of donors to these programmes unfortunately cannot be traced.

144 Details on organisational structures and responsibilities related to environmental governance in Tanzania are provided in the respective case study (see Chapter 7).

Ministry of Natural Resources and Tourism, Forestry and Beekeeping Division

Fiscal Year	Development expenditure			Recurrent expenditure	Total expenditure	Foreign as % of dev. total	Foreign as % of total
	local	foreign	dev. total				
2009/10	19	6 740	6 759	13 068	19 828	99.7	34.0
2010/11	0	3 287	3 287	13 354	16 641	100.0	19.8
2011/12	0	68	68	14 491	14 559	100.0	0.5

Source: Tanzania Budget Books (Government of Tanzania 2011a, 2011b, 2012a, 2012b, 2013a, 2013b).

Again, it needs to be stressed that the figures do not take into account the large sums of foreign funding provided outside the government system. Yet, they reflect the consistently high aid dependency of divisions concerned with environmental issues. The former director of environment in the Vice-President's Office confirmed that during his term in office more than 90% of funding for programmes was provided by donors. This made implementation reliant on continued support. At the time of our interviews, the Ministry of Natural Resources and Tourism experienced the consequence of this dependency when major donors withdrew aid due to recurrent corruption allegations, causing a serious funding crisis.

Without external resources, not only development programmes grind to a halt. In some cases, public entities are under-funded to an extent which imperils their core operations. The National Environmental Management Council (NEMC), established as a technical advisory, coordinating and regulatory agency in charge of environmental protection, struggles to meet its recurrent expenditures without donor money. According to a newspaper article citing the director-general, NEMC received only TSh 1 billion out of TSh 7 billion requested from the government in fiscal year 2011/2012 (Rugonzibwa 2012). An environmental officer working for the council delineated the situation as follows:

> *Even if you had the approval maybe that the government is giving one million, at the end of the day you are getting 200 000 thousand out of the million. So you find within the financial year, you have the promise, you have an approved budget, but the fund is not coming. (…) It is unpredictable when you are going to get the funds to implement the activities. That's why there are a lot of problems.* (Interview 59)

The fact that environment comes out at the short end in resource allocation is not surprising in a country with "tremendous needs and huge budget shortfalls" (Interview 46), as a World Bank environmentalist put it (see also

Mwalyosi & Sosovele 2001). External funding has become a substantial source of income for government units concerned with environmental issues. Hence, the dependency on donor support in the field of environment is significant.

In contrast to environment, education is a priority sector in Tanzania. As in South Africa, it has repeatedly received the largest portion of the government's budget in recent years, with shares fluctuating between 17% and 23% during 2008–2013.[145] As in other African countries, aid accounts for only a minor part of education spending (Samoff 2009). For the MoEVT, foreign contributions made up 8.5% of total expenditures in 2010/2011 (see Table 5) which implies a rather limited relevance of donor funding. However, the leveraging impact of external assistance needs to be considered. Education is a sector with high operational costs. Given that the bulk of resources are depleted by recurrent expenditures such as salaries and allowances, "there is little money for teacher education, textbooks, building construction and maintenance, even pencils, paper, and chalk" (Samoff 2009: 11). This is where donors come into play. While their contribution appears small in relation to the overall education budget, it makes up a significant portion of development expenditures. In 2010/11, foreign funds accounted for 60% of the education ministry's development budget, an increase compared to the previous two years where the share was between 45% and 50% (Policy Forum 2010a). Development programmes are thus highly dependent on donor support and subject to external priorities. At the time of our interviews, the Primary Education Development Programme suffered from decreased funding as a result of diminishing donor interest; the Higher Education Development Programme was shelved due to a lack of financial assistance. The fact that donors regularly fall short of meeting their pledges causes serious setbacks for the implementation of programmes.[146] The significance of external funding in the development budget makes donors more relevant than they may seem at first glance. In interviews in this study, Tanzanian policy-makers concerned with educational issues made clear that for them aid is a central source of revenue besides taxes. Assessing the financial impact of donors in the sector, one needs to consider that "a relatively small amount of money is a large portion of discretionary resources and purchases a great deal of influence" (Samoff 2009: 11).

---

145 See Policy Forum & HakiElimu (2011); Ministry of Finance (2012); United Republic of Tanzania (2012b); PER Macro Group (2013). Data on education spending as a share of total government budget provided by different sources vary. The discrepancy in figures, however, is marginal, amounting to 1–2%. In 2010/11, a sum of TSh 2 045 billion was destined for education, of which one third was allocated to the Ministry of Education and Vocational Training (MoEVT) and the remainder to the Ministry for Social Development, Gender and Children (MSDGC) and the Local Government Authorities (LGAs).

146 See Policy Forum (2010a). According to HakiElimu, a leading civil society organisation focusing on education in Tanzania, donors provided only 43% of their commitments in 2008/2009 (TSh 27.6 from 64 billion) and 48% in 2009/2010 (TSh 30.3 from 63.4 billion) (HakiElimu 2011: 4).

Looking at the health sector, the financial dependency is obvious at first glance. Table 8 displays external resources for health as a percentage of total health expenditure in Tanzania.[147] While in the mid-1990s, donor share was still less than 10%, it quadrupled in the new millennium.

Table 8: External resources as share of total health expenditure in Tanzania

Year	96	97	98	99	00	01	02	03	04	05	06	07	08	09	10	11
%	9	18	19	35	28	18	11	30	31	35	43	40	44	48	40	40

Source: WHO Global Health Expenditure Database (WHO 2014).

The share of external resources in the spending of the Ministry of Health and Social Welfare (MoHSW) ranges at around the same level, amounting to 38.5% of total expenditures in 2010/2011 (Ministry of Health and Social Welfare 2012: 14). As in the case of the MoEVT, the situation appears worse if one takes only the development budget into account: donors funded 97.8% thereof, which in practice means that the implementation of development programmes is almost entirely based on aid (Sikika 2011: 3). The fact that external money is largely earmarked and to a considerable extent provided off-budget leaves the ministry with little discretionary power over the use of development funding (Ministry of Health and Social Welfare 2009: 31). Although decision-makers complain about donors tying money to certain areas and topics, they hardly reject support – due to the budgetary situation of their ministry, "it is difficult for them to say no" (Interview 44), as a Tanzanian WHO officer put it. A retired health expert from Germany who had been working with officials in the health ministry for several years observed:

> *They say 'we have to take every penny we can get.' Never would someone say 'well, that actually doesn't fit'.* (Interview 73)

The dependency on external resources is particularly extreme in HIV/Aids governance. With a share of over 97% of expenditures, donors almost entirely finance the country's national response. Table 9 displays the appalling discrepancy between government resources and donor spending on HIV/Aids in the period 2006–2011.

---

147 The figures presented in Table 8 relate to all channels of health spending (i.e. government, the private sector and NGOs). Data were extracted on 20 February 2014 (WHO 2014).

Table 9: Government and donor expenditures on HIV/Aids in Tanzania

	2006/07	2007/08	2008/09	2009/10	2010/11
Government expenditures in TSh billion	22.0	23.0	14.0	12.5	11.0
Donor expenditures in TSh billion	282.0	383.3	566.9	566.3	431.8
Total expenditures in TSh billion	304.0	406.3	580.9	578.8	442.8
Government share of total expenditures in %	7.2	5.6	2.4	2.2	2.5
Donor share of total expenditures in %	92.8	94.3	97.6	97.8	97.5

Source: TACAIDS Public Expenditure Review 2011 (TACAIDS 2012: 1).

As the figures indicate, the dominance of external resources has slightly increased in recent years from an already high level in 2006/2007.[148] Just as in South Africa, the United States through PEPFAR and the Global Fund are by far the largest funders: in 2010/2011, they provided 91% of total aid on HIV/Aids of which the large majority was channelled outside the government system (TACAIDS 2012: 1), depriving the government of control and oversight. The absolute dependency on donors in tackling the epidemic poses a high risk for the country, making the implementation of the government's national programme, the National Multi-Sectoral Strategic Framework for HIV and Aids, highly vulnerable to external decisions and developments (see case study, Chapter 6).

Comparative assessment of sectoral financial strength

Drawing conclusions from budgetary figures is an intricate endeavour, given the lack of reliable and comparable data on government and donor spending at the sector level. Moreover, numbers always imply calculation and choice.[149] Therefore, we tried not to rely on aid shares in departmental expenditures as an indicator of donor impact in the respective sectors, but complemented the figures with additional quantitative and qualitative material. Aggregating the information we obtained for each sector, we assessed their financial strength as follows: in South Africa, education and health are strongest in terms of finances; donor money only plays a minor role in these areas, apart from HIV/Aids where aid is a relevant contribution. Environment was assessed as

---

148 Unfortunately, figures for earlier years which would allow a comparison of government and donor spending on HIV/Aids over a broader time span could not be found. Data presented in the public expenditure review for 2003, the earliest version we have on hand, are based on rough estimates and the authors stress that spending figures of both government and donors are incomplete and inconsistent (Foster & Mwinyimvua 2003). Making calculations based on these numbers seems unrewarding and questionable in terms of reliability.

149 See Rottenburg (2000). The constructed character of figures is discussed in Chapter 5 on legitimation and accountability pressures in the aid context.

weaker. Although from a national perspective, donor funding is marginal, it is a crucial source of income for environmental agents at national and provincial level. In Tanzania, education has the strongest position, although external money noticeably affects the implementation of national programmes. Health is more dependent on aid, with donors providing the bulk of the development budget. The weakest fields in our comparison are the cross-cutting issues of HIV/Aids and environment which are almost entirely financed from outside. Table 10 displays our assessment, with '++' indicating a high level of domestic resources (implying low financial dependency), and '--' a low level of domestic resources (implying high financial dependency) at the opposite end of the scale. Admittedly, this illustration is over-simplified and not devoid of subjective interpretation.

Table 10: Sectoral strength in terms of finances

		South Africa		Tanzania	
Environment		-		--	
Health	HIV/Aids	++	+	-	--
Education			++		+

Source: Authors' own illustration.

Administrative capacity

The implications of aid dependency for the bargaining power of recipients was a prime topic among interview partners. Yet, various narratives indicated that the financial situation is not the only structural condition that determines the scope of donor influence. A retired government member in Tanzania who previously held a high-ranking position in the Vice-President's Office-Division of Environment, a unit in dire need of external funding, summarised his experience as follows:

> *The extent to which [advisors] can influence the process depends on the strength the particular institution has. What carries the day is the arguments put on the table. If the technical advisor swallowed the arguments, it will carry the day. So it's important to have a strong national team to be able to see through the presentations of technical advisors, so that the nuances or deviations or preconditions can be addressed there, transparently.* (Interview 66)

His statement points to the significance of what can be termed 'absorptive capacity' as a crucial precondition for dealing with expert advice (i.e. the ability of recipients to scrutinise expertise for its quality, relevance and implicit interests). Absorptive capacity requires the availability of adequate technical knowledge and critical competencies in public administration, which enable civil servants to utilise instead of being swayed by external advice. The weaker recipient bureaucracies are in terms of the critical competence of their internal staff, the higher is the risk that policy processes are influenced from outside. One could paraphrase this second hypothesis with the comment of a Tanzanian policy-maker in the Prime Minister's Office referring to decision-makers in the senior government cadre:

> *If they're competent enough, they can really drive. But if they are not, they'll be driven.* (Interview 60)

The argument is based on the cognisance that the senior administrative cadre plays a substantial part in policy processes. Bureaucrats are not only the decisive agents in operationalising political decisions into strategies, implementing programmes and managing public service delivery; as coordinators and informants of their political leaders they are also potentially able to exert significant influence on the government agenda. In theory,

> *a well-institutionalized bureaucracy makes a vital contribution to the quality and coherence of decision-making through policy advice and the structuring of the decision-making process, even though the decisions themselves are taken outside the bureaucracy.* (Polidano 2000: 810)

In many developing democracies, however, bureaucracies are hardly capable of fulfilling this central policy function. While fragile institutions and low skills bases are legacies of the colonial rule in Africa, the erosion of the public sector was further exacerbated by decades of economic crisis.[150] Structural adjustment programmes imposed by the international financing institutions compelled staff lay-offs and retrenchments, leaving administration with financial and human resources barely sufficient to run government operations (Weissman 1990). Given sharp declines in wage levels and worsening working conditions, highly skilled and experienced civil servants fled out of the public sector, poached by the private sector and international organisations which offered salaries vastly exceeding government pay.[151]

---

150 See Bräutigam (1992); Bräutigam & Botchwey (1999); Ocheni & Nwankwo (2012).
151 See Olukoshi (1998); Bräutigam & Botchwey (1999).

In light of such developments, today's 'capacity gaps' identified in bureaucracies all over Africa should not be a surprise to donors whose policies and practices contributed to the problem. The common response of the international aid community has been to supply government organisations with advisors and consultants commissioned to assist policy-makers and senior officials. As outlined above, the expertise these professionals provide is inevitably infused with a distinct set of norms and values shared by the epistemic community of development experts; their advice must finally comply with the policy preferences and principles of their respective home organisation. From the angle of the recipient, it would thus be crucial to scrutinise advice offered in order to detect implicit interests and to assess its 'political robustness' (i.e. to examine whether it supports the domestic agenda and if respective recommendations are politically feasible). If this is not done, governments run the risk of adopting external policy ideas and concepts which may collide with the expectations of their constituencies or are just not implementable in the local context. Administrative capacity translated into absorptive capacity on the receiver's part is thus crucial in three respects: first, to prove that external advice takes local needs and interests into account; second, to make knowledge from outside applicable by adjusting it to the local context and conditions; and third for the reason that without addressees capable to take up and utilise expertise provided, expert assistance may fill gaps, but not help to increase the policy capacity of government bodies in the long run. Without a critical mass of competent civil servants, advice is reduced to a form of external interference perpetuating the dependency on foreign expertise.

This implication, however, is wittingly or unwittingly disregarded by donors who justify the deployment of experts exactly with the weakness of recipient bureaucracies. The state of public administration in developing countries has entered the limelight since, parallel to the rise of the 'new public management' paradigm in economics, 'good governance' emerged as a core issue on the aid agenda in the 1990s.[152] Although the latter has remained a fuzzy concept lacking a commonly shared definition, scholars have constructed a range of indices for measuring the state of 'governance' across the world. Most of them incorporate the quality of public administration into the assessment, focusing on

---

152 Since academic literature on these two concepts is too broad to be adequately summarised here, we point to only a few contributions: a central article laying the foundations for the concept of 'New Public Management' was Hood (1991); Hood and Peters (2004) provide a review on how NPM developed as a subject of administrative science and explore its intended and unintended effects on public sector reform. 'Good governance' as a core element of a new development strategy after the decade of structural adjustment was pushed to the fore by the World Bank (1989, 1992). Various scholars have discussed the relevance and implications of 'good governance' in developing countries, as, for instance, Appiah et al. (2004); Smith (2007); Kötschau and Marauhn (2008); Booth and Cammack (2013).

issues such as service delivery, management performance, resource efficiency, corruption or statistical capacity. Table 11 provides a compilation of the most widely known governance indices, displaying indicators related to public administration and the latest ratings of South Africa (SA) and Tanzania (TZ). In spite of using different methodologies, data sources and concrete variables, indices consistently rank the former higher than the latter. The Bertelsmann Transformation Index (BTI) – highly criticised for its normative and simplified approach of assessing governance systems – complements its numeric rating with narrative analyses. In the country report on Tanzania, the state of basic administration is delineated as follows:

> *The state maintains a basic infrastructure throughout the country. Administrative capacity however is weak and ineffective. Staff is poorly trained and often unprepared to carry out government goals; what's more, the administration suffers under political interference, a result of more than 50 years of one-party rule (despite, according to the constitution, the country's multiparty democracy established since 1992). As pay is low, administrative staff is uncommitted, often not accountable and susceptible to corruption.* (Bertelsmann Stiftung 2014c: 8)

South Africa is rated two points higher achieving a score of 7 for basic administration, which according to the BTI codebook indicates that "administrative structures of the state provide most basic public services throughout the country, but their operation is to some extent deficient" (Bertelsmann Stiftung 2014b: 17). The country report points to the following constraints:

> *The quality of administrative bodies varies considerably, with capacity generally declining from the highest to the lowest levels of government. Major technical and managerial skill shortages exist and have an impact on efficiency with which various levels of government execute their mandate. In addition, corruption, nepotism, and maladministration, which drain state coffers, are causes for great concern.* (Bertelsmann Stiftung 2014a: 8)

While the BTI surveys countries in transformation processes from all world regions, the Ibrahim Index on African Governance (IIAG) focuses only on African states. Despite the diagnosed deficiencies in administration, South Africa tops the IIAG ranking in the category Public Management with 76.9 points, and achieves the fifth rank out of 52 in Accountability. In both categories, the country scores much higher than Tanzania which ranges slightly above

Table 11: South Africa and Tanzania as assessed by governance indices

Indicator	Description	Methodology	Scale	SA	TZ
African Development Bank Country Policy and Institutional Assessment (CPIA 2012)					
Governance rating: Public sector management and institutions	Based on 5 criteria: property rights and rule-based governance, quality of budgetary and financial management, efficiency of revenue mobilisation, quality of public administration, transparency, accountability and corruption in the public sector	Expert assessment	1 to 6 (=best)	4.83	3.93
Bertelsmann Transformation Index (BTI 2014)					
Basic administration	Assessment of basic administrative structures as one criteria of 'stateness'	Expert assessment	1 to 10 (=best)	7	5
Ibrahim Index of African Governance (IIAG 2013)					
Accountability	Based on 7 sub-indicators on accountability, transparency and corruption in the public sector	Aggregation of various third-party data based on official figures and expert surveys	0 to 100 (=best)	65.2	42.1
Public management	Based cn 11 sub-indicators: statistical capacity, public administration, inflation, diversification, reserves, budget management, ratio of total revenue to total expenditure, fiscal policy, ratio of external debt service to exports, revenue collection, soundness of banks			76.9	57.2
Institutional Profiles Database (IPD 2012)					
Functioning of public administrations	Based on 14 sub-indicators: reliability of official economic information, transparency of economic policy, level of corruption, efficiency of tax administration, transparency in public procurement, functioning of the justice system, urban governance, influence of economic stakeholders, influence of donors, freedom to establish organisations, autonomy of organisations, capacity for state reform, capacity for sectoral reform, tax exemptions	Perception data gathered through expert survey	0 to 4 (=best)	2.41	2.37
Worldwide Governance Indicators (WGI 2013)					
Governance effectiveness	Based on more than 40 indicators covering the (perceived) quality of public service and bureaucratic capacity in terms of policy implementation and service delivery	Aggregation of various third-party data based on official figures and expert surveys	$-2,5$ to $+2,5$ (=best)	0.33	–0.69
Control of corruption	Based on 36 indicators covering the levels of corruption, transparency and accountability in the public sector			–0.15	–0.85

Source: AFD et al. (2012); African Development Bank Group (2013); Mo Ibrahim Foundation (2013); World Bank (2013c); Bertelsmann Stiftung (2014a).

the average level, but achieves only ranks 18 and 23, respectively.[153] In the African Development Bank's governance rating, Tanzania comes off slightly better in light of a smaller score difference to South Africa which is only superseded by Botswana in the country ranking. Referring to the Institutional Profiles Database and the Worldwide Governance Indicators, the discrepancy in administrative quality between South Africa and Tanzania appears even less pronounced.

This divergence of assessments hints at an important point regarding the use of governance indices: given that the strength of public institutions is not directly observable, all of them draw on proxy indicators which – as the term implies – can only indicate administrative capacity rather than give a realistic representation of it. The indicators are highly constructed and imply certain normative ideas of 'good governance' and sound public management. The level of accessibility to source data varies, and if one takes a closer look, one finds self-referential links across indices which to some extent call the validity of results into question.[154] Aside from such methodological flaws, the indices present our research with the problem that they do not allow for a sectoral differentiation. To our knowledge, there is currently no measurement of bureaucratic quality disaggregated by sectors. In order to delineate the strength of public administration in the different policy fields under investigation, we therefore turn to interview material which we complement with ministry workforce data and information extracted from government reports. As we already know from the governance indices presented above, South Africa is stronger in general than Tanzania with regard to public service performance. In the following section, we examine whether we find sectoral differences in administrative capacity within the two countries, particularly in terms of staffing levels and in-house expertise. Thereby, the focus is mainly on the relevant line ministries as frame of reference.

Sectoral comparison of administrative capacity in South Africa

For the sectoral comparison of administrative capacity in South Africa, we primarily look at the Department of Environmental Affairs (DEA), the Department of Health (DoH), and the two national departments responsible

---

153 The African average score was 53.4 for Public Management and 41.5 for Accountability.

154 The extent to which the different governance indices mutually resort to each other's ratings as source data or decision guidance is noticeable. To give just one example: for measuring 'governance effectiveness', the WGI rating takes scores of the AfDB CPIA into account, namely on the quality of public administration, the quality of budgetary and financial management and the efficiency of revenue mobilisation. The experts doing the assessment for the governance rating of the AfDB CPIA, in turn, are advised to draw on 'key sources of evidence' amongst which the WGI category 'government effectiveness' is listed (African Development Bank Group 2009).

for education, that is, the Department of Basic Education (DBE) and the Department of Higher Education and Training (DHET). As part of their annual reports, these ministries disclose data on human resources in their organisations. Table 12 provides a compilation of (filled) post numbers, vacancy and turn-over rates in 2011/2012. These figures reflect administrative capacity in terms of staffing levels: a high share of unfilled posts implies that the department has a rather insufficient number of officials to cope with the workload; a high turn-over rate of staff is obstructive insofar as it means a permanent loss of practical knowledge in the organisation. Judged on the figures presented below, Environmental Affairs is the strongest department in terms of its staffing level, although being affected by a high turn-over of personnel. With a vacancy rate of almost 30%, the Department of Health seems to be less adequately staffed, followed by Higher Education and Training with over 20% shortage.

Table 12: Staffing levels of South African line departments 2011/2012

	Posts total	Posts filled	Vacancy rate	Turn-over rate
Environmental Affairs	1 628	1 441	11.5%	10.6%
Health	1 819	1 293	28.9%	9.7%
Basic Education	823	628	17.1%	8.7%
Higher Education and Training	1 077	843	21.7%	7.6%

Source: Department of Basic Education (2012: 190/192); Department of Environmental Affairs (2012a: 142/144); Department of Health (2012: 186/189); Department of Higher Education and Training (2012a: 353/358).

There are various root causes for the problem of vacancies in the different departments. A common challenge for all departments is to fill vacant posts with adequately skilled applicants in line with the employment equity regulations. To overcome the racial discrimination and disparities in the labour market created under apartheid, the South African government pursues an affirmative action policy formalised in the Employment Equity Act which requires employers to ensure the equitable representation of previously disadvantaged groups in their workforce (Department of Labour 1998). The legacy of apartheid and its racially segregated school system, however, is still manifest in lower educational levels among the black population (Van der Berg 2007). Given that highly qualified professionals from the designated groups are scarce and attracted by higher salaries outside the public system, state organs are struggling to find suitable candidates for vacant positions. This is particularly an issue in environment as a knowledge area which previously was a "preserve of the whites" (Interview 8), in the words of a South African UNDP officer. A director in the provincial conservation authority CapeNature reported on the tedious search for black project managers with an environmental background:

We advertised up to four times to get someone. In the end we didn't get one and then fell back to appointing a white male. (Interview 13)

As this example indicates, filling vacant posts with adequately trained professionals is often a complicated and lengthy process for government departments which are under pressure to 'get equity figures right' (Interview 13). Aside from this structural problem pervading all government bodies, the departments face distinct challenges in sourcing and retaining in-house expertise; these challenges emanate from political and institutional developments in the respective policy fields.

The Department of Health, which in 2011/2012 had the highest vacancy rate of the entities compared, is still struggling to recover from the era under President Mbeki and his Health Minister Tshabalala-Msimang who became infamous for the denial of Aids and antiretroviral treatment. During their leadership, "capacity fled out from the government system" (Interview 27), as a civil society representative put it. Many knowledgeable and experienced officials left the department due to its controversial policies, draining into the private sector or international organisations. A South African who resigned from public service during that time to work for a foreign embassy instead told us:

I was a project manager in government working in the Aids unit. And I must say it was very, very nice – very exciting work. But at that stage we had this terrible minister of health – Manto Tshabalala-Msimang. (…) And in 2003 I found myself apologising for where I worked and when I caught myself I realised I can't do this anymore. (Interview 5)

When the new minister Motsoaledi came into office in 2009, he brought about a radical policy shift and initiated an organisational reform process reconfiguring administrative structures and staffing patterns. Nonetheless, it has remained difficult for the department to salvage the lost expertise. According to an HIV civil society activist, "very few people go in there other than as consultants" (Interview 27). The insufficient number of competent permanent staff severely weakens the administrative capacity of the department. This was mentioned as an issue by various South African interviewees with close contacts and working relations to the Department of Health, with one saying:

It's shocking, because you can count the skilled people inside the government on one hand. And the same skilled people are trying to do everything – writing a human resource plan, writing Aids plans, writing national health insurance. And they make a mess all of the time, because it's just too much. (Interview 27)

At the sub-national level, the situation appears even worse. In 2009, reports on the performance of provincial health departments revealed fundamental shortcomings, "ranging from strategic planning and leadership, through to financial management and monitoring and evaluation" (Barron et al. 2009: 8). While much has already been tackled by the vigorous new minister, challenges in health administration at both national and provincial level still persist.

Another field in which renewed governance structures are a major cause for current capacity constraints is education. The low staffing levels in the basic education department and in higher education and training are largely a result of the fact that the two entities were formed out of one ministry. When the national Department of Education was split in 2009, financial and human resources needed to be divided and apportioned to the two newly structured administrative bodies, leading to budgetary and staff constraints on both sides (Department of Basic Education 2011). At the time of our research, this organisational transformation process was still underway. The newly established Department of Higher Education and Training was particularly affected by a high vacancy rate which posed serious operational problems, as the Annual Report for 2011/2012 states:

> *The high number of vacancies inevitably had a negative impact on human capacity and therefore also on implementation. (...) The University Education Branch has severe capacity constraints which impact on the delivery of services. The most significant capacity problem is at a high level professional end. The post of Deputy Director-General remains unfilled. Of the nine director posts, only four are filled. In addition, some sections with high workloads have insufficient staff to cope with these.* (Department of Higher Education and Training 2012a: 143)

Interviewees from both the government and donor side confirmed that there is currently a huge vacuum at the higher education department, hampering policy development and implementation. The situation is thus equal to the one in the field of health: despite highly qualified individuals in office, administrative capacity is constrained due to an insufficient staffing level.

The Department of Environmental Affairs, in contrast, has a comparatively low vacancy rate and a strong team of competent officials. Various interview partners engaged in the environment sector highlighted the high degree of in-house expertise across government bodies at the national level, ranging from the line ministry to public entities such as SANBI. A UNDP programme manager praised his counterpart officials in these institutions as follows:

> *Extremely well capacitated, you know, there are knowledgeable people writing articles and stuff, globally respected. Some of them are part of the negotiating team on biodiversity perspective. When you run the projects through them, you can see these guys are in full control. You have less stress, they deliver, they know what they want, they know where they are going, they are pretty at the play. They are on top of the game.* (Interview 8)

The workforce of DEA and SANBI is largely made up of environmental specialists qualified with an academic degree up to the masters or PhD level; many are engaged in key policy platforms at the global level and strongly networked with the domestic and international science community. By way of example, a leading official in the biodiversity planning unit of the department sketched his professional background and work environment as follows:

> *Interviewee: I'm a conservation biologist. I've got two masters degrees, one from the UK. Presently, I'm a member of the Society for Conservation Biology. And I think that's my link with the technical academic research (…). I've been affiliated with the TWNSO, the Third World Network of Scientific Organizations as well. So again, that is keeping me up to date in terms of what is currently happening in terms of research. And that actually informs the way the government addresses issues because the cutting edge research is flowing into these processes, whether it's the minister's speech or the presentations or participation in these various platforms that do exist. My job is predominantly to mainstream some of that thinking into the national processes.*
>
> *Interviewer: 'Thinking' meaning scientific evidence?*
>
> *Interviewee: Yeah, scientific evidence, scientific concepts we hear on the international platforms of engagements because South Africa is very prominent in international circles in the sense that we have many multi-national environmental agreements. And our international work is quite robust because we're always engaging in the technical working groups of the CBD [Convention on Biological Diversity]. I'm a member of the Ad Hoc Technical Working Group 'Biodiversity for Poverty Eradication and Development'. And then there are other people as well deployed to various other technical working groups like SUBSTTA [Subsidiary Body on Scientific, Technical and Technological Advice] as well.* (Interview 15)

While in general South Africa has an outstandingly strong administration in the environment sector, interviewees raised some flaws pertaining to the knowledge base in government. First and foremost, as mentioned earlier, environmental expertise is largely held by a group of people which is not representative of the South African demographics; the expert community in both government and science is still racially skewed, and the number of black scientists coming out of university is very limited. Moreover, there is a stark discrepancy in capacity between national and sub-national levels, as a UNDP officer commented:

> *At national level they've got tall expertise, you know, PhD people leading policies and stuff. (…) But you go to the provinces and then it becomes obvious, never mind the local municipalities – to find a person who can be able to tell you how climate change links with the development work that they're doing sometimes can be a challenge.* (Interview 8)

The lack of environmental expertise in provincial and local government is particularly profound in distinct knowledge areas where specialists are required. The Environmental Sector Skills Plan for South Africa published in 2010 identified a scarcity of soil scientists, taxonomists, ecologists, environmental and resource economists, climate change scientists, or biotechnologists, amongst others (Department of Environmental Affairs 2010a: 19).

Despite such constraints related to the dispersion of (specialist) knowledge, however, the in-house expertise in government entities dealing with environment is substantial; this manifests itself in the fact that South Africa leads the way in certain areas such as spatial planning and in adopting innovative concepts of biodiversity management. In addition, there are well-established structures for policy dialogue and consultation in which domestic advisory bodies play a central role. In our sample, environment can thus be assessed as the strongest sector with regard to public administration and, hence, absorptive capacity.

Sectoral comparison of administrative capacity in Tanzania

Due to a lack of access to contrastable workforce data, assessing the administrative strength of sectors in Tanzania proves to be intricate. The shortfall of qualified staff is mentioned in literally all reports on sectoral performance in Tanzania. Most of them, however, remain superficial; very few authors support their claim with some sort of concrete evidence, which makes it difficult to differentiate the extent of the problem in different areas.

A comprehensive in-depth study on public sector capacity is available only for education. The Education Sector Human Resources Situation Analysis published in 2012 discloses detailed information on staffing levels on the delivery side of the education system (i.e. in schools and academic institutions, as well as on the governance side, i.e. authorities concerned with education at national, regional and district level). Aside from chronic shortages of teachers all across the system, the report reveals massive capacity gaps in the respective ministries, both in terms of numbers and expertise (Omari & Baser 2012). A case in point is the Department of Policy and Planning, a key unit within the Ministry of Education and Vocational Training (MoEVT). At the time the study was conducted, the planning section entailed only seven officials most of whom lacked training or experience in planning; out of the eight persons working in the Education Management Information System unit in charge of producing and processing educational data for the department, only four had adequate IT qualifications (Omari & Baser 2012). The lack of professionals with specialised training is also a sign of the generally low educational level of staff. As Table 13 indicates, less than 50% of the workforce holds an academic degree (including bachelors, postgraduate diplomas, masters or PhDs):

Table 13: MoEVT staff by educational level

Educational level	Number	Share of total
Certificate	142	34.6%
Ordinary Diploma	42	10.2%
Advanced Diploma	44	10.7%
Bachelors	70	17.1%
Postgraduate Diploma	20	4.9%
Masters	88	21.5%
PhD	4	1.0%
Total	410	100.0%

Source: Education Sector Human Resources Situation Analysis (Omari & Baser 2012: 171).

At the sub-national level, the situation looks similar if not worse: regional and district offices are affected by high vacancy rates and insufficiently skilled staff. The authors of the report made the observation that "many district education officers, even sometimes the primary and secondary DEOs [District Education Officers], were not comfortable in English" (Omari & Baser 2012: 179).

In addition to the weak bureaucratic workforce in the national ministry and local government authorities, governance in education has further been exacerbated by the lack of overall guidance. For years, a range of decisive leadership positions, including the Commissioner of Education, the Chief Inspector of Schools, as well as various director posts, were only filled with acting managers who were neither adequately qualified nor able to develop a strong steering capacity (Omari & Baser 2012) – "there are not the right people in the right position" (Interview 45), a Tanzanian expert working for the World Bank commented. All in all, the administrative capacity in education can be assessed as severely constrained.

The situation in health does not look much better if looking at the overall sector which is facing a serious human resource crisis (School of Public Health and Allied Sciences 2009). The Health Sector Strategic Plan III 2009–2015 illustrates the dimension of the problem with alarming numbers:

> *The total of staffing in the health sector stands at 35% of the actual need according to defined staffing norms. The available number of professional health workers in the public sector is 35,202 and deficit is 90,722 (…). There is an enormous shortage of human resources for health across all cadres: clinicians, nurses, pharmaceutical technicians, laboratory technicians, radiographers, physiotherapists, health officers and health administration cadres.* (Ministry of Health and Social Welfare 2009: 29)

The human resource scarcity also affects the Ministry of Health and Social Welfare as the main national governance body, translating into insufficient staffing levels, particularly in terms of certain specialists. At the time of our research, for instance, the ministry had only three health economists at its disposal who were hardly able to cope with the immense workload on their desks. Yet, while the administrative capacity is constrained in terms of numbers, the staff in office is said to be skilled and competent – an issue which was emphasised by various interviewees from both government and donor side. A Tanzanian WHO officer pointed out:

> *It is the numbers and the skills mix in the ministry which need to be made right. But the level of qualification is tough, certainly very high.* (Interview 44)

In a similar vein, a German health expert with years of working experience in Tanzania commented:

> *In the ministry of health as well as in the universities, we do have fairly competent people. The issue is, simply put: While in Germany we have 6 000 competent people, there are six of them in Tanzania. Those who are really capable are thin on the ground.* (Interview 73)

One of the few health economists within the Ministry of Health confirmed this outside perception from her perspective as follows:

> *We can manage. We're doing it. We really stretch ourselves, but it's not as serious as it was. (...) A challenge might be the shortage, but not the capacity – few people, many tasks, but not the capacity.* (Interview 54)

That the Ministry of Health, although being understaffed, can resort to a civil servant cadre which is comparatively strong in terms of in-house expertise is a crucial asset for health governance. There are however also constraints which hamper the overall bureaucratic performance: varying capacities in regional and district authorities which obstruct the implementation of policies and health service delivery, a high level of staff circulation and brain drain into international organisations and the private sector, and poor recruitment practices leading to intervals in which decisive positions are filled with acting officials who lack the confidence and competencies to assume leadership.[155] Yet, the dimension of such problems appears far smaller than, for instance, in education.

Rating the administrative capacity in environment is intricate insofar as different public entities are concerned with the matter – the Division of Environment in the Vice-President's Office, the Forestry and Beekeeping Division in the Ministry of Natural Resources and Tourism, the National Environmental Management Council and the Local Government Authorities, to name just the most important ones. A cross-cutting assessment made by internal and external evaluations is that overall, environmental governance is severely constrained by a shortage of qualified staff across all bodies, particularly at district level (Vice-President's Office 2007; Edwards et al. 2012; Nindi 2012). Similar conclusions were drawn by government and donor representatives dealing with environment-related issues such as climate change or forestry. A World Bank specialist put it straight, saying:

> *They just don't have enough people, they don't have the skills.*
> (Interview 46)

This statement hints at one important point made by many of those interviewed, namely that skills related to leadership, management, strategic planning and analysis are lacking in national ministries, rather than environmental expertise.

---

155 At the time of interviewing in 2013, the positions of the permanent secretary, the chief medical officer as well as the director of policy and planning within the Ministry of Health were filled with acting officials.

A Tanzanian programme officer working for the Danish Embassy commented on the capacity of her counterparts in government:

> *These guys are well trained experts. But in the field of leadership and management, there they have a problem.* (Interview 33)

At least for the Division of Environment, the claim that individuals in national bodies are well-trained can be confirmed with information on the educational profile of its workforce. In 2008 when the Human Resources Training Strategy for DoE was drafted, the unit had 54 employees made up of 38 professionals and 16 support staff. Three officials held a PhD and 29 a masters degree, that is, 60% of all staff were educated to masters degree level or higher (Draft Human Resource Training Strategy, VPO-DoE, April 2008, as cited by Inka Consult 2008: 7). Compared to the education ministry, where masters and PhD holders together made up only 22.5%, the DoE has a highly qualified team in terms of technical knowledge. Nonetheless, there is a fundamental flaw in capacity which a counsellor in the Finnish Embassy described as follows:

> *Having a kind of strategic view of the things – where do we want to move? What do we want to do? How do we make it happen? This kind of strategic thinking I see is very often missing.* (Interview 36)

In addition to the deficiencies in terms of these kind of competencies, the division of environment as well as other public entities are short of specialists in certain knowledge areas, as a high-ranking official admitted:

> *There are some emerging issues on climate change, for example, on the capture for greenhouse gases. We don't have experts in Tanzania. Even if we have, there are very few who are not ready to be employed for a long time period under contract.* (Interview 67)

Aside from climate change specialists, interviewees pointed to a shortage of professionals trained in issues such as resource and risk assessment, geographic information systems, or private forestry management. Given the scarcity of specialist knowledge, the deficiencies in terms of critical competencies and the enormous lack of adequately trained officials at sub-national level, the administrative capacity in the environment sector is severely limited.

Comparative assessment of administrative capacity in South Africa and Tanzania

The initial assumption was that administrative capacity on the recipient side is a crucial dimension determining the extent to which external experts are able to influence policy processes through advice, administrative capacity being understood as the strength of public entities in terms of their in-house expertise and staffing levels. Based on the findings presented above, we rank the capacity of administration in different policy fields as follows: the strongest area in the comparison is environment in South Africa, having a capable cadre of civil servants and in-house expertise at its disposal. The qualification levels of officials in health and education are similarly high, but the two sectors are affected by relatively high vacancy rates in line ministries, which to some extent limit their bureaucratic performance. In Tanzania, public administration generally suffers from insufficient staffing levels and a scarcity of specialists. While governance in health and environment stems from a small number of highly qualified individuals which ensures a certain level of in-house expertise, the education sector lacks a critical mass of competent staff at all levels. Table 14 displays our assessment, with '++' indicating a high level of administrative capacity, and '--' a low level of administrative capacity at the opposite end. Again, it is important to note that the table serves as means of illustration, not as a quantifiable scale.

Table 14: Sectoral strength in terms of administrative capacity

	South Africa	Tanzania
Environment	++	-
Health	+	-
Education	+	--

Source: Authors' own illustration.

Local knowledge base

Equally to the absorption capacity of administrations, the third dimension of recipient strength relies on the general educational level of a given society: we refer here to the strength of the local knowledge base in the widest sense, and more specifically to the size and quality of a country's science community. Again, the assumption is that a crucial condition for recipients to develop their own agenda without being driven from external advice is the availability of domestic sources from which alternative expertise can be obtained. The argument put forward reads: the stronger the local knowledge base and its voice in the policy discourse, the smaller is the scope of influence for outside actors.

This hypothesis implies two basic premises of democracy theories and sociology of science. The first is that in modern democracies, scientific knowledge serves both a problem-solving and legitimating function for political rule: it is required to find solutions for societal challenges and to demonstrate rational decision-making based on certified 'evidence' (Weingart 2003; Stehr 2010). The second is that scientific knowledge, despite its universal truth claim, is always – though to a varying extent depending on the discipline – contextual and culture-specific, transmitting certain constructs, beliefs and values of the epistemic community from which it is generated (Knorr-Cetina 1981; Knorr-Cetina 2007). For democratic governments, it is thus essential to have an endogenous knowledge base to draw on in order to take decisions informed by and sensitive to a society's historical, cultural and political imprint.

Many developing democracies, however, lack this fundamental requisite and resource of governance, given the weak state of their science systems. The persistent import of Northern knowledge is problematic insofar as it keeps them in a perpetual status of dependency, and restrains them from developing a genuine policy agenda which rests on their own societies' set of norms and experiences implied in local knowledge. As Girvan (2007: 40) points out,

> *autonomy – the right to choose one's path to development and to act in function of that choice – cannot be secured without a knowledge base. As long as the South is dependent for its development knowledge on the global centres of power, its own autonomy will be compromised.*

This argument does not convey the claim that autonomy emanates from "intellectual autarchy" (Girvan 2007: 32) which in a globalised world would neither be viable nor helpful. Instead, it makes the point that developing countries require a local knowledge base as a counterweight against the dominant body of knowledge provided by the North that transmits certain ideologies, shutting off alternative meaning and interpretation. Ideally, domestic science communities are able "to filter this [knowledge] through a conscious process of selection, evaluation and adaptation to local circumstances" (Girvan 2007: 32), and to provide the intellectual ground for problem solutions which take the existing social conditions into account. Without endogenous science systems which serve as absorptive and knowledge-producing entities, recipient governments are likely to be driven by external expertise, remaining "consumers (of knowledge) and implementers (of advice)" (Girvan 2007: 22).

As early as in 1969, the Advisory Committee on the Application of Science and Technology to Development of the UN Economic and Social Council stated in its 'World Plan' "that there is a fundamental necessity to build up indigenous scientific capability in the developing countries" (United Nations Economic and Social Council 1971: 102) which would enable them to define, analyse and solve nation-specific problems and boost economic production. The report expounds the problem of deficient knowledge production and points at the hurdles obstructing the development of solid science systems in developing countries. Today, the situation seems little better, if not worse in some respects. Africa's share in global science as measured in publication output has been steadily declining over the past 20 years, which reflects the widening gap of knowledge inequality between the Northern hemisphere and the global South (Mouton et al. 2008; Weingart 2006).[156] Despite some sporadic improvements, science in developing countries faces the same problems today as identified more than 40 years ago: a deficient research infrastructure, scarcity of human resources exacerbated by brain drain of scientists, poor science governance, and chronic underfunding which results in a destructive dependency on foreign financiers, to name just the major hitches (United Nations Economic and Social Council 1971; Mouton 2008; Mouton et al. 2008). Assessing the state of public science in the Southern African Development Community (SADC) region,[157] Mouton et al. (2008: 199–200) diagnosed a "de-institutionalisation" of science systems of which many operate in a "subsistence mode" struggling to reproduce themselves.

A country which counts as an exception is South Africa. With regard to scientific productivity, it is at the forefront of the continent and by far leading in the region (Mouton et al. 2008; African Union–New Partnership for Africa's Development 2010). Table 15 displays publication output and other indicators which are widely used to compare the strength of science systems across the globe, using data published by the African Innovation Outlook 2010 (African Union–New Partnership for Africa's Development 2010). A standard measure in this context is the gross domestic expenditure on research and development (GERD) as a percentage of the gross domestic product (GDP). While the countries with the highest research and development intensity in the world exceed 3% (e.g. Finland, Sweden or Japan), the African Union has recommended a 1% GERD/GDP ratio to its member states (Executive Council of the African Union 2006; European Commission 2014). Yet, among the countries reviewed by the African Innovation Outlook 2010, this target has only been reached by

---

156 According to Mouton et al. (2008: 199), "Africa has lost 11% of its share in global science since its peak in 1987; Sub-Saharan science has lost almost a third (31%)."

157 The SADC comprises 15 member states in southern Africa, namely Angola, Botswana, Democratic Republic of Congo, Lesotho, Madagascar, Malawi, Mauritius, Mozambique, Namibia, Seychelles, South Africa, Swaziland, Tanzania, Zambia and Zimbabwe (Southern African Development Community 2012). The bibliometric analyses by Mouton et al. (2008) did not include the Seychelles.

Malawi, Uganda and South Africa; the percentages of the remainder ranged between 0.20% and 0.48% which was achieved by Tanzania (African Union–New Partnership for Africa's Development 2010). A look at the human resource base in science reveals an even greater discrepancy between South Africa and Tanzania. With 825 researchers per million inhabitants (40 084 as headcount), the density of researchers in South Africa is more than ten times higher than in Tanzania, with only 67 researchers by million population (2 755 as headcount). As Weingart (2006: 173) argues, it is questionable whether such a small number of scientists can make up a "critical mass to even sustain an internal intellectual community, let alone a differentiated one".

Given the stark contrast in human resources for science, it is not surprising that there is a similar divide in terms of research productivity as measured in the number of publications. According to the Scopus database, South Africa produced 86 649 scientific articles during 1990–2009, around fifteen times as many as Tanzania (5 642) (African Union–New Partnership for Africa's Development 2010). Broken down per million inhabitants, the average annual output during 2005–2009 was 135 papers in South Africa against 12 papers in Tanzania (African Union–New Partnership for Africa's Development 2010).

Table 15: Research and development indicators for South Africa and Tanzania

R&D indicators	South Africa	Tanzania
Gross domestic expenditure on R&D (GERD) as % of GDP (2007)	1.05	0.48
Number of researchers (headcount)	40 084	2 755
Researchers per million inhabitants	815	67
Scientific output by country in papers listed in the Scopus database (1990–2009)	86 649	5 642
Average annual papers per million inhabitants (2005–2009)	135	12

Source: African Innovation Outlook 2010 (African Union–New Partnership for Africa's Development 2010).

Using the standard indicators for measuring research and development, it is evident that South Africa in general has a much greater scientific potential and higher level of research productivity than Tanzania, whose participation in the global science system – equivalent to most other African countries – seems miniscule.[158] Yet, one needs to consider that the set of indicators presented in the table above is tainted with a fundamental bias which discriminates against developing countries in several regards. First, it sets a Western

---

158 According to a bibliometric analysis based on the Scopus database and conducted by Arencibia-Jorge et al. (2012), Tanzania's share of the world scientific production from 1996 to 2009 was 0.03% while South Africa accounted for 0.39% in the same period.

concept of science systems and respective features as frame of reference for the assessment which has fundamental implications (Weingart 2006). For instance, the scope of databanks used to measure scientific output is limited to prestigious journals, most of which are published in the North (Gaillard 2010). Given that a large part of research findings of developing countries is disseminated in media and journals which are not captured by the common indexes, their contribution to global knowledge production is marginalised if solely assessed on the basis of the highly selective data sources. Hence, various authors point out that the standard indicators most probably fail to provide an adequate account of science in the developing world, emphasising the need for additional descriptors and narratives (Mouton 2007; Gaillard 2010).

In the following attempt to briefly sketch out the strength of science in South Africa and Tanzania by sectors, we therefore complement bibliometric data with qualitative information drawn from different reports and interview statements. Aside from delineating the size and quality of the local knowledge base in the respective fields, we also consider the extent to which institutionalised links to the policy sphere are existent.

The starting point of the analysis is Table 16 which presents publication output by relevant subject areas from 1990 to 2013 on the basis of scientific documents captured by the Scopus database:

Table 16: Scientific output by subject area in South Africa and Tanzania 1990–2013

Subject Area	South Africa		Tanzania	
	No. of papers	% of total output	No. of papers	% of total output
Health related				
Medicine	41 644	17.0	4 492	29.0
Immunology and microbiology	8 837	3.6	1 816	11.7
Health Professions	1 995	0.8	124	0.8
Nursing	1 660	0.7	167	1.1
Environment related				
Environmental science	13 587	5.6	1 137	7.3
Earth and planetary science	15 021	6.1	549	3.5
Education	1 552	0.6	81	0.5

Source: Scopus database.[159]

159 For the bibliometric data, the Scopus database was accessed on 11 and 12 March 2014. We did not limit the search to articles, but included all document types (e.g. conference papers or book chapters) as they also contribute to scientific output in a wider sense. Since education is not a subject area of its own in the Scopus database, we set the search condition that education must either be mentioned in the article title or be a keyword; we specified the results further by limiting them to those related to the subject areas social science, psychology, arts and humanities, mathematics and

Strength of Tanzanian science in health, environment and education

In the Tanzanian science landscape, the leading role of health is reflected by the composition of the country's scientific output: in the period 1990–2013, health-related areas (medicine, immunology and microbiology, health professions, nursing) together accounted for 42.6% of all publications. Environment is also a relatively strong research area, making up 10.8% if summing up contributions of environmental science and earth and planetary science. Education, in contrast, is almost insignificant in terms of publication output, with only 81 papers over a period of 14 years which amounts to a share of only 0.5%.[160]

Health research in Tanzania is conducted by government and private health research institutions of which the most productive and prestigious are the Muhimbili University of Health and Allied Sciences (MUHAS), the National Institute for Medical Research (NIMR) and the Ifakara Health Institute (IHI). While MUHAS is the only public university in Tanzania offering degree programmes in health sciences, NIMR serves as a parastatal entity under the Ministry of Health, mandated to conduct and coordinate medical research; the IHI is an independent non-profit organisation founded by the Swiss Tropical Institute which has acquired international renown, particularly for its contribution to malaria research. According to interviewees, the scientific capacity of these bodies varies; Ifakara is said to have the most capable cadre of highly skilled and well-trained scientists. A cross-cutting constraint, however, is the small human resource base of the relevant organisations. Referring to IHI, a Danida health advisor stated:

> *I think they've got some excellent people, but a few excellent people aren't enough to do a huge amount of work.* (Interview 34)

The small number of researchers is certainly a major cause of the limited capacity of health institutions. Another problem obstructing the production of policy-relevant science is their huge dependency on foreign financiers. While

---

computer science. The remaining articles clearly dealt with issues related to education. To prove the validity of results, we cross-checked the number and share of articles with those listed in Web of Science (WoS) under the category 'Education Educational Research'. In WoS, the timespan of article search was limited from 1995 to 2013, with 1995 being the first year accessible. Despite the shorter period, the number and share of documents listed was slightly higher for South Africa (1 691 articles; 1.3% of total); for Tanzania, absolute numbers were lower, but the share was equivalent (38 articles; 0.5% of total). Hence, while the results slightly differ, their scale is similar, supporting the argument that education is a rather minor research area in both countries.

160 The dominance of health and relative strength of environmental science in Tanzania have also been pointed out by previous studies using bibliometric data, as for instance African Union–New Partnership for Africa's Development (2010) and Arencibia-Jorge et al. (2012).

the Tanzanian government contributes some core funding, research activities are almost entirely financed from outside: from 2007 to 2010, NIMR did not receive any research budget from government side (Magesa et al. 2011); the Ifakara Health Institute states on its website that 80% of its annual income comes from competitive grants provided by foreign sources (Ifakara Health Institute 2014). Given this situation, focusing on national research priorities is more or less impossible, as a senior scientist working at IHI reported:

> *So basically, you can set your agenda saying I'll work in these areas. But working on what you really can't determine, because you are responding to a call for proposals.* (Interview 68)

Given that health research in Tanzania is mainly driven by external funders, it is not surprising that the uptake of findings by policy-makers is limited. Although IHI is increasingly recognised as a source of expertise by both government and donors, the exchange between research bodies and the Ministry of Health is still sporadic. Hence, the impact of Tanzania's scientific community on health is rather small, although there are "pockets of long-established research excellence" (Irikefe et al. 2011: 558).

Similar patterns, but an even more strained situation are found in the area of environment. The Sokoine University of Agriculture (SUA) in Morogoro and the University of Dar es Salaam with its Institute for Resource Assessment (IRA) are the most productive producers of environmental science in Tanzania.[161] While individuals working for these institutions are highly reputed scientists engaged in international research activities and expert forums, they are too few in numbers to build a sustained local knowledge base. Academic staff lack the time and financial resources for carrying out independent quality research on a larger scale. On its website, the Sokoine University of Agriculture indicates that 98% of its research activities are externally funded (Sokoine University of Agriculture Directorate of Research & Postgraduate Studies 2014). While we were unable to obtain concrete figures on IRA's budget and the share of foreign funding, a high-ranking staff member made the following statement on this:

> *The way it is, is that in the absence of donor support from outside, we cease even to be called researchers because there aren't much resources available.* (Interview 69)

---

161 The National Environmental Management Council (NEMC), the government's advisory and regulatory agency, is supposed to carry out research according to its mandate, but its output is miniscule. In the Scopus database, only nine articles in the period 1990–2013 are listed with institutional affiliation to NEMC.

Aside from occasionally contracting individuals for consultancies, the government does not regularly use the local science community available as a source of environmental expertise. There are a few, mostly donor-funded, initiatives to establish dialogue between policy-makers and scientists on environmental issues – as, for example, the 'Environment for Development' centre or the 'Decision Makers Forest Academy' – but their scope of impact is limited. All in all, Tanzania's local knowledge base in environment is small, and there are no structures in place through which national research findings would be disseminated to inform policy-making.

The weakest area in terms of scientific capacity, however, seems to be education. With only 81 articles over a period of 14 years, the output in this field is marginal. The University of Dar es Salaam is the most significant producer, accounting for almost 50% of all publications; the only other institution which has a double-digit number of contributions is the Tumaini University in Iringa. The figures confirm the perception articulated by various interviewees that educational research in Tanzania hardly takes place. A civil society representative described the state of the local knowledge base in education as follows:

> I'm going to say something politically incorrect. You are assuming there is a local expert community – I don't think there is one that is worth its salt. There are local experts, individual experts, but we don't have serious think tanks (…). The universities, I can't point you to a single department or programme of work that I can say, this is incredibly solid research and analysis and thinking and creative programme development. So what are universities, what is the state of our universities? We have expanded them dramatically to democratise access; they have become large factories of lecturing. Most professors and lecturers are busy doing consulting, and so you quickly do what you have to do at the university, often not even do that, you know, they're often away. If somebody did a careful noting of attendance, you'll find they are often away even for your basic lectures. And then they're going round doing consulting work, of which each piece may have some utility, but it doesn't add up to a body of work. So I don't think there is a local expert community in Tanzania (…). There are individual experts, but there is no community, there is no coherence. (Interview 70)

While interviewees from the donor side put it less bluntly, they consistently assessed the capacity of the science community in education as very low. Notably, the only one articulating that the local knowledge base would be sufficiently strong was a director in the education ministry who stated:

> *Well me, I think we have capacity (…). In the Institute of Education here which is working with the curriculum development, we have enough and learned sort of personnel. And we have people in the universities who have travelled widely. They have been engaged in different consultancies here and there, they are knowledgeable (...).* (Interview 49)

The Tanzania Institute of Education (TIE) the official referred to is a parastatal organisation under the Ministry of Education and Vocational Training in charge of curriculum development, teacher training, quality assurance and technical advice; it has a so-called 'Research, Publication and Consultancy Section' which is commissioned to conduct evaluations and research on educational matters (Tanzania Institute of Education 2014). While TIE is used by the government as a source of in-house expertise, it is not producing scientific output in a strict sense.

As both statements quoted above indicate, cooperation with university experts on education is limited to 'consultancies here and there'. From the perspective of various interview partners, there is no serious engagement between policy-makers and academia, and little receptiveness towards research on the part of the education ministry. A university professor of education commented in this regard:

> *You need a minister who shows interest. But we have (a) minister who I don't think shows interest in any research of the academic world.* (Interview 71)

This lack of interest on the part of the political leadership is reflected by the absence of a "formalised system" (Interview 45) facilitating exchange between policy-makers and scientists in education. In light of the interview narratives and the bibliometric figures presented earlier in the chapter, it can be said that independent educational research in Tanzania is almost non-existent; the impact of the country's few academic educationalists is narrowed down to consultancy work which does not result in the emergence of an endogenous local knowledge base.

Strength of South African science in health, environment and education

South Africa has a solid science community which in many fields significantly contributes to global knowledge production. Comparing productivity in terms of publications, health-related sciences are at the top of the three areas under review, accounting for 22.1% of the total output from 1990 to 2013 (see

Table 16), followed by environment-related sciences with 11.7% and, at the low end, education with 0.6%.

In health-related science and particularly in HIV/Aids research, South Africa has a whole range of universities which are internationally renowned for their scientific performance, such as the University of Cape Town, the University of Witwatersrand in Johannesburg or the University of Stellenbosch, to mention just the most prolific ones. In addition, the country has well-established parastatal bodies such as the South African Medical Research Council (MRC) and the Human Sciences Research Council (HSRC) which cover a broad spectrum of relevant subject areas. While these institutions deliver high-level and sometimes "global ground-breaking research" (Interview 27), as a civil society activist put it, they are yet faced with structural constraints typical of science systems in developing countries, namely a small human resource base and dependency on external financing. Expertise is stretched rather thinly, particularly offside the HIV/Aids research field. Reputed scientists are under constant pressure trying to cope with teaching obligations, generate third funding streams through conducting studies for multiple clients and respond to national priorities, while being dependent on foreign financiers. In HIV/Aids and TB research, for instance, more than 70% of the total funding comes from outside, less than 30% from local sources (Senkubuge & Mayosi 2013). Health research in South Africa is thus heavily influenced by the agendas of overseas sponsors; a senior scholar at the Institute of Infectious Disease and Molecular Medicine of the University of Cape Town stated upfront:

> *Of course you've got the potential conflict of who sets the agenda, who owns the agenda. And in a way I think we need to acknowledge that we've become scientific prostitutes in the sense that we are giving in to the highest bidder for our services. And it is actually much easier in the health field to get your money from abroad.*[162]

This issue of domestic underfunding was also raised at a National Health Research Summit held in 2011 to discuss the state of South Africa's health research and to make it more responsive to national challenges (Mayosi et al. 2011). The event was deemed an attempt to strengthen the ties between the health department and the science community after the breakup of relations during the Mbeki administration caused by the conflict around Aids and antiretroviral treatment. Health Minister Aaron Motsoaledi is perceived

---

162 This statement was made in the context of an exploratory interview for the research project conducted in 2007.

as hardly trying to establish a closer dialogue with the country's science community; as a professor at the University of the Western Cape commented:

> *That's a shift from a kind of vacuum at the centre to the re-emergence*
> *of a leadership that is willing to engage in a much more explicit way*
> *with South African knowledge communities, there's no doubt about that.*
> (Interview 28)

All in all, it can be stated that South Africa's local knowledge base in health is made up of a cadre of researchers which is small, but highly productive and increasingly used by policy-makers as a source of endogenous expertise.

The country's strongest scientific impact, however, is in environment-related disciplines. According to the Thomson Reuters Global Research Report Africa 2010, South African plant and animal sciences had the highest share of world publications (1.55%) out of any field in Africa, followed by environment and ecology (1.29%); the report further states that "many of South Africa's most highly-cited papers in this field pertain to climate change and its effects on plant propagation" (Adams et al. 2010). Among the most prolific producers are some which are also leading in health, such as the University of Cape Town, the University of Witwatersrand, and the University of Pretoria. Aside from a range of universities, parastatal bodies such as the Council for Scientific and Industrial Research (CSIR) with its Natural Resources and the Environment unit, as well as SANBI, are key contributors to environmental research. The science community operating within these institutions is regarded as "one of the tops in the world" (Interview 8), as a leading UNDP expert stated. Similarly, as in health, however, it is small in terms of human resources and still racially skewed, as an environmental specialist explained:

> *There is just a selective few individuals that are champions for the various*
> *initiatives. In terms of capacity, we don't have capacity in the sense that*
> *– it's lying only in a group of people and that group of people is not*
> *representative of the South African demographics. So in that respect, the*
> *skills development is needed – especially black scientists, it's very limited*
> *in the country, because science does not support a fast track transformation*
> *agenda.* (Interview 15)

In addition to this structural problem, there are some imbalances with regard to the performance in particular subject areas. Animal sciences are traditionally weaker than the botanical sciences, and there are some areas such as resource economics and biotechnology where expertise is scarce. Nonetheless, the South African science community in environment is broad enough to build a solid local knowledge base which substantially informs policy-making through its presence in advisory task teams or its contribution to the State of the Environment report. In 2012, the Department of Environmental Affairs published an 'Environment Sector Research, Development and Evidence Framework' seeking to further enhance and institutionalise the exchange between researchers and policy-makers (Department of Environmental Affairs 2012b). In short, environmental science in South Africa is highly recognised in academic and policy circles, both at the national and international level.

Finally, we look at South Africa's capacity in educational research. As the bibliometric figures indicate, its contribution to the overall science output is rather small, at least compared to health and environmental sciences. The most prolific producers in this area are again the well-known universities, with the University of Cape Town leading the way, followed by the universities of Witwatersrand, Pretoria and KwaZulu-Natal. Moreover, the Education and Skills Development Unit in the Human Sciences Research Council is a key body conducting studies on all kinds of educational matters related to schooling, teaching and learning from primary school to higher education. As an analysis of publications and academic projects indicates, South African educational research covers a broad spectrum of topics and disciplinary areas, ranging from educational theories to studies on classroom practice (Deacon et al. 2009). Yet, its methodological scope is rather narrow: in the period 1995–2006, "94% of education research has been small scale research, usually qualitative, often conceptual and frequently eclectic, (…) while hardly any (costly, time-consuming and often quantitative) large scale research has taken place, with only 1% of the database falling into this category" (Deacon et al. 2009: iv).

The authors of the analysis attribute the lack of longitudinal large-scale studies, which would provide more systemic findings, partly to the prevailing 'publish or perish' pressure on academics, but also

> "to the limited availability of research funding, the equally limited availability and often poor quality and unreliability of existing data, a widespread lack of research capacity and experience, and reduced time available for research due to increased teaching and administrative workloads." (Deacon et al. 2009: 14)

Despite constraints in terms of funding and human resources, however, educational scholars form a solid knowledge base which the government regularly draws on. There seems to be a frequent exchange between the two educational departments and the academic community through conferences and workshops (see, for instance, Department of Basic Education 2014a, c), and a variety of key reports informing policy decisions are compiled by university experts (see, for instance, Van der Berg et al. 2011). Hence, although the size and output of educational research in South Africa is small compared to other disciplines, it is recognised and used.

Comparative assessment of the local knowledge base in South Africa and Tanzania

On the basis of the bibliometric figures and qualitative information presented above, we rank the different fields under review as follows: environmental sciences in South Africa provide the strongest local knowledge base which substantially contributes to global science and has a strong presence at the national and international level. Although health sciences have a higher output in terms of numbers, the local knowledge base in this field is assessed to be weaker since it is highly concentrated on one particular subject, that is, HIV/Aids, and due to its dependency on external financing subject to the agendas of outside players. Educational research does not face this problem to the same extent, but the size and output of the research community is much smaller. We nonetheless rank it at the same level as health, since the core of educational scholars provides solid research which to a considerable extent informs policy-making. Tanzania's scientific capacity is much lower than that of South Africa which dominates African science in general. Given the prevailing lack of human and financial resources, science communities in Tanzania across all disciplines are struggling to maintain their basic subsistence, let alone to produce research under poor working conditions. Yet, "pockets of significant science" (Mouton et al. 2008: 200) are found, particularly in the areas of health and environment where small cadres of highly qualified scholars operate. In education, however, such a core of excellence is missing. While individuals in academic institutions do have substantial expertise, a science community in the common sense is non-existent. Table 17 displays our assessment at a glance, with '++' indicating a very strong local knowledge base, and '--' a very weak local knowledge base. Again, we want to make the remark that the table is an oversimplification and should be seen only as a tool of illustration.

Table 17: Sectoral strength in terms of the local knowledge base

	South Africa	Tanzania
Environment	++	-
Health	+	-
Education	+	--

Source: Authors' own illustration.

Chapter 7

THE IMPACT OF EXPERT ADVICE ON POLICY-MAKING IN YOUNG DEMOCRACIES: SECTOR STUDIES

There are, as was shown, significant variations between South Africa and Tanzania with respect to their financial power, administrative capacity and the local knowledge base and also across the different sectors. In the following chapter, we will investigate whether and how these differences impact on policy processes. It is of particular interest how the influence of external experts on these processes is conditioned by them.

Comparative empirical research is inherently confronted with diverse matters and material. Thus, the case studies presented below unavoidably differ in terms of their complexity and depth. Yet, they share some core themes and a broad texture. Each case is introduced with shortly delineating sectoral challenges and governance structures before sketching donors and their 'entry points' in the respective field. Then follows a detailed description of policy processes and players involved, with a particular focus on whether, how and in which roles external experts were engaged. While the narrations are not squeezed into a fixed grid, they are guided by some key questions, namely: At which stage and on which grounds (e.g. 'capacity gaps') did foreign actors enter the policy space? How did actors from government, aid organisations and academia position themselves and at which levels did they interact? Whose expertise and interests were finally taken up and reflected in policy decisions? The case studies are concluded with an assessment regarding external experts' impact on policy-making and governance in the field under review, taking the structural conditions found into account. A synthesis of findings that can be drawn from comparing the empirical accounts concludes this chapter.

Tanzania education: The hijacked agenda

Sectoral context

In the light of international goals for education, Tanzania's performance appears commendable at first glance: access to primary education is nearly 'universal', the completion rate stands high at 90%, and gender parity has almost been achieved (UNESCO Office Dakar and Regional Bureau for Education in Africa et al. 2011: 7). In secondary education, the Gross Enrolment Rate has gone up from 20.2% in 2006 (Sumra & Rajani 2006) to 35% in 2012 (UNESCO Institute for Statistics 2014), while in the same period enrolment numbers in higher education quadrupled (see Education Sector Development Committee 2012).[163]

Yet, this rapid expansion has put substantial stress on the education system, manifesting in plummeting literacy skills and mass failure in national examinations (see, for instance, Twaweza 2013; Uwezo 2013). While children have successfully been brought into school, they struggle to learn under deteriorating conditions in overcrowded classrooms without adequate furniture, basic learning material and pedagogical support (see Mhonyiwa et al. 2011); as of 2011/2012, the teacher-to-pupil ratio in primary education stood at 1:70 (Education Sector Development Committee 2012). The quality crisis in education has become a prime concern among educational stakeholders, sparking off serious dispute between the government and the aid community.

Governance structures

The two main authorities in charge of formal education from pre-primary to tertiary levels in Tanzania are the Ministry of Education and Vocational Training (MoEVT) and the Prime Minister's Office Regional Administration and Local Government (PMO-RALG). While the former is responsible for policy development, the provision of regulations and guidelines, standard setting, quality assurance and teacher training (Ministry of Education and Vocational Training 2014), the latter is mandated to oversee and coordinate the administration of schools which are managed by local government authorities (President's Office Public Service Management 2011). Hence, while MoEVT is the central body regarding policy issues, PMO-RALG is directly concerned with the day-to-day running of the school system. Both ministries collaborate with a range of other institutions concerned with educational

---

163 Total student enrolment in higher education increased from 40 993 in 2005/2006 to 166 484 in 2011/2012 (see Education Sector Development Committee 2011).

matters, such as the Tanzania Institute of Education (TIE) which develops curricula, teaching and learning materials, the National Examinations Council of Tanzania which designs and administrates national examinations and the Ministry of Community Development, Gender and Children dealing with Folk Education.[164]

Donor presence in the education sector

Compared to other policy areas, the number of donors engaged in education appears rather limited; as of 2012, the 'Education Development Partners Group' (ED-DPG) comprised seven active members, namely CIDA, DFID, Sida, UNESCO, UNICEF, USAID and the World Bank.[165] Depending on the respective focus of these organisations, representatives participate in one or more of the eight Technical Working Groups (e.g. 'Quality Improvement', 'Enrolment Expansion', or 'Resource Allocation, Cost Efficiency and Financing') to discuss issues coming up in these areas and to share information about their activities with ministry officials. If required, topics are brought forth to a higher-level task force and eventually to the Education Sector Development Committee chaired by the permanent secretary of MoEVT. While all actors are supposed to stick to this structure, both ministry and aid officials conceded that "it isn't really working that way" (Interview 30), and a lot of things are "sort of decided upon and shared outside" (Interview 40). Various interviewees reported that the tone of the 'dialogue' has become tense.

Understanding current aid relationships and the government's positioning towards the donor community requires an awareness of the history of cooperation. Tanzania has gone through different phases in this regard.

The rise and fall of Nyerere's 'Education for Self-Reliance' vision

When in 1961 the state of Tanganyika became independent, it inherited a society which was deeply affected by more than seven decades of imperialist rule. Both the Germans and British colonisers had installed a racially segregated formal education system whose main objective was to form a submissive yet productive workforce serving the external regime (Mushi 2009).[166] Very few Africans attained more than two years of formal education (Galabawa 1990).

---

164 Detailed information on mandates and functions of these institutions is provided on their websites: www.tie.go.tz/ (last accessed on 18 January 2015); http://www.necta.go.tz/ (last accessed on 18 January 2015) and http://www.mcdgc.go.tz/ (last accessed on 18 January 2015).

165 Moreover, GIZ and the World Food Programme are mentioned in some documents, but their engagement seems to be quite focused on cross-cutting issues (e.g. HIV prevention and awareness raising in schools) and specific concerns (e.g. community-led school feeding), respectively.

166 For a detailed account of colonial education in Tanzania, see Mushi (2009).

At independence, about 85% of the population could not read and write (*Nationalist Newspaper*, 24 August 1967, as cited in Bhalalusesa 2003). Aside from one university college affiliated to the University of London (which later became a constituent college of the University of East Africa), there were no higher education institutions in the country (Ngirwa et al. 2013).

Building a literate and capable citizenry became a central endeavour for Tanganyika's first post-colonial leader, Julius K Nyerere, who became Prime Minister in 1961 and was elected President in 1962. Himself a teacher prior to his political career, Nyerere considered education a fundamental pillar for realising his vision of a socialist state based on his philosophy of *Ujamaa* (the Swahili term for 'familyhood') which should free the society from the yoke of domination. Right after coming into power, *Mwalimu* as he was popularly called (meaning 'teacher' in Swahili), issued an Education Act which legally abolished all forms of discrimination in education, nationalised primary schools, streamlined school curricula and examinations, and promoted Swahili as the national language (Ministry of Education and Culture 1995). This first step of change was followed by the release of Nyerere's influential 'Education for Self-Reliance' policy of 1967. As a sequel to the Arusha Declaration, the document emphasised the essential role of education in ending external dependence and delineated the principles of the envisaged socialist education system; amongst others, it stated:

> *The education provided must therefore encourage the development in each citizen of three things: an enquiring mind; an ability to learn from what others do, and reject or adapt it to his own needs; and a basic confidence in his own position as a free and equal member of the society, who values others and is valued by them for what he does and not for what he obtains (…).*

> *The education provided by Tanzania for the students of Tanzania must serve the purposes of Tanzania. It must encourage the growth of the socialist values we aspire to. It must encourage the development of a proud, independent and free citizenry which relies upon itself for its own development (…).* (Nyerere 1967)

In Nyerere's vision, primary education was to become 'a complete education in itself', preparing students for life in a socialist society; an overhauled curriculum should include 'non-academic' subjects and practical activities such as agriculture and farming. Schools were to be integrated into villages and communities; education should be regarded as a process of lifelong learning rather than a formal system leading to white-collar skills (Nyerere 1967).[167]

A cornerstone of Nyerere's philosophy was the idea of compulsory and free primary education. Following the abolition of school fees as provided by the Musoma Resolution of 1974, the intake in primary schools almost doubled; by 1980, the gross enrolment rate stood at 98% (Galabawa 2001: 13). Galabawa, a Tanzanian professor affiliated with the University of Dar es Salaam, expressed the excitement about the government's successful campaign at that time as follows:

> *Both internal and external observers witnessed something akin to a miracle as enrolments in primary schools across the nation soared and the nation was gravitated in the frenzy to implement the call for education for all in a poor country committed to an equitable and fair provision of education to all the citizenry.* (Galabawa 2001: 17)

Yet, the 'miracle' of having all children in school entailed some serious drawbacks. Absorbing masses of new students required not only additional facilities and learning materials (which were not available), but also teachers. Since expanding teacher training was not sufficient to meet the exploding demand, the government introduced "teaching in turns, distance training of teachers and using secondary school students to teach in primary schools" (Galabawa 1990: 13). Such alternative measures, however, led to a serious decline in educational quality as reflected in the cognitive capabilities of school leavers. By the end of the 1970s, there was a public outcry about the 'falling standards' in the education system, with parents complaining about a "universalization of illiteracy" (Omari et al. 1983: 45).

The overt discontent about the deteriorating quality in education coincided with "a period of stress for Tanzania on many fronts" (Samoff 1994: 134) exacerbated by the global economic crisis during the mid-1980s. Initially the government had financed programmes such as the UPE campaign mainly from its own resources. Now it was forced to turn to foreign donors to maintain the system; as Samoff (2003: 380) illustrates, this shift had significant implications for educational governance:

---

167 The notion of life-long learning is not explicitly discussed in the 'Education for Self-Reliance' document, but prominently featured in later publications and speeches of Nyerere. In his New Year's Eve Broadcast on 31 December 1969, he particularly emphasised the importance of adult education and learning throughout life, stating: "Education is not just something which happens in the classrooms. It is learning from others, and from our own experience of past successes or failures (…). To live is to learn; and to learn is to try to live better" (Nyerere 1973: 138–141).

As the director of planning in Tanzania explained, planning had in fact become marketing. His task was less a process of exploring needs and developing strategies to address them than an effort to study the market of prospective funders. He then identified its priorities and value points, using that market knowledge to craft, advertise, and sell projects and programs. That strategy was perhaps effective for coping in difficult circumstances. Nevertheless, it entrenched the role of the funding agencies in setting national education policies and priorities. It also reinforced the status and influence of a particular set of actors within the country, not those with the clearest or most dynamic education vision or those with the most solid national political base but rather those who proved to be most effective in securing foreign funding.

When after a period of resistance (and Nyerere's replacement by Ali Hassan Mwinyi as president) the government gave in and began to adopt structural adjustment policies as required by the IMF and the World Bank (see Hyden & Karlstrom 1993), it was pressured to reverse fundamental features of the education system. In 1993, an inter-ministerial committee was commissioned to develop a new Education and Training Policy which should serve as a framework for both government action and donor support.[168] The final document released in 1995 clearly reflected the move from a socialist to a liberal vision of education geared to a market economy (Buchert 1997). The policy confirmed the re-introduction of school fees (promoted as 'cost-sharing mechanism'), encouraged private education providers to establish and manage learning institutions, and decentralised administration responsibility to the sub-national level (Ministry of Education and Culture 1995). The imprint of external agencies whose representatives provided comments and participated in discussions was manifest not only in the turn to privatisation and liberalisation, but also in the emphasis on issues such as gender equality and local autonomy which were key areas of donor support (Buchert 1997). Without any wider public discussion in the media or by parliament, the policy was approved by the Cabinet in February 1995. The respective amendment of the Education Act following in October finally provided the legal basis for a re-

---

168 Buchert (1997: 46–51) provides a detailed account of the different stages of policy formulation and actors involved therein, concluding that it remains an open question to what extent "certain areas were truly reflecting [government] thinking as compared to being imposed through agency pressure" (p. 51). According to her research based on interviews with stakeholders and observers, the document was perceived as a product of negotiation between technocrats in ministries and agency representatives; teachers, parents or students had not been invited to contribute their views to the debate.

structured education system which was now broadly in accordance with the ideas and principles prevailing in aid circles at that time.

Reform initiatives from 1995 onwards: Invading experts and a plethora of plans

The adjustment of Tanzania's macro and education policies to the international agenda paved the way for immense donor engagement in the sector. Adding up the activities listed by Buchert (1997), at least 86 education projects were carried out by different agencies during the 1990s, with the information provided not being exhaustive. The fact that the various funders, including the World Bank, UNICEF, EU, Danida, Norad, Sida, GTZ, Irish Aid, France, CIDA, the Netherlands, and the UK, operated largely disconnected from each other became a serious concern on both government and donor side (Buchert 1999). Proposing a 'sector-wide approach' (SWAp) as a new, 'harmonised' mode of assistance, the aid community pushed for the development of a comprehensive 'Education Sector Development Programme' (ESDP) which aimed to synchronise interventions and to pool resources for the implementation of the new Education and Training Policy. Yet, this was seen as an ambitious undertaking which – from the donors' point of view – was not doable by the ministry on its own. An education advisor working for Canada, herself being Tanzanian, expressed the sentiment in aid offices at that time as follows:

> *You see, there were new concepts coming around with the development. But then your counterparts are not talking that language. The challenge we also had was how much of the preparatory work should be done and who should do it? Even doing the needs assessment, doing the initial situation analysis to find out where we start, where we go? We ended up bringing a lot of TA [technical assistance] input – a lot. At a moment, that was a year we counted, I think almost between 25 to 30 different TAs were coming to do different things from different donors (…), and the ministry was like invaded, literally. And some donors even felt we should have offices in the ministry to make it feel that we are working with the government, for the government. So you go along the corridors of the government ministry, and you are seeing this mzungu and that one and this one. (Interview 31)[169]*

The fact that these 'mzungus' came not only with expertise but interests of their organisations was obvious; a Tanzanian consultant who had worked for the World Bank commented in this regard:

---

169 *Mzungu* is a Swahili term which is commonly used in East Africa for talking about or calling white people; literally translated it means 'someone who wanders without purpose/someone constantly on the move'.

It was not an easy one. I saw all of that game coming up, you know, every donor will see what they are doing is more important [and] how to push that onto the agenda. (Interview 32)

Many priorities outlined in the final draft published in 2001 obviously match what were key issues of donor concern and investment (United Republic of Tanzania 2001: 14). The focus on strengthening management capacity and introducing a computerised Education and Training Management Information System, for instance, reflected the technocratic-managerial approach to education championed by external consultants. Some paragraphs virtually read as if copied from donor documents; the following extract, for instance, more or less echoes the World Bank's human capital view on education as reflected in various publications of that time (see, for instance, World Bank 1988, 1995, 1999a):

> *The ultimate goal of any education and training system is to provide relevant and high quality education and training services to a broad range of clients in the most equitable, effective and efficient ways. This entails building the management capacity at all levels in the education sector.* (United Republic of Tanzania 2001: 20)[170]

The terminology used here indicates a stark conceptual shift: as opposed to the previous notion of education as a public responsibility with the aim to transmit "the accumulated wisdom and knowledge of the society" to the younger generation (Nyerere 1967: 1), education was now regarded as a 'service' provided to 'clients' that was to be managed 'in the most equitable, effective and efficient' manner. It is questionable whether this kind of wording was a deliberate choice of ministry officials or – what seems more likely – of technical assistants writing the draft.

The language used in such strategic documents is significant insofar as it structures and constrains the policy discourse; it conveys particular conceptions, directions and policy preferences (Samoff 1992: 67). In this case, the new emphasis on 'efficiency' and 'effectiveness'[171] implied the need to prioritise basic (understood as primary) education on the grounds that it had the highest 'rate of return' – an argument which had been pushed particularly by World

---

170 Nyerere, in contrast, had formulated the goal of a nation's education and training system as follows: "That purpose is to transmit from one generation to the next the accumulated wisdom and knowledge of the society, and to prepare young people for their future membership of the society and their active participation in its maintenance or development" (Nyerere 1967: 1).

171 For an early conceptualisation of 'efficiency' and 'effectiveness' in education which was published by the World Bank, see Lockheed and Hanushek (1994).

Bank economists (see, for instance, Psacharopoulos 1994; World Bank 1995) who deemed higher education with its high unit costs "a fiscal nightmare" (Youssef 2005: 20) in developing countries.[172]

Consequently, the first sub-sectoral plan developed as a sequel to the 'Education Sector Development Programme' addressed primary education. The so-called 'Primary Education Development Plan (PEDP)' (2002–2006) outlined four major goals, namely expanding enrolment, improving the quality of teaching and learning processes, building capacity and strengthening institutional arrangements for better educational planning and service delivery (Basic Education Development Committee 2001). While in the foreword, the involvement of "a variety of stakeholder groups" (Basic Education Development Committee 2001) in the formulation of the document was emphasised, it was regarded as mainly made by donors, first and foremost the World Bank which "allegedly [used] its Mozambique strategy as a template" (Holtom 2002: 24). It was also the Bank which was the largest external financier of PEDP, providing a grant of USD 150 million to be released over a period of three years; other donors (including the Netherlands, Canada, Sweden, Finland, Belgium, France, Norway, Ireland and the EU) pooled their resources and contributed around the same amount (USD 154 million) through a joint basket fund (World Bank 2005b: 4). Even though the latter was set up to support government priorities as outlined in PEDP, conflictual discussions on what the money should be spent emerged. A Tanzanian education specialist working for the Canadians remarked:

> *This issue of prioritisation then came up to be quite an issue. What is it that we want, and what is it that the government really wants? The biggest issue, for example, at that time – 2000 to 2005/6 – there was this huge enrolment taking place, all over the country (…). So the main challenge for the government was having classrooms' constructed. As donors we stood there and we said, 'We are not supporting construction work. We would like to see more inputs, but not buildings. So put your money into capital assets. Put your money in buildings, we'll come in with inputs.' So that's a clear case where the government's cry was on more construction (…), where if the government was left on its own – and*

---

172 An important point here is that 'basic education' for most donors meant primary (and lower secondary) education whereas for the Tanzanian government, the term included pre-primary, primary, adult, secondary, and teacher education. This divergence in definition led to tension, as an education advisor working for the Canadian embassy reported: "So there is already that conceptual issue: You have to argue between Canada and Tanzania: 'When we support you, this is what we mean'. So the issue becomes then: Who is the interlocutor there? And how do you interpret that?" (Interview 31)

knowing my government counterparts – maybe that is what they would have first done, put those structures in place. (Interview 31)

The decisive role of donors in determining the content of PEDP and the tight earmarking of resources in the basket dampened enthusiasm about the programme on the part of ministry officials. Observers of the process saw the insufficient internalisation – or to use the buzzword 'ownership' – of the programme by government bodies as a predictable consequence of external interference. Holtom (2002: 25) cites an aid representative (!) acknowledging:

PEDP was formulated mainly by donors and according to the donor programme, and donors have allocated their resources. So how can the Ministry of Education be involved in the process with 'their' ownership? Actually they cannot! And of course they cannot deny [accepting] aid from donors because, yeah, something is better than nothing.

Amongst ministry officials the sentiment that the education agenda had been 'hijacked'[173] by the donor community (particularly the World Bank) slowly but surely solidified.

A case in point which fuelled this perception was the abolishment of school fees which surprised Tanzanian officials, academics and civil society alike. As indicated earlier, the government had re-introduced school fees at the end of the 1980s as a condition of structural adjustment loans (Samoff 1994), with the result that enrolment rates dropped immediately (Mbilinyi 2003). Against internal critique, this decision was confirmed in the Education and Training Policy of 1995, with the education ministry allegedly anticipating that donors still advocated for cost-sharing mechanisms (Jerve 2006). Five years later, however, the World Bank suddenly signalled a reversal of its stance: in a late stage of preparing Tanzania's first poverty reduction strategy, the country director "announced to the President directly that the Bank had changed its position on user fees in primary education and was prepared to finance the shortfall in revenue" (Jerve 2006: 14). To the surprise of even high-level officials, the final draft of the strategy entailed the proclamation that "in a reversal of past policies, it is intended to abolish primary school fees, starting in FY 2001/2002" (United Republic of Tanzania 2000: 19). That this about-turn had not at all been discussed internally is reflected by the fact that after the release of the document the permanent secretary of the education ministry publicly deemed the passage a mistake (Jerve 2006). While civil society organisations welcomed

---

173 Both ministry officials and observers from NGO and academia are quoted using this notion in the context of the ESDP and PEDP processes; see Buchert (1997: 54) or Holtom (2002: 22).

this shift, leading academics who had advised against a blanket removal were shocked (Jerve 2006). Nonetheless, the commitment was confirmed in PEDP which followed shortly after (Basic Education Development Committee 2001).

The external influence on key issues in PEDP is particularly remarkable considering that the adoption of a sector-wide approach as introduced by the Education and Training Sector Development Programme and the establishment of a basket fund were actually meant to strengthen national leadership and foster "a new kind of partnership" (Basic Education Development Committee 2001: 21) based on consultation as opposed to conditionality. Therefore, a sophisticated 'dialogue' structure was put in place, ranging from technical working groups to sub-sectoral development committees to a high-level steering committee for education (see United Republic of Tanzania 2001: 70). Donors were 'invited' to participate at various levels in order to share information and provide policy advice. The cooperation should culminate in a joint annual review process of the education sector to evaluate the success of specific programmes and plans. The creation of these institutions as an attempt to align activities under the guidance of government was highly commended by stakeholders and observers; with similar mechanisms installed in other sectors (e.g. health), Tanzania was considered a forerunner in realising the new 'partnership' principles formalised by the 2005 Paris Declaration a few years later.

Since then, aid experts as members of the dialogue have routinely been involved in the development of various policies and programmes brought forth during a decade of reform, including two sequels of PEDP, equivalents in other subsectors and a revised version of the comprehensive Education Sector Development Programme.[174] Yet, there are strong indications that this 'new kind of partnership' has not grown as planned.

The return of the quality crisis: Frustration and frictions

By 2013, both government and donor officials conceded that while the institutions of the dialogue formally continued to exist, they were de facto

---

174 The list of pivotal programmes developed since 2001 includes (in chronological order of publication year): Primary Education Development Programme for 2002–2006 (Ministry of Education and Vocational Training 2008), Secondary Education Development Plan 2004–2009 (Ministry of Education and Culture 2004); Primary Education Development Programme II 2007–2011 (Basic Education Development Committee 2006); Education Sector Development Programme 2008–2017 (United Republic of Tanzania 2008a); Higher Education Development Programme 2010–2015 (Ministry of Education and Vocational Training 2010a); Secondary Education Development Programme II 2010–2015 (Ministry of Education and Vocational Training 2010b); Primary Education Development Programme III 2012–2016 (Ministry of Education and Vocational Training 2012b).

'barely functioning' (Interview 30). A Tanzanian education specialist working for Canada commented in this regard:

> *The membership or representation in those working groups is very, very erratic, if I may use that word. And I think to some extent the government is using it to its advantage. When they feel they need something to get that support, they will champion an issue, make sure it goes to the right channel, it's discussed and off it moves. If they are not really with you, (...) they may just decide, 'No, I'm not attending. I'm delegating my third level down to chair the meeting.' So there you are just talking.* (Interview 31)

In a similar vein, the education team leader in the Canadian Embassy remarked:

> *We find it very frustrating, because we try to follow these structures, but it's clear the government finds it very frustrating also. So it's not really working. (...) I think from their side, they really feel it's a donor imposed structure. And we feel like this is their structure that they created – so it is sort of both sides pointing fingers.* (Interview 30)

Given the high level of frustration on both sides, relationships between the government and donors were palpably strained. The worsening condition of primary education became the issue which exacerbated the frictions and sparked off serious dispute. The government had been praised for its 'outstanding achievements' made through its first Primary Education Development Programme for 2002–2006 (see Ministry of Education and Vocational Training 2008), but the evaluation of the second phase covering the years 2007–2011 produced rather disappointing 'results': pass rates for primary school leaving examination significantly declined from 70.5% in 2006 to 53.5% by 2010 which together with a constantly high number of drop-outs levelled down the transition rate to secondary education from 67.5% in 2006 to 52.5% in 2011 (Ministry of Education and Vocational Training 2012a: 90–95).[175] The poor performance was to a large part ascribed to the unfavourable learning environment found in many schools where teachers and pupils were squeezed into over-crowded classrooms with few desks, books and learning materials, housed in buildings which often lacked even basic infrastructure such as toilets and clean water (Ministry of Education and Vocational Training 2012a). The massive enrolment expansion which had previously been celebrated as a

---

175 The failure of learning was further documented by a study carried out by Uwezo, an education NGO which found out that many children in their last year of primary school were not able to read simple passages in Kiswahili or English or do basic arithmetic (Uwezo 2013).

success now turned out to negatively affect educational quality as reflected in plummeting literacy rates at both primary and secondary levels.[176]

The education crisis became a major issue in both public debate and donor–government relations. Media reports focused on the failure of learning and the resulting implications for the future of Tanzania's school children (see, for instance, Nkosi 2012; Kaijage 2013; Mgaya 2013; Tambwe 2013), whereas donor–government discussions rather turned on 'missed targets', as the following narrative of the DFID advisor reflects:

> *The evaluation which is commissioned by government overall is quite negative and pointed out that a lot of the resources weren't released by government, some particular things like the amount of school grants that were rewarded on a population, or school enrolment ratios which weren't delivered in full – it's been very large. They have missed many of the targets by (a) very large amount, particularly inputs around building buildings, deploying teachers, providing books … The government systems to decentralizing things haven't worked particularly well.* (Interview 35)

According to the DFID officer, the fact that the government had not nearly 'delivered' what has been expected created "a sort of difficult dynamic" (Interview 35) with respect to future aid. Major donors considered reducing budget and sector support through which PEDP II had mainly been financed, arguing that these modalities had failed to show results. The education team leader of the Canadian Embassy stated in this regard:

> *For the education side, we are looking at options. I don't know whether we will carry on with sector budget support, we might, we might not. This is exactly the discussions we are having right now in our team because there's pros and cons. I mean we are getting a lot of pressure – all donors, I think, are getting a lot of pressure to demonstrate results.* (Interview 30)

Similarly, the first secretary responsible for education in the Swedish Embassy reported:

> *At present, we really don't know when it comes to General Budget Support and so on, I think, that is clearly questioned by our Minister for Development Cooperation (…). So she has clearly stated we are not going to continue with GBS. This is not the government's official stand*

---

176 According to Wedgwood (2006: 4), observers with a morbid sense of humour allegedly jest that the abbreviation of Universal Primary Education 'UPE' in Tanzania stands for Ualimu Pasipo Elimu in Swahili, meaning 'teaching without education'.

at present – they are discussing this. That's why we had to prolong the present strategy. So there's an on-going discussion. We are trying to find a way within – not only focussing on General Budget Support but having a mix of modalities. (Interview 40)

DFID had already decided to significantly reduce its contribution to budget support on the grounds that its 2010 country programme evaluation "suggested that GBS was not the most effective way to deliver results in the current circumstances" (DFID Tanzania 2011: 3); in DFID's view, the 'unsatisfactory performance' of PEDP II corroborated this evaluation.

The donors' turn-around was not only based on the negative assessment report but followed a general trend reversal regarding aid modalities (see Chapter 5). They used the education crisis to legitimate the pulling out from joint funding mechanisms. This is remarkable insofar as the decline in quality was in a way a predictable implication of mass enrolment, as a DFID advisor acknowledged:

> *You could argue that perhaps it was never feasible to have such a major expansion against the MDG goals which are very much focused on gender equity and universal access (…). If you tried this in any country in the world, you wouldn't expect it to have anything like the same level of pass rates measured by a standard pass mark because you're putting huge pressure on the system to deliver the schools, the teachers, the learning resources needed. But also you're promoting up into the system children who come from very poor, underprivileged, remote, rural backgrounds, children entering primary schools who are much more likely to have illiterate parents themselves coming from very poor backgrounds. All of the things which are the best predictors of how well children do, how educated your parents are, how much opportunity you've got from other resources to help you learn. So clearly there are many more children who are coming in very disadvantaged, so the system is struggling to cope. So given that background, the government very reasonably can say, 'Well, what did you expect when you encouraged us to expand this way'.* (Interview 35)

Hence, although enrolment expansion had significantly been pushed by the aid community in order to achieve Universal Primary Education by 2015 (the second Millennium Development Goal), it was now the government which was held responsible for coping with the consequences and regarded as not taking sufficient action to improve the situation. Tanzanian policy-makers, on the other hand, felt unduly blamed, and perceived the announced reduction of budget support as a breach of agreement and sign of distrust; from their perspective, donors and their unreliable disbursements were at least partly at fault for the failure of reaching certain goals, as a high-level official in PMO-RALG remarked:

> *Three months you can continue discussing, you know, what and why the government is not up to its promises. But in actual fact, it is both. The government depends on collection (…). Tax payers, fine, that's one resource. The donors are another source – borrowing. Now, if the donor funds are not forthcoming and it was included in the budget, then that's the reason why we cannot get the amount of money this time.* (Interview 60)

In the course of tedious discussions over indicators, ratings (as essential 'triggers' for the release of aid money) and the reasons why targets were not met, donor–government relationships increasingly soured.[177] The friction between the two parties culminated when the education ministry in August 2012 distributed its PEDP III draft for comments – and received abrasive criticism from the 'Education Development Partners Group' (ED-DPG) which assessed the document as 'quite weak' (Interview 30), recommending

> *that significant changes need to be made (…) to ensure that it becomes a credible plan – attractive for both internal and external financing and an implementable plan that will deliver the human capital needed to put Tanzania on the right track to development.* (cited in Education Development Partners Group in Tanzania 2013: 19)

Amongst others, donors criticised the – in their view – unconvincing costing scenarios, deficient sector analysis and strategic orientation. Referring to the latter, the education team leader of the Canadian Embassy who acted as chair of ED-DPG in the interview commented:

> *It was a grouping of activities without a strategic orientation with a clear flow of: 'These are our objectives, and this is how we are going to do it'. It was just sort of a piecemeal document of well, we do much of these activities and we will do some of this, we do some of this. It didn't really have any coherence to it and it didn't seem to have any connections between obviously whatever is coming out of – when students leave primary, they should*

---

177 Given the numerous meetings dealing with rating frameworks and the like to 'measure' progress in education, Languille (2013) remarks that the "processes of performance quantification (…) contribute to crowd out the policy space of government staff: target setting and endless discussions over numbers are so time-consuming that no time is left to deliberate, in substance, upon the quality challenge and the policies to address it".

> *be prepared to go to secondary school, and there should be appropriate*
> *numbers who are passing to fill the places in the secondary and none of*
> *that had been considered. So there were some weaknesses in that way, and*
> *there was no monitoring framework at all which we felt was a major gap.*
> (Interview 30)

When donor representatives put forward their fundamental 'concerns' regarding the draft to the government, ministry officials made no pretence of their irritation which was a rather unusual reaction. Canada's education team leader attributed the blunt annoyance of his counterparts to a lack of receptiveness for critical feedback:

> *They were seeking editorial comments, I think. They said, 'Look, this is*
> *our plan'. But they were going through the formality of consulting, 'Let's*
> *consult the donors because we have to', but I'm not sure they were really*
> *interested in serious consultations – which is why when we came back*
> *with major revisions, they were kind of upset.* (Interview 30)

A second version circulated by the MoEVT by mid-October responded to some of the issues raised but still did not please the aid community. Given the – from their perspective – need for substantial changes, donors suggested resorting to experts to help rework and finalise the document:

> *We had said, 'Look, we think this isn't just something for comments, it*
> *really needs to be worked on a lot more.' And so we said, 'We are happy*
> *to help you with that, we can provide our experts to do that.' We can*
> *hire experts to do that, but in this case because of timing, we just said we*
> *all have experts here. And so the government thought that was a good*
> *idea and they invited a couple of us to provide technical expertise and*
> *to sit down in a room with their technical experts and they rewrote the*
> *document over a few days. They went off to another city and they just got*
> *it done.* (Interview 30)

To what extent the government, in fact, judged the use of external assistance a 'good idea' remains an open question; one can find at least indications that there were certain issues at stake which led the government to accept the suggestion, such as its application to the 'Global Partnership for Education'.

Eventually, a small group of ministry officials, civil society representatives and educational specialists provided by CIDA and UNICEF spent six days in Morogoro, a town around 200km west of Dar es Salaam, in order to rework the PEDP III document. As stated in the Minutes of the Education Development

Partners Group Meeting of 17th October 2012, the draft was "significantly revised" (ED-DPG 2012) in the course of the retreat exercise. Most notably, it now entailed a comprehensive costing and budgeting framework, as well as a logframe matrix including quantified targets – as, for instance, to raise the percentage of a cohort completing Standard VII (the last year of primary school) from 54.8% in 2012 to 72.8% by 2016 (Ministry of Education and Vocational Training 2012b: 48).

Interestingly, it also contained a passage insinuating that the government had given up the insistence on budget support for education; after reference to the Joint Assistance Strategy of 2006 which clearly emphasised GBS as the preferred aid modality, the text declares:

> *The Government has been encouraging Development Partners to channel their development assistance through General Budget Support (GBS) rather than basket funds and direct project support. However, the Government will continue to be flexible to accommodate assistance from Development Partners who have decided not to use the GBS funding modality but who are interested to support education interventions.* (Ministry of Education and Vocational Training 2012b)

It is questionable whether this concession of individual interventions derived from a changed government position or – what appears more likely – from donors' return to projects through which they are more easily able to trace their investments and put their flag on results.

The conditionality of consultation and the centrality of aid in policy-making

The PEDP III process reveals pervasive patterns which in their interplay severely affect educational governance in Tanzania. One pertains to the conditionality of donor consultation and the effects on the nature of interaction; another to the (perceived) dependency on aid money and the resulting implications for agenda-setting in education.

As to the former, the education team leader in the Canadian Embassy, reporting on the great deal of annoyance caused by the donors' feedback on the PEDP III draft, assumed that the harsh reaction of government officials derived from the fact that they 'were going through the formality of consulting' without actually seeking advice, but with the stance 'let's consult donors because we have to' (Interview 30). This perception is supported by various narratives of government officials. Asked to assess the usefulness of regular meetings with donors, the primary education director in the MoEVT responded:

*You know, sometimes it may not be useful – but they're the funders.
They're the ones who support you, so you have to go into negotiation.*
(Interview 49)

In fact, the 'dialogue' in the education sector (and similarly in other policy
fields) has been constructed as a requirement of budget support modalities
(i.e. GBS and basket funding for education). Clearly, the point of departure
for the institutionalised interaction between donors and the government is
the financial need of the latter. Hence, while the 'dialogue' is formally framed
as "an open space for discussions, challenges and agreements on technical
and policy issues" (United Republic of Tanzania 2012b: 1), it is inherently
based on a dependency relationship structured by financial power. From a
government perspective, policy discussions are primarily held to comply with
funding requirements and not because there is a genuine request for advice.
The 'process conditionality' (Gould & Ojanen 2005: 25) of donor consultation
renders actual demand for advice irrelevant. Against this background, it is not
surprising that ministry officials – as in the case of the PEDP III draft – were not
receptive to and were displeased about critical feedback.

The obligatory interaction with external experts forced upon the
government due to financial needs has resulted in a rejection of additional
technical assistance offered by donors. Referring to her ministry counterparts,
a Tanzanian advisor working for Canada reported:

*Consequently they have been refusing, at least in our sector education,
when you touch issues of – ok, we don't have money to do X, Y and Z,
but what you people need may be just somebody to take you through, so
that you know how to plan better, how to implement better. How about us
providing that resource, not in money, but we are bringing [someone] to
sit with you to do X, Y and Z? They are not very willing.* (Interview 31)

Since deliberation with donors has become an inevitable feature of educational
governance, the reflexive refusal of technical assistance can be interpreted as
an attempt to secure a last resort of autonomy on the part of policy-makers
whose discretionary power is markedly constrained. Ministry officials have
become used to bargain convictions against money, as a statement from the
director of Primary Education reflects:

*Sometimes you have to lose what your belief is. And the other side also has
to lose some of the elements … And you come to a place where you win a
little bit of it and the other side wins a little bit of it as well.* (Interview 49)

The understanding that the feasibility of policies and plans depends on the approval of donors is widely internalised among leadership ranks and civil servants in the education ministry. Many consider the government's scope of action as determined by the consensus and agendas of external funders who eventually hold the 'whip hand', as a high-ranking official in PMO-RALG pointed out:

> *You cannot implement unless you agree, and you have agreed this dialogue should be consultative, respecting one another, you need to listen to a colleague, you see. So there are times when these strategies and the policy get stuck to stand still because you have not agreed with the experts from the embassies, from the donor cooperation agencies.* (Interview 60)

Similarly, a senior official in the higher education department explained:

> *There's finance from someone who says, 'Yes, if you do this, I'm willing to convince someone somewhere to release that sum, so that you can do this'. But that 'this', what is it? Is it the real that you want? (...) But what you want to address, you have no funding for it.* (Interview 48)

Asked to give a concrete example, the interviewee pointed to the ministry's first Higher Education Development Programme (HEDP) approved in 2010 and covering the years 2010–2015. As the outcome of almost a decade of research, consultation and retreats, the document presented a detailed list of activities proposed to enhance access and quality in higher education, focusing on institutional reforms, service delivery and sustainability mechanisms (Ministry of Education and Vocational Training 2010a). Despite being commended for its clarity and thorough analysis (see Education Development Partners Group in Tanzania 2013), HEDP has not yet received much attention from the aid community. As the following statement reflects, the lack of support for implementing the suggested interventions caused much frustration among officials in the higher education department:

> *It is just in our shelves now. When it started, there was the idea that someone would fund that – none came up to now (...). But you have spent the department's budget for almost two years or so on that. Nobody came up and said yeah, I'm willing to even pick a portion in that, nobody is there. Of recent, we have been advised to go through it and – I don't know how to put it, but to make different portions, so that you can sell each portion separately (...). But even doing that, again we had to dig into the*

*department's budget to prepare that, in hope that someone would come up
to support that one.* (Interview 48)

The terms used here are telling: The government had to 'portion' its programme
in order to make it 'sellable' to external financiers. The fact that aid providers
showed little interest to buy-in is used as an explanation why HEDP was put
'on the shelves'. In this case as in many others, officials experienced themselves
as being at the mercy of the donors.

The dependency on external funding proved to be the predominant point
of reference across interviews with education policy-makers. The centrality of
the theme as the decisive condition structuring relationships and its use as a
legitimating pattern for action/inaction is striking. Although education is de
facto less dependent on foreign funding than other sectors (see Chapter 6), aid
money constitutes the prime concern of all actors in the field and the linchpin
of debate, as a Tanzanian education specialist emphasised:

> *So the resource issue becomes the driving – it's like you talk around the
> needs, you talk around, yes, a little bit on the priorities, but how much on
> those priorities.* (Interview 31)

The claim that aid money and resource flows have indeed become the prime
subjects of discourse is supported by various narratives and documents related
to the PEDP III process presented earlier; to iterate just two extracts for
illustration:

> *Now if the donor funds are not forthcoming and it was included in the
> budget, then that's the reason why we cannot get the amount of money this
> time.* (PMO-RALG official, interview 60)

> *Significant changes need to be made (…) to ensure that it becomes a credible
> plan – attractive for both internal and external financing.* (DPs cited in
> Education Development Partners Group in Tanzania 2013: 19)

The fact that 'development partners' called for significant changes of the PEDP
III draft on the grounds that it should be made 'credible' and 'attractive' for local
and foreign financiers points to the central role of aid as a frame of reference in
the education sector. In this particular case, PEDP III was considered important
not only for donor decisions on future budget support for education, but also

for prospective funding held out by the 'Global Partnership for Education',[178] a multi-lateral financing body which signalled it would allocate about USD 100 million if Tanzania applied; a successful application, however, required the endorsement of educational plans by 'development partners'. In their view, the first PEDP III versions were 'not good enough' to be approved, as a representative of the Canadian Embassy reported:

> We said, 'If you submit this, they are not going to accept it.' And we were quite confident that it wasn't good enough. (Interview 30)

Because of the ascribed and perceived centrality of external funding for educational governance, the assessment of policies and programmes against donor standards and agendas has become a common pattern. If need be – as obviously in the case of PEDP III – the government very pragmatically adjusts strategic documents or reports to make them 'fit' by including formal elements (e.g. tabular logframes) or the 'right' catch-words that match the aid community's current concepts. Often, the reframing is not even done by ministry officials but by technical assistants familiar with the terminology and formats required.[179] Gratifying funders in order to ensure that 'money flows' seems to have become a priority of policy-makers. Canada's education team leader commented in this regard:

> When there's a cheque on the horizon, again GPE is a good example, it's 100 million dollars, that caught their attention. (...) And then I do think they sort of figure out, 'Okay, what do we need to do to satisfy the donors so that we can get the money?' Yeah, I think that's a big part. (Interview 30)

The 'charade' of ownership in educational policy-making

The significance of donor agendas as a point of orientation, the focus on compliance with aid organisations' requirements and the intense involvement of external experts in formulating decisive documents infer that educational

---

178 The 'Global Partnership for Education' (formerly known as the Education for All Fast Track Initiative) is a multilateral financing mechanism providing grants to low-income countries aiming at accelerating the achievement of free, universal primary education. Its budget is made up of contributions from European and North American donor countries which are represented on the governance boards. The GPE secretariat is based in Washington.

179 Referring to the formulation of annual sector reports, an advisor in the Canadian Embassy explained: "Even though we say we read and we provide input, it is not quite just an issue of reading and providing input. Sometimes you are actually writing the sentences" (Interview 31).

policy-making in Tanzania has been externalised. This claim is supported by the first secretary for education in the Swedish Embassy who critically acknowledged:

> *We have all these very good policies and programmes and on paper, but it's not owned. It's very much from the outside.* (Interview 40)

Donors have become involved in policy-making to such an extent that it has become difficult to trace where priorities originate. After decades of interference, they find themselves in a situation where they are trying to guess whether there is a genuine government agenda and if so, what it looks like. An advisor working for the Canadian Embassy – herself being a Tanzanian – remarked:

> *My biggest challenge over the years has always been: What is the government thinking, when they sit on the other side and we are on this other side? They know their need; they know their priorities as a government. And that's why even right now, as we are talking, they are busy finalising their national budget speech for the year, so they will definitely have to go look backwards and forward. So they are planning! They have issued the Five Year Plans, now they are talking of a long-term plan, those things are on the table (...). The question is still, is that what the recipient government would wish to see happen?* (Interview 31)

In view of the well-entrenched involvement of donors over more than 20 years, it is hard for many to imagine what educational governance in Tanzania would look like if the government was in a position to decide and operate independently from external interference. The first secretary of education in the Swedish Embassy commented:

> *I've stated ... at least ten times in the dialogue from last year, 'What would happen if we suggested that we took time out and just supported the Tanzanian government to come up with a curriculum with a starting point from the Tanzanian context on the African continent. How would it look like? Would the subjects be the same? Would the content be the same?' And I've raised this question a couple of times. And then the government people say, 'Well, that's an interesting idea', but they know that the charade must go on.* (Interview 40)

The 'charade' going on in the education sector is outlined by a civil society leader who, similarly to the Swedish official, used the notion of an 'act' being played. The main protagonists are a "weak, distracted government not clear on what it wants" and donors who "start filling the gaps and trying to make things happen, because of the absence of strong clear government leadership" (Interview 70):

> *When that is not there in our government, the donors start stepping in. But we have to all pretend that government is in charge, in the 'driving seat'. So you live this kind of double life of officially everything has government stamps and leadership and so on, but in reality, the people pushing things are the donors.* (Interview 70)

The fact that donors collectively and individually start "creating what they want to see in Tanzania" (Interview 40) can be observed in various processes. Two examples, the push for re-entry of girls in schools and ICT in primary education, are briefly sketched.

"There are different, mixed feelings": The issue of pregnant girls in schools

By 2012, the large number of girls who dropped out of school due to pregnancy had come up as a serious matter of concern in Tanzania (IRIN News 2007b). According to media reports citing ministry statistics, 5 157 girls had to leave primary school in 2011 due to pregnancy even though no law explicitly prescribed the expulsion of students for that reason (Assey 2012; Robi 2012).

Donors strongly pushed the government to include a clear policy statement on the re-entry of teenage mothers into a revised Education and Training Policy, emphasising Tanzania's international commitments regarding gender equality and the right to education for all children. According to aid and government officials alike, the issue became a controversial point of discussion which was repeatedly put 'in and out' during the drafting process. An assistant director in the MoEVT Department of Policy and Planning delineated the sensitivity of the topic as follows:

> *The DPs are of the idea that the right should be given. But then … education stakeholders are many and they are different from cultural thinking. They think maybe from our culture it is not right if you do this. There are religious groups, they have different ideas, they say, 'No, once a girl has been pregnant to us, it's a sin' and so and so. There are different, mixed feelings.* (Interview 50)

Similarly, the director of Primary Education argued:

> *Me, I think that the entry programme is a good programme if you want*
> *to have every child in school. But the question is on how to implement*
> *that. Because education is cultural-based. And we have our culture. Our*
> *communities in Mtwara and Lindi have their cultures. And so I think we*
> *have to merge these two things. We want children to go to school but without*
> *compromising the culture of the children, the culture of the community*
> *of that particular, specific community. But also I think we should not do*
> *something that tomorrow will turn against us – that will speed up the rate*
> *of pregnancy, rather than stopping or rather than curbing the problem.*
> *And so I think those factors have caused this programme to delay. Because*
> *you take the idea to the parliament and find a lot of comments come in.*
> (Interview 49)

In fact, members of parliament seemed to be divided over the issue, with some arguing for alternative training of teenage mothers instead of bringing them back to the formal system. A commission formed to examine the matter reported that many teachers opposed the idea of allowing re-entry of girls with children (*Tanzania Daily News* 2012).

The government found itself caught between these positions. Perceiving resentment on the part of educational stakeholders, communities and religious leaders, the minister clearly signalled to donors that Tanzania was "not ready for this yet" (Interview 40). However, aid representatives continued to exert pressure, as a high-ranking official in PMO-RALG reported:

> *They say: 'You know you are late, you signed the human rights convention,*
> *you know, the rights of the child, a child must get this [education].' But*
> *you see: Good, we like it. But don't we need preparations for that? But*
> *some of these want it immediately. That's where we have a problem.*
> (Interview 60)

Clearly, educational decision-makers are aware of international obligations and of the necessity to deal with school dropouts, but they considered the implementation of a re-entry policy unfeasible, expecting little acceptance on the part of their constituency. According to ministry officials, the on-going disagreement on the subject led to the 'unsmooth running' of donor–government meetings due to 'some sort of resistance' among MoEVT representatives. During this research, the issue remained unresolved, and the Education and Training Policy continued to be revised. Commenting on the state of affairs, the PMO-RALG leader stated:

The ministry was forced to change that policy, but it's still in the draft. At least three years have elapsed without that policy being out. (Interview 60)

Waiting for computers: USAID's 'Tanzania 21st Century Basic Education Programme'

Another process which resulted in deadlock was USAID's 'Tanzania 21st Century Basic Education Programme', commonly known as 'TZ21'. Running from 2011 to 2015 with an overall budget of USD 94 million, the project's stated goal was to integrate information and communication technology (ICT) into primary education in order to enhance children's learning achievements (Embassy of the United States Dar es Salaam 2012). Similar to an equivalent project set up in Kenya, schools in two pilot areas – Mtwara and Zanzibar – are to be equipped with computers, learning and management software, with teachers and administrators getting trained in how to use the new technology.[180] Thereby, the project was closely aligned to USAID's new global education strategy which explicitly encouraged the use of ICT for achieving the goal of "improved reading skills for 100 million children in primary grades by 2015" (USAID 2009: 21).

When we met the USAID education team leader in his office on the US Embassy compound in May 2012, he was excited about the recent launch of the initiative on Zanzibar and the upcoming inauguration in the Mtwara region, stating that all partners were 'jazzed up' about the 'fantastic opportunity' to try out the 'totally experimental' approach: "There's the feeling 'let's do it, let's get started!'" (Interview 42).

The partners he referred to comprised a whole range of stakeholders: Creative Associates International, a US-based development firm which was contracted as implementing agent; Microsoft, Cisco and Intel, as well as two Tanzanian companies – UhuruOne and Zantel – which had been selected as technology supply companies; regional government authorities; and the national education ministries of Zanzibar and Tanzania Mainland.[181] With the

---

180 Initiated in 2009, the "Accelerating 21st Century Education" project in Kenya focused on providing PCs for classrooms, wireless internet connectivity, digital content, and ICT skills training for teachers (Microsoft News Center 2009; Kenya Ministry of Education 2012). In Tanzania, USAID chose Mtwara region due to its 'growing population, gas and oil', and Zanzibar due to the new US focus on investing in 'Islamic communities' as a strategy to prevent terrorism (Interview 42). According to the USAID education team leader, local officials from both places had asked USAID "to help introduce computer literacy", expressing concern "that the digital divide was widening between developed and developing countries and they didn't want to be left behind" (email correspondence 25 July 2015).

181 Upon reading the first version of this text, the USAID team leader emphasised that representatives from all five technology companies, as well as from the national and the regional governments of Mtwara and Zanzibar, were involved in the competitive selection process of the implementing

latter, he conceded, USAID had 'a rough time' during the design stage of TZ21 insofar as the MoEVT was 'not very enthusiastic' about the idea, and objected to the project approach in favour of budget support. Undeterred by the reluctance at the national level, USAID directly approached local authorities in the areas where the project should be carried out, and encountered 'very cooperative' counterparts. Eventually, when the opening of the project in Zanzibar went through the news, the MoEVT signalled interest in becoming involved; according to the USAID education team leader, the minister was suddenly thrilled by the initiative which he allegedly deemed 'incredible' (Interview 42).

Speaking to national government officials ten months later, we found little of that enthusiasm in the ministry.[182] Asked how the project was proceeding, the primary education director responded:

> *Well, the computers are still in Dar es Salaam. They have not been sent to Mtwara. I saw the computers for the first time when the vice-president went to inaugurate. But at the moment they are only in two schools – in Kambarage Primary School there in Mtwara, and the other one is at Naliendele, another school. There I found about two, three computers or laptops. And the rest of the computers have not been sent to Mtwara.*
>
> *Just last week I was talking to one of their representatives here. So I said, 'Do you think it's important for our ... computer personnel in here, to go and see the specs' – the computer specifications. Because the project is three years – sooner or later, it's going to come to an end. So what will happen if our people, our own people here, do not know the computers – specs of the computer, when they were made, where they were made and all these kinds of things?* (Interview 49)

While the director refrained from articulating blunt criticism, his dissatisfaction with the course of the cooperation was implied in various narratives. Aside from the annoyance about the deadlock in computer installation, a salient point seemed to be the fact that the MoEVT was only marginally (if at all) involved by its project 'partners', for example, in identifying or procuring the technical equipment which was meant to be supplied to schools. This was confirmed by a Tanzanian education specialist who had temporarily been

---

partner, Creative Associates "from the very beginning of the design of the activity" (email communication 6 April 2015).

182 We did not speak to officials in the regional governments of Mtwara and Zanzibar whose perspective on the project might be a different one.

contracted as an advisor for TZ21. Herself being highly critical about the way the project was carried out, she stated:

> *For ownership purposes, you would need also to bring into the process the government, the technical people, so that they know when we procure an equipment, let's say for the primary education, it should be of this kind because it cannot be an equipment that can be sent to secondary or colleges, you know, because of young children. Let that be documented and let that be a process that everybody understands. So there are a lot of implications of ICT implementation at the school level (…). But when you discuss with other people in the project, they don't see that.* (Interview 32)

An implication which had obviously not been considered and thoroughly discussed with national authorities concerned the incorporation of localised 'e-content' into the curriculum. While the delivery of education and the management of schools in Tanzania fall under the responsibility of local governments, the development of syllabi and learning materials is centrally done by the Tanzania Institute of Education (TIE), a parastatal organisation under the MoEVT. Already prior to the release of the government's ICT policy for basic education in 2007, TIE had designed an ICT curriculum ('Teknolojia ya Habari na Mawasiliano' or TEHAMA in short) to be applied in pre-primary and primary schools with adequate infrastructure (Ministry of Education and Vocational Training 2007). Thus USAID's aim to introduce externally designed ICT modules on TZ21 project sites seemed highly problematic to the director of Primary Education:

> *You cannot have a module which is not compatible to other modules that are applied in other regions in Tanzania, or a module that is not compatible with the curriculum that is being implemented. Otherwise you have to dismantle everything. And who is ready to do that? Nobody is ready for that; we are not ready for that yet. We may wish to review, revise our curriculum, but not because there is this one thing in Mtwara going on. It might be very difficult.* (Interview 49)

The potential deviation of curricula was not the only unresolved issue which caused irritation among MoEVT officials. Frictions also emerged with regard to suggested modifications of the ministry's Education Management Information System (EMIS). In order to strengthen school administration, TZ21 consultants, together with technology suppliers, had developed software for capturing real-time data on the attendance of teachers and students; in their view, the information collected through this tool could also be used constructively for

204

decision-making and planning if aggregated at the national level. Unluckily, the programme offered was not compatible with the system UNESCO had installed in MoEVT, amongst others, since its scope was restricted. Yet, USAID and other donors pushed the ministry to adopt their software solution and adjust the one currently in use. A senior director in the M&E unit who participated in the ensuing debate reported:

> *We told them: 'Look, here you have only collected the information for lower primary, from standard one to standard four. But here in the ministry we have a system which collects information from pre-primary to higher education institutions (…). Why can't you mainstream it to the ministry data base rather than the ministry mainstreams yours which covers only standard one to standard four level?' So there was some discussion.* (Interview 50)

The tensions arising on issues such as EMIS, ICT modules and procurement show a common pattern: the root cause of conflict can be found in a pervasive disregard of local institutions. Bypassing national decision-making entities, USAID drove forward a project in line with its own agenda but detached from the field it encountered. Against this background, the difficulties and frictions which emerged in the course of the operation were predictable.

TZ21 seems to be symptomatic for the particularity of 'ICT in education' as a policy subject in the Tanzanian context and its lack of local grounding. In fact, all-round table conferences and workshops held in previous years to explore the opportunities of ICT in education had been facilitated with donor support (see Nielinger 2006; Ministry of Education and Vocational Training 2007). A Tanzanian education specialist tentatively indicated that the ICT policy for basic education had primarily been created to please foreign funders, but apart from existing on paper, lacked political concern and feasibility. She supported her claim by stating:

> *The urgency of preparing that policy, you know, I remember it was not very systematically done because otherwise – by then I was in the World Bank – I would have heard about the process. Usually when it is time to prepare policy, you will know even if you are a donor that something is going on. I didn't hear about that until when something was there (…). Since that time up to now, that policy has not been developed for operationalization, in terms of operational guidelines at the school level, at the regional level or being budgeted for nothing. So as a donor, how will you prepare such a project? I mean the risks should have been seen by then.* (Interview 32)

At the time of writing, the project was still on-going. Aside from photo galleries with children in front of computers and anecdotes of 'success stories' on the project website (e.g. about communities mounting iron door gates in schools "to ensure the safety of the ICT equipment that will be installed" USAID & Creative Associates International 2014), no information on what TZ21 has actually achieved until now could be obtained (USAID & Creative Associates International 2014).[183]

Signs of resistance

Among policy-makers and senior officials in the MoEVT, there seems to be mounting resentment about being exposed to aid activities that consume staff time and energy, yet constantly result in failure. While Tanzanian government members are usually known for their outwardly calm countenance, their frustration has reached a level where it occasionally erupts, as the first secretary of education in the Swedish Embassy reported:

> *In our monitoring and evaluation technical working group last week, there was an outburst almost when the government officials said, 'We are so tired of all your projects and there's no sustainability, you, the development partners should really take responsibility' and so on. And then we said, 'Well, ok, we've tried to coordinate ourselves, but you could also say no, if you don't want the money. We come with all those proposals, but you should make sure that you say no if you don't want them.'* (Interview 40)

The claim that government counterparts did not make clear statements and did not direct donors in education was repeatedly brought up by interviewees in country offices and embassies. A Tanzanian education specialist who had worked for both the government and donors critically stated:

> *At the end of the day, it is the government receiving aid that has to be organized, and helping to guide anybody coming in. If the government is not going to do that, then you have all these scattered things.* (Interview 32)

In the experience of aid officials, most of the issues debated in policy discussions are brought up by themselves. Referring to the technical working groups

---

183 The external impact evaluation which was to assess the success of TZ21 was eventually "discontinued as the portfolio was realigned to focus more on reading to meet [USAID's] Education Strategy and respond to the BRN's [Big Results Now initiative's] focus on the 3Rs" (email communication with USAID official 28 July 2015).

and committee meetings which are formally chaired by the government, the Canadian team leader for education commented:

> To be honest I find a lot of the meetings are donor-driven. I'm not sure if it's because we are more impatient than they are. I mean it was often – this was interesting about being the chair [of the Development Partners Group], because it meant I would meet with their secretariat weekly (…), and we would sit down and say, 'Okay where are things at?' And they'd say, 'Well, we're going to do this'. They have a work plan, and they'd say, 'We'll do this that, this, that, this, that'. We'd say, 'Okay, what about this, this, this, this?' – 'Alright', and they'd start filling in all these other boxes they had apparently not thought about or not considered, it just seems like there was too much going on. So, I mean, I wonder if we said nothing, what would happen? Would nothing happen? I don't think so. I think they would eventually just pick up the slack and do something. But I think they've become very accustomed to us sort of setting the agenda, saying 'well, maybe we should do this then, this then and this then' and they say, 'Well, yeah, okay'. (Interview 30)

As the accounts above indicate, ministry officials seem to have adopted a conduct of compliance towards the aid community. Various circumstances lend themselves as explanations for the failing leadership. One reason preferably stated by donor representatives is the lack of capacity on the part of MoEVT, which – in their view – results in an ad-hoc way of working, devoid of prioritisation and forward planning.[184] In this reading, the failing leadership derives from deficient administrative strength.[185]

The ministry's lack of resolve can also be interpreted as a coping strategy in a relationship of dependence: based on accumulated experiences, many high-

---

184 The Canadian education team leader, for instance, stated: "When they focus to do something, they can do it. But they can only do one thing at a time. (…) And so, once your issue comes up, it's great because you get immediate action and it's, you know, pretty, pretty strong commitment and I mean there are very dedicated people who work long hours. So it's not that they're lazy or anything like that, but they do seem to be very sequential" (Interview 30).
Similarly, a Tanzanian education specialist remarked: "Things are done ad hoc, you know? Oh, the priorities today, oh, the minister wants this, oh this is that, oh … There's no concentration on the priorities that were set" (Interview 32).

185 That donors may exacerbate the ministry's human resource situation by poaching the most qualified and skilled education specialists was brought up by a Canadian official who commented: "I sometimes am a bit concerned; it's quite difficult to get good experts, I think. We've been lucky, I've been lucky. I have colleagues on different programmes who really struggled to get good experts. And I also worry, of course, if all the donors are hiring the best experts, who's actually running the system? Because I don't think - unfortunately, we try not to do this, but I think it's a reality that if you're really good at something, you're more likely to go on a job with the Canadians than with the government" (Interview 30).

ranking officials and policy-makers seem to have internalised the fact that overt objection against the aid community leads to nowhere and may eventually result in the withdrawal of money. As securing funding has precedence, concurring with donors opens up more room for tactical manoeuvring than taking an unequivocal stand. That this kind of strategy might be adopted is implied by a Canadian official who, when asked about the government's receptiveness to donor advice in policy meetings, responded:

> *Most of the time they are like, 'Yes, good idea, great, we will do something about that, we will think about that, we will include that in our next plan' – most of the time they receive it fairly positively. Whether things change, that is another story.* (Interview 30)

As the last part of the quote implies, agreement with donor suggestions is not necessarily followed by action. In fact, various reports from interviewees suggest that the ministry deliberately uses inaction and delay as a tool of resistance. The persistent postponing of a decision about how to deal with pregnant girls in schools and the resulting deadlock of policy revision can be seen as a case in point in this regard.

Jamming processes may help to thwart plans pushed from outside, but it does not really help to generate a local agenda, let alone execute it. Some observers claim that after years of external domination there is no local agenda left.

Conclusion

In a nutshell, the state of education governance in Tanzania could be sketched as follows: the need for foreign financing has legitimated an intense involvement of external actors in the policy space in which aid money has become the central preoccupation. The prevailing sentiment of being at the mercy of donors has paralysed leadership and administration which fails to set or refrains from articulating an agenda of its own. The pervasive entrenchment of donor interference in policy issues has blurred distinguishing what comes from within and what from outside. A civil society leader engaged in the education sector commented:

> *It's almost like you don't know now, the players, you don't know what is the truth and what is not the truth because we are all doing this act.* (Interview 70)

The government is formally ascribed the starring role in this 'act', but the scene is set by aid providers whose experts have become the pivotal protagonists of the play. Their role in driving forth policy and decision-making processes has become so central that an advisor of Tanzanian origin working for Canada critically remarked:

> *You ask yourself: When will this end? If we did leave this support, does that mean education in Tanzania would collapse? We don't have an answer, because we have always been there.* (Interview 31)

South Africa education: Exploiting outside expertise to create a local vision

Sectoral context

Education is one the most central topics of post-apartheid politics in South Africa. In its first *White Paper on Education and Training*, the new democratic government stated its conviction that education is an essential driver of transformation:

> *Appropriate education and training can empower people to participate effectively in all the processes of democratic society, economic activity, cultural expression, and community life, and can help citizens to build a nation free of race, gender and every other form of discrimination.* (Department of Education 1995)

The persistent prominence of education on the political agenda after 20 years of democracy arises from the massive challenges the country still faces in terms of building a society in which citizens are provided equal opportunities to attain well-being and prosperity. The development of South Africa's education system and its deficiencies cannot be understood without knowing about the role and structures of education in the apartheid era. Thus, before looking at current challenges, we sketch the educational politics of the apartheid regime whose devastating effects are still felt today.

Black South Africans had experienced educational marginalisation already during colonial times. The Bantu Education Act passed by the apartheid government in 1953 cemented the establishment of a segregated and suppressive education system. The racial law brought an end to the relative autonomy of mission schools attended by more than two-thirds of black South Africans at that time, centralising control over education in the Department of Native Affairs which imposed a curriculum designed to 'prepare' the African population for serving the white minority as labourers and workers (Fiske &

Ladd 2005). The then Minister of Native Affairs HF Verwoerd legitimised the Act before the South African parliament by stating:

> *There is no space for him [the "Bantu"] in the European Community above certain forms of labour (…). Until now he has been subjected to a school system which drew him away from his own community and misled him by showing him the green pastures of European society in which he is not allowed to graze. This attitude is not only uneconomic because money is spent for an education which has no specific aim but it is also dishonest to continue it.* (Verwoerd cited in Christie & Collins 1984: 173)

In the course of the apartheid rule, separate schools for each of South Africa's 'ethnic groups' were established, creating an educational hierarchy with 'whites' at the top, followed by 'Indians', 'coloureds' and 'blacks' at the bottom.[186] Governed by different authorities, the parallel systems differed immensely in terms of syllabi and ideological thrust, facilities and funding. By 1960, the per capita expenditure on education for whites (ZAR 144.57) was more than ten times higher than for blacks (ZAR 12.46) (Christie & Collins 1984). White students enjoyed conducive learning environments, while the remaining majority was confronted with overcrowded classrooms, dilapidated school buildings, a lack of text books and learning materials, and inadequate instruction. According to figures from 1987, 87% of teachers in black schools were underqualified (i.e. had achieved an educational level of less than Standard 10 and no Matric Certificate). The teacher-to-pupil ratio averaged 1:41, whereas in white schools it was about 1:16 (File et al. 1989).

The unequal conditions led to high discrepancies in terms of educational attainment, as reflected by data of the 1996 census:[187] taking persons aged 20 and older into account, two-thirds of the white population had achieved education at the level of Grade 12 (39.3%) or higher (26.8%). Almost all remaining had at least some secondary education; the percentage of people who had no schooling was marginal (1.1%). In contrast, among black Africans only one out of six had reached Grade 12 (12%) or higher, with the percentage in higher education being minimal (3.6%). Almost one out of four black Africans (24%) had received no formal schooling at all (Statistics South

---

186 The use of race as a form of classification in South Africa is still widespread in both official statistics and academic literature. As Spaull (2012: 2) states, "this serves a functional (rather than normative) purpose and any other attempt to refer to these population groups would be cumbersome, impractical or inaccurate".

187 The 1996 census was the first statistical exercise which provided accurate demographic and socio-economic data to describe South Africa's situation after apartheid. The statistical system under the apartheid regime was deeply distorted insofar as it was racially fragmented and disjointed (National Statistics System N/A).

Africa 2012: 34). While coloured people fared only slightly better, Indian/ Asian people were markedly better off regarding educational levels. Yet, all of them were structurally discriminated in the system imposed by the apartheid regime. The highly unequal educational opportunities translated into huge discrepancies in labour market status and income: as of 1996, only 3% of white people aged 15–65 were unemployed, as opposed to 23.4% of black Africans (Statistics South Africa 2004: 51). Of those black Africans who were part of the formal employment system, one third (33.3%) earned only R 500 or less per month, whereas only 5% of white employees had such a low salary (Statistics South Africa 2004).

The statistics above reflect the deep impact of apartheid rule on education in South Africa that over four decades "reinforced the inequalities of a divided society" (Msila 2007: 147). Twenty years after the end of the 'rogue regime', its legacies are not yet overcome. Although the Constitution of 1996 made education a basic right for every South African (Republic of South Africa 1996, section 29), many still face tremendous difficulties in fully utilising this right (Nevondwe & Odeku 2013), and educational opportunities continue to be racially skewed (Yamauchi 2005). Although significant progress has been made in terms of providing access – with a gross enrolment rate of 99% at the primary level – the quality of education remains at an alarmingly low level (Department of Basic Education 2014b: 7). In comparative international studies on literacy or numeracy (e.g. SACMEQ III or TIMMS 2011), South African pupils lag behind those in poorer African countries such as Ghana or Tanzania (Moloi & Chetty 2010; Human Sciences Research Council 2011).[188] This is even more concerning in light of the enormous differentials with respect to learning outcomes between historically 'white' schools (attended by a small minority of students from middle and upper class backgrounds) and former 'black' schools in township areas (attended by the majority of African children).[189] The persistent inequality is documented by various assessments; the National School Effectiveness Study (2007/08/09), for instance, found that Grade 3 pupils from former white schools scored higher on the same test than Grade 5 pupils at former black schools, indicating large discrepancies in learning achievements visible already by the age of eight (Taylor et al. 2012).

---

188 For an overview of empirical assessments on the quality of education in South Africa, see Spaull (2013).

189 As Yamauchi (2011) points out, high-quality schools situated in urban, well-off areas (with predominantly white residents) are neither geographically nor financially accessible for many African children. Hence, although racial segregation was abolished 20 years ago, the composition of students is still skewed along racial lines. While historically 'white' and 'Indian' schools have become more diverse, former 'black' schools remain racially homogeneous.

The appalling gap regarding learner performance, resources and teacher qualifications points to the "dualistic nature" (Spaull 2012) of South Africa's school system which seems to consist of two parallel subsystems:

> *One which is functional, wealthy and able to educate students; with the other being poor, dysfunctional, and unable to equip students with the necessary numeracy and literacy skills they should be acquiring.* (Spaull 2012: 14)

Given this situation, the lag of black youth in terms of educational attainment is little surprising. According to Møloi et al. (2014: 471), "almost 58.5% of whites and around 51% of Indians enter higher education. The rate for coloureds is 14.3%, while that for blacks is even lower at 12%". Many universities in South Africa are internationally recognised as "world-class academic institutions, at the cutting edge of research in certain spheres" (Moloi et al. 2014: 470). For the majority of learners, however, they are out of reach.

All in all, it appears that – despite massive resource shifts and several interventions put in place by the state – the South African school system in its current form contributes little to support upward mobility of the poor in the labour market (Van der Berg 2007). The economy, in turn, is severely affected by a shortage of skilled workers which hampers productivity and "reduces the country's capacity to develop a knowledge society" (Rasool & Botha 2011: 9). Providing equitable opportunities of education and training for all citizens in order to foster individual prosperity and economic growth has been on top of the political agenda since South Africa turned into a democracy; yet, it remains one of the greatest challenges for that country.

Governance structures

Since 1994, South Africa's institutional landscape in the field of education has been in a state of flux, with multiple bodies and structures being replaced, revised or recreated in the course of governance and policy reforms. Since 2014, the major policy-making bodies at the national level have been the Department of Basic Education (DBE) and the Department of Higher Education and Training (DHET); both were formed in 2009 when the former Department of Education was split into these two separate ministries. The DBE deals with primary and secondary education, early childhood development and adult literacy programmes; it provides national policy and legislative frameworks to give direction to the provinces which have their own education departments responsible for financing and managing schools in line with their needs. DHET is in charge of all post-school education and training components provided at universities, colleges and adult education institutions. It took over the Skills Development Branch from the Department of Labour, which shifted the Sector Education and Training Authorities (SETAs) concerned with workplace-related occupational training to DHET. An important role-player in this area is the National Skills Authority which liaises with SETAs and advises the minister of higher education on skills development matters.

Donor presence in the education sector

Similar to other sectors but certainly more pronounced, the nature and scope of aid for education and training in South Africa has shifted over time. One can roughly distinguish three different phases: the transitional era up to 1994, the period of system building until the early 2000s, and the phase of retreat lasting to the present. During the apartheid era, various countries such as Denmark, the United States and Australia supported non-state actors, which acted in opposition to the regime, by providing education grants and overseas scholarships, training programmes and study tours for blacks and anti-apartheid activists (King 1999). As will be shown below, this informal aid had a huge impact insofar as it put key actors of the democratic movements in touch with education and training systems in Europe and elsewhere which greatly impregnated their thinking. A witness of that time who participated in the exchange commented:

> Many people had studied in Britain and in America; they themselves had gone that route to study. So they came back believing in those systems because those systems had been the ones that had given them the step up. (Interview 20)

With the turn to democracy, the government and its administration – now staffed with many of those who had received support as civil society and union protagonists – became the main recipients of financial and technical assistance. Between 1994–1999, a whole range of bi- and multilateral donors addressed the education sector, amongst others Denmark, the Netherlands, Finland, Sweden, the United Kingdom, Ireland, Germany, Belgium, Japan, Canada and the United States (Ngeleza et al. 2000). The majority of their funding was spent on human resource development (e.g. teacher training), followed by school building, the development of new institutions (notably the South African Qualifications Authority), mathematics, science and technology programmes and curriculum development (Ngeleza et al. 2000). Hence, aid was used in almost all areas in order to build a new education and training system.

During what we demarcate as the third phase starting in the mid-2000s, both the scope of aid and the number of donors significantly diminished. After a decade in which new policies, institutions and structures had been put in place, many foreign supporters pulled back from the education sector or phased out ODA to South Africa in general. While the Department of Higher Education and Training continues to cooperate with a range of partners, the only donor from which the Department of Basic Education received additional funds during the fiscal years 2010–2013 was the European Union (Department of Basic Education 2011, 2012, 2013). The government went over to using the remaining aid resources for niche areas (e.g. inclusive education) or innovative pilot projects which would otherwise be difficult to undertake, given the pressure of national and provincial education budgets (Fölscher et al. 2010).

Starting from scratch: The creation of a post-apartheid education vision

Design of a policy to radically overhaul the South African education system had already started prior to the official end of apartheid. In the late 1980s and early 1990s, key players of the anti-apartheid movement began to liaise with counterparts and like-minded organisations abroad in order to develop visions for education in a new democratic South Africa. Funded by an NGO called Australian People for Health, Education and Development Abroad (APHEDA) and by the Swedish Sida, the National Union of Metalworkers (Numsa) and the Congress of South African Trade Unions (COSATU) carried out research projects which included travels to both developing and industrialised countries. The exchange with colleagues in Australia, in particular, heavily influenced the thinking of South African union leaders (Carton & King 2004; Badroodien & McGrath 2005).[190] A leading protagonist involved summarised the phase of policy exploration as follows:

> *We had ideas of what we wanted and how we wanted to do it – but we were keen to learn other ways, to hear ideas.* (Interview 20)

A unified attempt to conceptualise a future education and training system was undertaken in 1993 through the National Training Strategy Initiative (NTSI) which for the first time brought actors from the government in power and its opponents to one table. Faced with dysfunctional and racially divided schools, masses of illiterate and insufficiently trained people, and a fragmented governance system, including 19 disconnected departments of education, the

---

190 Details on the Numsa Vocational Training Project and the COSATU Participatory Research Project which had a great influence on the thinking of lead unionists are provided by Carton and King (2004) and Badroodien and McGrath (2005).

list of issues to be addressed was virtually endless. The challenges confronted with ranged from overcoming materially and symbolically the racial inequalities of the apartheid system to establishing a legitimate governance for all educational institutions, and from reducing spending on personnel to designing new curricula, assessment and accrediting procedures. Also, the national system of examinations and their results had to be reorganised and the teachers' capacity to participate and get engaged in these efforts developed (Christie 2006: 376).

The National Training Board, at that time an advisory body to the 'Minister of Manpower', formed a National Task Team comprising eight committees including representatives from the state, trade unions, employers, providers of education and training, the ANC Education Department, and the democratic alliance movement. Each of the eight working groups was commissioned to investigate a certain topic with a view to South Africa's situation, ranging from integrated career paths and certificates to legislation and financing.[191] Task group 7 was charged with compiling an international overview on 'systems building', drawing on experiences from industrialised countries, emerging markets and developing states (Heitmann 2010).[192] The research of this working group was supported by various donors, most notably Germany, which sponsored study tours to their own but also to other countries. Members of the task group thus travelled extensively to distil lessons and best practices from successful vocational education and training systems around the world. Their findings strongly shaped the principles and ideas adopted in the Discussion Document on a National Training Strategy Initiative which came out of the NTSI process in 1994 (National Training Board 1994). A key person who was part of the National Task Team described the influence of the international comparative work on the preliminary policy document as follows:

> *It's very hard to distinguish between what came from the other countries and what was the product of debate here. A lot of people were reflecting on the experience here and drawing bits and pieces, like: We like this Scandinavian work on women's training. So we had extensive sections from Scandinavia, where we said, look, we've got to train women to do traditionally male work and things like that. We knew that – but to see it in practice was very encouraging, and we thought now we can do this.*
>
> *And there were other things from other countries, I mean, we've known some stuff from some countries in Africa even who had come from a similar*

---

191 For a detailed list of the eight task groups established, see Heitmann (2010: 104–105).

192 The countries included in the analysis were Australia, Brazil, Germany, England, Malaysia, Singapore, Tanzania and Zimbabwe.

context to us. So that amalgam pot that had been created was captured into a policy document which included a chapter on international experience and was then used as a (…) first training document that had been agreed between the old apartheid officials and the new ones coming from the trade union movement. (Interview 20)

The centrepiece of the proposed model was a single National Qualification Framework which would fully integrate general education and vocational training in a system of life-long learning. Key to the concept was the idea that skills, knowledge and abilities would be measured against a general qualification scale which is so to speak 'blind' as to where those have been acquired – whether in a full-time or part-time school, at the workplace, by distance education, at college or university, or a combination of different sites. Most notably, it would also take into account learning that took place outside formal institutions and thereby "give value to the kind of learning people have already achieved in their lives" (Human Sciences Research Council 1995: 3, as reprinted in South African Qualifications Authority 2012). People would receive transferable credits for their competencies which would allow them to move across different fields and to progress within education, training and career paths. The features of the construct thus signalled a transformative endeavour which becomes apparent if one considers the prevailing conditions at the end of the apartheid era: the majority of the population had received few years of schooling and lacked formal qualifications which denied them access to and promotion in the labour market. The new model aimed at redressing the discrimination in education, training and employment opportunities by removing the "obsession with institutional learning as the measure of a person's worth" (Human Sciences Research Council 1995: 12, as reprinted in South African Qualifications Authority 2012). Instead, learning outcomes were to be the decisive denominator for qualification in a system which gives equal value to education and training.

Adopting the principles of outcomes-based learning, integration and progression, the NQF proposal was heavily influenced by education and training systems applied in other countries. In some Anglo-Saxon states, the concept of National Qualification Frameworks had evolved during the late 1980s. South Africa strongly followed the New Zealand model in that it envisaged a comprehensive framework for all sectors and a unified quality assurance system. Whereas the New Zealand model was favoured by business representatives, union members leaned on Australia's competency-based education approach which allowed for incremental learning (Keevy 2013); the latter was seen as a crucial aspect in the South African context, as an official who was member of the task team explained:

> *Within the trade union movement we had started (…) a policy debate and visited Australia in 1990 and they were talking policy ideas that I was extensively influenced by. I still think they were great, whether they were implementable in the form we thought, that's another story. But those [were] ideas which had to do with a national qualification framework and the ideas that workers could come in at a low level and could progress. Now the German system is more: you get a good schooling and then you train. In South Africa, you have many, many people who have not had a good schooling, so we were very keen to look at this progression idea that you might start as a semi-skilled worker [and] learn skills incrementally.* (Interview 20)[193]

Inspired by Australia's competency-centred approach, unionists advocated an outcomes-based system which would allow flexible career paths, offer lifelong learning opportunities and link education and skills ladders. Integrating general education and vocational training was deemed crucial to eliminate the hierarchy between the two. Labour representatives, sympathising with the German dual system, conveyed the view that in a new democratic South Africa vocational training "should stand alongside the academic tradition with its head held high" (Interview 20).

Although the blueprint NQF presented in the Discussion Document thus entailed elements which had been adopted from outside, it was widely conceived as a product of South African origin and debate. In part, this was a result of the National Task Teams' resolved adaptation of the findings from the international experiences into local policies. The team explicitly criticised the 'importation' of external models without adaptation to the local context as 'highly undesirable', emphasising that a future education system must "be *indigenous* to the needs of South Africa to suit our needs, cultures and values" (National Training Board 1994: 7 as cited in Carton & King 2004: 24). Nonetheless, it was seen as helpful to take cognisance of others' experiences. An actor involved commented on the extent of external influence as follows:

> *We were quite heavily influenced – but we were influenced because it served our purpose, it met a need for us (…). And whilst I don't see external influence in the sense of individuals come into play, I see those ideas straining a little against each other, trying to find the best of combination.* (Interview 20)

---

193 Referring to key role players, Carton and King (2004) describe in detail how the strong linkages between Australian and South African metal unionists evolved and how this exchange subsequently influenced the unions' positioning in the policy debate.

It is to be stressed here that external policy ideas and concepts were induced by committee members connecting with specialists abroad, rather than imparted by consultants from outside. Although foreign governments certainly had an interest in offering and promoting their own educational models to the emerging decision-makers of the new South Africa, their role was restricted to facilitating the process of policy exploration. International study tours and workshops created a space for knowledge sharing and selective borrowing that was not confined to the donors' own territories or expert communities but determined by local stakeholders (Carton & King 2004: 20). Hence, the policy document which came out of the National Training Strategy Initiative was seen as the outcome of a participatory, locally directed process, expressing a joint vision of post-apartheid education and training (Carton & King 2004).

Shortly after the first democratic elections in 1994, the newly formed Government of National Unity presented its *White Paper on Education and Training in a Democratic South Africa: First Steps to Develop a New System* to the public which broadly incorporated the principles of the Discussion Document (Department of Education 1995). In October 1995, the parliament passed the South African Qualifications Authority Act (No. 58 of 1995) which formally introduced an integrative NQF approach and created the South African Qualifications Authority (SAQA) as a parastatal body responsible for developing and implementing the NQF (Republic of South Africa 1995).

The Act thus laid the legal foundation for the transformation of the education system, institutions and structures such as quality assurance bodies, although new outcomes-based curricula and funding frameworks were still to be designed and set up. Coping with the scale of the radical reform would have been difficult enough for any administration, even in firmly established democracies. In South Africa, the situation was exacerbated by the fact that the authorities faced with this challenge were themselves in a state of flux, both in terms of structures and personnel. People from the democratic movement who entered bureaucratic bodies were highly committed to bring about change, but "did not, by definition, bring years of experience to the work of government administration" (Bird 2001: 266). They found themselves in a vibrant, but still fragile working environment and were confronted with a massive task which required both governance and specialist knowledge. The decision to approach donors for support was thus not only based on financial demand, but also on the need for external expertise, as a high-ranking official in the Department of Labour pointed out:

> *In order to change the whole system, we had to come up with a new legislation, new systems, processes, procedures and we wanted to deliver*

on a mass scale, we wanted to come up with a funding framework. And all those things could not have been achieved [without external support] because we didn't have local expertise. (Interview 22)

Bringing aid into line with the local agenda: The case of higher education

The two line departments in charge of education and training, the Department of Education and the Department of Labour thus entered into negotiations with the aid community which seemed eager to provide assistance. In the early years of democracy, "requests for educational collaboration were arriving virtually on a daily basis from prospective partners as large as the Russian Federation and as small as Croatia" (King 1999: 260–261). A high-ranking official who then worked for DoE described the dynamism of donor meetings during that time:

> *I must say that in the beginning it was like, it was a wonderful terrain to work in. You had 23, 24 partner countries all in one room and what we would do is, we would give them our priorities for the three years – this is what, where do you see yourself fitting in? Okay? America said: 'We want to do curriculum development'. Japan: 'Oh no, we will give support for schools (…)'. Germany: 'No, we have got skills, you know, yes, we can work with the Department of Labour and give a little support here to science education', for example. (…) So donor coordination meetings were critical – firstly, to share with them our plans, to get buy-in, to say 'look, this is where we get to go' or 'this is where we are going to collaborate with another donor'.* (Interview 21)

Naturally, not all went well in the beginning. In contrast to non-state actors, government authorities in the education and labour sectors had absolutely no experience in dealing with aid; hence, "the complex universe of development cooperation was an unknown quantity" for them (King 1999: 261). Aside from the pressure of meeting multiple donor requirements and procedures which, as one official stated, were a 'nightmare' during the first years, it proved difficult to get external assistance under control: the line departments soon realised that aid providers also used other entry-points to offer their services, particularly the provincial governments which were responsible for delivering reforms at the classroom level. Given that these implementing authorities did not sit around the table in national negotiations, aid projects often ran parallel and uncoordinated; in the worst case, high expectations were belied, as an official remarked:

Then you get a call later [from a provincial official] saying, 'but you know, Mr So and So came to our province, he promised us X, Y, and Z, I've never seen him again'. So we had to coordinate this thing much more effectively. And only after years did we manage to get the coordination. (Interview 21)

It also became apparent that donors, although being supportive of South Africa's transformative agenda, had their own interests and priorities. This was evident in that they clearly focused their support on areas which were historically relevant to them; a government official commented:

Obviously, the donors also had their own intelligence gathering – they knew exactly where and who they want to support, where their missionaries were before, and now they were closely related to those geographic areas and therefore they wanted to support them. (Interview 21)

For South African negotiators, it often turned out challenging to shift support to geographic and subject areas identified as being in particular need of technical assistance or funding. A case in point in which a mismatch of priorities became manifest was the struggle for aid to the higher education sector. From the government's point of view, higher education was a key issue to be addressed in order to foster national development and social change in post-apartheid South Africa. The first *White Paper on Education and Training*, recognising "the massive influence which higher education experts on the cultural, social, scientific, technological and professional formation of the country's leadership" (Department of Education 1995), emphasised the need to tackle the various challenges of the system, including fragmented structures, chronic financial pressure and absorption difficulties. Transforming the higher education landscape and advancing access to universities and tertiary learning institutions for students from historically disadvantaged communities were thus central concerns of decision-makers in the then Department of Education, as an interviewee involved pointed out:

Our view even at that stage when we were still a single department was that the heart of the system was higher education, was universities. If you get that wrong, you can't train – you can't train your intellectuals, you can't train your teachers, you can't train anyone. (Interview 21)

Yet, the focus on higher education was not in line with the international agenda of that time. The government's request for support targeting higher education reform engendered little response from the aid community. Only a few development partners, notably Finland and Norway, promptly catered to the priorities articulated by the Department of Education by setting up programmes which addressed higher education issues.[194] The majority of donors preferred to give resources for basic learning needs and schooling – hence for matters which had been strongly pushed by the international community since the Jomtien World Conference (1990) and the related Education for All movement during the 1990s (World Conference on Education for All 1990). Officials negotiating with donor representatives on behalf of DoE had to make strenuous efforts to attract assistance for higher education priorities from their international counterparts:

> *We kept on having to make overtures and to give more bides for higher education because they just wouldn't bid (…). A few scholarships were thrown in. But that wasn't what we wanted. We wanted budgetary support to reconfigure, restructure our higher education system. And I think that's what we managed to do and we got support.* (Interview 21)

The persistence of South African officials in bargaining aid evidently bore fruit. According to an evaluation of development cooperation during 1994–1999, 46% of official development assistance to the education sector was channelled to higher education (Ngeleza et al. 2000). The review team found that overall objectives of ODA were well aligned to those of the national and provincial departments of education, and that the distribution of aid "closely mirrored the prioritisation of the South African government" (Ngeleza et al. 2000: 14). The success of department officials in bringing aid into line with the South African agenda mainly rested on two structural advantages. First, despite financial needs, the education sector was not substantially dependent on donor money. Second, since many international players competed to be part of South Africa's educational transformation, government negotiators had a strategically advantageous position in which they were able to set the direction and conditions of support, as a former DoE official indicated:

> *We could be slightly cheeky to a donor to say 'no, thank you – another partner is going to come (…)'. And so we could push the envelope and say: 'No that's not what we want. We want this instead. We want you to support us in developing X, Y, Z.' I think in retrospect why we could*

194 Pertinent programmes set up to target higher education issues were the South African–Norway Tertiary Education Development Project (SANTED) which focused on enhancing access for and retention of people from previously discriminated groups and capacity-building of historically disadvantaged institutions, and the South African–Finnish Co-operation Programme in the Education Sector (SCOPE), which, amongst others, helped to transfer teacher education and training into higher education.

get possibly the highest percentage of support to higher education, to universities, was because we could be cheeky. We could tell the donors: Either you support it or not. But we can assure you that we will do it either way. (Interview 21)

The relative financial strength and the role as much-courted recipient enabled the Department of Education to strategically decide whose support and which kind to accept. In doing so, it adopted a rather wary attitude towards external expertise. Advisors or consultants were only brought in after thorough consideration for specific, clearly determined tasks; most notably, department leaders were vigilant about keeping foreign actors outside the centre of decision-making. As the following statement reflects, this caution had grown out of both a strong notion of self-reliance among the new leadership ranks and their awareness of the risks that advice from outside entailed:

So we had that possibility now to shape and to change things, to use our own policy-makers and we have had the years of international exposure and experience to develop our policies. So never did we have experts or foreign policy people in our policy discussions to decide and to determine the route that we are going to take. And it's not in a kind of arrogant way that we didn't want that, but we've understood also what has been happening in other countries. We have had obviously technical advice and expertise coming from all over the show [but] we've used that expertise to support our policy development agenda. (Interview 21)

There is one exception to this: in the area of vocational education and training decision-makers in charge have extensively drawn on external expertise to realise South African policy visions. In particular, the close and long-term cooperation with the German GIZ had a profound impact on policies and institutions addressing skills development in the new South Africa.

Expert involvement in constructing a new skills development architecture

When the democratic government came into power in 1994, it inherited an extremely poor skills regime which neither met the needs of society nor of the economy. With the majority of the population being insufficiently or inappropriately trained, the country faced a severe skills shortage across all sectors which had a negative effect on productivity and industrial competitiveness. The situation was a result of decades of apartheid rule under which institutionalised vocational education and training barely existed and non-formal skills training hardly provided prospects of qualification and employment (Heitmann 2010: 101–102). Thus, it became a central concern of policy-makers in the Department of Labour (DoL) that bore the political responsibility for occupational training to enhance the skills base of workers and unemployed citizens by creating a new, demand-driven skills development system.

Germany was the donor that, from the outset, lent its support to the envisaged reform. Already before entering an official agreement which defined skills development as one of three focus areas of bilateral cooperation, the German government had funded studies, invested in teacher training and supported the National Training Strategy Initiative in exploring vocational education and training systems in other countries. While by the mid-1990s almost all aid organisations had turned to basic education, the GTZ, as Germany's implementing agency for development cooperation, maintained its focus on skills development and offered significant in-house expertise in this field (Carton & King 2004).[195] When in 1996 the Department of Labour put in place a new chief directorate charged with developing policy and legal frameworks for a new skills development regime, it was agreed that GTZ would provide support to the process through a broad-based sector programme which included financial and technical assistance. In the course of the so-called 'Skills Development Strategy Initiative (SDSI) Support Programme' and related projects,[196] a close relationship between senior officials in the DoL and GTZ staff developed. The then head of the Pretoria country office became highly appreciated by key actors on the South African side for his flexibility in responding to the department's needs and his approach of catering advice to the local agenda. A decision-maker in the Department of Labour described the contribution of the GTZ director as follows:

---

195 As Carton and King (2004: 19) point out, GTZ obviously had a unique selling point at that time since the presence of donor staff with expertise on labour skills was significantly diminished by the mid to late 1990s: "Sida had only one vocational in-house expert left by the end of the decade, and DFID had none. Meanwhile the once very large staff of technical educators in the Bank had almost disappeared. CIDA too had no in-house professional capacity left. (…) Danida and Irish Aid, which were both to play important roles in relation to South Africa, drew more on the experience of Danish consulting firms and of FAS International Consulting (the commercial subsidiary of Ireland's Training and Employment Authority) than on their own staff."

196 The DoL has collaborated with GTZ since 1996 through various skills development and labour-market-related projects which in 2007 were merged under the umbrella of the 'Employment and Skills Development Service (ESDS) Programme'. Running until 2011, the ESDS programme focused on the development of skills development systems for the first (formal) and the second (informal) labour market and the establishment of a technology transfer network system for small and medium-sized enterprises (GTZ 2007). South African–German cooperation in that field took place also through other organisations such as the Centre for International Migration and Development (CIM), DED and InWEnt who seconded experts and provided training for college teachers and private company managers; moreover, German provincial states ('Bundesländer') such as Bavaria and Lower Saxony established an exchange of experts with partner provinces in South Africa (Department of Labour & GTZ 2008: 7).

He came to assist – he didn't come to tell us. And that was the big difference.
Because once you had a personal debate with him I think he was quick to
understand that the South African situation is completely different from
the German situation. (…) He would go out and research what is it that
we are trying to do and find out very good learning experiences from other
places – he would say 'look, this is what has happened in Sweden, this is
what has happened in, for instance, Zimbabwe, (…). I know this is what
you are trying but in these other places, this is how they approach this
issue and it seems as if you have got these options, these are consequences.'
And where he could not come up with a clear recommendation, he phoned
other people that he was working with to search for the solutions that
were used in their countries and what were some of the problems. And
he would get that information to us, so that we are able to get a balance.
(Interview 22)

In view of the internal capacity constraints of the newly established skills
unit in the Department of Labour, the assistance of GTZ in exploring how the
policy ideas for a new skills regime could be translated into action was highly
valued. Most effective: the advice provided by experts funded or employed by
GTZ was perceived as being geared to the local agenda, rather than driven by
external preferences. The German so-called 'dual system' with its combination
of theoretical and practical learning served as a central reference for advisors,
but that did not foreclose that experiences and models from elsewhere were
equally scrutinised for ideas and models that South Africa could take from
them to develop its own unique institutions.

The *Green Paper: Skills Development Strategy for Economic and Employment*
Growth in South Africa, presented in 1997, sketched out core elements of the
envisioned new system through which the government hoped to bring about
the urgently needed "skills revolution" (Department of Labour 1997). First
and foremost, it proposed the introduction of 'learnerships'. As opposed to
the previous apprenticeships which offered only a minimal level of theoretical
knowledge often unrelated to skills required at the workplace, learnerships
aimed at combining career-related learning in an accredited education and
training institution with practical on-the-job experience; having succeeded
in both areas, learners would obtain a registered occupational qualification
signifying their work readiness (Department of Labour 1997). A key feature
of the approach was that contrary to apprenticeships it appealed to a wide
range of learners in multiple occupational contexts irrespective of their age

and employment status (Kraak 2004).[197] As funding mechanism, a compulsory levy-grant scheme on payroll would be introduced; of the total revenue collected, 80% was meant to be channelled back to the sector via grants to enterprises that train, and 20% to a National Skills Fund to be used for strategic priority areas (Kraak 2004). The re-allocation of levies was to be managed by Sector Education and Training Authorities (SETAs)[198] which would replace the previous Industry Training Boards and function as intermediary institutions commissioned to coordinate skills development in their respective sector. A central role in the new system was given to the National Skills Authority (NSA) which would substitute the National Training Board as an advisory body to the government, responsible for defining skills development policies and priorities in consultation with the Department of Labour (Department of Labour 1997). Both SETAs and the NSA should be governed by multipartite boards composed of representatives from government, employers and trade unions (Kraak 2004); the 'social partnership' between these stakeholders was seen as a crucial principle in the post-apartheid skills regime (Heitmann 2010).

The mechanisms and institutions proposed in the *Green Paper* of 1997 were formally established through a range of laws passed in subsequent years, most notably the Skills Development Act of 1998 (Republic of South Africa 1998b) and the Skills Development Levies Act of 1999 (Republic of South Africa 1999). While the reform was an ambitious endeavour due to the mere number of innovations, the government was under immense pressure to set up the new architecture promptly in order to ease the social situation and relieve the stressed economy by delivering skilled workers. In view of the urgency of the reform, the dimension of the workload and the rather small cadre of experienced officials in the Department of Labour, decision-makers approached the aid community for support. External assistance was considered necessary to get the basic infrastructure and frameworks set up in a foreseeable time frame (Carton & King 2004). Hence, the DoL entered into agreements with a number of donors willing to provide financial and technical assistance, including GTZ, Danida, AusAid, Ireland Aid, USAID, the Netherlands Embassy, Korea, and the European Union; the latter accounted for the bulk of support, pledging EUR 46 million over a period of three years (Moodley & Vawda 2000).[199] Various stand-alone projects were started, but all

---

197 For a detailed itemisation of learnership features as opposed to the past apprenticeship system, see Kraak (2004: 120–124).

198 This is how the intermediary bodies were eventually termed. In the *Green Paper*, they were presented as Sector Education and Training Organisations (SETOs).

199 Out of the EUR 46 million committed by the EU, EUR 30 million were to be channelled to the DoL as work plan funds, almost EUR 14 million were set aside for consulting companies and the remaining kept for contingency. At that time, the EU support was the largest technical assistance programme of its kind in the world (Moodley & Vawda 2000).

of them were aligned to an operational strategy of the Department of Labour, the so-called Labour Market Skills Development Programme (LMSDP) which served as an umbrella framework for the implementation of the skills Acts. The Employment and Skills Development Chief Directorate which had designed the strategy took on an active leadership role in allocating resources to the different programmatic components.

Foreign funding significantly backed up the financing of the reform, but the delivery of expertise was the more substantial element of aid in the context of the LMSDP. The EU agreement alone covered more than eleven hundred consultancy months (Moodley & Vawda 2000). Experts from both South Africa and abroad were used to execute critical tasks for which the DoL lacked staff of its own. GTZ consultants, for instance, were contracted to develop detailed guidelines for learnerships, to assist in demarcating SETAs and to train National Standard Body members for their critical role in relation to the National Qualification Framework. Teams of specialists from different EU countries were commissioned to work on various technical issues, for example, to sketch technicalities of the envisaged levy grant system (Moodley & Vawda 2000).[200] All personnel brought in from outside had to report to the respective unit heads in DoL who issued directives, as a high-ranking official emphasised:

> *We told them what exactly we would have to achieve – and they would never do anything else.* (Interview 22)

Hence, although a large number of external experts were intensely involved in key issues of the reform, the process was led by the Department of Labour. The crucial point is that essential decisions were made before consultants were brought in to operationalise the nationally negotiated vision of a new skills system. The recourse to donor support allowed the government to speed up the implementation of reform by trying out and bringing to scale key innovative schemes (e.g. learnerships) within a narrow time frame and thus to meet its own deadlines (Carton & King 2004).[201] By the turn of the millennium, a radically revamped skills development architecture with a range of new

---

200 The EU project drew on consultancy consortia from several countries which were selected through a competitive bidding process (Carton & King 2004). The tendering procedure prescribed by the EU, however, was criticised not only for being lengthy and cumbersome, but also for disadvantaging companies from outside the EU. A review stated that "the perception in the DoL is that the criteria excluded many capable South African organisations from effectively competing" (Moodley & Vawda 2000: 34). In fact, almost all contracted companies were European.

201 A valuable project which helped to refine a new approach was carried out by Danida in KwaZulu-Natal where learnerships in the construction and tourism industries were tested; the experiences gained in that two-year pilot were taken up in the process of adjusting the learnership model before taking it to scale (Carton & King 2004).

institutions and governance bodies had been set up – from the perspective of key protagonists, it is unlikely that this would have happened at the same pace without external assistance.

Governance challenges, structural revisions and changing relationships

The integrative education and training system built by the first government of post-apartheid South Africa was internationally regarded as ambitious and ground-breaking; yet, getting this system to run and to deliver turned out to be challenging. While policies, laws and institutions had been put in place in quick succession, transformation on the ground could not keep pace. Difficulties emerged at various levels. Teachers in schools were struggling to implement the new outcomes-based curriculum (known as 'Curriculum 2005' and introduced in 1997), since they were unfamiliar with its concepts and felt alienated by its terminology (Chisholm 2003, 2005). The newly established SETAs faced severe governance problems, including financial mismanagement and fraud (Smith et al. 2005; Kraak 2008). Employers only slowly began to take up learnerships and showed little commitment to proactively invest in training (Moleke 2003). Although they generally embraced the new approach, many companies perceived processes as unduly bureaucratic and felt unprepared to offer learnership agreements (Mummenthey 2008). Hence, despite 'pockets of progress' in terms of enhancing the skills base and redressing apartheid's inequities, education and employment patterns remained racially skewed (Moleke 2003).[202]

A fundamental problem which indirectly contributed to the stagnation was the deep division between the Department of Education and the Department of Labour (Bird & Heitmann 2011). The decision to keep these two separate ministries – with the former being responsible for education and training in public institutions (i.e. schools, colleges and universities) and the latter for private providers of learning in the labour market – instead of merging them into one as expected in the early 1990s – had "serious ramifications, most importantly the failure of the new state to discard the political fiefdoms and territorial modes of working that characterised the divide between 'education' and 'training' in the apartheid state" (Kraak 2008). Both in a way pursued their own incoherent skills development agendas based on divergent philosophies, as a former DoL official pointed out:

---

202 Kraak (2008) delineates some successes achieved during the first phase of the National Skills Development Strategy; amongst others, more than 6 million workers out of a total employed workforce of 10,8 million people embarked on and finished structured learning programmes over a four-year period; moreover, almost 900 000 achieved a National Qualifications Framework Level One qualification through adult basic education and training in the workplace. Yet, as Kraak himself emphasises, other scholars have raised doubts about the validity of these government data.

> *The Department of Labour was influenced I think quite a lot by the German thinking about skilled training, vocational training in particular. But the colleagues in education were moving things by the British. So you had one department influenced by the Germanic tradition and another department influenced by I think the Anglo-Saxon idea. And that led to quite a lot of tension.* (Interview 20)

The discrepancies between the two ministries manifested in a range of laws and strategy documents issued by both sides which lacked interrelation and in some cases even contradicted each other (Allais 2006; 2010).[203] The tension between education and labour-side actors culminated when the minister of education in 2000 announced a first review of the National Qualifications Framework for which both departments shared responsibility. After much contestation as to whether there should be an assessment at such an early stage and what it should look like, an international study team comprising South African and foreign experts was commissioned to scrutinise the NQF with regard to its implementation (without probing its design) (Allais 2010). Finding that "broad malaise of discontent with the NQF and SAQA had taken hold among stakeholders" (Department of Education & Department of Labour 2002: 3), the authors provided a range of recommendations to overcome obstacles and take the process of implementing the NQF forward. Yet, the release of the report in 2002 was followed by years of inactivity and silence, although the DoE and DoL had brought themselves to publish a joint response in the form of a consultative document (Department of Education & Department of Labour 2003). Eventually, it took six years until an agreement was reached to make substantial changes through a set of (amendment) bills passed in 2008 (Allais 2010).[204] The reform provided for the split of the single, integrated NQF into three linked sub-frameworks managed by respective quality assurance bodies, namely Umalusi as Quality Council for General and Further Education and Training, the Quality Council for Higher Education (QCHE) covering the academic sector and the Quality Council for Trades and Occupations (QCTO) in charge of learning in a workplace context. Hence, while the NQF continued

---

203 Several scholars hint at incoherent or conflicting legislation and structures related to further/ vocational education and training, and the resulting confusion of role-players in the field. Allais (2006) provides a detailed account of conflicts over roles and responsibilities particularly with regard to quality assurance and certification. Bird and Heitmann (2011: 10) note that the Further Education and Training Colleges Act No. 16 of 2006 initiated by the Department of Education and the Department of Labour's Skills Development Amendment Act No. 37 of 2008 that followed shortly after did "not complement one another in any systematic way".

204 These included the National Qualifications Framework Act No. 67 of 2008, the General and Further Education and Training Quality Assurance Amendment Act No. 50 of 2008, the Skills Development Amendment Act No. 37 of 2008, and the Higher Education Amendment Act No. 39 of 2008 (Republic of South Africa 2008a, 2008b, 2009b, 2009c).

to exist as a 'meta'-framework and SAQA remained the national oversight and coordinating body, responsibilities and structures were significantly reconfigured (see Keevy 2013).

The complex task of establishing this new system was exacerbated by a major reorganisation of line departments which followed shortly after the legislative changes. President Zuma, who came to power in 2009, decided to divide the Department of Education into one for Basic Education and one for Higher Education and Training which would carry over skills development (hence also for SETAs and the newly established QCTO) from Labour (Khumalo 2009). Shifting the responsibility for all post-school education and training was seen as an attempt to overcome the persistent conflicts which had blocked progress over the past decade.

While many stakeholders welcomed this move, it involved the reallocation of staff which inevitably weakened administration in affected government units; in particular, the Department of Labour, which had lost the skills development branch to DHET, felt drained of experienced bureaucrats. In addition, it became evident how much the DoL and related bodies had relied on external expertise provided by long-standing partners. According to the head of the Employment and Skills Development Services (ESDS) Programme of GTZ who took the lead in 2009, the programme had about 120 consultancy contracts running at that time:

> *Small ones, big ones, but too many. And I've never experienced a project with so many contracts. And I was asking my predecessor, why do you have so many consultants employed? He said 'it's because there is no capacity with our partners'. (…) He had contracts with universities, with the research councils, all the experts in South Africa on skills development were on our payroll.* (Interview 2)

With the shift of political responsibilities, GTZ and other supporters turned towards new counterparts in the field. For DoL, this shift meant a severe loss of administrative capacity, as a decision-maker in the employment services branch pointed out:

> *Once [the programme] moved, the capacity disappeared and caused challenges (…). And that unfortunately is a setback because you can make that assumption if people who started were still there, but the minute they are gone through this transfer and so on, it's like going four years ahead and then six years back. It becomes a problem because all the senior people had left here, almost all of the seconded experts that were working here. So it becomes very difficult.* (Interview 22)

The technical assistants provided by GTZ and other aid agencies had functioned as an 'extra pair of hands' in various DoL units since the beginning of South Africa's education and training transition, but their support obviously had not resulted in a strengthened administrative capacity of their host organisation. Already by 2000 a team reviewing ODA had warned that the use of external specialists who executed key tasks instead of mentoring officials would result in 'minimal skills transfer' and pose a serious challenge for the DoL once projects ended (Moodley & Vawda 2000).[205] Almost a decade later, this scenario occurred, and the Department of Labour struggled to substitute the withdrawn specialists.

Yet, not only government authorities faced difficulties in the course of the restructuring process. Donors as well had to adjust their programmes and establish relationships with new partners who themselves were trying to gain safe ground. As of 2011, the previously much-lauded Employment and Skills Development Services (ESDS) programme of GIZ (formerly GTZ) had reached deadlock since GIZ representatives were unable to enter into a dialogue with DHET decision-makers. For the head of the programme in the Pretoria country office, this caused mounting pressure as he was unable to demonstrate progress and thereby legitimate the on-going operations before headquarters in Germany. In late 2011, his frustration had reached a point where he felt compelled to call in political authorities in order to enforce communication with DHET decision-makers:

> So now what I try to do is, when you don't get a response from a counterpart you invite for meetings (…), you use diplomatic interventions and this is what I have done. And diplomatic interventions I have to use in case, because it's a lot of resources. If let's say advisors are not needed, then I have to communicate this. I cannot just assume, ah, we have some progress here and there. You can cover up for 6 months maybe. But in this case, I really used the escalation ladder from zero to, I don't know, the highest level. There was one letter sent from our ministry in Germany through the Embassy warning 'if you don't come to a conclusion now, we will wind down the project', very clearly. Then they reacted. (…)
>
> And tomorrow we have consultations with Higher Education and Training. When I saw the people on the list that will come to the meeting,

---

205 The review team stated in this regard: "As the practice of Technical Assistance is new within the DoL, officials have minimal capacity to effectively and efficiently utilise and absorb technical assistants into project activities and tasks. (…) With the already extensive and intensive workload, and inadequate number of staff to execute tasks, skills transfer is an additional challenge" (Moodley & Vawda 2000: 15).

it's a shame. It's really a shame. Two people from international relations and only one technical person from the National Skills Fund; there's only one person who really knows about the subject. So I don't understand – we requested on the level of DG, please provide the DDGs for the meetings and technical people. (Interview 2)

The head of the GIZ programme felt uncertain about whether to interpret the bearing of the counterpart as a lack of leadership, sign of disinterest – or simply as the result of the persisting capacity constraints in the department, which, after two years since its formal inception, was still struggling to adequately staff the department. During 2011/2012, DHET's vacancy rate remained high at 21.73%, and many crucial positions at the senior level (e.g. directors) had not yet been filled (Department of Higher Education and Training 2012a).[206] In light of the fact that officials in place were already over-stretched with day-to-day operations, it is not surprising that donor meetings were not attended or repeatedly postponed, which left programme leaders somewhat in the dark about their new counterpart's vision. The GIZ director commented in this regard:

There was almost no donor coordination for the last two years. There was a DG, Mary Metcalfe, until September last year, then we have DG Qonde, and each of the DGs just had one donor meeting. And on donor side, we have an interest to know the policy of the department vis-à-vis cooperation, what are other development partners doing and all this kind of exchange. But it was very clear in our case that the Department of Higher Education and Training just didn't request for that. (Interview 2)

Discussing the GIZ's discontent and frustration about DHET's disregard, a high-ranking official who had closely collaborated with the Germans during her previous appointment in the Department of Labour provided the following explanation for the gridlock in cooperation:

---

206 According to DHET's Annual Report, the slow progress in staff appointment was caused by both insufficient funding and the difficulty in finding people with adequate expertise and experience: "The specialised nature of work in most of the areas of the Department necessitates the use of highly skilled people who are at some stages not readily available for permanent appointment and have to be appointed on contract for periods as may be required. (...) Some identified critical vacancies could not be filled due to limited funding. The prescribed time frame of four months for the filling of vacancies in some instances is not met or adhered to due to work pressure caused by the staff shortage in the HR section. We have identified a need for staff training and development and a request for the creation of additional posts was approved for filling in the new financial year" (Department of Higher Education and Training 2012a: 48–49).

I honestly believe it was a transitional problem that the German government got caught up in but which had nothing to do with them. What happened was the new department here was set up late 2009, it had to be staffed. There was a change of Director-General in the middle of that process, and that's a very important person in a new department. So that was still being sorted out. The new Director General, when he took over, he had to get his feel more secure around the policy debates and he didn't want to commit himself to projects and things before he had that. So I don't think it had anything to do with the German government or with any of the donors, I think it was a case of the department. What it reflects I think is that the South African government wants to lead any discussion – so it wants to be sure that it knows what it wants and why you're having a particular conversation. (Interview 20)

Eventually, the South African–German ESDS programme which had been running since 1995 ended in 2012. As a consequence of the tedious negotiations with DHET as counterpart during the last phase, GIZ decided to shift its focus to other players in the field when setting up a new programme called 'Skills Development for Green Jobs (SDfGJ)' (GIZ 2012b). While DHET formally remains one of the two 'lead executing agencies' (with the second one being the Department of Science and Technology), the actual cooperation takes place with other partners, such as the Office of the Premier in the Eastern Cape Province and the Manufacturing, Engineering and Related Services SETA (merSETA).[207] Both organisations are assisted in establishing 'green skills forums' in order to boost the 'green economy', with support including the secondment of advisors, study tours and training programmes.

Although GIZ promotes its new approach as a 'bottom-up strategy' with a "much greater potential for mainstreaming green skills" (GIZ 2012c), it is obvious that the shift towards this level was partly enforced by the fact that GIZ has lost its position in the policy-making space. While during the 15 years of cooperation with the Department of Labour, GTZ (as it was then called) had built itself up as an indispensable partner providing advice and assistance in the course of the education and training system reform, it was not able to transfer this relationship to DHET as the new political authority in charge. The reasons are at least twofold. First, the trust which allowed GTZ to be engaged in DoL processes rested to a significant extent on the personal bonds between key actors on both sides that had developed during more than a decade of

---

207 Moreover, the programme includes support to the Technology Innovation Agency (TIA) focusing on technology transfer which is a continuation of previous cooperation.

cooperation. The importance of this aspect was repeatedly addressed by interviewees involved, with one official stating:

> *It was a long-term partnership. If you speak to W. [the previous GTZ programme director], I know this is a strong point on his side that many donors work in the short-term, they go in, do a project and withdraw, and his feeling was always: No, you got to form partnerships at a personal level. And we certainly did form one with Werner.* (Interview 20)

As explained above, such social ties are a key element for advisory processes; yet, as they depend on "histories of interactions" (Nahapiet & Ghoshal 1998: 244), they cannot easily be passed on. Hence, it was not easy for the successor of the previous GTZ director to maintain the importance of the programme when he came into office in 2009 and even more difficult when it should be continued with DHET as the new partner.

Second, it seems that the nature of support sought by policy-makers in charge has changed. While they still signal interest in expertise and experiences from other countries, they seem to refrain from requesting direct advice and assistance in policy development. Instead of bringing in consultants from outside to provide 'hands-on' support to understaffed units, DHET appears to prefer a much looser form of cooperation, excluding external actors from decision-making. This is reflected by DHET's first major political undertaking of system reform in post-schooling education and training. The *Green Paper* released for discussion in early 2012 was largely a product of internal policy work (Department of Higher Education and Training 2012b). An extensive process of national discussion about the new post-school vision followed which included briefings, workshops and conferences with various stakeholders. International partners were invited to take part in some of these activities, but they did not play a decisive role therein. Moreover, the decision-making autonomy of the South African government was clearly evident throughout the process, as a GIZ interviewee commented:

> *In April [2012], there was a huge, international conference. We had two speakers here from BIBB [the German 'Federal Institute for Vocational Education and Training'] which was fine, that was great. But there were also Brazilians, people from Indonesia and Australia, six countries were represented, the Swiss as well. That means they [the South Africans] precisely pick what fits for them (…). And then it goes on: The South Africans have their own experts. Of course, they do not know the countries in great detail. But instead of bringing in consultants from Germany, they would compose a group of people travelling to Europe, visiting institutions,*

interviewing professors and practitioners, developers and others in ministries and organisations. They have money, they travel. (Interview 3)

The process of policy negotiation and refinement was firmly led by key actors within DHET (e.g. the Special Advisor to the Minister John Pampallis) who were assisted by a drafting team made up of six experts from South African research and advisory institutions, namely the Centre for Education Policy Development, the Centre for Researching Education and Labour of the University of Witwatersrand and Mzabalazo Advisory Services (Stuart 2014). After almost two years of consultation, in which nearly 200 public comments were received, the *White Paper for Post-School Education and Training* was finalised and approved by Cabinet in November 2013 (Department of Higher Education and Training 2013c). One of the main challenges it aims to address is providing prospects for young people who have hitherto fallen through the cracks, that is, the 3.4 million aged 15 to 24 currently not in employment, education or training (so-called 'NEETs'). To cater for youth and adults who have never attended school and therefore were excluded from further studies at colleges or universities, a new institutional type of 'community colleges' is envisaged, which is expected "to facilitate a cycle of lifelong learning in communities by enabling the development of skills (including literacy, numeracy and vocational skills) to enhance personal, social, family and employment experiences" (Department of Higher Education and Training 2013c: 22). Moreover, the previous further education and training (FET) colleges are to be rebranded Technical and Vocational Education and Training Colleges on the grounds that this name "better reflects their nature and better defines their main role in the diversified post-school education and training system", as DHET argues (Department of Higher Education and Training 2013c: 12). Turning TVET colleges into "institutions of choice" which constitute "the cornerstone of the country's skills development system" (Department of Higher Education and Training 2013c: 12) is a prime endeavour of the government which sets itself ambitious targets: by 2013, it wants to have 2.5 million students enrolled in TVET colleges (as compared to 500 000 in 2011), 1 million in community colleges (from 265 000 in public adult learning centres in 2011), and about 1.6 million students in universities (from just over 937 000 in 2011). At the time of writing, it is too early to assess the likelihood of success.

Conclusion

When assessing the impact of foreign aid on education and training in post-apartheid South Africa, the judgement has to be differentiated: certainly, financial and technical assistance significantly helped to revamp structures at a pace which would not have been possible had the government relied on its own resources. Also, study tours sponsored and/or facilitated by donors conveyed models and ideas from abroad which inspired the thinking of key protagonists involved in shaping a new system for the country. Despite extensive foreign support, however, "the overall negotiation for a new skills architecture has firmly been in South African hands" (Carton & King 2004: 31). That policy-makers, while drawing on external expertise and resources, managed to retain their decision-making autonomy appears to rest on at least four reasons. First, the sector was not financially dependent on donors. This is not to say that additional funding was not needed; yet, aid did not make up a substantial part of the budget. This allowed negotiators to tell international financiers:

> *Either you support it but we can assure you that we will do it either way.*
> *It's just going to take a slightly longer because we'll have to wait, but we*
> *will do this.* (Interview 21)

Second, education in the broadest sense was a prime topic on the aid agenda; given that bi- and multilateral organisations competed to be part of South Africa's education transition, government officials could select those which were most responsive to local needs and priorities. Third, policy-making authorities concerned with education and training seem to have adopted a careful approach towards advice and assistance from outside which is reflected by the following statement of a DHET (and former DoE) official:

> *The experts that we had, that we used, were very few. And (..) they*
> *were coming in towards (…) the end (…) of the process to advise and*
> *give support and so forth. But (…) they were never sent through to the*
> *conceptualization of the direction.* (Interview 21)

Finally, it seems that the participation of various stakeholders with strong voices in the South African education and training landscape has mitigated the scope of direct influence from outside. While the vested and sometimes contradictory interests of education and training providers, trade unions and employers may have decelerated the pace or even blocked processes, such frictions enforced national negotiation about concepts developed internally or adopted from elsewhere. The academic community played a distinct role therein.

All in all, in the field of education, the South African government was able to create its own vision and system, although it resorted to aid for both expertise and money. The fact that many institutions and structures were repeatedly revised in the course of reform indicates that the system put in place was not 'perfect' and entailed flaws which became evident in implementation. A DHET official, however, stated:

> *We've made mistakes; some of them were really unintended consequences of our policies. But those were our own mistakes. It's worse what has happened in Tanzania because of the Bank's and other agencies' interference.* (Interview 21)

Tanzania health: The normality of foreign involvement

Sectoral context

The health situation in Tanzania has improved significantly in recent years. Life expectancy at birth rose from 51 years in 2002 to 61 years in 2012 (World Bank 2014c).[208] Within the same period, infant and under-five mortality substantially declined; according to UN estimates, the rate of children dying between birth and five years of age decreased from 114 to 54 per thousand live births (UN Inter-agency Group for Child Mortality Estimation 2013). These positive trends are largely attributed to a high coverage of immunisation, expanded vitamin A distribution, and an increased use of insecticide-treated bed nets to prevent malaria which helped to reduce the prevalence among children under five from 18% in 2008 to 9% in 2012 (UNICEF Tanzania 2010; TACAIDS et al. 2013).

Whereas much progress has been achieved in terms of child survival, maternal health remains an unresolved challenge. Tanzania's maternal mortality rate is one of the highest in the world: in 2010, an estimated 8 500 women died while being pregnant or giving birth (UN Maternal Mortality Estimation Inter-agency Group 2010).[209] While most of these deaths are caused by obstetric complications, the poor quality of health services and the existence of infectious diseases – most notably malaria and HIV/Aids – indirectly contribute to the persistent high number of cases (Shija et al. 2012).

As one of the most perilous health problems in Tanzania, malaria continues to be the country's major cause of morbidity and mortality. Although interventions in malaria control show signs of success, the tropical disease still

---

208 According to the World Bank's World Development Indicators database, the average life expectancy at birth in developing countries of sub-Saharan Africa was 56.4 in 2012 (World Bank 2014c).

209 In 2010, the maternal mortality rate was estimated to be 460 per 100 000 live births (UN Maternal Mortality Estimation Inter-agency Group 2010).

leads to about 60 000 deaths per year, of which 80% are children under five years (Massero 2013). The fight against HIV/Aids seems similarly challenging. Despite huge efforts undertaken since the disease was declared a 'national disaster' in 1999, the HI virus continues to spread in Tanzania.[210] Even though knowledge about how to prevent transmission is relatively common, it is estimated that more than 100 000 Tanzanians are newly infected each year (Interview 62; UNICEF Tanzania 2014). The prevalence of HIV among the population has only marginally dropped in recent years (TACAIDS et al. 2013); as of 2011/2012, 1.6 million people were living with HIV/Aids (United Republic of Tanzania 2012a).

An impediment to scaling up interventions to combat the multiple epidemics is the massive shortage of health professionals in the country. As estimated in the Health Sector Strategic Plan (2009–2015), there is a lack of more than 90 000 health workers which amounts to a deficit of 65% (Ministry of Health and Social Welfare 2009). The on-going human resource crisis is seen as one of the greatest obstacles hampering the implementation of Tanzania's ambitious health sector reforms (Kwesigabo et al. 2012).

Governance structures

At the national level, the two main authorities dealing with health issues in Tanzania are the Ministry of Health and Social Welfare (MoHSW) and the Prime Minister's Office Regional Administration and Local Government (PMO-RALG). While the former is mandated to provide overall policy guidance and quality control, the latter is responsible for overseeing the delivery of district health services which form the centrepiece of the system and are managed by local government authorities (Ministry of Health and Social Welfare 2009).

For the fight against HIV/Aids, the government set up the Tanzania Commission for AIDS (TACAIDS) in 2001. Established as an independent department under the Prime Minister's Office, TACAIDS has been mandated to provide strategic leadership, formulate policy guidelines, advise the government, and coordinate the implementation of the national response to the epidemic (TACAIDS 2014a). As the central institution for policy-making and resource mobilisation in the field of HIV/Aids, TACAIDS has become the focal point for donors engaged in HIV/Aids-related activities.

---

210 The first three Aids cases on Tanzania mainland occurred in 1983. By the end of 1999, it was estimated that more than 2 million people were infected with HIV. At that point in time, then President Mkapa called the epidemic "an extraordinary crisis that requires extra-ordinary measures to deal with it" (TACAIDS 2014c).

Donor presence in the health sector

Health and HIV/Aids are policy fields which are both characterised by a high 'donor density' in Tanzania. As of 2014, the 'Development Partners Groups' in the two areas – DPG-Health and DPG-AIDS – each comprised more than 15 members, including major bilateral funders such as the United States, Canada, Germany, the Netherlands, and Denmark, as well as multilateral bodies such as the World Bank and UN agencies (Development Partners Group Tanzania 2014a). Experts from these organisations interact with senior government officials through various Technical Working Groups (TWGs) which were established when a Sector-Wide Approach (SWAp) was introduced (see later in this chapter). TWGs in health focus on issues such as district and regional health services, health financing, and public private partnerships; in the field of HIV/Aids, they concentrate on prevention, care and treatment, impact mitigation, and evaluation, amongst others (interviews 32, 61, 62). Aid representatives also take part in higher-level forums concerned with policy-making and resource allocation, for example, the SWAp Technical Committee, the Health Basket Financing Committee or Tanzania's National Coordinating Mechanism for the Global Fund (see Ministry of Health and Social Welfare 2009; TACAIDS 2014b). As will be shown, donors exert significant influence on decision-making through such structures and beyond, both in health and HIV/Aids.

Tanzania's health system after independence

When Tanzania became independent in 1961, the country's health system consisted of only a few hospitals and private doctors accessible to a small elite living in urban areas; the majority of the population relied on traditional healers and missionary centres (McIntyre et al. 2008). Providing essential health services for all became a major endeavour of the first post-colonial leader, Julius K Nyerere. Following the Arusha Declaration of 1967, the government made public healthcare free of charge, and invested in building health facilities in rural areas. Between 1969 and 1978, the number of state-operated rural health centres more than tripled, and as a result of increased training, the health workforce grew significantly (Wangwe & Rweyemamu 2001). The government financed the system through tax and donor funding; private for-profit practice was limited and later even prohibited by law on the grounds that health was seen as the sole responsibility of the state, assisted by faith-based organisations (McIntyre et al. 2008).

When in the course of the economic crisis during the 1980s, Tanzania was forced to adopt structural adjustment policies as required by international finance institutions, the health sector experienced a sharp decline in government spending, "with real per capita expenditure falling by 46% in the decade to 1988/89" (Kumaranayake et al. 2000: 360). In order to maintain the system, user fees were re-introduced, and the ban on private services was lifted, which "led to a rapid increase in the number of private health providers, many of them informal and unregistered" (McIntyre et al. 2008: 872). By the early 1990s, Tanzania's health system was fragmented, underfunded and hardly functioning; while the country had a relatively wide network of facilities, these often lacked basic equipment, personnel and essential drugs to care for patients (Wangwe & Rweyemamu 2001).[211]

The road to reforms

Tanzania was not the only African country which experienced a deterioration in health services at that time. In its 1993 'World Development Report', the World Bank highlighted the poor performance of health systems in developing countries with low cost-effectiveness, inefficiency and mismanagement, and called on governments and the aid community to invest in health sector reforms (World Bank 1993). In the same year, donors held a consultative meeting in Paris where the need for reform in Tanzania was discussed. Shortly after, a joint workshop with officials from the Ministry of Health was organised, following which a working group was established (Semali 2003). With funding from the World Bank and Danida, the group produced the 'Proposals for Health Sector Reform' (1994),[212] the Strategic Health Plan for 1995–1998 and the Health Sector Reform Plan of Action 1996–1999, which sketched out major problems and suggested interventions to tackle them. In the process of developing these pivotal documents, officials regularly consulted with aid representatives whose support was deemed crucial for realising the reforms.

Aside from being involved in revising and adjusting reform plans, donors in parallel began to test the feasibility of new tools and financing mechanisms through aid initiatives; the World Bank, for instance, carried out a pilot project introducing a community health fund in Igunga District, and the GTZ conducted a study on district planning and management in Tanga Region (Semali 2003).[213] Following a series of 'joint missions', the government and donors eventually agreed on a final 'Programme of Work' (PoW) for the period 1999–2002 which outlined eight priority areas of reform: the decentralisation

---

211 As of 1985, an estimated 90% of the Tanzanian population lived within a 10km distance of a health facility which indicates a relatively wide coverage at that time (Hingora n.d.).

212 The Proposals for Health Sector Reform were approved by the cabinet in March 1996 (Burki 2001).

213 For a detailed description of the various projects and studies carried out to test different reform proposals, see Semali (2003).

of authority to the districts which should be given full responsibility for the organisation and delivery of health services; the establishment of a referral system with back-up secondary and tertiary hospitals to support primary healthcare; the transformation of the national Ministry of Health into a facilitative policy organisation with a normative and standard-setting role; addressing the human resource shortage; ensuring central support systems are in place; diversifying health financing through insurance systems, cost-sharing mechanisms and user fees; providing for an 'appropriate' mix of public and private healthcare services; and 'restructuring' the relationship between the Ministry of Health and donors (Ministry of Health 1999).

Regarding the last point, donors and the ministry had finally arrived at the decision to move towards a 'Sector-Wide Approach' (SWAp) with the aim "to dilute the administrative and planning burden of multiple systems imposed through the various donor-led approaches, and to promote coordinated planning and resource management" (Burki 2001: 13). The basic idea behind this was that stakeholders in health would collaborate to back the implementation of a shared programme under government leadership. After tedious negotiations, some of the 'development partners' – namely Danida, DFID, Swiss Development Cooperation, Ireland Aid, Norway, and the World Bank, later on joined by Germany, the Netherlands and Canada[214] – also embarked on pooling resources in a basket fund which would be used for agreed priority areas and disbursed through the government system (Mapunda 2003).[215]

With the introduction of the new modalities, a range of 'dialogue' mechanisms were set up, including a SWAp Committee which would meet biannually to review the overall reform process, a Basket Financing Committee to approve disbursements and review budget execution on a quarterly basis, and various technical working groups to discuss specific topics such as hospital reforms, human resources for health, and performance monitoring (Burki 2001). The establishment of these multiple forums implied an institutionalisation of external engagement in health policy-making which enhanced rather than reduced donor interference.

---

214 The number and composition of basket fund contributors changed over time; as of 2014, these comprised Canada, Denmark, Ireland, Switzerland, UNFPA, UNICEF and the World Bank (Development Partners Group on Health 2014).

215 Donors staying outside the basket justified their decision in terms of internal rules and regulations which would prevent them from merging funds, whereby the loss of 'control' and 'visibility' was considered a major barrier (Hobbs 2001).

The role of donors in the sector-wide approach

Introducing the SWAp and the health basket at around the turn of the millennium, Tanzania was seen as a forerunner in experimenting with new, 'harmonised' aid modalities which became popular with the donor community at that time. In cross-country studies, the arrangements adopted in the health sector were deemed 'most advanced' and highly commended for increasing government 'ownership' (Brown 2000: v).[216] Protagonists involved in donor–government interaction also perceived a positive shift in relations. A retired official who then served as chief medical officer in the Ministry of Health remembered:

> *With the new thinking of the health sector reform, one of the big changes was from thinking in terms of 'a donor and a project' to 'donors agreeing and putting the money in one budget' and getting also the government budget together to say 'ok we have this money, what shall we do'? What shall we do? Not what shall I do? Big difference!* (Interview 53)

Similarly, a GTZ representative who at that time strongly championed the new approach remarked:

> *During the good years of the SWAp, we talked to each other, like 'what are you doing, what are we doing, how do we put that into the overall strategy' – there was no 'donor agenda', but a national programme. It was a mutual process, we had a certain model in mind, we were kind of a 'dream team' which advocated for comprehensive primary health care, district health services, so the overall direction was fairly clear.* (Interview 73, translated by authors)

The 'dream team' in that context comprised a number of like-minded aid experts and key figures in the health ministry who, sharing the same vision and convictions, pushed forward reforms in the following years. The same group also worked out the subsequent Health Sector Strategic Plan 2003–2008 which more or less set out to follow up on the PoW priority areas, though with a greater focus on ensuring the delivery of essential health packages at district level, sharpening the role of the central ministry, and tackling the human

---

216 This was emphasised by a research report commissioned by the WHO which investigated the status of SWAp arrangements in Cambodia, Vietnam, Mozambique, Uganda and Tanzania in early 2000. In the case study on Tanzania, the author noted that "despite high aid dependency, government ownership of the programme is growing and national commitment to sector programmes and public expenditure reform create a positive environment for health SWAp expansion" (Brown 2000: v).

resource shortage (Ministry of Health 2003). Moreover, the fight against HIV/ Aids which had become a "serious problem on the country's economy and development" (Ministry of Health 2003: viii) was for the first time taken up as a 'special' strategy.

Overall, there seemed little dispute about the 'rightness' of reforms within the Ministry of Health, but they were considered as being driven by a rather small cadre of senior officials in the Health Sector Reform Secretariat who closely collaborated with donor experts, particularly from those organisations that contributed to the health basket (Hobbs 2001; Holtom 2002).[217] Through the newly established forums, the latter were closely involved in developing policies and plans, doing situational analyses and 'helping' to think about what should be done; a health specialist in the Netherlands Embassy described his and other donor colleagues' contribution as follows:

> *We definitely assisted and facilitated the whole process around a new policy, a new strategic Health Sector Strategy Plan, which – I don't want to say that those are seen as the most important documents by the Tanzanian ministry, but they're definitely key documents.*
>
> *And for example, we, a number of DPs [development partners], helped to analyse (…): There are good gains in infant and child mortality, how do we sustain that? We do not see these gains yet in maternal health, why is there way too slow progress in that area? Has it to do with family planning, new diseases, non-communicable diseases… (…).*
>
> *In that case a small group of donors helped to formulate strategic plans, and made sure that at all levels monitoring and evaluation became more important, that evidence-informed decisions became more important.* (Interview 38)

The regular encounter with government officials through the various technical working groups and other forums enabled donor experts not only to impact on *how* issues were discussed (e.g. by promoting 'evidence-based' decision-making), but also *which* issues were put on the agenda. In particular, the so-called 'Troika' of the DPG-Health, a body comprising three elected officials from member organisations commissioned to advocate donor positions, had direct access to key figures in the Ministry of Health which could be used

---

217 In contrast to donors, national stakeholders such as research communities, faith-based organisations, the private sector or civil society were only marginally or not at all involved in the early stages of the reform process (Semali 2003).

to turn the spotlight on issues of (donor) concern. A Dutch Embassy official reported:

> *As the Troika, initially, we had a monthly meeting with senior management at the ministry, with the PS [Permanent Secretary], the chief medical officer and the directors. And they started then a monthly meeting – maybe it was then forced by us that they had that meeting – where they started the first half hour with us and then they went on with their own meeting. Even at that meeting, you would constantly raise priorities how you perceived them. Are they always taking and act upon that? No. But often, you will find that they act.* (Interview 38)

As the statements above indicate, the SWAp dialogue mechanisms provided aid experts with the opportunity to become legitimate participants in the policy discourse and shape the agenda through formal discussions. At the same time, however, informal negotiations continued, with a lot of "side-meetings" (Interview 61) taking place behind the scenes. The entry of global health initiatives with massive financial power eventually depleted the potential for concerted action under Tanzanian guidance, particularly, but not only, in the field of HIV/Aids.

The rise of global HIV initiatives and their impact on HIV and health governance

At around the turn of the millennium, HIV/Aids in Tanzania had become a massive "social and economic problem with devastating impact on national development" (TACAIDS 2014c). Although the creation of TACAIDS in 2001 helped to shift HIV/Aids onto the political agenda as reflected by a considerable increase in domestic and foreign funding (Foster & Mwinyimvua 2003: 4), Tanzania remained far from reaching budget levels required to finance the national response outlined by the country's first National HIV/Aids Policy (Prime Minister's Office 2001) and the related National Multi-Sectoral Strategic Framework on HIV/Aids 2003–2007 (NMSF) (TACAIDS 2003).[218] The World

---

218 Reliable and comprehensive information on HIV/Aids spending before 2004/2005 is hardly available; only then, HIV/Aids was given a separate code in the Tanzanian budget. In their Public Expenditure Review: HIV/Aids Multi-Sectoral Update for 2004, Foster and Mwinyimvua (2003) emphasised that both government and donor reports lacked complete and accurate figures on HIV-related expenditures. The data they were able to compile indicated an increase of TSh 4.75 billion in government spending from 2001/02 to 2002/03, almost entirely accounted for by the establishment of TACAIDS. Moreover, the authors estimated that HIV/Aids-related aid channelled through government agencies increased by 107%, and aid directed to NGOs by 326%. Although the total amount of HIV/Aids resources which could be traced had almost doubled, it was considered "still less than half of the levels that have been estimated to be needed" (Foster & Mwinyimvua 2003: 15).

Bank was the first donor to come up with the prospect of additional money, offering a loan of USD 70 million to be used over a period of five years (2003–2008) under the umbrella of its Multi-Country HIV/Aids Programme (World Bank 2003). Given the massive financing gap, the government accepted the project, yielding to the Bank's pressure, despite reluctance among its own ranks and resentment on the part of the remaining donor group which feared losing influence (Holtom 2002). The then chairman of TACAIDS remembered the situation he found himself in as follows:

> *When the World Bank was coming in, they came in with a lot of funds. And so I was having a meeting predominantly with the donor group. And they began complaining that since the World Bank is stepping in, you are paying attention to the World Bank and forgetting us and you follow World Bank dictation, etc. So I was quick to point out to them that this is a Tanzanian programme and I'm head of this programme and therefore it's going to be, you know, home-based. I don't care where the money comes from, but we are going to make sure that it is Tanzanian-led and -oriented.*
> (Interview 64)

Whether enforced by Tanzanian negotiators or for other reasons, the World Bank indeed broadly catered the Tanzania Multi-sectoral Aids Programme (T-MAP) to the government's priorities. The focus was on prevention and mitigation measures, and institutional support for TACAIDS which was charged with coordinating project-funded activities and submitting annual work plans and progress reports (World Bank 2003).

The Bank undoubtedly made itself the lead agency in the field of HIV/Aids by providing by far the largest share of resources, but it did not keep this position for very long. Shortly after T-MAP started in 2003, a range of global players entered the scene: the Global Fund for AIDS, TB and Malaria (GFATM), the US President's Emergency Plan for AIDS Relief (PEPFAR), and the Clinton HIV/AIDS Initiative (CHAI), all together large-scale, vertical funding schemes offering enormous amounts of money. The Global Fund in its third round awarded Tanzania a total of USD 87 million for 2004–2008, PEPFAR held out the prospect of disbursing up to USD 100 million annually, and CHAI promised to raise a sum of USD 539 million over a period of five years (Barry et al. 2003). The hitch in these offers, however, was that resources were tightly earmarked; large shares – in the case of PEPFAR 55% – were destined to scale-up care and treatment, irrespective of the government's actual prioritisation of HIV prevention and AIDS control. The fact that both local and foreign experts deemed the provision of life-long antiretroviral drugs neither feasible at that point in time[219] nor affordable in the long run did not prevent US representatives from advancing their agenda – a stance which outraged the remaining aid community, as a former GTZ representative recalled:

> *Interviewee: The Americans had written a programme stating: 'We have realised that HIV/Aids is a problem in Tanzania. We Americans know how to fight HIV/Aids, and we will fight HIV/Aids in Tanzania.' No mention of Tanzanians or other actors. Nothing. It caused a scandal – at that time I was the acting chair of the donor group and there was a meeting where all non-US donors left, saying this is unacceptable (…).*
>
> *Interviewer: How did the Tanzanian side react to that?*
>
> *Interviewee: Well, there you encounter the actual problem and the limits of rational advice: When big money is on the horizon, there is a decision of the president or the minister and all the experts – Tanzanians, Europeans, Chinese, WHO, whoever else – stand in the corner with no say anymore.*
> (Interview 73, translated by authors)

Being confronted with an increasing number of people dying of Aids, the government decided to accept the funding offers and to accommodate the requirements of the respective donors. The Clinton Foundation, for instance, demanded a new National Care and Treatment Plan (NCTP), although the Ministry of Health in March 2003 had produced a Health Sector HIV/Aids Strategy which entailed a detailed care and treatment section. Drafted by experts from the Clinton Foundation, together with Tanzanian officials and approved by the Cabinet in October 2003, the NCTP set highly ambitious goals: whereas the MoH strategy had proposed to put 13 000 patients on treatment until the end of 2006, the 'Clinton' plan increased this number to 151 000 (United Republic of Tanzania 2003; Hutton 2004).[220] While the authors pointed out that the plan neither implied "a radical redirection of policy" nor replaced any "of the careful planning and wide-ranging action which the United Republic of Tanzania has taken" (United Republic of Tanzania 2003: 1–2), it did throw

---

219 A Tanzanian expert who then worked for the US government at the Center for Disease Control and Prevention commented: "We were advising: 'yes, we should start care and treatment, but the focus should also be to strengthen the systems, because you cannot throw the ARVs [antiretroviral drugs] in the air and then they go and look for the mouth where to go into'. That is exactly an example I gave in the same way. But it was a push that we want ART [antiretroviral treatment] (…) and the budget was: more than 50% should go to the drugs. And the remaining should go to prevention, the agency costs and whatever. So it remained very little…" (Interview 68)

220 The actual number of patients put on treatment fell far behind this ambitious target; according to TACAIDS information, 54 264 were on ART by end of October 2006 (TACAIDS 2014d).

over previous targets and schedules set by the Ministry of Health, and put treatment centre stage in Tanzania's Aids response.[221]

Not only the Clinton Foundation imposed rigid conditions to its funding. PEPFAR in its early phase had a strict rule that only ARVs approved by the US Food and Drug Administration (FDA) could be procured with the programme's funds, which excluded the purchase of most low-cost generic drugs (Dietrich 2007).[222] Tanzania's policy, however, was to give preference to generic alternatives which were ten to 40 times cheaper than the brand-name drugs provided by the US pharmaceutical industry (Venkatesh et al. 2012). The conflict led to difficult negotiations, as the then chief medical officer remembered:

> *Interviewee: USAID just said 'no' to generics and we said 'no' to non-generics because this would have been against the drug policy. But at the end we agreed.*
>
> *Interviewer: You agreed?*
>
> *Interviewee: Yes, we agreed. We had to come to a compromise.*
> (Interview 53)

In late 2004, Tanzania started a nation-wide care and treatment programme financed mainly with money from the new HIV/Aids initiatives.[223] Overshadowing the government and the remaining donors all together in terms of funding volumes, PEPFAR and the Global Fund in a short space of time became the main sponsors of the overall Aids response: by 2007, both together accounted for almost 80% of total expenditures on HIV/Aids (cf. TACAIDS' 2010 Public Expenditure Review, Table 18).

---

221 The participation of the Ministry of Health in drafting the new plan is said to have been limited; a study found that "there has been a certain amount of MOH leadership and ownership in this process, but this is still far from desirable levels" (Hutton 2004: 13).

222 In May 2004, the FDA introduced a tentative approval process for essential generic antiretroviral drugs; yet, the number of generics eligible for purchase through PEPFAR only slowly increased. For details on PEPFAR's changing drug policy and regulations, see Venkatesh et al. (2012).

223 Despite large volumes of aid channelled through the new global HIV/Aids initiatives, the programme had a slow start (IRIN News 2006). Treatment figures remained well below the ambitious targets set by the National Care and Treatment plan; by 2007, 136 700 patients – only about half of the number envisaged and 22% of those eligible for ART – received antiretroviral drugs (National AIDS Control Programme 2008).The lack of qualified medical staff, persisting stigma and low voluntary counselling and testing rates were seen as major challenges hampering the scale-up of ARV provision.

Table 18: HIV/Aids expenditures in Tanzania in 2007

Expenditures on HIV/Aids	in TSh billion	as share of total in %
Domestic expenditures	22.0	5.5
Foreign aid	380.0	94.5
thereof United States Government (PEPFAR)	230.3	57.3
thereof Global Fund	89.9	22.4
Total expenditures	402.0	100.0

Source: TACAIDS (2010: viii/22).

While the entry of new donors meant a stark increase in funding available for HIV/Aids interventions, it did not give the government a greater scope of action insofar as the money was channelled outside Tanzania's budgetary system. The bulk of Global Fund and PEPFAR money was disbursed through NGOs and US agencies, leaving the government with little control over resource flows and clarity on what was being done in the country (TACAIDS 2010), as the Director of Finance at TACAIDS remarked:

> *In the first phase when they started in 2004, nobody knew what the US government was doing (…). It was like when they come to the meeting, people will ask them and they will not be able to explain.* (Interview 61)

For the government, the lack of information on how the money was spent and where it went created problems not only with respect to resource allocation and planning, but also in terms of accountability. The TACAIDS' director of finance commented:

> *When USAID funds Non-Governmental Organizations, that money goes outside the system. And the way the government operates, you cannot capture that unless the money is passing through the government (…). But we've also discussed with US government that it's very important for us to be accountable; and for them as well. Because if the money does not pass through the government machinery, it means it is not being reflected in the books of parliament and parliament passes the budget though the money is outside, and therefore they cannot follow how it was worked on and how it is accounted.* (Interview 61)

Although TACAIDS officials reported that as a result of tedious negotiations information sharing on the part of US representatives has improved the problem of insufficient public oversight over large proportions of HIV/Aids funding still has not been solved. From fiscal years 2006/07 to 2010/11, the share of off-budget expenditures (i.e. expenditures which are not captured by the national exchequer system) actually increased from 78% to over 85% (TACAIDS 2010, 2012). The fact that the Tanzanian government lacks discretionary authority over the larger share of financial resources spent on HIV/Aids makes it impossible to use budget allocation as a steering tool (United Republic of Tanzania 2012a). It also explains the discrepancy between policy statements and resource flows: although prevention was again prioritised by the Second National Multi-Sectoral Strategic Framework on HIV and Aids covering the years 2008 to 2012 (TACAIDS 2007) and further pushed onto the agenda by the formulation of a National HIV Prevention Strategy (Prime Minister's Office 2009),[224] it received less than a quarter of the overall HIV/Aids funding (23%) in the period 2008 to 2010 (TACAIDS 2012). The TACAIDS chairperson commented:

> *It shouldn't be like that. The priority is HIV prevention. And HIV prevention should be allocated more money than treatment. We know that treatment is prevention, but at the end of the day, we'll continue treating more people if we do not prevent!* (Interview 63)[225]

That more than half (59%) of HIV/Aids funding was spent on treatment, care and support can be attributed particularly to the United States' strong emphasis on this. The government's recent attempts to obtain a shift in PEPFAR spending patterns had only a limited effect. The TACAIDS director of finance described the difficulty in prevailing against the US agenda:

> *I know when we were designing PEPFAR 2 which started around 2009/2010, they wanted to fund more treatment and we wanted to fund more prevention (…). It was hard – it was hard, because for them it's easy to account for how many test kits and how many drugs you have sent to Tanzania, because you can physically count them. But on prevention programmes, actually for any donor it's hard, because you just educate people and you cannot measure it easily, you know.* (Interview 61)

The explanation that the US as well as other donors preferred to support treatment due to their internal legitimation pressure was also used by TACAIDS' director for policy and planning who remarked:

---

224 For a detailed analysis of the formulation process of the HIV Prevention Strategy and related interests, see Hunsmann (2013: 146–175).

225 The 'treatment as prevention' agenda the interviewee refers to was pushed when a clinical study funded by the US National Institutes of Health found that treatment of a person living with HIV reduced the risk of transmission to partners by 96% (*The Lancet* 2011). The United States in particular strongly promoted the finding and highlighted the idea of 'treatment as prevention' in its PEPFAR II Blueprint released in 2012 (United States of America, Department of State 2012).

Any external support, they operate result-based. Prevention – whether based on condoms, whatever intervention, STIs and alike, these interventions are becoming very unpopular because the impact you don't see now, you will see later. It takes longer to see the results. But if you put someone on ART, you monitor for one year, he or she recovers – that is the outcome. You can say now they are healthy living, doing her or his duty. So that's the result. (Interview 62)

As a result of the massive amounts of aid provided for the scale-up of treatment, the number of people receiving antiretroviral drugs increased from 23 951 in 2005 to 432 293 in 2012 which corresponds to 61% of those eligible for ART (World Health Organization et al. 2013; TACAIDS 2014d). While the rapid expansion of ART coverage was judged a notable achievement which saved the lives of many, it implied a substantive absorption of financial and human resources in a system which already faced a severe shortage of health workers, money and equipment for the supply of basic services. Health officials found it highly problematic that the roll-out of HIV care and treatment negatively affected other areas in terms of staff and budget availability. The head of Health Care Financing in the MoHSW remarked:

When you focus your money on HIV, you know the impact: attraction of staff from other programmes to HIV, because you have money here. But again, the problem cannot be really solved because HIV patients should go to the labs which are not functioning. So you are focusing on an area which also depends on other areas (…). So the challenges are there. (Interview 54)

This statement hints at one of the most problematic issues related to the entry of global health initiatives in Tanzania: they not only shifted the bulk of the HIV budget to treatment but also skewed the overall resource allocation in health towards HIV/Aids at the expense of other crucial areas and prevalent diseases (Hutton 2004). Imposing conditions and their own agendas, the new HIV players undermined the efforts and main goal of the newly established SWAp mechanism, namely to achieve a more harmonised form of health governance under which all stakeholders would act in concert. As in other recipient countries, the emergence and dominance of these actors in Tanzania profoundly impacted on both policy-making and aid relationships in the way of distorting national priorities and distracting the government from assuming leadership (Biesma et al. 2009).

The current state of aid relations in health and HIV/Aids

The reforms in the early 2000s were meant to increase national 'ownership' and to establish a new kind of partnership between the government and donors. However, the state of affairs ten years after seems far from ideal. The sophisticated dialogue structure which has repeatedly been refined and revised over the years exists primarily on paper. A Danida advisor placed in the MoHSW expressed her frustration about constant delays of meetings:

> *The actual policy dialogue between the partners and the ministry has been very weak. It's been very poor. I mean the Troika has had to fight to meet with the management to discuss how things are going. And meetings are barely kept on schedule – meetings that are supposed to happen within the SWAp all of which are kind of conditions for the basket funding (…). And it's not very much as an advisor that you can do other than kind of remind people that now there is a commitment to have a meeting, that it's important.* (Interview 34)

The meetings referred to in the statement above include, amongst others, the various technical working groups and the Technical Committee of the SWAp (TC-SWAp) which was meant to serve as a joint monitoring and advisory body of the health sector (Ministry of Health and Social Welfare et al. 2009). Commenting on the functioning of these forums, the first secretary for health and HIV/Aids in the Netherlands Embassy stated:

> *Some of them work relatively well – M&E [Monitoring and Evaluation] because we have an initiative there, HR [Human Resources] is working relatively well, not so effective though. There're other ones who hardly meet (…). Officially we still have four TC-SWAp meetings a year. Now if you have two, it's much.* (Interview 38)

Both interviewees attributed the lack of adherence to meeting schedules first and foremost to management challenges in the Ministry of Health, pointing to unfilled positions, a high staff turn-over and an 'ad hoc' way of working which kept their counterparts 'constantly running'. These problems were explained primarily in terms of inappropriate organisational structures, poor human resource management and a general lack of administrative capacity in the MoHSW. But the first secretary in the Netherlands Embassy also blamed the aid community for exacerbating the situation:

It's also partly caused by the various partners who are coming in and out, etc. Because if you now look at the dialogue structure, the idea was that we would not as partners bother the government too much beyond those structures. That was the idea. If you had interest in HR, then you would be active in the HR group. [But] of course development partners still have their own direct lines. And strong governments, they would say more often 'sorry, but…' You don't have to be too Stalinist on that, but it shouldn't be that you are constantly busy. (Interview 38)

The fact that donors on their part do not comply with the agreed working arrangements and principles – such as to limit their interaction with decision-makers to the formal dialogue in order to reduce 'transaction' costs and to increase transparency – was confirmed by various officials. The TACAIDS director of finance and administration, for instance, referring to the Finance and Auditing Technical Working Committee for HIV/Aids, reported:

Apart from that committee, we have side meetings with bilaterals, for example, to discuss their funding and some of the issues they want. Because sometimes some of the development partners (…), they still want to do some of the things separately. So we accommodate them and we have these meetings and agree on various issues. (Interview 61)

The continuation of bilateral 'backdoor' meetings and the persisting endeavour by donors to push individual interventions not only absorb immense staff time from the Tanzanian administration, but subvert transparent negotiation and concerted action as envisaged by the SWAp code of conduct and the respective terms of references for the DPG sub-groups Health and AIDS (see Development Partners Group on Health 2006; Government of Tanzania & Development Partners 2007; Development Partners Group on HIV/Aids 2013). Although 'development partners' themselves have set up and signed these rules, they seem little committed to adhere to them. Commenting on the deficient compliance and the difficulty of 'speaking with one voice', the head of the German health programme and then chair of DPG Health remarked:

Harmonisation is partly an arduous process since naturally each organisation, each country is driven by its headquarters, by the capital where political processes take place; and a change of minister can have quite an effect. This applies for Germany as well as for other countries – when governments and ministers change, foci and priorities are likely to shift. (Interview 37, translated by authors)

Both Tanzania's health reforms and its Aids response are highly vulnerable to the shifting priorities and preferences of external funders, given the considerable dependency on aid money. This has been particularly palpable in recent years when three of the largest contributors to the health basket, together accounting for about one third of the estimated budget pledged for 2011/2012 (Government of Tanzania & Health Basket Partners 2011),[226] almost simultaneously announced a reduction or termination of their support. The Netherlands decided to cut the number of its recipient countries from 33 to 15. Tanzania was informed that Dutch aid would phase out (Netherlands Ministry of Foreign Affairs 2011). Norway decided to withdraw from health in order to focus on five other priority areas (environment, climate and forest, management of natural resources, fiscal issues and illegal capital flight, human rights and democracy) (Norwegian Agency for Development Cooperation 2014). Germany informed the government that it would scale back the overall financial volume of support to the sector and pull out from the health basket (GIZ Tanzanian German Programme to Support Health 2011). Approached upon this decision – which seems remarkable insofar as Germany had been instrumental in setting up this mechanism – the head of the German health programme responded with noticeable unease:

> *Yes, in fact there has been a change of tack which indicates that political decision-making processes are not always coherent with technical advisory approaches (...) And quite recently, indeed, Germany in bilateral governmental consultations made clear its position that we pull out of basket funding. The partner was sitting on the other side and emphasised the importance of this contribution, asking 'please do not withdraw, it is important for the health reform programme which runs until 2015 and we thought Germany would stay and provide support'. But there was a political decision (...) towards which we now have to orientate ourselves.*
> (Interview 37, translated by authors)

For policy-makers and senior officials in the MoHSW, Germany's and other donors' decision to terminate support was more than untimely insofar as it severely threatens the implementation of the Health Sector Strategic Plan III (2009–2015) which calculated on increased rather than reduced contributions

---

226 The health basket side-agreement for fiscal year 2011/2012 estimated that partners would pledge an amount of USD 115.81 million; thereof, the Netherlands was expected to contribute USD 21.29 million (EUR 15.00 million), Germany USD 9.93 million (EUR 7.00 million) and Norway USD 5.40 million (NOK 30.00 million) (Government of Tanzania & Health Basket Partners 2011).

from foreign funders, particularly through the health basket (Ministry of Health and Social Welfare 2009). In the view of the chief medical officer, the withdrawal of major funders jeopardises the progress under way:

> *In the reduction in childhood deaths, there has been a downward trend very fast. There is also a downward trend in maternal deaths, though it is not as fast. But we believe that with all these developments, the speed will definitely pick up. And this is where we will start now showing the countries, our partners, there is the impact or the outcome of their support (…). [If the partners] pull out now, then definitely they will be doing a great disservice to all these efforts and the processes and the achievements that are starting now to emerge.* (Interview 52)

Not only decision-makers in the MoHSW fear a setback through a decrease in foreign funding. Officials at TACAIDS face a similarly worrisome situation with respect to shifting aid priorities, as the chairperson of the organisation noted when interviewed:

> *The reality is right now, funds are getting less (…). When I joined TACAIDS in January 2007, there were lots of resources, particularly from the World Bank, very flexible resources so that we could say 'NGO so and so, you're just starting and your work is on orphans, I think this is very good because nobody has gone to that area. Please take this money, this is how you report, this is how you will be audited, go ahead.' Right now you cannot do that anymore. So the writing is on the wall that the shape is different, the interest is different and people have other priorities.* (Interview 63)

Since 2011, TACAIDS has been confronted with budget cuts from several key donors: The United States and Germany decided to reduce financial aid for HIV/Aids-related activities, and Denmark and Canada announced they would terminate their support for the Aids response (i.e. the National Multi-Sectoral Strategic Framework) by 2015 (GIZ Tanzanian German Programme to Support Health 2011; *Tanzania Daily News* 2013). Moreover, the Global Fund cancelled its next round of funding due to insufficient pledges of its members, informing recipients that no new grants could be financed until 2014 (IRIN News 2011b). In response to decreasing aid volumes and the imminent phase-out of long-standing partners, the chairperson of TACAIDS has repeatedly called for increased efforts to raise domestic resources, warning that a failure to get prompt replacement for the funding would result in a 'heavy blow' affecting the achievements made in the fight against HIV/Aids within the last 20 years (*Tanzania Daily News* 2013).[227]

Aid dependency and its implications

The centrality of aid for the implementation of health reforms and the national Aids response seems widely internalised among leadership ranks in the responsible organisations. Given that about 97% of the health ministry's development budget and the overall budget for HIV/Aids is financed from outside (see Chapter 6), programmes and initiatives which do not conform to donors' expectations are unlikely to be realised. As a consequence of this experience, government officials appear to have accepted that policy-making and planning is done in close consultation with experts from the respective funding agencies. This is reflected by statements from the finance directors of TACAIDS and the MoHSW, respectively, who commented:

> *HIV/Aids in Tanzania is heavily funded by donors and therefore it's very important to have that relationship (…) – I would say that we have a very, very close relationship in everything that we do.* (Interview 61)

> *The way we have built our dialogue structures – we discuss technically with partners, we plan technically together with them, that's how it has been meant to be; we don't just go up while we have not shared with the working groups. That's how we work.* (Interview 54)

Aid representatives were outspoken about the fact that despite all rhetoric of 'partnership' the whole dialogue is based on the government's financial needs. A Tanzanian World Bank specialist bluntly stated:

> *It is inevitable that the government has a dialogue with the donors because there is a gap. If there wasn't a gap, if the government was self-sufficient, then probably it would not need any that kind of discussion.* (Interview 47)

The dependency relationship underlying the dialogue latently shapes the outcomes of discussions insofar as government officials are forced to reach some sort of agreement with donor representatives in order to maintain room

---

227 As an attempt to mitigate its donor dependency in the field of HIV/Aids, the government is in the process of establishing an Aids Trust Fund through which it hopes to mobilise more local resources (Lamtey 2012; Kassim 2014). At the time of writing, however, the fund was still not effective.

for manoeuvre. Faced with extreme resource scarcity, rejecting 'advice' of 'development partners' is hardly an option for decision-makers. That money is openly used as a lever to give 'technical' arguments more clout was bluntly confirmed by a Tanzanian health expert working for WHO:

> *External experts would normally use the muscle of their financial support – 'if you don't do this, then I think I would advise my government not to give more money'. So the national experts will not win that war although they might have reasons behind it (…). So we have seen sometimes the agenda of external experts prevails simply because of the financial side of it.* (Interview 44)

This statement suggests that the mechanisms established in the context of the SWAp reform with the aim to strengthen Tanzanian leadership have not been particularly effective. Even in the case of the health basket fund which was set up to increase the government's steering capacity and control over resources, donors are said to strongly determine what the money is used for, depriving the MoHSW of its discretionary authority. The WHO officer, himself a former ministry member, alleged the following examples:

> *In terms of diagnostics, what is important in the hospitals [is that] there are x-rays. In its policies, the ministry says we want to rehabilitate x-rays – and we [the development partners] say 'no, that one, we are not buying it'. (…) And then we go to the health basket fund and we say, you forgot to put iodine (…), we will give you money for that. The minister has not even requested that!* (Interview 44)

In both the health sector and the field of HIV/Aids, the government's capacity to exercise leadership in terms of defining its own priorities seems strongly limited, with donors still earmarking aid for specific purposes even though this contravenes the agreed principles of cooperation. Assessing the government's options in terms of reacting against the dominance of external funders, aid officials acknowledged that in the current setting it seems to have little choice. The health programme manager of GIZ rhetorically asked:

> *There is a health system which is utterly underfinanced (…). So don't you take what comes along to at least support some of the most essential pillars?* (Interview 37)

In a similar vein, a Danida consultant placed in the MoHSW remarked:

*It has to be a very confident ministry that will kind of turn down money –
even if it's contrary to its own policies.* (Interview 34)

Yet, not all interviewees agreed with the 'no choice' narrative. Contrary to the
aid officials quoted above, a Tanzanian health specialist with ten years of work
experience in the MoHSW argued:

*You can say no! It does not always send the money away. But many
people are worried that if you say no, then the support will go away.*
(Interview 68)

There is an additional factor that further weakens the government's stance
towards donors: senior officials in the administration seem to encounter aid
experts with a sort of resignation based on the experience or mere assumption
that they are eventually dependent on the donor community's consent. This
sort of pre-emptive submissiveness was observed by the former executive
chairman of TACAIDS who criticised:

*The natives are not sufficiently strong to impress upon the donor
organisations that 'this is what we want and this is how we want it'
(…). I notice that some of the people, some of the officials who get their
assistance, they sort of say 'well, he has the money, he wants to do this and
that, well, why don't we cut a long story short, and let's agree with him'.
That's where things go wrong.* (Interview 64)

Given the perceived precedence of securing aid, officials in the MoHSW and
TACAIDS appear to have internalised a conduct of compliance towards the
donor community. The fact that 'advice' from aid experts is seldom contested
would also explain why there are rather few occurrences of serious disputes in
policy discussions, as interviewees from both sides noted. While in the official
narrative, the lack of conflict is represented as an indication of the harmonious
relationship of 'partners' in health and HIV/Aids, it can also be interpreted as
a sign that aid dependency has eroded recipients' resistance.

Conclusion

Analysing Aids policy-making by investigating the formulation process of the
HIV prevention strategy, Hunsmann (2013: 169) came to the conclusion that
"international donors are not merely 'influencing' AIDS policy in Tanzania;
they are *co-constitutive* of its very existence". The observations of this case
study not only support the finding that there is no sphere of independent,

endogenous policy-making in HIV/Aids, but suggest that this also applies to the health sector in general. A retired official, previously director of policy and planning at TACAIDS, stated:

> *I don't think we have policies really that are purely national (…) because it's a process and this process always involves the partners. They have a say there, they do have a say.* (Interview 65)

With the introduction of the SWAp and related mechanisms, aid experts have become legitimate participants in the policy discourse with a strong voice in defining priorities and setting the agenda – as opposed to national stakeholders from civil society, the private sector or the research community whose role therein seems if at all marginal. While the dialogue forums in health and HIV/Aids were actually established to reduce donor influence and induce "a more distant form of advice" (Interview 73) it de facto brought aid actors closer to decision-making insofar as it entrenched their participation in policy development, analysis and evaluation. Given the intense engagement of donors in decision-making processes, it is questionable whether the new partnership approach has increased national leadership in health and HIV/Aids governance as claimed by its proponents, or rather weakened it by institutionalising external interference.

South Africa health: Rebuilding relationships with local and external experts

Sectoral context

With an estimate of 5.26 million people living with Aids (roughly 10% of the population) as of 2013, South Africa counts the highest number of HIV infections in the world (Statistics South Africa 2013). At the same time, the country faces a high incidence rate of tuberculosis (TB) which has more than doubled since 2001 (The Lancet South Africa Series Executive Summary Core Group 2009). While the large numbers of HIV and TB cases would be enough to put any nation under stress, three other 'colliding epidemics' – chronic illness and mental health disorders, injury and violence-related deaths, and maternal, neonatal and child mortality – exacerbate the situation; the fact that the 'quadruple burden of disease' falls on a system which is still characterised by inequity and fragmentation makes matters worse (The Lancet South Africa Series Executive Summary Core Group 2009). The persistent inequality caused by apartheid is manifested in the huge discrepancy between the 'first-class' health services provided by private suppliers financed through medical schemes and out-of-pocket payments, and the dismal conditions in tax-funded public facilities which the vast majority of the population relies on. It is also reflected by a skewed distribution of health workforce between the private and the public sector, as well as between urban and rural areas (McIntyre et al. 2008). In the latter, the chronic shortage of qualified staff is particularly severe.[228] Overall, the Department of Health identified a deficit of about 83 000 health professionals in 2011 (Department of Health 2011b).[229]

Despite the challenge of multiple epidemics, systemic flaws and a severe workforce crisis, the government has achieved notable successes since Health Minister Aaron Motsoaledi assumed office in 2009. Life expectancy at birth increased from 54 years in 2005 to 60 years in 2011, and the under-5 mortality rate per 1 000 live births significantly declined from 56 in 2009 to 42 in 2011; both developments are attributed to the extensive roll-out of antiretroviral treatment and massive efforts in the prevention of HIV mother-to-child transmission undertaken by the new administration (Bradshaw et al. 2012; Mayosi et al. 2012). Although immense problems remain, the health improvements brought about in recent years give rise to positive outlooks. In an article published by *The Lancet* in late 2012, authors assessing the changing health conditions in South Africa came to the conclusion that "for the first time in two decades, this progress instils a basis for hope" (Mayosi et al. 2012: 2040).

Governance structures

The structures of health governance in South Africa are outlined by the National Health Act of 2003 which provides the framework for a uniform system encompassing public and private health establishments (Republic of South Africa 2004b). According to the Act, the overall responsibility for healthcare in the country lies with the Department of Health (DoH) which as the national line ministry provides strategic guidance to the sector by setting norms and standards, developing policies and plans, and monitoring their implementation. The provinces in turn are directly responsible for delivering and overseeing most health services from primary care level to specialised

---

228 McIntyre et al. (2008) provide numbers which reflect the huge disparity: in the public sector, there are 4 200 people per general doctor, 10 800 people per specialist, and 620 people per nurse; the private sector, in contrast, counts only 590 people per general doctor, 470 people per specialist, and 100 per nurse. Overall, "the majority of health care professionals work in the private sector, despite serving the minority of the population" (McIntyre et al. 2008: c).

229 The human resources situation in health is exacerbated by the brain drain of health professionals to foreign countries, with an estimated attrition rate of about 25% per year (Department of Health 2011b: 31). As of 2003, there were more South African medical practitioners working abroad (8 921 in Australia, Canada, New Zealand, United Kingdom, United States) than counted in the public sector (7 517) (Department of Health 2011b: 22/32).

hospitals; each provincial government has its own health department with considerable autonomy in terms of resource allocation and programme implementation (Mills et al. 2012).

The health departments at the national and provincial levels are supported by health councils which are assigned to provide advice on health policy matters; the Act further established consultative forums comprising representatives of key stakeholders from the public and the private sector, civil society, academia and donors (Republic of South Africa 2004b).

The highest advisory and coordinating body on HIV/Aids is the South African National AIDS Council (SANAC) which was formed in 2002 to strengthen the country's multi-sectoral response to the epidemic. After a decade in which SANAC existed in name but was more or less dysfunctional, the organisation underwent a major reform process initiated in 2012, through which its mandate was expanded and its structures were radically revamped. As an independent entity, SANAC brings together ministerial leaders, provincial government members and civil society actors from nineteen sectors who are represented in the decision-making plenary chaired by the deputy president. A small secretariat is supposed to facilitate and coordinate the work of the different SANAC institutions such as the Programme Review Committee which monitors implementation, technical task teams which process scientific findings and the Civil Society Forum which was established to foster dialogue and information sharing. The secretariat is also expected to support provincial and district AIDS councils and to help mobilise domestic and international resources. This makes it a focal point for the aid community.

Donor presence in the health sector

As a focus area and 'cross-cutting issue' of many aid organisations, HIV/Aids receives by far the largest amount of external resources provided for health in South Africa, "often in conjunction with support related to other sexually transmitted infections and tuberculosis or primary health care in general" (Fölscher et al. 2010: 59).

According to a spending assessment covering the years 2007/08–2009/10, aid for HIV/Aids and TB interventions amounted to ZAR 5.57 billion (approximately USD 693 million) almost half of which was sourced from the US President's Emergency Plan for AIDS Relief (PEPFAR) programme (see data cited in Republic of South Africa 2012: 92 and SANAC 2013: 3). Hence, considering the scope of financial contribution, the US government stood out as the preeminent player in the field, followed by the Global Fund to Fight AIDS, Tuberculosis and Malaria, the Netherlands, the United Kingdom through DFID and the European Commission. All together, these five organisations accounted for 82% of external funding. The list of donors which contributed smaller amounts and technical assistance is extensive, comprising more than 14 bilateral and seven multilateral agencies (see Republic of South Africa 2012: 93/95).[230]

Given the significant number of foreign actors engaged, it is remarkable that only two of them, namely DFID and the EU, support the health sector beyond HIV/TB, and that aside from informal information-sharing there has been little coordination until recently.[231] In order to improve the harmonisation and alignment of donor activities with the national agenda, the DoH in 2011 launched an 'Aid Effectiveness Framework for Health in South Africa' which provided for the establishment of joint planning and coordination forums (Department of Health 2011e). At the time of our interviews, these institutions did not yet fully work as expected; both DoH officials and donor representatives, however, expressed the sentiment that communication had already improved, pointing to a renewed political leadership and cooperative spirit emerging after an era in which donor–government relationships had broken down.

HIV and health governance in post-apartheid South Africa

From today's viewpoint, the history of health governance in post-apartheid South Africa can be told in three chapters structured along the respective response to the country's most perilous disease: the first is about the initial years of democracy in which the rapid spread of HIV urged the government to take the issue onto the political agenda; the second covers the era of Aids denialism under the Mbeki administration resulting in a deep crisis of government legitimacy and break up of relations with the science and the donor communities; the third starts with the change of leadership in 2009 which paved the way for a radical policy shift initiated by a "passionate" (Interview 11) new health minister with a "powerful presence" (Interview 27) in the DoH and beyond.

Motsoaledi's coming into office is widely regarded as the crucial turning point for HIV and health governance in South Africa. In order to provide the background for conceiving the paradigm shift he brought about, pivotal

---

230 These included the governments of Australia, Austria, Belgium, Canada, Finland, France, Germany, Ireland, Italy, Japan, Norway, Spain, Sweden, Switzerland, as well as IOM, UNAIDS, UNFPA, UNHRC, UNODC, WHO and the World Bank (Republic of South Africa 2012). In addition, various international foundations such as the Bill and Melinda Gates Foundation, Caritas, Red Cross, Médicins sans Frontières, Open Society Institute and the Ford Foundation provided funding and assistance (SANAC 2013).

231 The only informal arrangement which has existed since around 2009 was the so-called EU Plus Working Group in which donors from European member states shared information about their activities, but without any government participation (Interview 5).

developments prior to his term are briefly sketched out before focusing on recent policy processes and the involvement of aid experts therein.

An epidemic on the rise: The spread of HIV in an era of health system transformation

When the first democratic government took over power in 1994 a central endeavour was to overcome the "racially discriminatory, fragmented, and poorly coordinated" (Benatar 1997: 1537) health system inherited from the apartheid regime. The *White Paper for the Transformation of the Health System in South Africa* released in 1997 envisaged a unified national system centred on comprehensive primary healthcare (PHC) at the district level. In order to redress past inequalities, emphasis "should be placed on reaching the poor, the under-served, the aged, women and children, who are amongst the most vulnerable" (Department of Health 1997). The realisation of reform, however, was hampered, first and foremost by the vast lack of human resources and managerial capacity in the public sector (Coovadia et al. 2009). As in other ministries, the new cadre of civil servants in the health department comprised often highly engaged but inexperienced officials "with little knowledge of large bureaucracies, let alone how to achieve innovation through these bureaucracies" (Schneider & Stein 2001: 726).

Such institutional constraints also impaired the implementation of the first National AIDS Plan (NAP) which was developed by the National AIDS Committee of South Africa (NACOSA) and adopted by the Department of Health in 1994 (Schneider & Stein 2001). With its emphasis on the need to adopt a multi-sectoral response and human-rights centred approach, the document represented to many an ideal policy, combining "the technical with the political" and being "comprehensive, practical and carefully costed" (Schneider & Stein 2001: 725). The fact that the fight against Aids was declared a 'Presidential Lead Project' signalled high-level commitment to combat the epidemic and granted preferential access to resources from the government's Reconstruction and Development Programme for related activities (Schneider & Stein 2001).

Yet, the plan did not materialise as expected; in hindsight, many observers attributed the failure to achieve the ambitious aims to the fact that the human resources at the government's disposal in the throes of transition had been greatly over-estimated (Schneider & Stein 2001; Butler 2005; Wouters et al. 2010). Lacking skilled and experienced personnel, the administration struggled to translate the plan into action and to effectively use the resources set aside by the government and donors. Of the ZAR 53 million allocated by the EU for the implementation period 1995–1996 only ZAR 7 million (equivalent to

13%) had been disbursed by May 1997 (Schneider & Gilson 1999; Schneider & Stein 2001).

Due to the inability to put intentions into practice and emerging policy contestation among Aids players[232], HIV rapidly spread during Mandela's presidency, with prevalence among adults aged 20–64 rising from 1.5% in 1994 to 9.7% by 1999 (ASSA AIDS Committee 2011).[233]

Mbeki and Tshabalala-Msimang: The era of Aids denialism

When after South Africa's second general elections in 1999 Thabo Mbeki took over power, "the HIV/AIDS epidemic had already taken on horrifying proportions: approximately 4.2 million South Africans were living with HIV, and an additional 1600 people were infected daily" (Wouters et al. 2010: 176). Right after assuming office, Mbeki directed the development of a new five-year HIV/AIDS & STD Strategic Plan which was finalised in January 2000 (Department of Health 2000). While the pace of its formulation seemed to signal the new leadership's commitment to tackle the increasing Aids problem, the plan lacked clear activities, timeframes and budgets, and thus remained "somewhat generalised in terms of what is to be done and how resources are to be prioritised" (Grimwood et al. 2000: 292); most notably, it kept quiet about concrete treatment options. A novelty put forward was the establishment of a multi-sectoral South African National AIDS Council (SANAC) with the mandate to advise the government on HIV/Aids and STD policy and to oversee and enforce implementation (Wouters et al. 2010). That the institution was to be formed by representatives from government and civil society was widely commended; yet, when it came to the appointment of members, lead activists and renowned academics were excluded (Schneider 2002; Fourie & Meyer 2010).

Mbeki's relationship with the Aids and biomedical community had already been strained by his key role in the Virodene affair and his publicly articulated claims about 'toxic side-effects' of antiretroviral drugs (Baleta 1999).[234] Tensions culminated when Mbeki convened a Presidential Aids Advisory

---

232 Serious disputes in the Aids context emerged about the *Sarafina 2* awareness play project (1996), the quack remedy Virodene (1997), Aids notification plans (1997) and antiretroviral therapy for pregnant women (1998). For details on these controversies, see Schneider (2002).

233 Results extracted from the ASSA2008 AIDS and Demographic model of the Actuarial Society of South Africa, Summary (Prov) Output as downloaded on 22 July 2014 from http://aids. actuarialsociety.org.za/ASSA2008-Model-3480.htm.

234 In 1997, researchers from the University of Pretoria presented Virodene as an allegedly 'breakthrough' treatment to cure Aids. Mbeki as deputy president was a key actor supporting the group despite strong scepticism on the part of the South African biomedical community which he accused of retarding access to life-saving therapy. Due to insufficient evidence and toxic risks, Virodene was eventually rejected by South Africa's Medicines Control Council (Schneider 2002).

Panel to re-examine causes and solutions to the epidemic, inviting a group of 'dissidents' who denied the link between HIV and Aids. Mbeki's championing of the latter evoked massive critique on the part of the local and international science community. Internal pressure led the president to withdraw from the debate, but not to reverse his stance (Schneider 2002).[235]

Mbeki's agenda was pushed forward by his Health Minister Manto Tshabalala-Msimang who persistently rejected the roll-out of antiretroviral treatment, portraying it as 'poison' and promoting unproven alternative remedies instead (Nattrass 2008). Even after being forced by the Constitutional Court to make ARVs nationally available to pregnant women as means to prevent mother-to-child HIV transmission (PMTCT) and being pressurised by the Cabinet to introduce highly active antiretroviral therapy (HAART) for Aids-sick people, the minister continued to promote alternative remedies and preached the alleged benefits of garlic, olive oil and lemon juice for curing the disease (see Heywood 2003; Wines 2004; Nattrass 2006a, 2006b, 2008).[236] Comparing the number of persons who received ARVs between 2000 and 2005 with an alternative of what would have been reasonably feasible in the country during that period, a study later estimated that more than 330 000 lives were lost due to the government's reluctance to provide antiretroviral treatment (Chigwedere et al. 2008).

During the era of Mbeki/Tshabalala-Msimang, the Department of Health's relationships with other actors in the Aids field broke down completely. The local science community and civil society formed alliances internally and internationally to push forward PMTCT and ART programmes on the ground, supported by foreign donors who channelled their aid to NGOs and research projects, bypassing the ministry.[237] The cleavage between the central leadership and lower levels of the system became apparent in that doctors backed by medical associations and provincial governments openly defied the national policy by supplying ARVs to patients (IRIN News 2002; Stoppard 2002).

---

235 For a detailed analysis of the public discourse on the matter and its implications for the relationship between politics and science, see Weingart (2002).

236 The government was taken to court by the Treatment Action Campaign (TAC) which launched a constitutional challenge when the government restricted the provision of the antiretroviral drug Nevirapine to pregnant women for the purpose of preventing mother-to-child transmission of HIV. TAC alleged a violation of the right to healthcare services as granted by the South African Constitution. In 2002, the Court ordered the Minister of Health and the nine Health Members of the provincial Executive Committees to extend the availability of Nevirapine to state hospitals and clinics and to launch a national programme 'without delay'. A detailed summary of the case is provided by Heywood (2003); all official documents related to the litigation are provided on the website of the International Network for Economic, Social & Cultural Rights (http://www.escr-net.org/docs/i/403050, last accessed on 18 January 2015).

237 For an analysis of HIV/Aids-related donor funding to South Africa in the period 2000–2005, see Ndlovu (2005).

In the light of increasing domestic and international pressure following the health minister's speech at the Toronto Aids conference where she reaffirmed her renitent stance, the Cabinet eventually transferred the responsibility for Aids policy to Deputy President Phumzile Mlambo-Ngcuka (Nattrass 2008). This shift of authority and the sick leave of Tshabalala-Msimang in late 2006 opened up a 'window of opportunity' (Kingdon 1984) to overcome the impasse. As chairwoman of SANAC and the inter-ministerial Aids committee, Mlambo-Ngcuka drove forward the development of a new strategic plan, incorporating Aids specialists who had previously been excluded from the policy terrain (Timberg 2006).[238] After extensive consultations with health professionals, scientists, activists and officials from various sectors, the HIV&Aids and STI Strategic Plan for South Africa 2007–2011 (commonly abbreviated as NSP standing for National Strategic Plan) was finalised by an expert task team and approved by the Cabinet in May 2007 (Venter 2007). In contrast to the preceding document, the NSP set clear targets, such as halving the rate of new HIV infections and providing treatment, care and support to 80% of all HIV-positive people and their families by 2011 (SANAC 2007). The plan was praised by health experts, donor representatives and activists alike for its ambitious goals and vigorous commitments which signalled a clear policy shift (IRIN News 2007a; Sapa & AFP 2007). A key actor involved in drafting the document was more critical about the actual soundness of the strategy and expressed the importance of the NSP for civil society at that time:

I don't think it was a perfect policy paper – people say that, but it wasn't. The current five-year plan was something we forced as a way to give us power to shape the policy and implementation agenda. So with that plan at the beginning of 2007, we just threw everything into it, because in 2007 Manto Tshabalala-Msimang was still the Minister of Health, Thabo Mbeki was still the president – they've been forced to back down, but they were still there. So we didn't have strong grounds. So the new strategic plan came along and we said, ok, ARVs, male circumcision, prevention of mother-to-child transmission – let's just put everything in, because if it's in there (…) it would strengthen our hand if we had to litigate, if we could go to the courts and say, look, the Cabinet has agreed to this as a matter

---

238 Another key protagonist in that process was the Deputy Health Minister Nozizwe Madlala-Routledge who during Tshabalala-Msimang's sick leave in late 2006 spoke out against her own government, admitting Aids "denial at the very highest level" (Bevan 2006). Together with the deputy president (allegedly an old friend of hers) she pushed for policy change, reaching out to civil society and scientists whom her absent superior had refused to consult. In August 2007, Madlala-Routledge was sacked by President Mbeki on the grounds of an unauthorised trip to the International AIDS Vaccine Initiative Conference in Madrid and "her inability to work as part of the 'collective'" (Sosibo 2007).

of policy, why is it that they are not prepared to do it when it comes to implementation? (Interview 27)

The NSP was a strong symbol of policy change, but realising it with still reluctant protagonists in key positions proved challenging. Implementation was also hampered by the fact that expertise had "fled from the system" (Interview 27), as a civil society leader put it. Under Tshabalala-Msimang, experienced officials had left the health department on the grounds that they felt unable to justify the institution's policy against their own conviction. A former official who had worked in the Aids unit quit public service in 2003 for this reason:

> *I found myself apologising for where I worked and when I caught myself I realised I can't do this anymore.* (Interview 5)

The era of Tshabalala-Msimang as head of the department ended in September 2008 when Mbeki resigned after losing support of his own party. Interim President Kgalema Motlanthe immediately dismissed Tshabalala-Msimang and replaced her with Barbara Hogan, one of the few ANC members of parliament who had spoken out openly against the Aids denialism of the Mbeki government (Gilbert & Cherry 2008).

Shortly after taking office, the new health minister in a landmark speech before leading scientists, clinicians and activists explicitly acknowledged the causal link between HIV and Aids and commended the contribution of science and civil society in the fight against the epidemic (Treatment Action Campaign 2008). She also actively approached the donor community which over years had been 'chased away' by her predecessor, as an official in the Swedish Embassy put it, requesting for the renewal of cooperation:

> *She asked us to do a lot of things, because she realized that we put ourselves in order and we knew what was going on. And one of the things she asked us was to do a mapping to see what money was going where, which we did, and she also asked us to assist with technical assistance and to assist with money.* (Interview 5)

Hogan's cooperative stance and commitment to a decisive response to the Aids epidemic evoked much enthusiasm among donors, activists, and health professionals; after her first 100 days in office, the head of the Southern African AIDS Clinicians Society assessed her as "absolutely superb", stating that "she hasn't put a foot wrong" (Kapp 2009: 291).

Despite such praise and to the disappointment of many, Hogan's term as health minister ended after only nine months. In the course of a cabinet shuffle in May 2009, the newly elected President Zuma moved Hogan to the less influential public enterprises portfolio, replacing her with the largely unknown medical doctor and previous provincial education minister Aaron Motsoaledi (Smith 2009; Wouters et al. 2010). While his successor had put an end to the era of Aids denialism, the new health minister faced the dual challenge of bringing the epidemic under control and turning South Africa's deteriorated health system around.

Paradigm shift in HIV and health governance

Given Zuma's statement about showering after having sex with an HIV-positive woman[239] and the fact that he removed the popular 'hero' Hogan from the DoH, experts raised doubts whether the course prompted by the interim administration would be pursued under this president (*The Lancet* 2008). Yet, there were signals that he seriously aimed to follow that direction. In a speech at the World AIDS day commemoration on 1 December 2009, Zuma proclaimed a set of changes and initiatives which signalled a radical break with past policies. Aside from pledging increased prevention efforts, he announced a massive testing campaign and a drastic expansion of access to treatment. With effect from April 2010, all children under one year would get antiretroviral drugs if tested HIV-positive; ARVs would also be made available to pregnant women and people with both tuberculosis and HIV having a CD4 count of 350 or less (The Presidency 2009).[240]

The new criteria for ART eligibility literally mirrored the revised recommendations on treatment, prevention and infant feeding in the context of HIV which the WHO had released only one month earlier (World Health Organization 2009a). According to a British advisor in the Department of Health, officials had even arranged a conference call between the WHO and the Presidency "to make sure every single line was totally in line with the international guidance because they were so paranoid of being criticised, because they'd gotten it so wrong before" (Interview 1).

Not only the new ART guidelines, but also other decisions presented by the president were informed by analysis and advice from specialised aid agencies:

---

239 In 2006, Zuma was on trial for an alleged rape of an HIV-positive woman. In his cross-examination, he testified that after having 'consensual sex' he took a shower thinking this "would minimise the risk of contracting the disease" (BBC News 2006). Zuma was eventually cleared of the rape charge but rebuked by the judge for "totally unacceptable" behaviour (Peta 2006).

240 CD4 cells are white blood cells which are essential for the human immune system. If depleted or reduced through an HIV infection, the body is highly vulnerable to opportunistic illnesses and other infections. The CD4 count of a healthy adult ranges from 500 to 1500 cells per cubic millimetres of blood; an HIV-positive person with a CD4 count of less than 200 is diagnosed as having progressed to Aids (NAM Aidsmap 2014). Until 2009, access to treatment in South Africa was limited to those patients who had reached this stage.

shortly after taking office, the health minister had requested the UN to assist the national department in conducting an assessment of the health sector's HIV/Aids response and a mid-term review of the NSP (see SANAC 2010). Specialists from UNAIDS and WHO partnered with senior officials of DoH to undertake these exercises which brought up a range of recommendations, such as to integrate HIV and TB services at the primary healthcare level, shift care and treatment tasks to nurses and auxiliary health workers, introduce a fixed-dose combination of ARVs and modify procurement costs (World Health Organization South Africa 2009; Interviews 6, 11). To the surprise of the experts involved, the government demonstrated an unexpected high level of receptiveness to their advice. A UNAIDS specialist commented:

> *All the recommendations have been addressed to a large extent, so they were very responsive to everything (…), and it's been very nice to see that responsiveness, I must say.* (Interview 6)

After a decade of confrontation and disconnect from the global health community, the South African government seemed anxious to regain legitimacy by aligning national policies to international standards and by revitalising cooperation with international players. The latter were now considered key partners for realising the new health vision of the '10 Point Plan' which had been released as soon as the new administration was in place. The plan outlined the top priorities for the sector. It emphasised the need to provide strategic leadership, implement a National Health Insurance, improve the quality of health services and accelerate the HIV/Aids response (Health Systems Trust 2010).[241] The commitments were later formalised in a 'Negotiated Service Delivery Agreement' which entailed concrete targets to be achieved by 2014 such as increased life expectancy and reduced maternal and child mortality (Department of Health 2010).

The new health minister's and his director-general's approach to the aid community to assist in implementing the targeted initiatives was perceived as a paradigm shift in country offices and embassies. A South African official who at that time still worked for the US government commented:

---

241 The 10 Point Plan lists the following priorities: provision of strategic leadership and creation of a social compact for better health outcomes; the implementation of a National Health Insurance; improving the quality of health services; overhauling the healthcare system and improving management; improved human resources planning, development and management; the revitalisation of physical infrastructure; accelerated implementation of the HIV and Aids strategic plan and the increased focus on TB and other communicable diseases; mass mobilisation for the better health of the population; review of drug policy; strengthening research and development (see Health Systems Trust 2010).

I remember very well during the old administration, the international donors used to have a meeting outside the department where they would discuss strategies on how to assist the department and one of the biggest barrier by that time was that they were not really welcomed (…). But when the new administration came into place, it came up with ambitious plans. We want to put everybody on treatment to get rid of the backlog, we want to improve the sites, we want to come up with new programmes. And the new administration was very open because they went outside to all these donors and said: 'This is the challenge that we have and this is our plan, where do you fit into this, what can you do?' That's when all the donors came and said now 'we can offer this, we can do this, we can do that'. (Interview 17)

This statement hints at two notable aspects pertaining to the renewal of relations. First, the way the government addressed potential partners signalled that the new decision-makers were willing to re-assume leadership and fill the void in which the health department had been deadlocked for a while.[242] They 'opened the door' to the donor community, but at the same time made it clear that the government's agenda would be the frame of reference for support.

Second, the fact that donors were immediately able to pledge assistance indicates that they had not been 'passive' while being excluded from the policy terrain and 'waiting out' Mbeki (Fourie et al. 2010). Instead, they had prepared themselves for leadership change by refocusing portfolios and setting aside resources which they offered as soon as new political protagonists entered the scene.[243] Technical agencies such as WHO and UNAIDS had put HIV specialists in place ready to provide policy advice if requested.[244]

How external expertise and money was utilised in the course of subsequent reforms is illustrated by two exemplary processes outlined in the following section, namely the development of the National Strategic Plan 2012–2016 and the introduction of the National Health Insurance system.

---

242 A DFID advisor who entered the health department in 2009 remarked: "When I first arrived (…), things were quite messy here, it was very difficult. The previous minister had left, there was a big vacuum, the director-general had been moved out, it was almost anarchic. There was no sense of who was in control" (Interview 1).

243 DFID and GIZ, for instance, came up with new Aids and health-related programmes which were agreed in 2009/2010, namely the SARRAH programme (Strengthening South Africa's Revitalised Response to AIDS and Health) and a Multi-sector HIV and Aids Prevention Programme (MHIVP).

244 Both the medical officer for HIV/Aids in the WHO country office as well as the UNAIDS senior policy & programme adviser interviewed for this research started their work in South Africa in 2009.

External experts' involvement in developing the NSP II

As indicated, the coming in of Motsoaledi meant a complete about-turn not only of politics, but also of donor–government relations in the field of health and HIV. A DoH official illustrated this by saying:

> *Immediately all the donors came into the department again, you could see the faces of people whom you couldn't see during the old administration. You couldn't see them. But now they are all in the building, they are welcomed and there is continuous working together and collaboration.* (Interview 17)

Within a short period of time, external experts particularly from UN bodies such as WHO, UNAIDS or UNICEF established close working relationships with key officials in the DoH and SANAC whom they immediately assisted in setting up initiatives such as the mass HIV Counselling and Testing (HCT) campaign launched in 2010 (SANAC Secretariat 2010).[245]

When the term of the NSP 2007–2011 for South Africa's Aids response was coming to an end, a pending task on the agenda was the development of a succeeding document. Preparations for the process of policy formulation began in early 2011, though not in a very coordinated way, as a DFID advisor remarked:

> *SANAC was approaching people for bits of work and it was very, very messy and not sustainable, and no one knew who was doing what. So we agreed to form a group of development partners that had funds or resources, and together with SANAC and UNAIDS – UNAIDS took on quite a strong role earlier on in helping to coordinate that – we formed a group and created a matrix of who would support what. So SANAC said they wanted consultants in these provinces and they wanted someone working on the national desk, and then we provided expertise as part of that.* (Interview 1)

In the following period, SANAC received technical assistance at various levels, with experts being deployed and funded by a range of donors including DFID, Sida and specialised UN organisations. A senior policy & programme advisor of

---

245 The government launched the national HIV Counselling and Testing (HCT) campaign in April 2010 aiming at encouraging citizens to know their HIV status and access counselling and treatment. While the ambitious goal of getting 15 million people tested by June 2010 was not reached, the initiative was still praised as the largest scale-up of HCT world-wide, with over 13 million being tested and 400 000 people initiated in ARVs within one year (Bodibe 2011; Mbengashe 2012).

UNAIDS was commissioned to assist the SANAC CEO in drafting a first road map for the whole NSP process which was taken to the Programme Implementation Committee for approval and subsequently presented to the plenary to be endorsed. The first key activity organised was a two-day think tank meeting in April 2011 where representatives from government departments, civil society and donors met to deliberate "what should be in the NSP, what's the evidence showing us, what's the guidance, where should we be going" (Interview 6), as a UNAIDS advisor put it. The discussions were informed by findings from a range of analyses which had been conducted since 2009, such as the mid-term review of the first NSP for 2007–2011, the review of the health sector response, a national Aids-spending assessment, and comprehensive technical reports on the status of the epidemic, current policies and prevention efforts (see Fraser-Hurt et al. 2011; SANAC 2011a, 2011b). All of these studies had been realised with external funding and immense technical support, most notably from UNAIDS, WHO and the World Bank which had provided experts to coordinate and compile the evidence gathered.

This brought to light that since the development of the first NSP, approximately 1.5 million people had become newly infected with HIV, and despite massive expansion of treatment an estimated 2 million had died of Aids-related causes. It was strongly suggested that the only way to overcome the epidemic was "to rapidly intensify HIV prevention efforts so as to virtually halt all new infections" (SANAC 2011a: 5). The latter recommendation matched well with the new UNAIDS global strategy 'Getting to Zero' which the UNAIDS country director presented to participants of the think tank meeting. Aside from setting the target of zero Aids-related deaths and discrimination by 2015, it advocated for high-quality, cost-effective HIV prevention programmes to reach zero new infections (UNAIDS 2010).

After two days of consultation, delegates arrived at some basic decisions. The three 'zeros' should be adopted as long-term vision of the NSP which for the first time should explicitly integrate tuberculosis, given the outstanding high co-infection rate of HIV and TB; moreover, prevention should become a prime pillar of the response. In August 2011, a first draft NSP was disseminated for public comment. In the following months, the editorial team received more than 100 written submissions from a broad range of organisations and individuals with diverse interests. Key issues of contestation which emerged in the process of consolidation related to the nature and scope of the policy document – how broad or specific it should become, what kind of concrete targets it should include (and how many), and to what extent it should or must be costed (Treatment Action Campaign & Section27 2011: 14). Some civil society organisations such as Section27 strongly pushed for costing and budgeting the plan to ensure implementation and be able to hold the state accountable in terms of resource allocation (Section27 2011). In their view, the new NSP would need to serve as "a plan that people actually refer to rather than just (...) a symbol" (Interview 27), as a lead Section27 member put it, arguing:

> *A symbol was good for a point. But that's not what we need now. Now we need a plan that will actually guide implementation.* (Interview 27)

Other stakeholders, however, had a different conception of what the document should be, envisaging a framework strategy with overall goals and objectives rather than a detailed plan. A senior advisor representing the EU on the SANAC Programme Implementation Committee which oversaw the writing process commented:

> *This is something that we found with working through the document time and time again, bringing people back again and again that this is not a plan, it's a strategy! Because people want to go further every time. And I think the consultants that we have – they've chopped down every time and said no, this is not a plan, this is a strategy. The provinces and the people who are going to execute this, they will make this a plan.* (Interview 5)

The final version, approved by the SANAC Council in mid-November 2011, comprised a chapter on costing which estimated financial requirements at ZAR 131 billion (equivalent to USD 16 billion) for the whole period (SANAC 2011c). However, it was explicitly emphasised that the amount should be indicative, "with detailed implementation plans being developed separately by the sectors and provinces" (SANAC 2011c: 76) by March 2012.

On World AIDS Day in December 2012, the 'National Strategic Plan on HIV, STIs and TB 2012–2016' was officially launched by the president (IRIN News 2011a). The four key objectives forming the basis of the response were to address social and structural barriers to HIV, STI and TB prevention, care and impact; to prevent new HIV, STI and TB infections; to sustain health and wellness; and to increase the protection of human rights and improve access to justice (SANAC 2011c).

Despite some criticism on specific aspects,[246] the new NSP was widely commended by actors from the government, civil society and donors who

---

246 The Treatment Action Campaign and Section27, for instance, criticised insufficient attention to tuberculosis throughout the document, claiming that "TB has been integrated more deeply into each successive draft of the NSP, but often still seems overwhelmed by HIV" (Treatment Action Campaign & Section27 2011: 7).

particularly lauded the process through which the policy was produced. A South African HIV specialist in the Swedish Embassy commented:

> *All of us pitched in, and we all supported this and we all funded this (…). I think a lot of people have worked really hard to get this together in a year's time. It was a consultative effort, which has never really in the past been so much consultative like this time, and I think this was under the leadership of the minister and the new DG and other role players in the Department. I think it was really, really positive.* (Interview 5)

Even the usually highly critical Treatment Action Campaign (formerly attacked as a 'disgrace' by Tshablala-Msimang) stated that the "NSP 2012–2016 has been developed through an unprecedented degree of collaboration between civil society and the Department of Health, under the auspices of SANAC", and proclaimed that it marked "the beginning of a new era in the response to HIV, TB and the social drivers of these epidemics" (Treatment Action Campaign & Section27 2011: 1). After a decade in which the cooperation between government and other players had completely broken off due to the leadership's counteraction to international consensus on HIV/Aids, the NSP process signalled that South Africa was coming 'back on track'.

Creating a South African National Health Insurance system

A second undertaking which marked Motsoaledi's first term in office was the establishment of a National Health Insurance (NHI) system. That process has so far significantly been informed by expert analysis and international 'evidence'.

The idea of introducing some form of mandatory health insurance had been taken up several times in South African history, even long before its democratic transition. During the 1990s, several policy proposals were brought forward, but not followed up further (McIntyre 2010).[247] At its 2007 policy conference in Polokwane, the ruling African National Congress passed a resolution which called for the realisation of a National Health Insurance system (African National Congress 2007). Yet, only two years later, the NHI emerged as an explicit priority on the government's agenda. In his first budget speech as health minister, Motsoaledi justified the envisaged reform as follows:

> *The present system of healthcare financing can no longer be allowed to go on, because it is simply unsustainable. No way can we perpetuate a*

---

247 The different proposals over time are outlined in the *Green Paper* on the NHI; see Department of Health (2011d: 12–14).

*system whereby we spend 8.5% of the GDP whereas 5% caters for 14%
of the population or 7 million people, on the remaining 3.5% caters for
a whopping 84% of the population or 41 million people. Nowhere in
the civilised world can you find that state of affairs; the present model
of healthcare financing is just outright primitive, and we are going to
abandon it. (…)*

*Hon Chairperson, what is NHI? – it [sic] is a system of universal
healthcare coverage where every citizen is covered by healthcare insurance,
rich or poor, employed or unemployed, young or old, sick or very healthy,
black, white, yellow or people of whatever [persuasion].* (Parliamentary
Monitoring Group 2009)

In late 2009, Motsoaledi established a Ministerial Advisory Committee (MAC)
made up of 25 individuals with a cross-section of skills and expertise, including
lead South African scientists, health practitioners, government officials,
representatives from the pharmaceutical and medical schemes (health
insurance) industries, and 'international' (i.e. foreign) health experts. Led by
the CEO of the Human Sciences Research Council, the committee was given
the task to compile recommendations regarding the NHI design and relevant
health system reforms.

After one-and-a-half years of preparation (and considerable public
speculation), the government presented a first policy paper on the NHI. Issued
in August 2011, it outlined the vision of an integrated healthcare system in
which everyone would have access to appropriate, efficient and quality health
services provided through appropriately accredited and contracted public and
private providers. Financial risk protection for the whole population was to
be ensured through a mechanism of cross-subsidisation, whereby funding
contributions would be linked to an individual's ability-to-pay and benefits
would be in line with an individual's need (Department of Health 2011d). In
view of the need for a "complete transformation of healthcare service provision
and delivery" and a "radical change of administration and management", it
was proposed to phase in the NHI over a period of 14 years, whereby the first
five years would be used to establish core institutions and to introduce core
features at selected pilot sites (Department of Health 2011d: 5).

The launch of the *Green Paper* on the NHI was followed by immediate
action on the part of DoH, such as entering stakeholder discussions and
setting key interventions scheduled for the first phase of implementation.
Thereby, it received substantial assistance delivered through the DFID-funded
'SARRAH' (Strengthening South Africa's Revitalised Response to Aids And
Health) programme. Negotiated in 2009, SARRAH was set up as a programme

channelling technical and financial support to strategic initiatives related to South Africa's health sector reforms. The budget of GBP 25 million was placed at the disposal of the national health department for selected priorities agreed with DFID. A central role in this flexible arrangement was given to a senior advisor from the UK who was seconded to the DoH with the dual mandate of advising high-ranking decision-makers and overseeing SARRAH-funded activities. HLSP, a UK-based, internationally operating firm specialised in consultancy, project management and policy advice in the health sector, was contracted to supply expertise and administrative support as requested by DoH leaders.

The NHI became a key area for which these services were used. The range of tasks carried out by contracted specialists in the course of conceptualisation and implementation is comprehensive. The compilation of technical support and consultancies specifically addressing NHI matters was provided in the first four years of the SARRAH programme (2010–2013). The information was drawn from project briefs available on the programme's website as of 1 August 2014. Since not all activities might have been documented in this form, the list should be understood as indicative rather than fully comprehensive:

Table 19: Expert support to the NHI process through SARRAH 2010–2013

Description / Purpose	Time frame	Provider
Logistical support for the Ministerial Advisory Committee on NHI	01/2010–12/2012	HLSP, N James
Consultancy for the provision of support services for the NHI communications strategy	03/2010–05/2012	Meropa Communications
Technical support for the purchasing sub-committee of the NHI Ministerial Advisory Committee	09/2010–11/2010	Team of consultants led by L Gilson & K Grant
Consultancy services for the purchasing sub-committee of the Ministerial Advisory Committee	09/2010–08/2011	J Miot
Project planning and management support to the DoH project team	12/2010–12/2011	J Katzke
Technical assistance to district specialist task team	04/2011–10/2011	K Jacobs
Consultancy on development of packages of services to be provided on NHI pilot sites	03/2011–12/2011	L Ngubane, K Grant, D Whittaker, J Katzke
Project manager to coordinate work related to district clinical specialist teams	08/2011–01/2012	N Bandezi
Expert advice to the Office of the DG in developing NHI health-purchasing implementation steps	09/2012–09/2013	S O'Dougherty
Project manager to the Office of the DG in coordinating the national community outreach programme	10/2012–03/2013	E Paulus
Technical support for General Practitioners initiative	2012–2014 (sic)	SARRAH team

Description / Purpose	Time frame	Provider
Technical and logistical support to NHI road shows in 11 NHI pilot districts	2012–2013 (sic)	SARRAH team
Provide revised national costing of NHI pilots	01/2013–03/2013	PricewaterhouseCoopers
Consultancy to DoH on strengthening management arrangements of central hospitals	02/2013–04/2013	S Hayes
Rapid assessment of the status of the 11 NHI pilot districts	02/2013–05/2013	SARRAH technical leads and consultants
Technical support for establishing prototype PHC facilities	08/2013–11/2013	S Asmal

Source: Project briefs available on the SARRAH website accessed 1 August 2014.[248]

Categorising the assignments listed above, one can broadly differentiate between facilitating activities and analytical work, which was assigned to experts outside the DoH. They provided either administrative support or technical input. The former mainly helped to drive forward the NHI process insofar as consultants were commissioned to organise meetings and events, to ensure that timetables were adhered to, or that written documentation was distributed to all stakeholders. Such tasks were the main components of the logistical support for the Ministerial Advisory Committee, technical assistance to the district specialist task team or the project management support to the DoH project team. In the latter case, for instance, the consultant was expected to "develop and maintain a planning process and secure timely contributions and revisions from team members and stakeholders; monitor and report on project implementation plans with timelines, critical path and risk management; facilitate all Project Workgroup forums and record deliberations and findings for the Project Leader" (SARRAH 2011a).

While these kinds of assignments required strong administrative/managerial skills, the second type presupposed specialist knowledge of a highly technical nature and analytical abilities. Experts were commissioned to generate 'evidence' in the form of reports, analyses and assessments to be used for refining NHI components. The range of documents produced includes six technical papers on resource allocations and purchasing strategies distributed to the Ministerial Advisory Committee; a report for the director-general on the proposed packages of services to be available under the NHI with details on how these services could be delivered through a purchaser/provider split; a study to determine frameworks and modalities for contracting private sector general practitioners in public clinics; a revised national costing of the NHI; an assessment of 'ideal' primary healthcare facilities; a rapid appraisal of the 11

248 http://www.sarrahsouthafrica.org/ABOUTSARRAH/SARRAHprojectbriefs.aspx (accessed on 18 January 2015).

NHI pilot districts after 12 months, covering their status in terms of quality, hospital reforms, primary healthcare (PHC) re-engineering, infrastructure, human resources, management performance, referral systems, and cooperation with private doctors. The list could be further continued. Notably, most of the analyses supplied through the SARRAH programme were done by renowned health experts from South African academic institutions such as the University of Witwatersrand or the University of Cape Town. Hence, while the expertise was mobilised by external agencies (i.e. DFID/HLSP), it was largely provided from 'locals' with national and international research experience contracted to serve as consultants to the DoH.

Nevertheless, external health system ideas did play a significant role as points of reference in the development of the NHI. Many of the commissioned studies delineated 'lessons learned' outside South Africa, pointing out how models worked or did not work in other countries. The *Green Paper* on the NHI explicitly refers to international evidence and experience.[249] Following the release of the *Green Paper*, DFID organised three study tours to the UK where high-level decision-makers such as the minister and DoH's director-general met with their counterparts and visited health institutions to gain an understanding of the British system (SARRAH 2011b, 2012a, 2012b). Together with the EU, DFID also co-sponsored and facilitated an international conference held in Johannesburg where experts from aid organisations, foreign universities and health ministries presented experiences from a range of developing and developed countries, including South Korea, Thailand, Turkey, Ghana, Germany, Australia, France and the United States. The event was attended by high-level decision-makers including the minister and the director-general, senior government officials, experts from academic institutions and private sector representatives (see Department of Health 2011c). In her concluding speech, DG Matsoso highlighted that the "lessons shared were eye-opening" (Department of Health 2011c: 43), and that insights gained would be considered in the process of refining the South African NHI system.

The conference took place in early December 2011 and was a key event in the phase of public consultation on the *Green Paper* which formally ended on 30 December 2011. By then, the DoH had received over a hundred submissions from various stakeholders; main points of criticism were a lack of public deliberation in the initial stage of policy development, and vagueness with respect to crucial aspects of the reform, such as cost implications and the future role of private schemes (see, for instance, Helen Suzman Foundation 2011; South African Private Practitioner Forum 2011; Van den Heever 2011). In early 2014, the minister announced that the release of an NHI *White Paper*

---

249 See, for instance, Department of Health (2011d: 27/3).

which would shed light on such details was 'imminent' (Kahn 2014a; at the time of writing, the much anticipated document had not yet been disclosed, but was said to be 'in the final stages', Jadoo 2014; Kahn 2014b).

Patterns of current health governance

The processes of NSP and NHI development were described in sufficient detail to illustrate the paradigm shift within the DoH which represents a radically changed stance towards the use of scientific knowledge and expert advice. In contrast to the preceding administration, the new leadership extensively draws on local and external expertise, adopting a governance approach which bears a number of characteristics.

First of all, it strongly features scientific knowledge as the point of departure for policy development. Documents such as the National Strategic Plan for HIV/ Aids and the *Green Paper* on the NHI entail numerous references to studies and analyses whose findings are used to justify decisions. The following extracts are exemplary for the prevailing pattern of argumentation:

> *The NSP's goals and strategic objectives are guided by evidence from various reports, including the Know Your Epidemic (KYE) report, a situation analysis of TB in the country and other epidemiological studies. These studies identified key populations that are most likely to be exposed to or to transmit HIV and/or TB (…). Within each strategic objective, these key populations will be targeted with different, but specific interventions, to achieve maximum impact.* (SANAC 2011c: 13)

> *Evidence has demonstrated that those who are not adequately covered by any form of health insurance are among others women; children; the elderly; low income groups etc. It is for this reason that coverage should be extended to all these populations.* (Department of Health 2011d: 12)

Whereas the previous government had openly questioned the robustness of evidence put forward by the mainstream science community, it is now used as the main means of legitimation for policy decisions. The importance of underpinning decisions with consensual scientific knowledge was also emphasised by the chief director of the HIV/Aids unit in the DoH who stated:

> *We pursue evidence – evidence that's relevant, that's closer to the issues. We understand evidence is not sufficient; it has to deal with values and other issues. So we're not ideological about what we're trying to do. Our starting point because of the burden of disease that we need to fix [is that]*

there are some things that we know that work and we want people to help us to do that. (Interview 19)

Although the DoH director seemed wary of conveying the impression that the government blindly followed evidence without scrutinising it for its relevance and embedding it into the social context, his statement affirms the significance of scientific knowledge as a reference point in policy-making.

A second feature which was manifest in both the NSP and NHI processes is the strong orientation towards international guidance; the uptake of WHO's ART guidelines and of universal coverage as an overall objective of the health system (promoted by the WHO since 2005) illustrates efforts to realign policies with the international agenda. After an era in which the government deliberately ignored recommendations from global health players, decision-makers in the DoH seemed eager to demonstrate that this has changed with the new leadership, as a DFID advisor pointed out:

> *They went out of their way to make sure absolutely everything that they did was totally in line with international policy (…). HIV/Aids is the most obvious one but in other areas as well. And they are at pains to point out that they stick to international guidance. So when WHO suggests changing the CD4 count, the level at which you start treatment, South Africa takes it on immediately and they've been very proactive in keeping up with international best practice because they have this terrible history together. So they've gone to the other extreme now, they can't now do enough in line with international guidance.* (Interview 1)

The fact that alignment with international guidance has become an imperative in the health department is reflected by the statement of a director who emphasised:

> *Whatever we are doing has got to be internationally accepted (…); we need to make sure that we meet the international standards.* (Interview 18)

The new orientation towards scientific knowledge and international guidance has come along with an openness towards external assistance and receptiveness to advice which can be seen as the third characteristic of the current governance approach. In both the NSP and the NHI processes, the DoH extensively drew on advisors and consultants to realise the envisaged reforms. In seeking facilitative and analytical support, however, decision-makers seem selective in terms of whom to approach for what kind of tasks and on which terms.[250] Commenting on the consultants coming into the DoH, a senior official emphasised:

> Whatever work they are doing, it's work that is a directive of the Director-General or the minister. So they don't come here and want to do their own things. (Interview 18)

The statement points at what can be seen as the fourth outstanding feature of current health governance, namely the strong guidance executed by DoH leadership ranks, both in terms of setting the agenda and directing experts in supporting the department's policy work. Various advisors engaging with the DoH reported on the firm stance of their South African counterparts. A UNAIDS specialist commented in this regard:

> They do close the doors if they don't think you're useful. And they don't miss their words, they say it clearly – they fire the consultant on the night. (Interview 6)

Since the DoH has been severely weakened in its capacity through the brain drain of specialists, it now depends on the support of outside experts to manage the massive reforms envisaged. Yet, it seems as if decision-makers use external assistance in a deliberate way, namely as a means to get things done quickly and to figure out *how* to achieve objectives rather than *which* objectives to achieve. This is reflected by a statement of the health department's chief director for HIV/Aids who explained:

> You find that when the problem is quite substantial, you tend to spend your time on the things that need to be fixed today. So, what do experts and technical advisors do? My sense is that what they do is really look in the manner how we're doing things and say: 'Look, there is one aspect, if you would do this, this will release many of those things that you need to do.' So, it's like finding the disconnect between the things that we really want to do, the capacity that we have and the thing that's holding us back not do it (…).

> They can do the analysis of the composition of my finance, they can tell, look, you know, if you're saying this where you want to go, in the manner how your budget is right now, it is unlikely you get there (…). When we

---

250 A review of the SARRAH programme, for instance, reports that in many cases the DoH took over responsibility for the appointment of consultants, "and instructed DFID and HLSP accordingly" (Wright 2012: 13).

hit bottlenecks on quality – when we're not achieving our coverage, when we're not being able to actually attract the right people and reach the right people, then there is some analysis that needs to be done (...) – that's the role that they can actually play. (Interview 19)

In this narrative it becomes clear that external experts are ascribed a facilitative function, rather than a determining role in policy development and implementation. The chief director of the HIV/Aids unit used a fitting metaphor to illustrate this approach in a nutshell:

These people for me, when they come in, they are co-pilots; they're not driving the plane. (Interview 19)

Re-building relationships: Government interaction with the local science community

As mentioned earlier, decision-makers in the DoH increasingly resort to members of the South African science community when seeking assistance, which indicates that after almost a decade of schism between government and academia, relationships are slowly building up. Yet, the lack of 'histories of trust' and of institutionalised dialogue still hamper the full utilisation of local knowledge resources. Various interviewees raised the issue that policy-makers tended to request support from donor organisations although expertise was locally available. A WHO representative in the Pretoria country office reported on her experience:

South Africa is asking us for expertise when we use their South Africans to send elsewhere. So it's like the proverbial biblical saying 'the prophet is not known in his own home' acts here. (Interview 12)

Aside from the still existing disconnects between the political system and academia, another problem lies in the fact that the South African knowledge community in health is strong with respect to scientific performance, but small in terms of numbers (see Chapter 6). Given multiple obligations, the capacity of scientists to serve as advisors in policy processes is severely limited, as a professor at the University of the Western Cape stated:

South African knowledge communities have an absolute place – there's just not always enough of it and enough time. You know, I mean in a place like this, a) it's quite difficult to travel to Pretoria for a meeting, b) we're training people and the universities have loads of other things to do, so the ability to provide the very kind of flexible, immediate expertise when it's needed in very short time frames – the donors do that and mobilise it from international consulting communities. (Interview 28)

The local knowledge base is too small to cope with the burden of disease in South Africa. The lack in capacity of expertise is thus filled by aid organisations which source specialists from their country offices and from global expert networks.

Conclusion

As shown by using the examples of the Aids plan and the National Health Insurance reforms, external experts do have a presence in the current era of South African health governance. Providing advice, analysis and administrative support, they impact on policy development and implementation in various ways. Yet, they do so at the request of leaders who demonstrate a high level of steering capacity both in terms of setting the agenda and dealing with donors. Not being dependent on aid money, decision-makers are able to determine the conditions of support and to be selective with regard to whom to approach for assistance. At the same time, a strong local science community and vocal civil society limit the risk of external interference.

The fact that South Africa's HIV and health policies have been radically revised and adjusted to international standards is less the result of outside pressure than of the government's attempt to regain credibility in the global health arena and to redress the failures of past policies. In the reform of the health system, UN bodies such as WHO and UNAIDS have gained considerable influence, "not so much because they've come in and sought to be influential, but because what they have produced has been picked up internally and used to develop policy" (Interview 27), as a civil society leader put it. In a similar vein, a professor at the University of the Western Cape remarked:

I would say (...) it's not a kind of very overt and forceful colonisation of ideas; it's a process of harmonization and emulation. (Interview 28)

The policy shifts of recent years can thus be interpreted as a process of deliberate alignment pursued by a health administration which is characterised by both a high degree of receptiveness to expert advice and science and a considerable degree of autonomy in setting its own agenda.

Tanzania environment: Opportunistic adaption

Sectoral context

Tanzania is by comparison a rich country in terms of environmental wealth with respect to its natural ecosystems of forests, grasslands, savannah, wetlands, rivers, lakes and the Ocean (United Republic of Tanzania 2012c). The world-famous Serengeti National Park is only one of several biodiversity hotspot areas.[251] Tanzania's territory is home to numerous endemic animal and plant species (United Republic of Tanzania 2009): by 2003, 10 008 plant species, 316 mammals, 229 breeding birds, 335 reptiles, 116 amphibians and 331 fish species had been counted in the country (UNEP 2014). Although almost 30% of the terrestrial area and around 10% of territorial waters are protected (IUCN & UNEP-WCMC 2011), large parts of the natural habitat are at risk: many biosphere reserves such as Mount Kilimanjaro are severely affected by land degradation (Temba 2012). Coastal and marine areas are suffering from pollution and erosion that have led to a decline in living resources (United Republic of Tanzania 2009). To this is added over-harvesting, illegal logging, bush fires, and detrimental cultivation practices leading to rapid deforestation (United Republic of Tanzania 2009). According to the FAO Global Forest Resources Assessment 2010, Tanzania is among the top ten countries that had the largest annual net loss of forest area world-wide between 2000 and 2010. (FAO 2010b).[252] Poverty is seen as the main cause driving the persistent exploitation. The former director of the Forestry and Beekeeping Division sketched the linkage between poverty and deforestation as follows:

> *People are heavily depending on [forests] for their livelihood. They don't have another support. They don't have another alternative, they need to survive. Sometimes climate change is causing havoc here. Crops don't produce when they are about to produce. Drought at flowering stage or at the fruiting stage, maize and everything collapses, what do you do? And you need to see your children surviving. So the alternative is to harvest a tree (…).*

---

251 Other areas that are known as biodiversity hotspots are the Eastern Arc old Block-Mountain Forests (Usambara, Nguru, Uluguru, Ukaguru and Udzungwa Mountains); the coastal forests (e.g. Pugu, Rondo); the Great Lakes for Cichlid fishes (lakes Victoria, Tanganyika and Nyasa); the marine coral reef ecosystems; and the ecosystems of the alkaline Rift-Valley Lakes (e.g. Natron and Eyasi) (United Republic of Tanzania 2009).

252 From 2005 to 2010, Tanzania lost 403 000 hectares per year, equivalent to 1.16% of the total forest area (FAO 2010a).

In Dar es Salaam and other cities, 90% of the household energy is charcoal. You can't use electricity, it is very expensive. You can't use gas, it is very expensive. And sometimes availability of gas is a problem, acquisition of the gadgets, they are very expensive. So for a normal person, middle income and others – they use charcoal. Then those guys in the rural areas, they know there's a big demand for charcoal. Some business people are going in the rural areas looking for charcoal. So if you cut more trees for charcoal making, you earn something. (Interview 58)

Forest and nature degradation is a huge problem in Tanzania, threatening not only more than 700 plant and animal species, but also the livelihoods of large parts of the human population.[253]

Governance structures

The structures of environmental governance in Tanzania are laid down by the Environmental Management Act (EMA) of 2004, which frames environment as a horizontal policy issue cutting across various sectors. Line ministries such as the Ministry of Natural Resources and Tourism, which is also responsible for forests, are required to manage environmental matters in their respective areas. The Act, however, established the director of environment and his unit – the Division of Environment in the Vice-President's Office (VPO-DoE) – as the focal body in charge of policy-making, coordination and oversight under the overall leadership of the minister of environment. EMA also specified the mandate of the National Environment Management Council (NEMC) which serves as the leading technical advisory and regulatory agency. Aside from conducting and coordinating research, its main functions are to enforce compliance with environmental quality standards by reviewing and monitoring environmental impact assessments. As in other policy areas, the actual implementation of policies and legislation falls under the responsibility of local government authorities (United Republic of Tanzania 2004).

Donor presence in environment

Since 2004, donors supporting and carrying out environmental activities in Tanzania have collaborated in the so-called 'Development Partners Group on Environment', or DPG-E in short. As of 2014, it comprised ten bilateral funders, namely Belgium, Canada, Denmark, DFID (UK), the European

---

253 According to the IUCN Red Lists 2012, 302 plant species and 408 animal species are currently threatened, including species classified as critically endangered, endangered and vulnerable (IUCN 2012a, 2012b).

Union, Finland, France, Germany (and GIZ), Norway and USAID, as well as five multilaterals, namely UNDP, UNEP, UNESCO, the World Bank and the African Development Bank. Depending on their focus, these aid providers are related to sub-groups on climate change, natural resource management or environment in general. The members of these groups are supposed to interact with their main counterparts in government, that is, the Vice-President's Office – Division of Environment and the Ministry of Natural Resources and Tourism, through the established dialogue structure including meetings on thematic areas, cluster working groups, and discussions related to general budget support (Development Partners Group Tanzania 2014b). Yet, at the time of research, participants admitted that these forums did not work as they should. Government officials complained about being unduly occupied with aid meetings, and donor representatives were upset about the absence of policy-makers in the same and the consequent slow pace of decision-making. Overall, relationships seemed tense, with both sides accusing the other for not adhering to the agreed conditions of dialogue and cooperation.

The making of environmental policies in Tanzania

Environment conservation has always been a playground for external actors in Tanzania. Under colonial rule, the British imposed preservation policies which restricted human activities in designated game parks and nature reserves. After independence, a range of external organisations such as the World Wildlife Fund (WWF) and the German GTZ took over and divided up the funding and management of national parks, while Tanzania's first President Nyerere supported the expansion of protected areas primarily in order to boost the country's tourist industry (Levine 2002).

With the Brundlandt Report 'Our Common Future' published in 1987 by the World Commission on Environment and Development, the notion of 'sustainable development' ascended to the international agenda, and environment gained centre stage as an issue of global concern (World Commission on Environment and Development 1987). For Tanzania, this translated into generous funding offers arising in the run-up to the 1992 Earth Summit in Rio de Janeiro, as the former Director of Environment remembered:

> *When at that time, in 1991 January, these negotiations for the Earth Summit were going on, it gave rise to several meetings at the global level, at the regional level within Africa, at the sub-regional level, and at national level (…). And in order to be able to understand the process and to contribute meaningfully, you simply had to get time to participate, to travel – and that's expensive. So in Tanzania, I put up together a team*

of – at that time, I think it was twelve technical people from various ministries, and also representations from NGOs. And you couldn't have the government to support these travels because per diems and flight tickets are expensive. I was simply fortunate that there was such a climate of giving from the donors – it was basically the donors who were just covering everything. They simply wanted me to produce the list of people that were going. So I wrote a letter, 'this is what I want'. They were just happy to support. (Interview 66)

Amongst the major aid providers sponsoring the participation were UNDP, the Netherlands, and Nordic countries such as Sweden. According to the former director of environment, their support enabled his delegation to take part in the summit's preparation as well as in negotiations on the three Rio Conventions on biodiversity, climate change and desertification. From his perception, Tanzania was thereby given a voice in the global discourse.

The increased donor interest in environment not only yielded new programmes and funding mechanisms (e.g. the Global Environment Facility), but also brought forth new conditions. The World Bank, for instance, made environmental impact assessments of varying depth obligatory for the approval of projects, and it required IDA borrowers to formulate 'National Environmental Action Plans' which Tanzania endorsed in 1994. As in many other recipient countries, this donor-initiated document led to the foundation of the subsequent national environmental policy. Aside from identifying six urgent problems – land degradation; lack of accessible, good quality water; environmental pollution; a loss of wildlife habitats and biodiversity; deterioration of aquatic systems and deforestation – it framed environment as a cross-sectoral issue and set overall policy objectives (United Republic of Tanzania 1997). The role of the lead organisation in the process of policy development was given to the Division of Environment in the Vice-President's Office, which received substantial assistance from the Danish government.[254] Although, according to the former director of environment, the Danes did not set any conditions related to the policy content, it is remarkable that their financial support justified the presence of Danida representatives in policy discussions, as the following statement reflects:

They supported the process. And I don't remember any incident where we had any preconditions given by the Danish on what we should say in our policy. There was nothing like that. Of course, because they provided

---

254 The Division of Environment was established in 1991 under the Ministry of Natural Resources and Tourism. It was transferred to the Vice-President's Office in 1995 to give it more political clout (Death 2012).

funding, they would be interested in the process to ensure that the money they are giving is being put to good use. And so we would bring them on board in terms of the meetings we'd hold for our discussions and they would be giving their views. (Interview 66)

The policy was primarily shaped by national consultations and a range of workshops attended mainly by government officials, donor spokespersons and a few NGO activists. Despite

a clear bias toward an elite understanding of the problems of the environment and their solutions, (...) there was little public or private controversy over the guidelines and plans of the National Environmental Policy when it was finally adopted by the Cabinet in 1997. (Elliott-Teague 2011: 849)

In the subsequent years, environment as a policy issue came to the fore on Tanzania's agenda; the increasing importance can partly be attributed to the active lobbying of intellectuals with influence in political circles (Assey et al. 2007), but also to an enhanced engagement of international organisations which supported environmental champions "to express their views" (Interview 66) and financed government activities. According to the then director of environment, donors accounted for over 90% of the funding for environmental programmes and projects undertaken by his unit.

The Division of Environment also received external assistance in the course of two policy processes which took place in parallel in the early years of the new millennium: the development of the Environmental Management Act (EMA) and the poverty reduction strategy known as MKUKUTA. Donors backed up these processes through two major initiatives: the 'Institutional and Legal Framework for Environmental Management Project (ILFEMP)' designed to prepare environmental legislation, and the 'Integrating Environment Programme' aimed at 'mainstreaming' environmental issues into MKUKUTA. The former was primarily sponsored by the World Bank, USAID, Sida and the WWF; the latter was supported by UNDP, UNEP, Danida, DFID and the Norwegian government (Assey et al. 2007; Elliott-Teague 2011). Both initiatives were officially housed in the Vice-President's Office, and included the use of national and foreign experts for various tasks.

The ILFEMP project started in 1998 with a team comprising an American technical advisor and three Tanzanian specialists from different research institutes commissioned to review the institutional framework of environmental management, and, in the second phase, to draft a respective bill (Elliott-Teague 2007).[255] The process involved consultative meetings with representatives from government ministries, non-governmental organisations and donors. Supporting studies and background papers were produced by individually hired scholars (Elliott-Teague 2011). After two years of analysis and discussion, the team published a report outlining viable options for institutional arrangements. Interestingly, they rejected initial donor concerns over institutional structures as unjustified (Elliott-Teague 2011). Taking up the report's recommendations on future legislation, an expert group paid by the World Bank and made up of two members of the University of Dar es Salaam, the executive director of the Tanzanian law organisation LEAT (Lawyers' Environmental Action Team) and the chief parliamentary draftsman in the Attorney General's Office, developed a Bill which went for Cabinet approval. After a brief public hearing, the Environmental Management Act was finally passed by parliament in 2004 (Elliott-Teague 2007).

The use of local expertise, the wide range of stakeholder workshops held and the fact that the final drafting team consisted of solely Tanzanian actors suggest that the act indeed reflects a national perspective on how environmental management should be organised.[256] There is no evidence that international assistance for the preparation and formulation of the law presupposed any concrete policy demands (Elliott-Teague 2011). Yet, donors were intensely engaged in the process, pushing for the development of environmental legislation. It is questionable whether, without their sponsoring of the review and drafting process, EMA would have been developed in this form and at that pace.

A similar 'pushing effect' of external assistance was attained through the 'Integrating Environment Programme' related to the process of developing Tanzania's National Strategy for Growth and Reduction of Poverty (MKUKUTA). Initiated in 2003, the aim of the programme was to make sure that the policy considered environment as a key component in poverty reduction efforts.

The idea of 'mainstreaming environment' internationally came up at around the turn of the millennium when a number of influential World

---

255 According to Elliott-Teague (2011), the Tanzanian experts consisted of Dr PJ Kabudi, a member of the Faculty of Law at the University of Dar es Salaam as well as the chair of the board of directors of a non-governmental organisation called the Lawyers' Environmental Action Team (LEAT) who was brought in as the legal expert and project coordinator; Dr Suma Kaare who at that time was affiliated with the Economic and Social Research Foundation and served as the institution's specialist, and Mr Deo-Gratias Gamassa, an ecologist at the College of Wildlife Management, who was hired as natural resources expert. The foreign member of the ILFEMP team changed. Finally, the position was filled by an international consultant from Great Britain.

256 The final team preparing the EMA draft consisted of two members of the Faculty of Law at the University of Dar es Salaam, the acting executive director of the Lawyers' Environmental Action Team LEAT and the chief parliamentary draftsman in the Attorney General's Office (Elliott-Teague 2007).

Bank publications such as the environmental strategy 'Making Sustainable Commitments' (World Bank 2001) established linkages between environment, poverty and growth, and made the claim that these needed to be better addressed in developing countries policies (see also World Bank 1996; Bojö & Reddy 2002; Dale 2005).[257] The aid community broadly adopted this agenda, and UNDP together with UNEP launched a global 'Poverty-Environment Initiative' through which governments in developing countries would be assisted to include environmental objectives into national plans and budgets (Bass & Renard 2009). Tanzania was one of the pilot countries receiving financial and technical assistance for this purpose. The Vice-President's Office, which was assigned to coordinate the mainstreaming efforts, got a full-time advisor from the UK who played a central role by disseminating environmental information and analyses, keeping the process on track and assisting the MKUKUTA drafting team (Assey et al. 2007).[258] Donors' technical leads provided input through their participation in the Environment Working Group which was established "to improve consensus amongst environmental stakeholders" (Assey et al. 2007: 18), bringing together representatives from government, the private sector, civil society and aid organisations. Moreover, the programme funded a range of analyses which substantially informed the MKUKUTA document, such as a review of expenditures on environment (Vice-President's Office 2004) and the development of indicators of poverty-environment linkages (Vice-President's Office 2005).[259] Ultimately, the MKUKUTA entailed at least 15 environment-related targets (Rutasitara et al. 2010: 12), ranging from 'reduced land degradation and loss of biodiversity' to 'improved access to clean and safe water' and 'reduction in harmful industrial and agricultural effluents' (United Republic of Tanzania 2005: 37, 33, 46). Progress in achieving these targets was to be measured against mostly quantitative indicators as specified in the MKUKUTA log-frame and monitoring master plan (United Republic of Tanzania 2005; Ministry of Planning, Economy and Empowerment 2006).

---

257 The World Bank's publication list on the environment-poverty nexus has become too vast to be reflected here. Amongst others, the Bank has issued a range of 'Environment Strategy Notes' as well as an 'Environment Matters' series with annual reviews, all of which are accessible on its website. In 2012, the Bank launched its new environment strategy for the next decade (2012–2022) (World Bank 2012e).

258 The post of the 'Poverty-Environment adviser' was filled by David Howlett, a DFID specialist on food and climate change policies who during 2002–2005 had been seconded to UNDP (Assey et al. 2007).

259 The report on the poverty-environment indicators was contracted to two UK-based and one Tanzanian institution, namely the Environmental Resources Management (ERM) London, the Institute of Resource Assessment (IRA) Dar es Salaam and Oxford Policy Management Limited (OPML) Oxford (Vice-President's Office 2005). The public expenditure review was contracted to NORPLAN Tanzania Branch, a consulting company linked to the Norwegian firm Multiconsult (Vice-President's Office 2004).

UNDP/UNEP assistance continued during the implementation of MKUKUTA with a focus on reporting and generating statistics on environmental conditions (UNDP & UNEP 2014). Through the Development Partners Group on Environment, experts from various agencies and embassies substantially contributed to developing the subsequent strategy MKUKUTA II for the period 2011–2015, as a UNDP environmental specialist in the Dar es Salaam office sketched out:

> *At the point where you are doing sector reviews, partners are invited to provide their input. At the point where they are harmonizing and (...) finalizing the final document, donors are also invited – the entire plan is presented to stakeholders and you input in it. So we are mainly involved and we provide the input. And sometimes they may ask for even writing, so you provide that writing.* (Interview 41)

Concrete 'input' was provided, for example, in the form of comments on priority results areas which strongly proposed including climate change and sustainability aspects into operational targets (DPG 2010). In the final document, various references to these matters can be found. One strategy to reduce income poverty (goal 2), for instance, foresees "integrating, harmonizing and coordinating environmentally sustainable policies and strategies for growth in key growth sectors, including climate change adaptation and mitigation" (United Republic of Tanzania 2010: 42).

Tanzania's 'environmental mainstreaming' work has been widely praised as a success and has been promoted as a 'best practice' case in various reports (see, for instance, Assey et al. 2007 and Dalal-Clayton et al. 2009). All in all, Tanzania's environmental policies, legislation and programmes are regarded as "very advanced" (Interview 36) by the international community.

A look beyond intentions and official narratives

Looking at government action related to environmental management as opposed to intentions, however, reveals a picture that starkly contradicts the success story told about Tanzania in aid publications. A review assessing the progress made during MKUKUTA I found persistent problems "relating mainly to knowledge gaps and change in mind-set on the importance of environment. Lack of accurate data, capacity limitations in terms of requisite professional skills to suit the different sector situations as well as financial resources still remain major setbacks" (Rutasitara et al. 2010: v). Several interviewees from donor organisations pointed to an appalling discrepancy between policy statements and (perceived) government action; some bluntly conceded that this divergence may partly derive from their organisations' interference in environmental governance. A natural resources specialist in the Finnish Embassy was outspoken about the obviously divergent agendas of local and external players:

> *Many of the policies and legislations that exist have been pushed by development partners. And the government has put a minimum of interest on that because they have another kind of agenda and another kind of economy where they work.* (Interview 36)

For officials concerned with environmental issues in ministries and parastatal bodies, the lack of interest and support on the part of the government is manifested in deficient resources allocated for environmental interventions. A senior officer working at the National Environment Management Council stated:

> *The integration of environment in most of the development plans is there. But in the budgetary process, that's not happening. It is just in the documents, but we don't see really the commitment. (…) So that's the problem. It is acknowledged that environment is very important for the poverty reduction efforts, but whenever it comes to the resource allocation, it is not one of the priority sectors.* (Interview 59)

A retired director who had led the Forestry and Beekeeping Division in the Ministry of Natural Resources summarised his experience:

> *The government has so many other priorities. Environment, forestry is not among the priorities. The priority here it is agriculture, it is energy, it is education and water, infrastructure. So those are the sectors heavily covered by the government, but forestry is not among them. So, you see, you get more money from donors, from workshops, consultancies. You analyse the situation through the consultant, you get the reports – but you can't put those reports into action, simply you don't have that ability. So that is the difference.* (Interview 58)

Given financial constraints and insufficient staffing levels in public entities, environmental policies and legislation are hardly put into practice. A case in point in this regard is the Environmental Management Act.

The Environmental Management Act: "Great", but "ineffective"

The Environmental Management Act – according to a World Bank employee a "great act" that "is fantastic" – became operational in 2005. Yet, the progress in implementing institutional reforms prescribed by the Act is slow. By 2007, only a few ministries had established environmental sections as required, and none had prepared environmental action plans (Government of Tanzania & Danida 2007). Compliance with the environmental impact assessment system, a central component of the Act, remains poor, which partly derives from a low awareness of regulatory requirements among local government bodies and the fact that violations are rarely penalised (Sosovele 2011).[260] Public authorities seem unable to fulfil the functions assigned to them by the environmental law, given the lack of a "clear and proper mandate to institutions and personnel with autonomous positions" (Pallangyo 2011: 517) as well as insufficient human and financial resources. An NEMC officer told us:

> *Our institution, it has the mandate to oversee that the act is being enforced (…). But if we don't have the funds to actually implement it on the ground, then really you find that we have a problem. Because I think there was the expectation that the government would provide support in terms of implementation of the act, but that is not the case.* (Interview 59)

In order to boost the execution of the new legislation, the Vice-President's Office in 2006 proposed an 'Environmental Management Act Implementation Support Programme', in short EMA-ISP. The idea of the programme was to establish a basket fund which would increase financial resources. The anticipated 'medium-term outcome' of the programme was to create an "enabling framework for EMA implementation – i.e. through policy harmonisation, planning, environmental assessments, enforcement, reporting, and awareness creation – (…) that significantly improves environmental management in Tanzania" (Government of Tanzania & Danida 2007: 54). In light of the broad assistance received from technical and financing agencies for the development

---

260 According to EMA, public and private investors are obliged to commission an analysis of potential environmental effects in the process of planning development projects. Only registered experts are authorised to conduct such environmental impact assessments (EIAs), and the National Environment Management Council is mandated to review and oversee compliance with the EIA requirements. The legislation for this system is in place, but it is not yet working in practice. A recent study found that "even the central government was implementing construction projects that fell under mandatory EIA list, without subjecting them to the EIA process" (Sosovele 2011: 129). The author of the study found a low degree of awareness of the EIA requirements among decision-makers in Dar es Salaam municipalities, stating that "up to 40% of those interviewed admitted to have no basic knowledge of the act and EIA regulations" (Sosovele 2011: 129).

of EMA, decision-makers in the Vice-President's Office anticipated various 'partners' to sponsor the programme.

The interest on the donor side, however, was unexpectedly low. Only Denmark joined in 2007, pledging assistance in the amount of 35 million Danish kroner (around USD 6 million at that time) over a period of five years and thereby covering 15% of the estimated programme costs. In 2011, Canada came on board, with a contribution of USD 2.75 million approved until 2013. A retired high-ranking official who had initiated the programme in the Vice-President's Office surmised shifting agendas of donor governments as a major reason for the meagre support:

> *In the development of the programme, we had all the donors together and the Canadians were looking at it. The Embassy here was for it, they had to convince their bosses in the centre in Canada; and that depends on the politics in the centre, and depends on which priorities they have. Sometimes priorities change, sometimes an initiative begins well – and then there are things called elections (…). You have a change of government and this change of government comes with different policies saying now we are getting out of environment, now I think we are looking at gender, you know. Those kinds of things can actually happen.* (Interview 66)

At the time of our interviews, frustration was high on all sides – government officials were disappointed about the lack of funding and donor staff at Danida despaired about poor progress. A mid-term review conducted in 2010 recommended a 'refocus' of Danish support in order to achieve visible results until the end of the programme:

> *Given the lack of success in establishing a functioning basket fund for support to EMA-ISP, the slow pace of implementation of on-going activities, the rapid development in some sectors (i.e.: the increased focus on agricultural productivity) and possible new needs in these sectors as a result, the ASR [Annual Sector Review] team strongly recommends a "refocusing" exercise. The ASR finds it urgent to look for the most appropriate modality to ensure that there will be documented results/ outcomes in the last three years of Danida's support to EMA implementation.* (Danida et al. 2010: 9)

Notably, government and donor actors concerned with EMA-ISP stated different root causes for the strained situation. An official at NEMC underlined the lack of financial resources as the major obstacle in implementing the Act and the programme, whereas the Danida officer in charge pointed to the lack of capacity in the Tanzanian counterpart institutions. Her narrative on the problem is cited at length, since it entails a number of implications which are discussed below the quotation:

> *Interviewee: Things have not been smoothly, because the capacity is very weak there. We did a capacity assessment for the Vice-President's Office and NEMC. The report just said their staff is overstretched, they need a support, technical support. And still they couldn't accept that.*
>
> *Interviewer: In which field of knowledge do they have the greatest needs where you would say that should be something that has to come from outside?*
>
> *Interviewee: We are not there to monitor day-to-day activities because that would be micro managing from the mission point of view. We are assessing the type of reports we receive, the quarterly reports, the annual reports, the work plans and budgets that we get. If you submit to us your annual work plan and we review it three or four times – what would your judgement be? There is a problem here. Because here is an individual coordinating for ten ministries to prepare everything – and you get various different reports with a different format, though they have a standard format.*
>
> *Then you look at the type of activities people are planning to implement – at times they are out of scope. Then you look at the person that is coordinating the programme, you look at his work, at his knowledge, and the skills and the capacity, is he a team leader? A real team leader, because a team leader has to be flexible and tolerant. How is he coordinating the crew? How are the people that he is coordinating responding to the issues that he is raising? Those are the things that we look at in general. And we find that maybe they need someone else to assist. And then, as the time goes, he's trying to pull back and assist them to have that ownership. So you feel also the ownership is not there, you just get the ownership when they want the disbursement of funds.*
>
> *And now at the coming in of Canadian CIDA, the review team felt that no, the programme is suffering. There is very slow implementation; we get very low quality reports. And so we feel there is need for someone to come in and assist you in various areas. Especially they didn't have a standard monitoring and evaluation system. If someone could come in and help them with that, maybe things would move.* (Interview 33)

In her statement, the Danida programme officer indicates some important aspects pertaining to the understanding of 'capacity' and the nature of bureaucracy on the donor side. The fact that the capacity of government bodies is assessed on the basis of reporting, planning and management performance implies a strong technical perspective on public administration. The problematic framing of incongruent reporting formats and the missing monitoring and evaluation system confirms this notion. Adopting such a technical view – no reference to the content of the reports was made – it logically follows that if someone helped to settle administrative deficiencies, 'things would move'. Consequently, the mid-term review urged the Danish Embassy to draw on the expertise of an international technical assistant, suggesting to contract a *"process consultant, expert in results-based programming (…) with immediate effect"* (Danida et al. 2010: 7, italics in original).

This kind of argumentation implies that the main reason for the poor implementation of the programme is insufficient administrative capacity. What it seems to ignore, however, is the political nature of the issues at stake. Given that environmental management is handled as a cross-cutting issue involving various ministries which often pursue conflicting objectives (e.g. an increase in agricultural production or industrial investment vs. environment conservation), it is obvious that institutional reforms entail difficult negotiation processes. The constant delays in planning and approval procedures and the absence of key actors in decision-making meetings support what can be seen as an indication of a low priority of the EMA implementation on the Tanzanian agenda, or simply as a sign of the complexity of cross-sectoral governance.

Through the technical lens of aid providers, however, such political intricacies seem to be blanked out. Danida's and CIDA's joint response to the lack of progress was to strongly push for an advisor to be embedded in the Vice-President's Office who should drive forth the process and 'assist them to have that ownership'. The negotiations about technical assistance turned out tediously, given that VPO officers in charge did not see a need for external support. Danida's programme manager described the situation as follows:

The Vice-President's Office – in principle, they don't want advisors. They feel that they have the capacity to implement activities on their own. And later on, they said 'No, we don't want an international advisor, we want a local advisor. But still, if you want to bring in an advisor, the funds to support the advisor's role should not come from the programme. You should outsource somewhere, but not use the same funds (…).'

And so they have accepted now to have an advisor, but not long term, they want a short term advisor. We have just received the draft terms of reference. We are now in the process of reviewing and seeing how we can bring in an advisor, because we would like the advisor to start in July. (Interview 33)

Donors seemed unhappy with this arrangement, which might also have resulted from the experience that the 'contextual analysis' delivered by a short-term advisor in the inception phase of the programme passed unheeded:

> *After the advisor left, the report was kept on the shelf, it was never revised. And so you find now, the start of the programme had a lot of challenges. From the beginning, they did not want to have a technical advisor. So for that case, the programme has also been affected by not having a technical advisor to assist them, also how the report should look like.* (Interview 33)

In 2014, Danida and CIDA funding for EMA-ISP was about to be phased out. At the time of writing, there was no final report publicly accessible which assessed the impact of technical assistance and the progress of the programme until external support ended. In light of the extensive donor engagement in the development of the Environmental Management Act and its international promotion when it was adopted, it is remarkable that the aid community's interest in the actual implementation of the Act seems to have faded away. In line with the changing global agenda, the focus of donors in Dar es Salaam appears to have shifted towards a new prime topic on the rise, namely climate change mitigation and the related REDD+ process. Once again, Tanzania is among the pilot countries in which the feasibility of a new international approach is being tested.

The emergence of REDD+ and the spread of related aid programmes in Tanzania

REDD+ is the commonly used term for an envisaged global mechanism of channelling payments to developing countries which effectively contribute to climate change mitigation. REDD stands for 'Reducing Emissions from Deforestation and Forest Degradation'; the plus indicates that aside from a reduction of greenhouse gas emissions, conservation, the sustainable management of forests and the enhancement of forest carbon stocks are considered as rewarding mitigation efforts.

REDD+ evolved in the course of various high-level meetings related to the United Nations Framework Convention on Climate Change (UNFCCC). While the role of forests as greenhouse gas reservoirs has long been recognised, halting and reversing forest loss as an approach of the global climate change regime was formalised in the Bali Road Map agreed by the 13th Conference of the Parties in 2007 (UNFCCC Conference of the Parties 2008).[261] Although details of REDD+ continue to be negotiated and a financing mechanism is not yet in place, the concept has been taken up by the aid community which promptly designed a range of programmes in order to 'prepare' the potential beneficiaries.

Norway was at the forefront of donor countries incorporating REDD+ into its development work through the 'International Climate and Forest Initiative' which the government established in 2008. According to the environment counsellor in the Norwegian Embassy in Dar es Salaam, Norway had a great interest in getting Tanzania to participate:

> *Tanzania was already chosen as one of the countries that we wanted to try this out. And why Tanzania was chosen was because we wanted to have African countries and also wanted to have countries with dry forests. So Congo Basin is part of this initiative, but also then Tanzania and Zambia. It was in the beginning three countries on each continent. So very early the Embassy here, the ambassador started dialogue with the government in this country to see if there was an interest. And it was.* (Interview 39)

In April 2008, the governments of Norway and Tanzania signed a letter of intent on climate change collaboration for which Norway pledged 500 million Norwegian Kroner (equivalent to USD 83 million at that time) over a period of five years, with the money being destined for policy development, pilot projects, and research related to REDD+. Shortly after, Tanzania was also selected to join the World Bank's Forest Carbon Partnership Facility through which financial and technical assistance is channelled to countries preparing for REDD+. In 2009, the United Nations came in with the UN-REDD programme, a collaborative partnership of FAO, UNDP and UNEP launched with the objective "to assist developing countries to build capacity to reduce emissions and to participate in a future REDD+ mechanism" (UN-REDD Programme 2011: 1). Other REDD+ related aid projects which started at around the same time included Finland's support to the first comprehensive forest inventory in Tanzania, the so-called National Forest Monitoring and Assessment, and the Clinton Foundation's Clinton Climate Initiative with a focus on the development of social and environmental standards for the implementation of REDD+ activities. In sum, donor commitments for REDD+ efforts in the period 2009–2012 amounted to USD 93.5 million (Kaijage & Kuhanwa 2013).

---

261 Already the Kyoto Protocol of 1997 referred to the "promotion of sustainable forest management practices, afforestation and reforestation" (United Nations (1997), Article 2) as a measure to achieve quantified emission limitation and reduction commitments.

The generous supply of assistance fostering REDD+ processes in Tanzania can be explained by the fact that the country serves as an ideal field of experimentation for this new approach: with 35.3 million hectares, the country is endowed with vast forest resources which cover almost 40% of the mainland area (United Republic of Tanzania 2012d: 5). Given an annual deforestation rate of 1.16%, forests are at a high risk (FAO 2010a). Aside from the 'appropriate' natural conditions which make Tanzania predestined for the new international approach, the preceding involvement of various donors in the country's forestry sector might have been a factor boosting the prominence of Tanzania as a forerunner of the REDD+ regime.

External influences on forest governance in Tanzania

The history of foreign engagement in Tanzania's forestry sector dates back to the early 1970s. Since forestry and related industries played an important role in their own economies at that time, Scandinavian countries which favoured Nyerere's socialist vision of *ujamaa* were among the first to provide assistance by first sending experts and later on channelling money to Tanzania's forestry administration, research and training institutes.[262] Until the 1990s, their support focused on the expansion of village forestry and the commercialisation of forest plantation and logging activities, emphasising the potential of forestry for economic development. With the rise of 'sustainable development' on the international agenda, donors such as Sweden and Finland reframed their aid towards environmental aspects of forestry. At the programmatic level, this meant that support to state-led forestry industries was gradually phased out, being replaced by initiatives promoting community-based approaches and privatisation, and their incorporation into policies and law. In the course of this paradigm shift, 'Participatory Forest Management' evolved as the favourite theme of forestry-related aid in Tanzania.

The notion of Participatory Forest Management (or PFM in short) subsumes a range of different concepts and arrangements varying from country to country.[263] The basic idea of the approach is that local communities should be involved in the management and utilisation of natural forests and woodland, which in Tanzania, as in many other states, has historically been an exclusive domain of the central government. During the 1990s, various

---

262 By 1972, ten Swedish forestry experts to Tanzania worked for the government's Forest Division and the Tanzania Wood Industries Corporation (TWICO) paid by Sida; in the mid-1970s, Sweden accounted for almost 90% of the Forestry and Beekeeping Division's and TWICO's combined budget (Katila et al. 2003).

263 In the understanding of the FAO, "participatory forestry refers to processes and mechanisms which enable people with a direct stake in forest resources to be part of decision-making in all aspects of forest management, including policy formulation processes" (FAO 2012).

donors, including Sweden, Finland, Norway, Denmark, Germany, UNDP and the World Bank started to pilot participatory management through a range of projects in different districts, while at the same time advocating and providing support for a comprehensive reform of policies and legislation. In 1998, the old forest policy which had been carried over from colonial rule was revised and a new version approved (United Republic of Tanzania 1998). This was followed by a new Forest Act passed by parliament in 2002 (United Republic of Tanzania 2002). Together, the new policy and legal framework meant a substantial change in forest governance in that it decentralised authority and formally allowed communities to own and (co-) manage forests under a set of arrangements. The Act notably encourages private sector involvement, and embraces the principle of subsidiarity, stating that the responsibility of forest management should be delegated to the lowest possible level. The reforms were widely praised by the donor community which lauded Tanzania for having "one of the most advanced community forestry jurisdictions in Africa as reflected in policy, law and practice" (Blomley & Ramadhani 2006: 94).

In the years following the policy change, Participatory Forest Management spread from a couple of pilot sites to being implemented in various districts across Tanzania. By 2008, around 2 300 villages engaged in PFM under joint or community-based forest management arrangements covering almost 4 million hectares equivalent to 11% of the total forest land (Blomley & Iddi 2009).[264] Research conducted in recent years has found slight signs of improved forest conditions in PFM sites as reflected by increased basal areas and declined forest disturbance by human activities, and pointed to a few examples where villages have begun to see economic potential from forest management (Blomley & Ramadhani 2006; Blomley et al. 2008; Ngaga et al. 2014; Treue et al. 2014). Yet, the same studies also document a wide range of constraints and problems which seem to overshadow the improvements gained, ranging from persistent exploitation, illegal logging and elite capturing of benefits to massive governance shortfalls and pervasive corruption at all levels.

Officials commenting on the situation referred to the lack of financial and human resources for controlling what is happening on the ground. Donor staff, in contrast, expressed that the government has little incentive to enforce compliance with its own legislation, given the vested interests of individuals and collusive networks in forest activities. A counsellor in the Finnish Embassy commented in this regard:

---

264 Under Joint Forest Management agreements, ownership remains with the government while communities co-manage a designated forest area and in turn get shared benefits and user rights. Under Community-Based Forest Management arrangements, "villagers take full ownership and management responsibility for an area of forest within their jurisdiction and declared by village and district government as a Village Forest Reserve" (Blomley & Ramadhani 2006: 94).

> *There are politicians who interfere in the affairs of the ministry all the time. And the only person that could make any changes is the Minister for Natural Resources, not the others because they are more or less administrating, they are technicians. And as much as they want to change the things – even the director of FBD [Forestry and Beekeeping Division] when he was there or the CEO of TFS [Tanzania Forest Services Agency] – as much as they want to change things, there are limits to that. Because you always have somebody, a politician coming there and asking for favours and make sure that this functions like this, and this, and this. (…) There are lots of people who are looking for their own good. So the policy, the legislation and programmes are very good in Tanzania, very advanced. But they cannot function properly because of political interference – they cannot, absolutely.* (Interview 36)

A donor-financed report authorised by the Ministry of Natural Resources and Tourism in fact found evidence of "self-dealing, nepotism and cronyism involving timber trade" (Milledge et al. 2007: 11) permeating all government levels, as well as "high levels of collusion, organisation and protection between different government institutions and the private sector" (Milledge et al. 2007: 12); the authors of the study concluded that "current policy, as set out in the formal laws and regulations governing the management of these resources, was systematically being manipulated by domestic and foreign private sector interests in concert with senior Tanzanian and foreign government officials" (Milledge et al. 2007: 2).

The outcomes of aid to the forestry sector: Discontent and frictions

Having spent around USD 30 million on introducing PFM in Tanzania (Treue et al. 2014), donors were rather dissatisfied with the state of forest governance at the time of our research and perceived the government as insufficiently committed to put any effort in changing the situation. A counsellor at the Finnish Embassy expressed the common discontent on the donor side as follows:

> *All the funding for the community based forest management has been coming from the development partners. The government has not funded it as such at all. So I mean it's very clear that they have the policy and the legislation on this. But it's a clear sign if there is no funding from the government for this type of activity – they don't see it as a priority.* (Interview 36)

Budgetary figures do not confirm the claim that the government did not fund Participatory Forest Management "at all", but they do show a significant imbalance between local and external resources: during 2005–2008, the government allocated around USD 16.8 million for development programmes of the forestry sector, while donors provided more than twice as much, namely USD 35.6 million which accounted for 68% of the total budget (Akida et al. 2012).[265]

Aside from the small financial contribution from the government, the slow progress in implementing activities seriously disgruntled staff in country offices and embassies under pressure to deliver results and disburse appropriated funds. As indicated by the following statements, their explanations for the various deadlocks ranged from capacity constraints to disinterest and deliberate jamming on the part of their Tanzanian counterparts. With regard to the first of these obstacles, a Danida officer commented:

> *At the PMO-RALG, it's one officer responsible with forest activities. And it is not only one donor who is supporting participatory forest management. For instance, you have Finland, you have Denmark, you have the World Bank. It's over 60 districts in the country implementing Participatory Forest Management. But in the sector coordination, you have one component leader. Can this one person manage three different donors with three different headquarter demands? Those are the challenges that you see in terms of capacity.* (Interview 33)

Whilst acknowledging the additional burden donors put on already overstrained government units, the interviewee still complained about the lack of engagement as reflected by the absence of leading officials in environment working group meetings:

> *You expect the people who should come to these technical meetings are directors, but they send in junior officers who are not decision makers or policy-makers. Then you have the steering committees, where you expect the permanent secretaries will be there for you to discuss the policy implementation. Then they bring in junior officers, not directors. But this is the meeting where decisions have to be made. So there is also that*

---

265 In the Tanzanian Five-Year Development Plan 2011–2016, the discrepancy between projected local and external resources is even wider, with the government being expected to provide USD 1 million (TSh 1 548 million) against USD 8 million (TSh 13 131 million) from development partners. According to the plan, the forestry sector would require an amount of TSh 71 563 million for the fiscal years 2011/12–2015/16; the open balance is to be covered by other sources such as the private sector whose contribution is not reflected in the figures (President's Office 2012).

weakness in not understanding the significance of the programme in that particular organisation. That is what you also see. (Interview 33)

From donor experience, the only way to get their counterparts in government engaged is to provide tangible incentives in the form of individual payments to those attending the meetings and events. This practice, however, seems to have got out of control, resulting in a situation where the pace of programmes has become solely dependent on the extra amounts paid. Yet, it proves difficult for donors to abolish the incentive system they have created, as the Danida officer spelled out:

We have reached a point where developing partners say 'no, we will not give you top up allowances, we're not giving you seating allowances, we're not giving you honorarium. Now, here's a project that does not support that'. But this is an officer who is not only responsible for this project; he also has to look at this project. Now this project pays more. Do you expect him to assist you in this? He is paid less. But there is a five days meeting where he will be paid 400 000 in the end of the week. Where will he go? (Interview 33)

The sentiment that the 'per diem' culture has seriously affected programmes in the forestry sector in a detrimental way was not only expressed by the Danida officer. Her colleague in the Finnish Embassy also raised the issue, reporting on the support for Tanzania's National Forest Programme which had been developed with Finnish assistance a decade ago. In order to boost its implementation, Finland set up a project which was supposed to run from 2009 to 2011 and included a grant of EUR 6 million to be channelled through the MNRT. By 2012, however, only EUR 3 million had been used, with the result that the project was extended until 2014. Commenting on the disbursement difficulties and the poor financial management on the part of her counterparts, the counsellor in the Finnish Embassy stated:

With the Ministry of Natural Resources, it's not very easy to have a good relationship because things are not moving. (…) And there are reasons for that. And I can only guess because I am not in the ministry. But for me, it's very much a deliberate thing. I mean people – it's not rocket science. They could make those systems work. They know how to work them. But there is a lot of mismanagement of funds. Funds are directed to different directions where they shouldn't go. And then I also think it's deliberate that they were only able to use half of the money that we were giving them for two years – they used it in three and a half years. And you know, somehow in my mind the idea is that if it lasts for six, seven years, it's easier to get more daily allowances, all these per diems, discussion workshops organized and so on. So it kind of dilutes the whole thing. (Interview 36)

The fact that the use of funds in the context of the National Forest Programme lacks transparency had already been attested by a review conducted in 2010. It found that documentations for training sessions, workshops and meetings were missing, funds had not been audited and procurement procedures had not been followed (Karani 2010). The on-going problems with regard to the financial management of MNRT and PMO-RALG finally led the Finnish Embassy to re-allocate the remaining project resources towards service providers and private sector companies in the forestry sector, arguing that:

This is the only way to support something that works instead of continuing this very confrontational relationship with them [the ministries]. (…) It doesn't take us anywhere if we just continue doing audits. I mean, it's difficult to give them money and see all the time that the audit reports are bad and their financial management is not in place and so on. So we try to find those alternatives where can we work. (Interview 36)

Finland was not the only donor that withdrew funding from the Ministry of Natural Resources and Tourism due to concerns of financial accountability and deficient progress. The World Bank had a similar experience with its Forest Conservation and Management Project starting in 2002 with the objectives to scale up participatory forest management, to get an endowment fund in place and to improve service delivery by establishing the Tanzanian Forest Services Agency, amongst others. With the MNRT as 'implementing agency' on the government side, the World Bank disbursed almost USD 35 million until the project ended in 2009. The 'Implementation Completion and Results Report' rated outcomes as 'moderately unsatisfactory', indicating significant shortcomings in the operation's achievement of objectives (World Bank 2010c). Asked for the Bank's reaction to the negative assessment, the senior environmental specialist in the Dar es Salaam country office commented:

Well, I can tell you with regards to that, we stopped financing MNRT. I mean right now there are no programmes or whatsoever with MNRT through the World Bank. So I think for a variety of reasons, because they weren't able to deliver, because there were all kinds of corruption problems, I mean there was serious mismanagement of funds and – walk down the street and you'll hear the same answer. (Interview 46)

As most aid agencies and embassies suspended funding or terminated cooperation with MNRT in the aftermath of corruption cases and allegations, the ministry faced a serious crisis at the time of research. The withdrawal of external assistance substantially weakened the MNRT not only in financial terms, but also with regard to its political influence in the evolving REDD+ regime.

The changing nature of aid to the forestry sector under the REDD+ regime

The aid community's turning away from ministries towards other players in the forestry sector, notably NGOs, private industry and academia, had significant implications for both the direction of resource flows and the power relations in the context of the REDD+. Norway as the most instrumental donor driving the process determined not to channel any funds of its REDD+ portfolio through the government, justifying the decision in terms of the misuse of aid money in its previous natural resources support programme.[266] Instead, the available resources were transferred directly to NGOs implementing pilot projects, universities carrying out research and the secretariat of the National REDD+ Task Force. That the latter was established at the Institute of Resource Assessment of the University of Dar es Salaam and not in one of the key ministries assigned with the political authority to deal with climate change and forestry (i.e. the VPO-DoE and the MNRT) was to a significant extent the result of Norway's objection to placing this central institution in one of the government ministries. Commenting on this arrangement, the counsellor in the Norwegian Embassy stated:

> *Interviewee: This current process, of course, is part of government responsibility. But instead of having the secretariat within any of the ministries, it's at the university. So that is also kind of giving the authorities support without channelling funds directly to the ministry.*

> *Interviewer: Is this a unique case due to this corruption case?*

---

266 From 1994 to 2006, Norway financed the so-called 'Management of Natural Resources Programme' in Tanzania, spending around USD 60 million, about USD 5 million per year. After 12 years of support, a final evaluation raised doubts about the use of funds; subsequent audit reports of a Danish consultancy firm found evidence of massive mismanagement and corrupt practices, such as (double) payments of per diems and allowances for workshops which did not take place as indicated, the coverage of undocumented travel expenses, and the purchase of over-priced or non-existent goods and services, amongst others (Jansen 2009). As a consequence, Norway stopped funding to the Ministry of Natural Resources and Tourism which was responsible for the programme.

Interviewee: Yes, as far as I know from the Norwegian side, it is, this kind of set up. Because usually they work much closer with the relevant sector ministry.

Interviewer: And does that harm your processes?

Interviewee: Of course some will think that we have a closer cooperation when the money is following the dialogue, so it might be. I mean, we know that the Ministry of Natural Resources very much would like also to have funds, of course. I also know that in some meetings, the ministry has not met. I should not say that they are boycotting, but almost…that's suspicion. That might be because of this arrangement, but also I think it's mainly because it's an on-going competition between the Ministry of Natural Resources and VPO about who should be in charge. It's forestry and climate change. Forestry, it's within MNRT, climate change in VPO. So they are competing all the time. And for that reason, actually it is nice to have a body outside both of them. I think several times that it is not so bad, it's a solution. Actually it might be very good. And also, now having this direct support to NGOs has secured the kind of bottom up process for the development of the REDD strategy. We feel that now the NGOs also have strong voice into the process. (Interview 39)

In fact, NGOs such as the Tanzania Forest Conservation Group were strongly bolstered by the piloting role given to them by the aid community. Through implementing projects on the ground, they have gained sufficient strategic power to substantially influence REDD+ processes at both the local and national levels (Manyika et al. 2013). Already in the early phases of REDD+, it has become evident that their policy preferences are not necessarily congruent with those of the government-focused task force.[267] In view of the vested interests of local actors seeking to profit from future forest carbon trading and the external influence of foreign financers, one can assume that "both strategic behaviour and power struggles may lead to political legitimacy concerns and subsequently affect the effectiveness of the chosen governance structures" (Manyika et al. 2013: 77). Another indication for struggles behind the stage is the fact that despite a long, consultative process, Tanzania's REDD+ strategy approved in 2013 did not clarify "many unresolved and thorny issues such

---

267 This is drawn from Manyika et al. (2013: 76) who found that governance structures proposed by NGOs "contradict what has been proposed at national led REDD+ governance process". According to the authors, the case studies analysed reflect that "pilot projects envisage selling Carbon credits directly to the international markets, and thus propose establishment of their own local/project level Carbon credit marketing strategy, which does not necessarily link with the NRTF [National REDD+ Trust Fund] proposed at national level".

as legal gaps, tree/carbon tenure, benefit sharing and financial mechanisms" (Nordeco & Arcacia 2013: v).

All in all, it seems that the REDD+ process in Tanzania is heavily driven and orchestrated by the aid community which during 2009–2012 accounted for 95% of the funding for related activities (Kaijage & Kuhanwa 2013). Donor-financed expert engagement ranged from delivering studies and providing administrative support to preparing strategies and commenting on drafts. Preparing Tanzania for the REDD+ regime was primarily a concern of the developed countries – the potential buyers of carbon credits – rather than a national request.

Considering that Tanzania would potentially benefit from a future carbon trading market under the REDD+ regime, it is certainly true that the government was interested in getting engaged with donors on that matter. A retired official from the Forestry and Beekeeping Division delineated the decision-makers' stance as follows:

> *Donors are part and parcel of the REDD development process, globally and nationally. (…) REDD is not a one-sided business. We are talking of selling carbon and where are the markets for carbon? They are not in Tanzania; if they were in Tanzania, they would be very limited. So much of it will be a global market and at a particular point in time, we'll need to negotiate with those.* (Interview 58)

Whether aside from the prospect of additional financing, the Tanzanian government sees the overall objective of REDD+ (i.e. mitigating climate change by reducing emissions from deforestation and forest degradation) as a national priority, is another question. A high-ranking director in the VPO-DoE gave a very clear answer in this regard:

> *For us, for the government, our priority is on poverty reduction. But donors maybe want to reduce the greenhouse gas emissions by implementing some projects here. They will say, 'why don't you say climate change?' But they're not giving us a room to say what the priority issue is. Although they may say: 'You guys, you don't see people are affected by drought and you are facing a lot of floods in some parts, why don't you consider climate change as a priority issue'. That's an imposed priority issue! It's not an intrinsic priority issue. A genuine priority issue in our country, a genuine one is the one which is thought to come from the government. And that's why I was saying: For the government, poverty reduction is a priority issue and the means to reduce poverty or to ensure food security*

and nutrition. If it involves climate change, fine, then let's address climate change. (Interview 67)

"Tell me what you have money for, and I'll tell you what my priorities are"

As this account indicates, the evolvement of REDD+ put Tanzania under significant pressure to adjust its policies to the new paradigm (i.e. to reframe forest management as a matter of climate change mitigation). That aid is used by the international community to leverage such policy shifts is evident in respective changes to the funding portfolio. A Tanzanian environmental specialist at NEMC reported on the current situation:

> *Every donor now is running with climate change. Even now here in Tanzania there are other things, we have a lot of problems here – like the desertification, we have land degradation, we have a lot of erosion, but that ones are not receiving attention. (…) It's climate change now on top of the agenda, even if you go to the UN organizations, what is being supported is climate change now. It's the order of the day.* (Interview 59)

In response to the ever-shifting aid agenda, Tanzanian decision-makers concerned with environment and natural resources appear to have adopted what could be called a 'chameleon' strategy, strategically framing their priorities according to the respective donor preferences in order to access money. A director in the VPO-DoE commented on this:

> *You see, donors have their own political propagandas. If you can come up with a strong statement that climate change is a priority issue – for them, it is an advantage that now they can give you a lot of money. Maybe you can use that to address poverty – where in principle they won't be happy, if you direct the big share to address poverty issues, because if you talk of poverty issues, it has its own parameters which may not tally with the climate change parameters.* (Interview 67)

While at the surface, it may seem as if the government does not set clear priorities, various narratives of government officials indicate that for strategic reasons these are not openly communicated to the aid community. The tactical manoeuvring of decision- makers seems to have evolved from their experience that national requests are neglected by donors pursuing their own agenda, as a previous director of the Forestry and Beekeeping Division pointed out:

They come with already predetermined activities to be done – we can support this, we can support this, regardless of its impact on whatever you want to achieve on the ground. (…) On the issue of climate change, we said like in Dar es Salam here, it is the question of access to affordable energy. They made a study here in Dar es Salam to be able to network the use of natural gas which we already have here. Five years ago, they would have needed USD 35 million to be able to do that. And if they had connected maybe 70% of the households here in Dar es Salam, our demand for charcoal would have gone significantly down. But who is giving that money? You go to the government which says oh, we don't have that, sorry, our budget, we have so many issues to respond to. You go to the donors who say: 'Ah no, this is not my priority or I don't have that money'. (…) They may have the money but if that money does not fit into their programme of work which has been already agreed through the parliament and the other decision-making machinery – to change it, it's not so easy. (Interview 58)

Learning from the recurrent neglect of their actual demands, decision-makers in Tanzania's environmental authorities have adopted a stance of 'take what you can get' which is clearly recognised by staff in country offices and embassies. An interviewee in the Norwegian Embassy resignedly stated:

I think here you can ask them for anything. Are you interested in? And they will say yes. (Interview 39)

The environmental specialist in the World Bank's Dar es Salaam office put this notion even more bluntly:

If you ask here, give me what your priorities are, they say 'well, you tell me what you have money for and I'll tell you what my priorities are'. (Interview 46)

Conclusion

As the detailed description of previous and current policy processes has shown, aid has been an essential driver of environmental policy-making in Tanzania: the majority of environmental policies and laws have been stipulated and financed by the donor community whose experts were substantially involved in its development. The immense external engagement helped to shift the issue on the country's political agenda, but it has also narrowed down the decision-makers' autonomy in the policy space, with aid providers using their relevance as financiers to push priorities in line with their own portfolios. A professor at the University of Dar es Salaam commented:

> *On the forest management part, you see in some areas the forests are being well managed, so I wouldn't totally say that the support that is given from the foreign countries is useless. But I think the only thing is that we would wish to see that, okay, you give resources, but you allow for the locals or rather the nation to set priorities – what they think is a priority; even within the forest sector, how one would like to be supported, for example. There should be a leeway for the respective nations to dictate on what needs to be done.* (Interview 69)

As they have experienced that their agenda-setting authority is constrained by the dominance of foreign funders, Tanzanian decision-makers have adopted a strategic stance in dealing with them: the alignment of priorities to the prevailing aid agenda enables them to secure resources which are direly needed in the underfunded sector. What then happens on the ground is another story. The appalling gap between policies and implementation may thus be seen not only as a result of deficient capacity and budget constraints (as it is usually explained and certainly true to some extent) but also one of tactical manoeuvring on the part of recipients who thereby aim to preserve discretion, while being dependent on aid.

South Africa environment: On top of the game

Sectoral context

Occupying only 2% of the earth's land surface, South Africa is one of the world's richest countries in terms of natural habitat, home to 10% of the planet's plant species and 7% of all reptile, bird and mammal species (Department of Environmental Affairs and Tourism 2009). Exceptionally high levels of biodiversity can be found in three hotspots: the Succulent Karoo, the Maputaland-Pondoland-Albany hotspot, and the Cape Floristic Region. The latter is unique insofar as it is the only floral kingdom world-wide that falls entirely within the borders of a single country (Conservation International 2013).

Yet, Red List assessments indicate alarming figures: around 20% of freshwater fish and mammals and 15% of birds face a high risk of becoming extinct in the near future. Already under threat are 2 500 (12% of all) domestic plant species. Nearly half of the country's wetland ecosystem types which are vital for ensuring water quality and regulating water supplies are critically endangered (Driver et al. 2012). While nature degradation, invasive alien species, pollution and waste, over-exploitation of resources and climate change are seen as the main drivers of habitat loss, the tension between conservation measures and conflicting interests evolving from an emerging economy is a core problem in the country (Driver et al. 2012). A director in the Department of Environmental Affairs described the major challenges with regard to preserving biodiversity as follows:

> *I think the biggest one is probably covered under the broad term sustainable development where the biggest threat is the economy – the question how do we protect and enhance and reap a benefit from sustained ecosystems (…). We're grappling with rhinos, with species management, and that is the one thing that is keeping us all running a lot in the biodiversity space. We are grappling with issues of land use and land use change and what that then means; with issues of mining and protected areas, and how to make a case for conservation versus the extractive use.* (Interview 14)

Reconciling environmental protection with economic growth is a challenge many emerging countries are confronted with. Yet, it is a particularly sensitive issue in South Africa, given its long, but problematic history of conservation. Under colonial and apartheid rule, racial policies led to the forcible removal of thousands of South Africans from their ancestral land. Black communities were 're-settled' to make way for game parks open exclusively to whites, while the majority of the population was deprived of access to desperately needed natural resources (Crane et al. 2009). The fact that "billions of rands were spent on preserving wildlife and protecting wild flowers while people in 'townships' and 'homelands' lived without adequate food, shelter, and clean water" (McDonald 2002: 1) reflects the perverse politics of that time. As a result, "the *environment* was seen to be a white, suburban issue of little relevance to the anti-apartheid struggle. At worst, environmental policy was seen as an explicit tool of racially based oppression" (McDonald 2002: 1, emphasis in original).

When the new democratic government came into power in 1994, it made huge efforts to replace the destructive approach of the apartheid regime with a re-framed notion of environment as a human rights and development issue. This is reflected by the South African Constitution of 1996 which in section 24 grants all South Africans the right:

> (a) to an environment that is not harmful to their health or well-being; and

(b) to have the environment protected, for the benefit of present and future generations, through reasonable legislative and other measures that
  (i) prevent pollution and ecological degradation;
  (ii) promote conservation; and
  (iii) secure ecologically sustainable development and use of natural resources while promoting justifiable economic and social development. (Republic of South Africa 1996)

This paradigm shift went along with the development of a whole set of environmental policies and laws. Following an extensive process that comprised widespread national consultation, the *White Paper on Conservation and the Sustainable Use of South Africa's Biological Diversity* (1997) and the National Environmental Management Act (1998) outlining the principles of environmental governance in the new democratic South Africa were formulated.

Governance structures

The National Environmental Management Act of 1998 (or NEMA in short) is internationally regarded as one of the most progressive legal frameworks for environmental management. It articulates the idea of environmental justice and emphasises the principle of public participation in section 2(4) where it states:

Environmental justice must be pursued so that adverse environmental impacts shall not be distributed in such a manner as to unfairly discriminate against any person, particularly vulnerable and disadvantaged persons; (...)

The participation of all interested and affected parties in environmental governance must be promoted, and all people must have the opportunity to develop the understanding, skills and capacity necessary for achieving equitable and effective participation, and participation by vulnerable and disadvantaged persons must be ensured. (Republic of South Africa 1998a)

The Act defines environment as an area of cooperative governance which means that legislative and executive powers are allocated to various line functionaries at the national level (e.g. the Department of Environmental Affairs, the Department of Water Affairs, the Department of Mineral Resources or the Department of Energy) as well as to provincial and local authorities.

In order to ensure alignment of governance efforts, NEMA stipulates that all spheres of government and state organs concerned with environmental issues "must co-operate with, consult and support one another" (Republic of South Africa 1998a).[268]

The lead authority mandated to formulate, coordinate and monitor the implementation of national environmental policies, programmes and legislation is the Department of Environmental Affairs (DEA) which since 2009 has operated under the newly established Ministry of Water and Environmental Affairs. The work of the department is supported by statutory bodies such as the South African National Parks (SANParks), which is charged with overseeing and managing conservation in South Africa's national parks, and by the South African National Biodiversity Institute (SANBI), which plays a crucial role as a consultative body. SANBI was established through the National Environmental Management: Biodiversity Act 10 of 2004. It has been given a broad mandate, which aside from maintaining botanical gardens, includes carrying out and coordinating research, reporting on the status of biodiversity and providing science-based policy advice to environmental stakeholders at all tiers of government (see Republic of South Africa 2004a, section 11). Hence, SANBI also closely works with environmental departments and conservation authorities in the provinces (e.g. CapeNature in the Western Cape), particularly in the context of bioregional plans and programmes, which will be illustrated in the case of CAPE.

Donor presence in environment

The circle of donors providing aid to environmental issues in South Africa has – compared to other sectors – always been rather small. The limited extent of external support in the first years of democracy was not necessarily caused by a lack of donor interest but by the fact that the lead agency on the government side, the Department of Environmental Affairs and Tourism (now Department of Environmental Affairs), was in a state of institutional flux and officials were "initially cautious and reluctant to engage" (Albertyn & Fakir 2000: 45). An evaluation of ODA conducted in 2000 identified ten donor agencies which had invested in environmental projects by then, namely DFID, Finida, Norad, USAID, GTZ, the Netherlands, and the Danish Cooperation for Environment and Development (DANCED), the most active bilateral aid provider. Multilateral players engaged were the European Union, UNDP and the Global

---

268 Although the principles of cooperative environmental governance are widely endorsed, various scholars have shown that the current environmental governance and policy regime in practice is highly fragmented which hampers effective service delivery (see, for instance, Kotze 2006; Du Plessis 2008).

Environment Facility which has been the largest source of international funding for environmental activities over the past two decades (Albertyn & Fakir 2000). From 1994 to 2012, South Africa received GEF grants amounting to USD 108.1 million for national projects, plus USD 2.7 million for smaller programmes executed by civil society and community-based organisations. USD 288.7 million were spent on regional and global projects in which South Africa participated (Global Environment Facility 2012).[269]

By 2012, the group of donors active in environment had been significantly reduced. Most of them had phased out their conventional ODA to environment in South Africa, having shifted the focus to other topics and new forms of partnerships. The major players remaining are the World Bank and UNDP as implementing agencies for GEF-financed programmes.[270] The nature of cooperation and the contribution of experts in this setting may be illustrated with the example of what is seen as South Africa's most influential undertaking in the field of environment, the CAPE programme.

The making and implementation of the CAPE programme

Following the policy change in the early years of the democratic transition, South Africa was granted USD 12.3 million by the Global Environment Facility in support of the 'Cape Peninsula Biodiversity Conservation Project'. Running from 1998 to 2005, the project was mainly carried out by SANParks and WWF-South Africa who were assisted and supervised by the World Bank. The bulk of the funding was directed at the creation of the Table Mountain National Park and the expansion of the Table Mountain Fund. USD 1 million was assigned for preparing a long-term strategy and action plan to protect the biodiversity in the Cape Floristic Region (CFR). The process began with a phase of stock-taking and analysis. During the initial phase, scientists from the University of Cape Town were commissioned to assess the current state of biodiversity in the terrestrial, marine and freshwater ecosystems of the CFR. Experts of the Council for Scientific and Industrial Research reviewed the legal, policy, institutional, financial, social and economic aspects affecting conservation

---

269 The Global Environment Facility has been set up as an independent financing mechanism providing grants and concessional funding to cover incremental costs of measures targeting global environmental benefits in the areas of biodiversity, climate change, international waters, land degradation, ozone layer depletion, and persistent organic pollutants. As of 2014, the organisation comprised 183 member states. South Africa joined the GEF when it became a democracy in 1994.

270 The GEF term 'implementing agencies' is to some extent misleading insofar as the role of the IAs (as, for instance, the World Bank, UNDP or UNEP) is focused on assisting and overseeing the actual implementers which are usually government bodies or NGOs. In GEF terminology, the latter are called 'executing agencies'.

in this area (Younge & Fowkes 2003).[271] The recommendations contained in these studies were taken up by a team comprising consultants and technical staff of executing agencies such as the Western Cape Nature Conservation Board (today known as CapeNature), DEAT and SANParks who formulated a first draft strategy. Their preliminary version was scrutinised and refined by representatives from government, the private sector, civil society and the local science community during a three-day workshop held in early 2000 (Lochner et al. 2003). The revised draft was then circulated to around 1 500 individuals before its final release as the 'Cape Action Plan for the Environment' (CAPE) which comprised the following main objectives:

> *To establish an effective reserve network, enhance off-reserve conservation and support bio-regional planning;*

> *To develop methods to ensure sustainable yields, promote compliance with laws, integrate biodiversity concerns into catchment management and promote sustainable nature-based tourism;*

> *To strengthen institutions, policies and laws, enhance co-operative governance and community participation, and support continued research* (CAPE Project Team 2000: 3)

Nationally and internationally, the CAPE strategy was seen as the outcome of a successful regional planning exercise. Part of the success was ascribed to the extensive public consultation with a large number of disparate stakeholders whose commitment was deemed crucial to ensure that the strategy would be financed and internalised in the long term. In order to achieve the necessary 'ownership' of local actors, it was attempted to keep external players at the side-lines of the process. According to members of the organising team, outcomes "were consequently only translated into a log frame format and presented to international role-players once local buy-in was secured" (Lochner et al. 2003: 31).

Hence, although the development of the CAPE strategy was substantially funded from outside, the involvement of donor experts – for example, the World Bank task team leader or consultants funded through GEF resources – was limited to administrative backing and supervision. A CapeNature official described their part as follows:

---

271 For a detailed list of the reports and their respective recommendations, see Younge and Fowkes (2003).

They did bring in some expertise but it was more expertise in terms of funding, project management and that kind of thing, and they did make use of local expertise or local scientists in terms of developing the original strategy. And so we went through a whole process within which we agreed on what we want to do with this funding. So it wasn't forced on us, it was part of a broadly negotiated process. There were lots of arguments at that stage between the scientists locally, you know, the one group saying no we must go in this direction, the other one saying we must go in that direction. And so the GEF experts played a facilitating role in trying to find a common ground. (Interview 13)

Although the outcomes were broadly accepted and the parties involved pledged to realign existing resources around agreed priorities, it was clear that turning the strategy into action would require external funding, at least in the first phase of implementation. The action plan designed for the initial five years called for an investment of ZAR 812 million (equivalent to around USD 107 million at that time), of which ZAR 487 million (ca. USD 64 million) needed to be sourced from outside (Cape Action Plan for the Environment 2000).[272] In order to attract financiers, an international conference was held in September 2000 where core projects related to priority areas outlined in the strategy were presented. All proposals had been developed by or in close collaboration with the respective South African institutions that would execute them (Cape Action Plan for the Environment 2000; Younge & Fowkes 2003).

Amongst the largest aid providers responding to this request was the GEF which in subsequent years approved a range of supporting activities, such as the Agulhas Biodiversity Initiative, the CAPE Biodiversity Conservation and Sustainable Development Project as well as investment through the Critical Ecosystem Partnership Fund (CEPF).[273] The World Bank and UNDP were commissioned to oversee the interventions and ensure compliance with GEF requirements. According to the programme developer of the CAPE Coordination Unit, experts of both organisations particularly assisted in hooking up proposals with the international agenda to make projects 'sellable' to the GEF:

---

272 Rand was converted into USD using the exchange rate on 31 December 2000 (7 595:1).

273 The Critical Ecosystem Partnership Fund was launched in 2000 as a partnership between the Global Environment Facility (GEF), the World Bank, the John D and Catherine T MacArthur Foundation, and the government of Japan with the aim to provide grants to NGOs and the private sector for undertaking conservation activities in biodiversity hotspots. As of today, it is also supported by Conservation International, L'Agence Française de Développement and the European Union.

C [...] from the World Bank and N [...] from UNDP were very involved in putting together the application to the GEF, so they helped us frame it and package it, you know, 'the GEF's not interested in this, but they might be interested in that', 'frame it like a programmatic approach', 'build on another phase here' – that sort of thing. Having said that, it did come on the back of this twenty-year strategy that we had already. So it wasn't like they were coming in fresh with their own new ideas. (Interview 25)

One of the biggest policy changes leveraged through donor-funded CAPE initiatives was the introduction of 'biodiversity stewardship' as a new tool of managing South Africa's protected areas network. Evolving on a few pilot sites in the Western Cape Province, the concept was rapidly taken up into national policies and legislation.

The evolvement of 'biodiversity stewardship'

Analyses conducted in the context of CAPE found that while 80% of priority conservation areas in the Western Cape region were in private and communal hands, few mechanisms were in place to secure the conservation of threatened species and ecosystems outside the formal reserves managed by the state. It was recognised that especially in view of the fragmentation of landscapes, government authorities would not be able to link the sites flagged as critically endangered and build conservation corridors without bringing private and communal landowners on board (Ashwell et al. 2006). In 2002, the Botanical Society in collaboration with CapeNature initiated a small pilot project in order to develop and refine workable stewardship arrangements with farmers owning land of high biodiversity importance. The stewardship concept rests on the idea that instead of buying up land to protect threatened habitat, conservation authorities offer a range of cooperation agreements to land owners who are willing to conserve biodiversity through sustainable land use for which they are rewarded with tangible benefits.[274] Central to the concept is that land owners do not cede any ownership rights, but remain the custodians and key users of their properties. They voluntarily decide whether to enter an agreement and which of the available options to take, with categories ranging from informal, flexible agreements to legally binding, long-term contracts which demand a higher degree of commitment but qualify for more substantial incentives

---

274 CapeNature has defined stewardship as follows: "Stewardship refers to the wise use, management and protection of that which has been entrusted to you or is rightfully yours. Within the context of conservation, stewardship means protecting important ecosystems, effectively managing invasive alien species and fires, and grazing or harvesting without damaging the veld" (Cape Nature Conservation 2003). This definition has been widely adopted throughout the country.

such as tax deductions and advanced management assistance (Cadman et al. 2010).[275]

While landowner engagement initiatives existed before – with little success due to cumbersome procedures and a lack of legal security – the Conservation Stewardship Pilot Project helped to simplify and sharpen the stewardship concept by exploring feasible models on three pilot sites in the Cape Floristic Region (Ashwell et al. 2006).[276] Although the project closed in 2004 without having contracts signed, it had a substantial effect insofar as it informed subsequent bioregional programmes concerned with the creation of conservation corridors by involving the private sector and communities (e.g. the Agulhas Biodiversity Initiative or the Succulent Karoo Ecosystem Programme).[277] Several of these activities were greatly driven forward by external funding, in particular from GEF and CEPF. For international investors, South Africa's stewardship approach fitted neatly with the globally emerging paradigm of 'mainstreaming' biodiversity into production sectors and development planning (see, for instance, Petersen & Huntley 2005; Global Environment Facility 2010a; Huntley & Redford 2014). Hence, the concept was promoted by the aid community as an efficient tool to 'establish the foundations of the biodiversity economy' (World Bank 2011b).[278]

In fact, the stewardship programmes carried out in the context of CAPE have leveraged significant changes in land-use planning and helped to expand protected areas. Through contracts with private landowners and communities, the area of (critically) endangered ecosystems under conservation in the Cape Floristic Region increased from 16 115 hectares in 2004 to 61 603 hectares in 2011 (World Bank 2011b: 31). The models and guidelines developed in the Western Cape were adopted by other provinces such as the Eastern Cape, KwaZulu-Natal, and Gauteng, and they were taken up by the Department of Environmental Affairs which set up a 'Biodiversity Stewardship South Africa' programme to establish and strengthen provincial stewardship initiatives

---

275 Aside from the landowner's willingness to put effort into conservation and accept land-use limitations, the biodiversity value of the land is a determining factor for which types of arrangement are being offered by authorities. The highest stewardship category under which land is declared a nature reserve requires that the site contains ecosystems, habitats and species which are critically important and endangered.

276 The pilot sites of the Conservation Stewardship Pilot Project were the Agtergroenberg near Wellington, the Bot River Valley near Grabouw and the Lower Breede River area near Swellendam (Ashwell et al. 2006).

277 According to the Project Completion Report compiled by the Botanical Society, no actual agreements had been signed at project completion, but several were pending for final legal processing (Botha 2004).

278 This term was used in the World Bank's final report on the GEF-funded 'Biodiversity Conservation and Sustainable Development Project' which targeted the expansion of stewardship arrangements and the development of financial incentives for environmental services, amongst others (World Bank 2011b).

(Department of Environmental Affairs and Tourism 2009b). Having been tested and proved on the ground, the concept was gradually incorporated into South Africa's environmental policy and legal frameworks. While the Protected Areas Act of 2003 and the Biodiversity Act of 2004 laid out enabling provisions for piloting the approach, biodiversity stewardship was featured as a key conservation mechanism in strategic documents such as the National Biodiversity Framework (Department of Environmental Affairs and Tourism 2009b) and the National Protected Area Expansion Strategy (Department of Environmental Affairs 2010b).[279] Moreover, the government developed a national Biodiversity Stewardship Policy and Guideline Document as well as a framework for fiscal incentives encouraging conservation through the custodianship of land (Republic of South Africa 2009a). By 2014, biodiversity stewardship has taken hold as a strategy to secure South Africa's threatened ecosystems. The experiences and results achieved so far have received much attention from the international community which promotes the Western Cape as a pioneer of innovative conservation approaches (Cadman et al. 2010; Müller & Fourie 2011).

The role of donors in the CAPE process

Biodiversity stewardship is just one example of a concept which in the course of CAPE implementation triggered a step-by-step change in the country's conservation regime. In both government and donor publications, CAPE is praised for its achievements with regard to policy reform. A UNDP expert engaged in the process from the beginning explained its effect as follows:

> *What happened with the CAPE programme is that it tested things, it was an early starter, which then progressively got injected into the national policy process. Prior to the CAPE programme starting, all there was in terms of policy for biodiversity was a White Paper. We then subsequently had two Acts, the Biodiversity Act and the Protected Area Bill and then we have the National Biodiversity Framework. All of this was sort of infused into that.* (Interview 7)

---

279 The National Environmental Management: Protected Areas Act 2003 creates a legal framework for the management of South Africa's protected areas network and outlines a range of conservation categories and related governance options. The crucial provision it entails with regard to the stewardship concept is that it allows private and communal land to be declared as protected areas, given the consent of the owner (Republic of South Africa 2003). The National Environmental Management: Biodiversity Act 2004 provides an array of planning tools for assessing the state of biodiversity such as the National Biodiversity Framework; the categorisation of threatened ecosystems helps to focus interventions on priority areas to be conserved and to identify sites for biodiversity stewardship (Republic of South Africa 2004a).

International bodies attribute part of CAPE's success to the 'catalytic support' they provided to the process. In its Country Portfolio Evaluation for South Africa, the GEF emphasises that

> *key policy, strategy, and legislation changes such as SANBI's expanded mandate, the National Biodiversity Strategy and Action Plan (NBSAP), the National Environmental Management Biodiversity Act, and the National Environmental Management: Protected Areas Act have been funded directly or catalyzed or informed by GEF investment and projects.*
> (Global Environment Facility Evaluation Office 2008: 62)

Promoting its contribution through the 'Biodiversity Conservation and Sustainable Development Project', the World Bank on its website reports that aside from channelling grants it supplied "the expertise and technical knowledge of several experts" (World Bank 2013a). While such statements remain at a very general level, a closer look reveals that the role of donors in implementing the CAPE strategy has in fact been very specific and limited, both with respect to financial and advisory support.

In terms of funding, the initiatives carried out in the context of CAPE mainly stemmed from local sources. The share of foreign contributions in major projects did not exceed 40%, while the remaining budget was provided by government authorities, the private sector, South African NGOs and academic bodies (cf. Table 20).

Table 20: Local and foreign resources in GEF-supported CAPE projects

Project	Period	Local sources		Foreign sources	
		in USD m	% of total	in USD m	% of total
Cape Peninsula Biodiversity Conservation Project	1998–2005	92.02	87.1	13.65	12.9
Agulhas Biodiversity Initiative	2003–2010	7.22	61.2	4.57	38.8
Biodiversity Conservation and Sustainable Development Project	2004–2010	51.40	82.4	11.00	17.6

Source: World Bank (2006: 22); Child (2010: 41); World Bank (2011b: 27).

Although external funding appears relatively modest, it had a significant effect from the perspective of the actors involved, insofar as it enabled them to experiment with ideas – e.g. the stewardship concept – for which they did not have allocations from the state (Cadman et al. 2010). The establishment of a shared, publicly accessible database (the Biodiversity Geographical Information System) and a facility disseminating biodiversity information to underpin land-use planning, for instance, was primarily made possible through foreign money and support, as a leading official at SANBI acknowledged:

> *We would not have been able to win the case with our government in terms of our funds to say actually the way forward is to have an information facility that can be accessible to researchers, to the public, to the citizens, unleashing this information and bringing it in the public eye. We wouldn't have been able to make the case to our government at the time – and they [the donors] were able to pioneer that kind of idea.* (Interview 24)

International funding coming in through CAPE helped both national and provincial authorities to pilot initiatives, but it also entailed bureaucratic burdens. Referring particularly to the World Bank, interviewees from DEA, SANBI and CapeNature criticised the cumbersome requirements related to financial management and procurement which partly blocked implementation and made processes overly complex. Yet, since their institutions are generally underfunded, officials nonetheless weighed the value of accessing additional financing higher than the administrative challenges related to it, as the statement of a SANBI director reflects:

> *We have learnt how to overcome those [challenges], so I would play those down rather than play those up. We're wiser now, we won't go into another GEF grant without setting up a coordination unit that's big enough to really do it – whereas the other way around we did that, and our team ended up being stretched beyond, so were all of our other partners. So, you know, now there are great benefits to show, and as time passes the bitterness of being so under the hammer all the time by the donors sort of evaporates a bit and you can see the positive impact.* (Interview 25)

Similarly, a leading official at CapeNature commented:

> *We did benefit a lot from being part of international funding and we feel we're now getting to the stage where we know how to play the game, so to speak. You've got to understand how it works, you have to be able to know how to play the game to get the benefits and I think that applies both sides, for the funder but also for the recipient. And we're definitely more mature now in terms of how to deal with these kinds of things than we were ten years ago, without any doubt.* (Interview 13)

According to interviewees, South African authorities went through a 'steep learning curve' in terms of handling the different requirements associated with grants channelled through the World Bank and UNDP. While the main role of the latter was to function as a conduit for GEF money, they also served as a source of expertise, particularly with regard to innovative approaches tested and adopted in other countries. One example mentioned by officials was the provision of best practice cases and international experiences around 'payments for environmental services' (PES) schemes which compensate land users for maintaining and enhancing the flow of ecosystem services. Since SANBI and CapeNature considered including such a scheme in a future financial incentive system targeting sustainable land management, there was an interest in how PES mechanisms were set up elsewhere. Given their links to PES programmes carried out in Costa Rica and other Latin America countries, the World Bank and UNDP were able to present examples and facilitate exchange with experts and practitioners from abroad who shared their lessons learned. Such kind of input was perceived as very useful on the South African side, with officials appreciating the "global perspective" (Interview 24) their international partners brought in.

While in the course of CAPE and related initiatives a range of workshops and study tours on specific topics took place, technical assistance was used to a rather limited extent, and if so in many cases provided by South African experts affiliated with public and private research institutes. To give just one example, when SANBI required a consultant to develop a feasible PES model, the six-month assignment was given to an internationally renowned resource economist from the University of Pretoria. Experts from abroad were mainly used for progress reviews and evaluations because they "require an outsider's perspective" (Interview 7), as a UNDP representative argued. In the case of the 'Biodiversity Conservation and Sustainable Development Project', for instance, final reports were compiled by an expert from New Zealand and a British consultant (see Tortell 2010; World Bank 2011b).

The most regular collaboration throughout the lifespan of CAPE initiatives took place between members of the CAPE Coordination Unit housed at SANBI and permanent staff in the UNDP country office, with the latter acting as interlocutors for both managerial and technical issues related to GEF-funded programmes. Despite challenges in terms of ensuring compliance with reporting and management requirements which put all actors under pressure, interviewees from both sides spoke in high terms of the quality of cooperation and the relationship that has evolved. A SANBI official summarised her experience as follows:

> *I think it's a very complementary relationship. I think they bring us insight into what the international agenda is, and they bring us some clues as to what's happening in other places of the world. They're able to help us frame funding applications – for example, there's a big project on the Agulhas Plain that has received climate change adaptation funding. And if it were not for N and his colleagues at UNDP, we wouldn't have even figured out that we could frame our work in that way. At the same time, what we give the UNDP and the World Bank is practice of this international agenda wish list. So they came up with a concept of mainstreaming – and a couple of years ago, I presented on mainstreaming at a GEF meeting and we were the only project at that stage that was putting these policies into practice. (…) So we bring them that nice hook into a developing paradigm but with all the capacity and all the experience and all the skills of the teams of people that work on these projects.* (Interview 25)

The high capacity of government officials particularly within SANBI was in fact highlighted by UNDP representatives in the Pretoria country office. A programme officer concerned with UNDP's environment and energy portfolio in South Africa commented:

> *When you run the projects through them, you can see these guys are in full control. You have less stress, they deliver, they know what they want, they know where they are going, they are pretty at the play, you know. They are on top of the game.* (Interview 8)

As these statements indicate, both government and donor representatives perceived the cooperation as taking place at eye level, with South Africans taking the lead. Summarising the role of international players in CAPE, it can be stated that aside from providing and channelling funds their main contribution was to mobilise expertise and to facilitate knowledge exchange by using the global networks of their organisations. External actors did give technical input in designing and implementing initiatives, but they did not play a decisive part in decision-making and policy processes. The priorities of CAPE and the policy changes it brought about were largely an outcome of local negotiation informed by national science and practice. This is not to say that findings and experiences from outside were disregarded. In fact, South African actors expressly appreciated advice provided by foreign specialists and scholars, but apparently external expertise was only taken up at a stage when the broad agenda was already agreed upon. This ensured that despite the use of foreign aid CAPE remained a locally driven process. The fact that CAPE partnerships and initiatives persist while major donor projects have ended can be seen as an indication supporting this view.

Entering the second phase of CAPE

It should not be concealed, however, that the gradual phasing out of international financiers did entail problems for authorities who struggled to find alternative sources of funding and to retain staff recruited in the course of CAPE projects. A leading official of CapeNature described his organisation's situation during this phase of transition as follows:

> We could take up, I would say, about 50% of the people that were part of the CAPE project in terms of project managers and so on but we couldn't take all of them and absorb them as part of the process. I think SANParks were even worse off, you know, they took a very small percentage on. So I think the goal there was to create this kind of workforce of expertise and make it part of the organisational structures, but it didn't in all cases work out like that. (Interview 13)

Such challenges, however, did not bring an end to the partnerships established in the course of CAPE. At the end of the first ten-year phase, most participants signalled a willingness to continue the cooperation, as a member of the coordination unit at SANBI reported:

> Early this year [2011], we asked everybody, do you want CAPE to carry on or should we just close it because the project is done now, and all of the partners said they wanted it to carry on. They're all engaged, they still come to the meetings, it's no longer about implementing a project, it's about all of the other things that we need to do to get alignment around conservation and development in the Cape Floristic Region. (Interview 25)

At the beginning of the second phase of implementation, 23 government entities and NGOs were signatories to the CAPE Memorandum of Understanding (Cape Action for People and the Environment 2011). Although this does not give evidence of proceedings on the ground, it indicates at least formal commitment and can be seen as a sign that the strategy has gained a high degree of legitimacy across environmental stakeholders.

Harnessing external ideas for the local agenda

While CAPE originally emerged as a regional programme, national authorities such as the Department of Environmental Affairs and SANBI played a crucial part in the process. Both authorities are known for taking a strong stance in dealing with donors. A UNDP programme officer exemplified this:

> *We recently had a project for which the EU was proposing to give between USD 500 000 and USD 700 000, and USD 30 000 for the preparation of a small concept about the project. It was on climate change mitigation. The government said, 'no, we don't want it'. We wrote so many letters and they said no (…). We've got a couple of ideas which we pushed, which we thought they were good and innovative – the government just said 'we're not interested', (…) they say 'you can go back with your money', and that's it. So it's an interesting dynamic.* (Interview 8)

The fact that aid offers are rejected by government officials is noticeable insofar as environmental authorities do face financial constraints, with many relying on external resources to fulfil their mandate (see Chapter 6). CapeNature, for instance, needs to source 40% of its budget externally. Yet, in the course of CAPE, decision-makers have come to the point where donor support comes at a high cost to their organisation if not aligned to its core business. A high-ranking director stated:

> *In the early stages of CAPE, (…) some of the projects were not entirely what we needed, they were a bit off the mark. But through the process we learnt, and nowadays, for example, we wouldn't take on international funding projects unless it speaks directly to our research needs or our capacity-building needs or protected area expansion objectives, whatever the funders aim at, so we've become much more choosy in terms of what we accept as a funding.* (Interview 13)

The policy not to engage with foreign funders unless their support fits South African priorities is also promoted at the national level. A leading official at SANBI strongly emphasised the importance of setting and defending the local agenda against donors irrespective of financial imbalances:

> *If you understand what your agenda is, what you want to achieve and you say this is your agenda then you can engage with donors on a more equal footing. But if you don't have that understanding and you haven't got the confidence to put it on the table, then of course people who are*

cleverer than you can come and tell you what to do (....). It's a two-way thing, it's not – you're not a victim here, you know, victim, victim, victim... And somebody comes along and we just take the money. So it's a two-way street. We have to have more confidence in what we see are our solutions. We must have the confidence to also absorb other best practices in the world but not take it holus-bolus. We must have the confidence and ability to say to donors, 'there you are, let's work together'. (Interview 24)

That environmental agents in South Africa do in fact adopt such a firm attitude towards donors and advance their own proposals for cooperation rather than accept external suggestions was repeatedly confirmed by staff in country offices and embassies. An environmental specialist who previously worked as a first secretary for the Norwegian Embassy in Pretoria reported about her former South African counterparts:

They know what they want, and then they know also which country they want to use for support. At least it's the picture of what I experienced. For instance, they approached the Norwegian Embassy to have some support for pollution control in Durban where they have refineries and so on. And Norway was not so much into pollution control. So we said, 'oh, Denmark is doing this, so why do you come to Norway'? And they said 'No. First, Denmark is coming in with too many experts. We don't want these to overtake our ministry. And we have been on the internet, talking with a Norwegian institution that has this kind of instrument that we want to use. That's why we are coming to you'. So, I have many stories like that. They are doing their homework to see where to find the best technical advice or solutions or at least what they think has to be done, then they start a dialogue. (Interview 39)

This account points to a salient feature of environmental agents' dealings with aid: *they* define not only the need and area of support, but also whom to approach, what to request and which conditions to set. The ability to show this kind of leadership seems to rest to a large extent on the highly capacitated cadre of experts in environmental authorities.

Negotiating expertise: The absorptive capacity of experts in environmental authorities

Assessing the capacity of environmental entities such as DEA and SANBI, a UNDP expert pointed out:

> *Some of these guys who are managing various sectors of government are now well capacitated. It's been 15 years now and we're starting to see an emergence of young, assertive people, who when you come and say we are gonna do a workshop or do this, they say, no, that's not capacity-building. We only like your idea (…). So in that context I think they are forcing organisations like ours to become innovative and to come up with good approaches. We can't just sell anything anymore. You can't just say something and everybody says it's good, it's good. No. Now there are people who can say, no, this is not good.* (Interview 8)

From a donor perspective, the strength of environmental authorities in terms of in-house expertise and capacity is a double-edged sword. On the one hand, it simplifies the cooperation if aid projects are administrated by capable counterparts in recipient institutions. On the other hand, the pace of interventions is often slowed down due to lengthy negotiation processes which a director in the biodiversity unit of DEA explained as follows:

> *It's because we are adding some value to the process. We just don't accept it, we question it, we will say 'what are the implications for this' and 'it's a duplication', this and that. And so that's why we take long and it's often perceived as if we are delaying processes or not being proactive enough to harness opportunity. But I think it's about questioning why this is done.* (Interview 15)

The frictions emerging in the joint preparation of projects are not necessarily caused by contradicting objectives but are sparked off by the divergent use of concepts and terminologies, with government and donor experts trying to frame interventions in line with their own agendas and paradigms. Conflicts of this sort have recently emerged in the context of designing applications for the fifth GEF replenishment. For the period 2010–2014, South Africa was offered an indicative resource envelope of USD 52.65 million accessible for interventions in the fields of biodiversity, climate change and land degradation (Global Environment Facility 2010b). Preparing project proposals, experts from DEA and international partners had different conceptions about both approaches and issues to be prioritised, as the following narrative of a ministry official reflects:

> *Interviewee: There was a lot of pressure for us to make decisions about how we want these projects to run as a programme approach or as an individual project approach. And the country's position is that we need to use these GEF resources to empower smaller organisations so that they*

can build capacity. And then UNDP came with their approach to say 'no, we want to be the big player in this whole process, we want to take on a programmatic approach rather than a project, or a smaller project approach'. So there was much conflict in that respect because we didn't see the merit in actually taking on a programmatic approach as opposed to a project approach. But eventually, I don't know whether we saw the light, but we gave in in the sense that we took the programme approach because some of the implementing agencies in the country supported it. (…)

Interviewer: But there wasn't a struggle about the content or the priorities?

Interviewee: There was a conflict of interest in terms of the content as well. Certain things were duplication and belonged to other branches within the country or within the department, so then we had to start channelling, choking and changing things. For example, green economy: Green economy is a concept and a project that is driven by a different branch and not the biodiversity branch. So we had to change things to make them aligned with our priorities. Say, we need to remove green economy from the concept and maybe include it under some other way, like valuation of biodiversity for example – which is one and the same thing, but again, it's aligning with the national priorities. And also terminology, you know, to include the priority areas – for example, GMO [Genetically Modified Organisms] that is one of our priorities. From the outside perspective that wasn't a priority, so we had to fight for the space for GMOs in the project.

'Protected areas' and 'stewardship' as well: Those are two concepts that are very often interchangeable. But 'stewardship' means something different in South Africa. It's about voluntary participation of land owners and it's outside the protected areas, and 'protected areas' is a formal designation of protected areas [owned by the state]. So those content issues did emerge.
(Interview 15)

Frictions around divergent terminologies for 'one and the same thing' might seem trivial at first glance. Yet, since wording conveys meaning, it has significant implications for the nature and legitimacy of activities, particularly in the realm of environmental governance. Recognising the nuances of technical language and paradigmatic underpinnings is thus crucial in the context of setting up policy-related government programmes, even more so if they are prepared with the assistance of aid experts who bring in their own organisations' interests.

How easily initiatives can be infused with 'external' concepts from outside becomes evident in the case of the Grasslands Programme. South Africa's grasslands biome has been identified as one of the spatial priorities for conservation action that is particularly threatened by productive activities such as agriculture, coal mining and forestry (Department of Environmental Affairs and Tourism 2005). In response to this finding, SANBI requested GEF funding for the design and implementation phase of a programme targeting the integration of biodiversity objectives into the major production sectors operating on South Africa's grasslands biome. A South African official involved in the process remembered how the notion of 'mainstreaming' was pushed into the proposal:

> *So we developed the concept and then the UNDP came in and said 'no, we need to make this concept more sexy', that were the words that they used. So they added some terminology of 'mainstreaming in production sectors' and all sorts of things. And it didn't go down well in the initial stages.* (Interview 15)

While the programme was launched in 2008 to run until 2013, the 'mainstreaming' notion only slowly gained acceptance in both environmental policy circles and production sectors. A mid-term review conducted in 2011 remarked that benefits were achieved on a very limited scale and criticised that some targets were so unrealistic that it was recommended to drop them altogether (Tortell 2011). Still, the experiences gained from the Grasslands Programme were presented at several international conferences and workshops, amongst others at a side-event of COP 11 in Hyderabad where – according to a participating DEA official – the initial insubstantiality of the concept was acknowledged:

> *The UNDP people (…) admitted that when they did take the concept note of the Grasslands Programme, they actually didn't know what they were doing and it was a major risk to actually take this approach. So if the government knew that it was something that was uncharted territory, they wouldn't have bought into it at all, because it's a major risk: How do you ensure that such a programme is actually going to provide tangible benefits for our grassland conservation? And so it was just a concept, a pie in the sky that they actually sold to us. And again, it comes back to officials like myself trying to make sense of some of those abstract concepts. And we make sense of it with the knowledge that we know – and sometimes we're not convinced, but then we try to pull it together.* (Interview 15)

That such kinds of experiments do not result in major failures can to a significant extent be ascribed to SANBI's and DEA's institutional strength. The presence of civil servants possessing a high level of technical knowledge, together with a sound understanding of national and international agendas, seems to make environmental authorities in South Africa less prone to being "swayed off the path" (Interview 25) while being advised and assisted from outside. Having learned from experience, government officials indicated a high awareness for the need to scrutinise and adjust external models and approaches, as a DEA director commented:

> *UNDP comes in with this concept – but it needs to be shaped and aligned with the national processes. (…) And sometimes those concepts are too bizarre to actually be adopted by the South African people. So if it can't be adopted, it's not going to be a success.* (Interview 15)

The targeted use of external expertise and the impact of local consultation

Given that national authorities can revert to a cadre of highly skilled specialists, one can hardly find technical assistants embedded within the organisations. Asked whether there are any advisors deployed to DEA, an official responded:

> *In the ministry itself, there is very limited [use] of those (…). And I think we don't have a permanent person that would be sitting here. Actually I think once the concept paper and everything is developed, then they move away from the project and the rest is us that implement it (…). So we don't have them constantly influencing what is happening.* (Interview 16)

If external experts are requested, they are contracted for a rather short time period and to carry out a specific task outlined by the recipient authority. According to a UNDP officer the recipient authority is adamant that they are the ones setting the conditions for support:

> *In some instances you find that we do the contracting for them. But they will formulate everything you need like what they want this person to do and then they will also be responsible for monitoring the performance of this particular person. Immediately once you say you are going to supervise this person, and you put the money, they say 'oh, even if the money is yours, no, we have control of the person'.* (Interview 8)

Foreign specialists brought in for consultancies are in most cases paired with local experts from government or research institutes. The policy drafts or studies produced usually pass through an internal discussion and public consultation process before being taken up to the political decision-making level for approval.

The National Environmental Management Act (NEMA) explicitly provides for public participation in policy development, and various structures have been set up to integrate stakeholders from the national and provincial governments, communities, the private sector and science. Platforms which enable the articulation of interests and views on environmental issues include the national Wildlife Forum, which brings together the government and the wildlife industry, the Peoples and Parks conferences, which deal with community concerns, or the 'Rhino Dialogues', which were initiated in 2012 in response to the deteriorating rhino poaching crisis. Although the scope of influence stakeholders are able to exert through such structures varies, it is clear "that public participation has become a basic feature of environmental decision-making" (University of Cape Town 2007: 78). A director at DEA commented on the required consultation processes:

> *In the case of biodiversity, to a large extent your stakeholders are polarized, so you actually never get them all on the same page and agreeing. But we do have an extensive process prescribed within the Act of what constitutes public consultation and that would need to be taken into account. So our stakeholders are the public, the users, fellow government departments where we need mandate's clarity sometimes, industry if there are impacts of an industry, communities. So we try to ensure that we've got really as many voices as possible. (…) So, when we present the report to our minister to take a decision, she can safely say that we have really consulted and have on record the views of all these constituencies.* (Interview 14)

Public involvement, in a way, counter-balances the impact of external expertise. An example is South Africa's green economy modelling report. Following a first national summit on the issue held in 2010, DEA requested a scoping study which would outline potential opportunities and options for a transition to a green economy in South Africa. On behalf of DEA, UNEP commissioned two policy analysts from the US-based Millennium Institute and two researchers affiliated with the South African Sustainability Institute and the Centre for Renewable and Sustainable Energy Studies of Stellenbosch University for technical assistance. This team finally conducted the modelling exercise and prepared the report, but the priority sectors, targets and scenarios to be included in the analysis were defined in the course of a workshop attended by South African policy-makers, economists and researchers. Moreover, various government departments contributed to data collection (UNEP 2013). Hence, although the assessment process was co-financed and supported by UNEP,

UNDP and the European Commission, the 'South African Green Economy Modelling Report' launched in 2013 was substantially shaped and informed by local actors.

Conclusion

All in all, a fairly clear picture emerges with regard to environmental policy processes in South Africa: although being financially supported through aid, these processes are firmly led and driven by local actors. Environmental authorities rely to some extent on external financiers, at least in emerging areas which are not (yet) established enough to receive budgetary allocations. The strength of recipients in defending their agenda-setting and decision-making autonomy despite this dependency derives from different sources. First, there is the comparatively high level of in-house expertise within government bodies which are staffed with a cadre of civil servants able to scrutinise and adjust policy concepts suggested from outside. If necessary, they are able to defend decisions against external pressure. Second, there are established internal advisory and public consultation mechanisms which mitigate external influence insofar as they ensure national deliberation. Due to the strong voice and interaction of local stakeholders from government branches, the private sector, civil society and not least the science community, the impact of donors in environmental policy-making is fairly limited.

It's not all about the money: Synthesis of findings

In the preceding six case studies, we explored the impact of aid-related expert advice on policy-making in South Africa and Tanzania. 'Impact' is used here (and can only be used) in its qualitative meaning, that is, in terms of the effects of external engagement on the agenda-setting and steering capability of recipient bureaucracies. The key question addressed was: what enables young democratic governments to retain their agenda-setting autonomy, that is, to define and defend own priorities, while relying on aid, notably expert advice? Against a background of previous findings and theoretical considerations three structural conditions were assumed to be decisive in this regard: the recipient's financial status; its administrative capacity, especially to absorb advice from external experts; and the local knowledge base (i.e. the strength of the internal science community). The assessment of South Africa's and Tanzania's relative strength with respect to these indicators revealed variance not only between the two countries but also across the three sectors: education, health and environment (see Chapter 6).

There are, as the case studies showed, remarkable differences in the way countries that receive aid and advice from outside deal with donors. This may not be surprising, given that each area of governance has its own history of aid relationships and experiences which impact on the way recipients position themselves towards the aid community. Although the cases are distinct, their comparison allows the identification of fairly clear patterns in which certain structural conditions are responsible for strengthening or weakening governments' ability to remain sovereign in their policy-making while dealing with donors. It is instructive to highlight the effects of these conditions with empirical findings before we conclude, glancing at the role of recipient agency in a given context.

Financial strength

Financial strength or, the opposite, financial dependency is certainly the dimension which is used most often to explain donor–recipient relationships. It is argued that governments which rely heavily on foreign funding have little power to defy policy pressures exerted by the aid community (see, for instance, Bräutigam 2000; Gould 2005a; Mkandawire 2010). The case studies provide indications that this thesis partly applies, but also suggest that finances are neither the only nor necessarily the decisive condition for recipients' bargaining positions.

In Tanzania, empirical evidence which supports the dependency narrative is found across all sectors. The fact that aid accounts for the bulk of ministerial development budgets and for more than 97% of HIV/Aids expenditures inevitably coerces authorities to reach consensus with funders if they want to maintain some scope of action. Policies and programmes which are not 'endorsed' by donors become irrelevant if they cannot be implemented due to lack of money. The stark dependence on aid lends itself as explanation why decision-makers feel forced to consult with aid experts and usually follow their 'advice' – which tends to be an implicit requirement for cash disbursement – even if this means the need to adjust priorities and plans according to external funders' priorities. The uptake of climate change as a priority issue, the formulation of a new HIV/Aids Care and Treatment Plan, or the repeated revision of the Primary Education Development Programme III are just three examples of this kind of alignment which appears to be driven by the necessity to secure foreign funding, rather than by actual conviction on government side.

In South Africa, one finds a very different setting. This is not too surprising given that aid as a share of budgets is much lower, currently around 1% of national departments' expenditures. Decision-makers particularly in education and health showed themselves quite aware of the fact that their scope of action is not delimited by donor money, although that is valued as an additional source of finance. The relative independence from aid enables them to take a strong stance towards potential funders when it comes to defining priorities and setting the conditions of cooperation. If donors do not agree and withhold support, it may affect the pace of policy implementation but not compromise implementation as such.

While this applies to the health and education sector (or at least to major reforms carried out in these fields) the situation is different in the environment sector where national bodies and provincial authorities do face financial constraints and often rely on external funding to realise important programmes. However, this does not seem to affect the sovereignty of environmental actors: despite requiring resources from outside, they take a firm stand towards international players. Although environmental entities have received substantial grants particularly from the GEF and have closely collaborated with experts from the World Bank and UNDP, they have been able to retain control over the agenda and keep external actors out of decision-making spheres; the CAPE process delineated in this study can be seen as a case in point.

The examples of the South African environment sector and to some extent also of HIV/Aids, an area where financial and technical assistance continues to play a role, challenge the thesis that the recourse to aid inevitably results in a loss of policy autonomy. They also refute what seems like an irrevocable fact in Tanzania, namely that recipients need to accept external involvement in the policy space in return for money. Various statements of government officials indicate that this corollary is taken as given and is internalised across leadership ranks in Tanzanian authorities (cf. Interview 49, Chapter 7; Interview 54, see Chapter 7; Interview 61, see Chapter 7; Interview 66, see Chapter 7).

Although the sectoral variance regarding the level of dependence is considerable, the similarity of statements from ministerial representatives is notable. One could have expected that leaders in education where aid amounts to 'only' 8.5% of total and 60% of development expenditures (considering MoEVT figures in 2010/11) might have a different position than decision-makers in HIV/Aids whose programmes are almost entirely financed by the aid community. However, this does not seem to be the case. Quite contrary to the assumption that due to their relatively high domestic budget the Tanzanian educational actors would take the strongest stance towards donors, they clearly showed signs of resignation with respect to defending a local agenda. Whereas officials in HIV/Aids at least tried to convince donors to support national policy priorities (as exemplified by the treatment/prevention struggle), officials in education seem to have lost confidence in raising objections due to the perception of being at the mercy of external funders.

The observations that (a) South African environmental actors successfully retain their policy autonomy despite relying on aid and (b) the Tanzanian education sector seems particularly weak in agenda-setting, although being 'better off' than others in terms of finances, suggest that financial strength is not necessarily the (only) determining factor of recipients' ability to maintain the lead in policy-making while being advised from outside.

Administrative capacity

Looking at the South African environmental sector, a feature which obviously plays a crucial role in policy processes is the outstanding administrative strength of authorities dealing with donors. Whether it is the national Department of Environmental Affairs, the South African National Biodiversity Institute as an advisory body or the provincial agency CapeNature, all of them are known for being staffed with highly knowledgeable and skilled officials who encounter experts from the aid community at eye-level in terms of environmental expertise. Given that these actors possess both specialist knowledge and a sound understanding of national and international agendas, they are able to scrutinise and challenge policy ideas presented to their organisations by international funders – as a UNDP officer remarked, "there are people who can say 'no, this is not good" (Interview 8). This kind of 'absorptive capacity' of the administration – that is, the capacity to receive, competently interpret, adapt to local circumstances and implement advice from outside – is based on the quality of internal expertise and has been a major factor why the policy changes leveraged through CAPE were an outcome of exploration and negotiation by local stakeholders, although the programme was heavily co-financed from outside. The ability of environmental authorities to guide such processes and to keep control over the engagement of external actors, including the rejection of proposals which do not support the South African agenda, rests to a significant extent on the capacity of their own expert cadres.

A notable point is that administrative strength does not necessarily mean to have in-house expertise for all spheres of responsibility on hand. Particularly in emerging knowledge areas entities such as DEA or SANBI face 'capacity gaps' which require assistance from outside. But these organisations determine the tasks assigned to consultants themselves (e.g. the compilation and interpretation of data or the development of planning tools required), and clearly delimit the scope of assistance. While external experts are commissioned to carry out analytical work or prepare recommendations, they do not get engaged in decision-making processes. Instead, their deliverables are validated by officials who deduce policy implications and put them forward for discussion. Absorption capacity, in other words, appears to be a major factor why environmental agents in South Africa remain firmly in control of their agenda, despite resorting to financial and technical support; the risk of being swayed by foreign actors is mitigated by a strong administration in the environmental sector.

In other fields of governance, the scope of influence for external experts tends to be greater. Due to their limited in-house capacity, line departments in health and education rely much more on sourcing policy advice (as opposed to mere technical assistance) from outside. Advisors and consultants supplied by aid organisations have played a significant role in past and recent reform processes in these sectors. In the course of establishing a new skills development system or preparing the National Health Insurance, for instance, they were not only used to elaborate technicalities of implementation, but also to provide expertise and advice in early stages of policy exploration. The ideas and concepts conveyed through experts from outside markedly shaped the policies and schemes adopted by the South African administration.

Yet, it needs to be emphasised that despite using advice at various stages, authorities in health and education have held the upper hand in making policy choices. While strategic decisions taken in the course of reforms were certainly informed by external expertise, they remained nonetheless locally 'driven' for at least two reasons. First, decision-makers were not burdened with substantial financial needs and could thus pick or reject recommendations without being concerned about funders' reaction. Second, despite limited in-house capacity, recipient authorities were strong enough to determine general policy objectives and direct advisors accordingly.

This kind of steering capability often appears to be missing on the part of the administration in Tanzania. Due to the immense shortfalls of qualified staff in national ministries (with deficits being even worse at lower levels), the latter are struggling to carry out intellectual work without financial and technical assistance. This does not mean that policy and planning units are void of skilled officials; one can find highly knowledgeable individuals with an impressive training background and years of experience who are able to undertake the analytical exercises and studies required. Yet, the number of such specialists is just insufficient. The fact that at the time of research the Ministry of Health and Social Welfare had only three health economists at its disposal (with one of them being the permanent secretary) indicates the dimension of the problem. The scarcity of specialists has two implications for recipient organisations: their ability to develop an endogenous policy vision which is essential to direct the aid community and its experts is severely constrained, and they are also hardly capable of thoroughly investigating the advice put forward by external actors and – where appropriate – to disprove their arguments with own analyses.

The lack of steering and absorption capacity opens up a wide space for external experts to affect sectoral agendas and decision-making, as the examples in the case studies illustrate. Health sector strategic plans and educational programmes have been strongly shaped by advisors and consultants who provided 'evidence' in the form of situational assessments, statistics, expenditure reviews or evaluations. In many cases, policy recommendations were taken up almost unfiltered in the sense that they were included one-to-one into policies and strategic frameworks. One explanation as to why decisive documents (e.g. the Education Sector Development Programme) frequently mirror external concepts and priorities is that the contribution of ministry staff in the course of their preparation is often more nominal than substantial, and that internal processes of critical validation are non-existent.

As the comparison of cases in South Africa and Tanzania shows, it is not the use of aid-funded experts per se which allows external influence but the absence of absorptive and steering capacity in recipient authorities. The latter seems even more problematic if there are no vocal stakeholders who are able to challenge external policy proposals, thereby supporting their own administration to defend its agenda.

Local knowledge base

The availability of a local science community which is able to play a critical part in policy discourses and to serve as a source of alternative expertise was suggested as a third factor determining the recipients' strength to set their own agendas. Sector studies from both countries confirm the relevance of this dimension through both positive and negative examples. Again, the CAPE process which has brought about significant policy changes in South Africa lends itself as case in point: aside from participating in public consultations, scientists from local academic institutions were involved by carrying out research required to understand the state of biodiversity and socio-political conditions affecting conservation. Their results were crucial for developing policies and approaches fitting the particular context in which they were meant to be applied. Many of the analyses conducted in the course of CAPE were financed with grant money from the GEF or other external financiers; yet, they were contracted out to South African researchers holding knowledge of both environmental issues and country-specific peculiarities. The utilisation of local scientists as producers of policy-relevant expertise clearly limited the 'import' of external views into the process.

The example of CAPE thus suggests a more general conclusion: the availability of local expert communities potentially helps recipient authorities to keep foreign actors out of decision-making spheres and thus to preserve their agenda-setting authority, even if they rely on donor funding. While the environmental sector in South Africa serves best to illustrate this finding, it is also supported by other cases: the fact that the South African health administration invited the HIV community to participate in developing the second National Strategic Plan for AIDS, and used academics from within the country to provide advice and consultancies in the process of preparing a National Health Insurance system seems to have strengthened its ability to re-assume leadership in policy-making. Various donors supported these processes with financial and technical assistance, but their impact on decision-making remained limited.

The Tanzanian environmental sector serves as a third example. The National Environmental Policy and the Environmental Management Act – despite being funded from outside – were drafted by local experts from government and academia. These documents, therefore, clearly reflect a national perspective on how the environment in Tanzania should be conserved and managed. Although there are a number of reasons for the failure of implementation, including conflicting interests in the political realm, deficient budgets and staff constraints, it is not a matter of 'imposed' priorities which hinders execution. On the contrary, environmental authorities, most notably the Division of Environment in the Vice-President's Office, have repeatedly been trying to get support for implementing its policy and legal frameworks. In this case the cause of failure was that the aid community had shifted its attention to new issues.

The significance of local expert communities manifests itself not only where they have contributed to policy processes, but also where they are either non-existent or simply not utilised. The former applies to the Tanzanian education sector, the latter to health. In both areas, foreign experts commissioned by aid agencies have taken over the function of feeding decision-making bodies with 'facts' which suggest certain policy choices – for example, to introduce 'treatment as prevention' or to focus educational investment on the primary level due to its high 'rate of return'. Under the rule of the current imperative of 'evidence-based' policy-making, recipients have little to argue against such recommendations if they cannot present 'counter-expertise' to support a dissenting position. The lack of local explanations for social problems such as the current quality crisis in education or a lack of sexual behaviour change despite widespread HIV awareness opens up room for donors to give reasons and provide solutions which fit the paradigms prevailing in their headquarters. If their reasoning is not scrutinised by actors within or outside the administration, recipients risk becoming fields of experimentation for the aid community's newest ideas and approaches – USAID's ICT project in primary education is a case in point.

Overall, the investigation of educational and health policy-making in Tanzania indicates that the absence or non-involvement of local science communities tends to weaken policy-makers' ability to contest advice put forward by the aid community. Since they are, in principle, able to play a crucial role as knowledge producers and critical examiners of outside expertise – as observed in the policy fields of environment or health in South Africa – it is even more questionable why expert cadres available (e.g. in the field of health) are not used more effectively.

The effects of structural conditions and recipient agency

Taking a comparative perspective on the six case studies from South Africa and Tanzania, a general conclusion can be drawn: all of the conditions we focused on – financial strength, administrative capacity and the local knowledge base – do in fact appear to have a determining impact on recipients' control over sectoral agendas. What needs to be emphasised here is that it is not *one* of these conditions but – as Whitfield and Fraser (2010) have concluded from similar research (see Chapter 1) – their 'intersection' which seems to be decisive. A higher degree of financial dependency does not necessarily result in a loss of control but can to a certain degree be compensated by a strong administration which uses the local science community to define and defend its policy choices against outside advice. Equally, being better off in terms of finances does not prevent external influence if authorities are unable to scrutinise donor recommendations for their responsiveness to the local agenda, and/or continue to rely on foreign advisors and consultants who provide evidence for policy decisions.

In other words: it follows from these observations that it is insufficient to explain external influence on policy-making with a single factor since there is no one-dimensional causality. Using only aid dependency as a justification for weak recipient leadership would thus mean to disregard other conditions from which governments could potentially gain strength to keep control over their policy space. That some senior officials in Tanzania nonetheless tend to do so, hints at an important aspect pertaining to the effect of structural conditions, namely the significance of subjective interpretation and consequent agency on the recipient side. As Whitfield and Fraser (2009: 39) have pointed out, "conditions do not determine the outcome of any negotiation in a mechanistic sense". While they do provide resources or constraints which delimit the bargaining power of decision makers, it also matters how the latter react to them.

The case studies from Tanzania have shown that recipients confronted with largely similar conditions choose different strategies of dealing with donors.

In education, officials seem to have adopted an attitude of submissiveness towards aid experts whereby resistance is expressed through deliberate postponing of decision-making; in health, leaders rhetorically keep promoting national priorities while at the same time accommodating funders' demands; in environment, decision-makers embark on tactical manoeuvring, framing priorities to the aid agenda while following their own route in implementation. All these strategies primarily aim at maximising aid which in the light of the existing budget deficits is a justifiable objective. The downside of executing such strategies is that to a greater or lesser extent policy autonomy gets lost.

The question is whether this is an inevitable consequence of receiving aid – the cases from South Africa indicate that it is not. As delineated in the sector studies, all three fields at times faced unfavourable conditions. Particularly during the early years of transition, authorities were short of money and experienced officials, and thus they relied on funding and expertise from outside. Nonetheless, decision-makers took an assertive attitude towards donors, maintaining their sovereignty in agenda-setting. While other factors (e.g. diplomatic interests) also came into play, the aplomb demonstrated by South African leaders led external actors to accept and support national policy visions. This observation supports Whitfield and Fraser's finding that while structural conditions largely explain variation in recipients' ability to retain control over the agenda, "a significant degree of variation is due to the confidence of recipient governments to turn their conditions into negotiating capital" (Whitfield & Fraser 2009: 364).

Individual decision-makers in Tanzania, too, possess this kind of confidence which enables them to interact with aid experts on a par, although they have few resources to draw on. Yet, here an attitude of resignation among decision-makers in government is pervasive. Senior officials are more likely to cede policy-making and planning to aid experts who feed 'national' strategies with their own 'solutions' for development. Overcoming the acquiescence prevailing among leadership ranks may be a first step in constraining external actors' scope of influence, despite adverse structural conditions.

Chapter 8

THERE IS NO SUBSTITUTE FOR LOCAL KNOWLEDGE: SUMMARY AND CONCLUSION

This book began by referring to the repeated critique and persistent failure of expert advice that has become a prime tool of foreign aid, with the rise of the 'knowledge for development' paradigm. We argued that the chronic ineffectiveness of 'technical assistance' – the label under which advisory activities are commonly subsumed – does not primarily result from deficient implementation (as it is often suggested by evaluation studies) but from structural constraints that frustrate knowledge transfer in the context of development cooperation. Moreover, the engagement of external experts in the policy space of recipient countries must be considered dangerous for young democracies insofar as it opens up room for outside interference; ultimately, thus our thesis, posing a threat to the legitimacy of these countries' governments as they risk losing control over their own policy agendas. Using South Africa and Tanzania as sites of empirical investigation, we aimed to identify the conditions which determine recipients' ability to retain their agenda-setting autonomy. We sought to identify general impediments that explain why aid-related expert advice keeps developing countries in a status of dependency, rather than making them self-reliant as is claimed by the aid community.

The inherently political nature and especially the vested interests attached to aid are key explanatory factors in this regard (see Chapter 4). Donor governments use development assistance as a device to promote foreign policy and economic objectives. Thus, expertise provided in this setting is inherently not as 'neutral' as is usually claimed by those who emphasise its 'evidence-based' grounding. The extent to which advice is tied to donors' agendas varies depending on their policies and organisational set-ups. In any case, it needs to be at least broadly in line with the political views of the funding governments.

Since the preferences of the latter shift with elections, as well as with global trends and fads in aid policies, priorities and modalities of aid frequently change. This ephemerality is detrimental to advisory processes insofar as they require a certain degree of continuance and stability if they are to have any sustained impact (see Chapter 5).

The linkage between aid and politics also explains the supply-driven nature of expert activities which has consistently been criticised as a major flaw by assessment studies (see, for instance, Forss et al. 1988; Berg 1993; Royal Ministry of Foreign Affairs Norway & Asplan Analyse 1994; Williams et al. 2003; Land 2007; European Commission 2008; World Bank Independent Evaluation Group 2008). Most of these reports call for a greater involvement of recipients in identifying their needs or defining the terms of reference for external support. However, such suggestions, we have argued, will not solve the root cause of the prevailing mismatch between demand and supply (see Chapter 5). For donor governments and their respective implementing agencies, placing experts in recipient authorities not only helps to support policy ideas that conform to their own political convictions but also to trace the use of their taxpayers' money. Some donor governments (e.g. the US) make that a condition of their aid programmes. To cede decision-making over expert assistance to beneficiaries in order to increase local 'ownership' and commitment would mean to give up control and influence. From the donor perspective, this would counteract efforts to legitimate aid spending and to prove accountability vis-à-vis domestic constituencies. Therefore, expert advice in aid will remain oriented at funders' interests, even if recipients are formally being given more say.

Another set of problems are flaws pertaining to expert employment: the absence of clear concepts of knowledge transfer on the donor side, an insufficient fit of advisors' expertise, experience and competencies, and adverse employment conditions that impede the building of trust and social ties (see Chapter 5). In view of such constraints, external experts at best fill gaps in recipient authorities, but contribute little to 'capacitating' counterparts as it is purported by aid providers. In actual fact, the latter profit from this failure insofar as their support would eventually become obsolete if knowledge transfer was achieved.

A third root cause of the inefficacy of expert advice was identified in the unequal relations that – despite all rhetoric of 'partnership' – continue to exist in development cooperation (see Chapter 5). The imbalance which derives from the situation that one party depends on the assistance of the other – be it financially or in terms of specialist knowledge – is reinforced by the fact that advisory relations in aid are structured along a knowledge hierarchy which places 'international' (i.e. Northern) over 'local' knowledge. It manifests itself in stark discrepancies concerning the quality and credibility accredited to expertise. Aid agencies perpetuate this hierarchical classification through procurement practices that marginalise expert communities in recipient countries and solidify the pre-eminence of their own expert cadres. The obvious status difference between 'international' advisors and their counterparts in government authorities hampers the building of relationships which would allow for knowledge transfer, exchange and mutual learning.

The intricacies resulting from hierarchical relations and vested interests underlying aid partly explain why decades of 'technical assistance' have had so little impact in terms of 'capacity-building', and why technocratic suggestions are unlikely to increase its effectiveness. The intrinsic constraints of aid-related expert advice delineated in this study account for its failure to help recipient governments in becoming independent. Policy-makers in developing countries, thus, continue to rely on experts financed and provided by donor agencies. The persistent presence of external actors in their policy space, however, implies the constant risk of foreign interference in decision-making. The sector studies from South Africa and Tanzania (see Chapter 7) document the close involvement of aid experts in policy processes but also show that the extent to which they are able to shape agendas varies considerably. Recipients' ability to retain the lead in decision-making is to some extent dependent on the degree of their financial dependence. Our analysis revealed that it is also determined by the strength of their administrations and science communities in the respective fields. Also, the finding that policy-makers who faced similar structural conditions positioned themselves differently towards the aid community, for example by adopting an attitude of resignation or by employing strategies of resistance, hinted at the significance of agency within a given context (see Chapter 7).

All in all, the case studies show that external advice has different effects on young democracies. The case of the Tanzanian education sector most strongly supports the initial thesis that such advice threatens the legitimacy of governments insofar as it makes decision-making responsive to the preferences of foreign actors rather than to those of domestic stakeholders. The orientation towards donor demands undermines the 'input' legitimacy of educational governance. 'Output' legitimacy is undermined since programmes developed from outside largely fail to bring about substantial change. The fact that the government formally bears the blame for policy failure in education, although decisions are largely driven by donors, hints at the accountability problems entailed in the reliance on external advice. The dominance of aid experts has narrowed down if not eliminated the space for endogenous policy thinking in responsible authorities. Unable to provide a genuine policy vision, leaders seem to have lost control over the country's education agenda to the expert cadres of foreign funders.

The Tanzanian education sector represents the most extreme case in our study, but indications for a loss of policy-making authority were found in the fields of health and environment as well. The case studies from Tanzania thus substantiate the claim that aid-related expert advice potentially jeopardises the legitimacy of democratic governments if these are not able to maintain their decision-making autonomy to advance their own agendas. That this is possible in principle, *if* recipients possess resources that allow them to scrutinise external expertise and adapt it to national policy visions, can be seen in South Africa. In all three fields under investigation, policy-makers have managed to retain the lead in decision-making despite drawing on external assistance. Yet, as repeatedly pointed out, the country is a rather unusual case, given its outstanding financial and institutional strength. Most young democracies in sub-Saharan Africa rather face conditions as found in Tanzania. Hence, the risk that their governments similarly lose (or have lost) legitimacy due to their dependence on donor funding and advice is high.

The findings of this study indicate the pertinence of this peril. Yet, it would be overstating the case if we do not admit to some weaknesses in the empirical approach. First, the loss of legitimacy has to be theoretically inferred rather than actually being 'measurable'. The limitations of the scope of empirical inquiry did not allow us to ascertain the public acceptance of policies or the assessment of government performance by citizens. Such evidence would provide ultimate proof of the thesis that loss of control over agenda-setting actually puts the legitimacy of young democratic regimes at risk. Obviously it could only be gathered by large-scale surveys in each country. It is important to note that the scarcity of social science research and public opinion polls in developing countries not only poses a problem for research on the link between government policy positions and citizens' preferences, it is also problematic for the democratic system insofar as important indicators of representation are missing.

An auxiliary approach for investigating to what extent policy agendas reflect local concerns (as opposed to priorities of foreign actors) would have been to include parliamentary debates about sectoral challenges and reform proposals into the analysis. This might have been feasible for South Africa where records of parliamentary committee meetings are provided online in English. However, access to Tanzania's National Assembly records requires Swahili skills not at our disposal.

Given these constraints, we tried to mitigate this missing evidence by including the perspectives of academics and civil society activists who, while counting among elites, can be considered part of 'the public'. In fact, they theoretically represent the vocal public which influences public discourses and shapes public opinion. The focus of the investigation is on tracing the policy interests of two groups of actors, namely the government (represented by policy-makers and senior bureaucrats) and donors (represented by experts of aid agencies in their various roles). Thereby, we classified the interests of the former as 'local' and those of the latter as 'external'. To be sure, this is a generalisation that oversimplifies reality. Yet, it helped to reconstruct struggles over policies and to understand which side was more successful in shaping the outcomes of the discourse. The fact that we primarily relied on the protagonists involved in such processes to give an account of their own and others' roles meant that no 'unbiased' material (if such exists) to draw on was available. Using expert interviews in spite of their methodological limitations (see Chapter 2) allowed us to carry out sector studies in two countries, and to include past and present policy processes. The variety of cases, in turn, helped to reveal general complexities of expert advice in the aid setting, as well as to identify conditions which determine its effects. Similar empirical research covering other aid-receiving countries in Africa and other world regions would be instructive to test the generalisability of findings and their validity in different contexts, nationally, culturally, economically and with respect to the pertinent aid policies. It would surely be advantageous if this research was carried out by or in collaboration with local scholars who might have a deeper understanding of historical developments, social realities and the political scenes in their countries than researchers from the North.

Much literature about aid emanates from political science and economics, and focuses on its political and institutional effects in recipient countries. This study contributes to the debate with insights from the sociology of science and provides a new perspective which highlights the complexities of knowledge transfer as the ultimate aim of expert advice. While international organisations have been promoting knowledge transfer through expert advice as the new panacea for development, this study provides explanations why in most cases it fails to be of use for recipients, or, even worse, has a detrimental impact on the fragile fabric of their democracies.

It needs to be emphasised at this point that we do not insinuate that harming recipients' institutions is the intention of anyone involved in the aid business. Most experts we met in country offices, embassies and government authorities conveyed the impression that they truly sought to help their South African or Tanzanian counterparts in coping with the massive problems related to healthcare, education systems or the environment. Some advisors were themselves highly critical of their own organisations' practices, and seemed seriously interested in how to bring about change. The findings of our research, however, suggest that providing developing countries with experts from outside will not achieve this change, irrespective of the commitment and good will of individual actors or attempts to refine approaches. This conclusion sounds rather pessimistic and in a way prompts the withdrawal of a large amount of aid immediately. In fact, the results of this study tempt one to dissuade donors from continuing to supply advice to countries that obviously lack the absorptive capacity to adequately deal with it.

It would probably be more constructive to use the available means to support the knowledge communities in developing countries so that these become able to produce a critical mass of local experts who qualify as producers and critical scrutinisers of expertise. This support does not necessarily need to (or should better not?) be delivered through conventional aid programmes since these are invariably affected by conflicts of interests and accountability pressures that undermine their actual objectives. It could, instead, take the form of investment that facilitates institutional cooperation between research centres, be they university-based or 'think tanks' outside the academic system. It could also be provided in the form of educational scholarships that enable students to enter higher education paths, notably not only abroad (which, most often, means in the North) but in their own countries. It could mean making funding available for the setup of new university programmes that are locally designed and oriented at the specific country challenges. None of these suggestions are new, but they seem to have faded from the spotlight of foreign funders. One reason, probably the most important one, is the difficulty in gaining visible results from such kind of investment in a relatively short time, the kind of tangible evidence that can be demonstrated to the taxpayers/voters at home. In terms of value for the societies of developing countries, however, such a strategy is likely to have more effect than using 'parachute experts' from outside to provide technical assistance that all too often does not respond to these countries' political agendas.

Examples that hint at the potential of science-related initiatives can already be found. In Tanzania, cooperation between the Muhimbili University College of Health Sciences in Dar es Salaam, the University of Heidelberg (Germany) and GTZ in the early 2000s led to the introduction of a first Master of Public Health Programme. Producing a crucial cadre of public health specialists, the annual course is still being offered by the School of Public Health and Social Sciences, and the two universities have continued collaboration and exchange. In South Africa, remarkable achievements regarding the transformation of the higher education landscape were accomplished through the so-called 'South Africa Norway Tertiary Education Programme' (SANTED). Starting in 2000, it aimed at improving the access, retention and success of previously disadvantaged students, enhancing the administrative and academic capacity of selected universities, and facilitating regional cooperation. When the programme formally ended in 2010, it had – despite a comparatively small amount of foreign investment – catalysed structural changes and institutional linkages spanning 16 universities in South Africa and the SADC region (see Gibbon 2014).

It is certainly difficult to 'measure' the impact of such initiatives directly. However, the fact that they outlast the time frames of external support indicates a degree of sustainability which many aid projects are lacking. The value of students who benefit from better education opportunities in their countries and empower their societies through building an endogenous knowledge base must not be underestimated just because it cannot be easily expressed in numerical terms. The long-term profit from building 'human capital' in developing democracies through strengthening their higher education systems should be considered by those who have the means to provide support but also by the governments in these countries themselves. Surely, investing in tertiary education may seem like an unaffordable luxury for decision-makers facing a myriad of social problems that require attention and budget. This may explain why some science systems in sub-Saharan Africa are underfunded to such an extent that they operate "in a 'subsistence mode' where they struggle to reproduce themselves" (Mouton et al. 2008: 200). Their absolute dependency on foreign funders in many cases bars them from playing a systemic role insofar as they are unable to set their own research agendas independently from external influences (Mouton et al. 2008). To carry out science in response to local needs, universities would need to be "backed by long-term commitment of adequate resources from government and the private sector" (Girvan 2007: 33). The provision of domestic means for research and higher education is critical because

> *only on this basis do external support and collaboration stand a chance of success. In this, as in all other areas, external inputs cannot substitute for internal effort.* (Girvan 2007: 33)

It needs to be acknowledged that many African leaders increasingly try to put science on their political agendas. Although these endeavours have not always or not yet been translated into budgets, newly formulated policy frameworks and intensified efforts to produce data on science and technology systems signal rising awareness of their potential (see NEPAD Planning and Coordinating Agency 2014). At the same time, however, it is noticeable that this potential is often reduced to stimulating economic growth through innovation, whereas the value of science communities for policy-making and governance is neglected. This manifests itself in the weak and sometimes non-existent links between the political sphere and academia. Various researchers we met for this study, particularly in Tanzania, complained about the disinterest of decision-makers in their findings. Such complaints, of course, are neither new nor confined to developing countries, and the tense relationship between science and politics has been a topic of debate for a while (see Barker & Peters 1993; Bechmann 2003; Lentsch & Weingart 2009b). Yet, the disregard of local knowledge by policy-makers in young African democracies is specifically distressing insofar as an important resource that could strengthen their sovereignty is left unexploited.

Certainly, expert communities in developing countries are still small in many fields and require internal and external support to grow. They nonetheless constitute a source of expertise that – if tapped by their governments – could contribute to decreasing the dependence on advice from outside and to abolishing the asymmetry between foreign and local experts. For young democracies, using the knowledge and capacity of their own societies seems indispensable if they want to find and realise their own policy visions.

References

Adams, J, King, C & Hook, D (2010) Global Research Report Africa. Leeds: Thomson Reuters

Adamson, MR (2006) The most important single aspect of our foreign policy? The Eisenhower Administration, foreign aid, and the Third World. In: KC Statler & AL Johns (eds) *The Eisenhower Administration, the Third World, and the Globalization of the Cold War*. Lanham, Md: Rowman & Littlefield. pp. 47–99

Adler, PS & Kwon, S-W (2002) Social capital: Prospects for a new concept. *The Academy of Management Review* 27(1): 17–40

AFD, DG Trésor, CEPII & University of Maastricht (2012) Institutional Profiles Database. Available at http://www.cepii.fr/institutions/data/IPD_2012_%20EN.xlsx [accessed 26 February 2014]

African Development Bank Group (2009) Assessing governance: Staff Guidance Note on the governance rating of the bank's country performance assessment. Operational Guidance Note. Tunis: African Development Bank Group

——— (2013) *Country Policy and Institutional Assessment*. Formatted CPIA Dataset, released 2011, last updated 27.01.2013, Abidjan, Tunis. Available at http://cpia.afdb.org/ResourceCenter/Default.aspx. [accessed 27 February 2014]

African National Congress (2007) 52nd national conference: Resolutions, Polokwane

African Union–New Partnership for Africa's Development (2010) *African Innovation Outlook 2010*. Pretoria: AU–NEPAD

Agrawal, A (1995) Dismantling the divide between indigenous and scientific knowledge. *Development and Change* 26(3): 413–439

AIDS Healthcare Foundation (2013) South Africa: 1,000 protest U.S. AIDS funding cuts. Los Angeles: AHF. Available at http://www.aidshealth.org/archives/15911 [accessed 23 January 2014]

Akida, A, Mnangwone, I & Lyimo, L (2012) *Financing for Sustainable Forest Management in Tanzania: Country Case Study*. Indufor, Helsinki

Albertyn, C & Fakir, S (2000) *Development Cooperation Report II for South Africa 1994–1999: Evaluation of ODA to the Environment Sector*. Pretoria: National Treasury

Alesina, A & Dollar, D (2000) Who gives foreign aid to whom and why? *Journal of Economic Growth* 5(1): 33-63

Alexander, R (2008) Education For All: The Quality Imperative and the Problem of Pedagogy. *CREATE Research Monograph (20)*. London: Consortium for Research on Educational Access, Transitions and Equity

Alexopoulos, AN & Buckley, F (2013) What trust matters when: The temporal value of professional and personal trust for effective knowledge transfer. *Group & Organization Management* 38(3): 361–391

Allais, S (2010) *The Changing Faces of the South African National Qualifications Framework: NQF Country Study*. Geneva: International Labour Organization

Allais, SM (2006) Problems with qualification reform in senior secondary education in South Africa. In: M Young & J Gamble (eds) *Knowledge, Curriculum and Qualifications for South African Further Education*. Cape Town: HSRC Press. pp. 18–45

Anderson, T (2008) *South-to-South Consulting: Africans Offer International Perspective*. Cambridge, Mass.: USAID. Available at http://pdf.usaid.gov/pdf_docs/pnaeb085.pdf [accessed 5 November 2013]

Aning, K (2010) Security, the war on terror, and Official Development Assistance. *Critical Studies on Terrorism* 3(1): 7–26

Antweiler, C (1998) Local knowledge and local knowing. *Anthropos* 93(4-6): 469–494

Appiah, F, Chimanikire, DP & Gran, T (eds) (2004) *Professionalism and Good Governance in Africa*. Oslo: Abstrakt forlag

Arencibia-Jorge, R, Araujo Ruíz, JA, Hung Llamos, BR, Corera Álvarez, E & Rodríguez, ZC (2012) *Scientific Development in African Countries: A Scientometric Approach 1996–2009*. Project report. INASP, Editorial Universitaria, Ministerio de Educación Superior, Oxford, Havana

Argote, L & Ingram, P (2000) Knowledge transfer: A basis for competitive advantage in firms. *Organizational Behavior and Human Decision Processes* 82(1): 150–169

Ashwell, A, Sandwith, T, Barnett, M, Parker, A & Wisani, F (2006) Fynbos Fynmense: People Making Biodiversity Work. *SANBI Biodiversity Series (4)*. Pretoria: South African National Biodiversity Institute

ASSA AIDS Committee (2011) *ASSA2008 AIDS and demographic model of the Actuarial Society of South Africa: ProvOutput*. Actuarial Society of South Africa. Available at http://aids.actuarialsociety.org.za/scripts/buildfile.asp?filename=ProvOutput_110216.zip [accessed 22 July 2014]

Assey, P, Bass, S, Cheche, B et al. (2007) Environment at the Heart of Tanzania's Development: Lessons from Tanzania's National Strategy for Growth and Reduction of Poverty. *Natural Resource Issues Series (6)*. London: International Institute for Environment and Development

Assey, S (2012) A critical analysis of the expulsion of pregnant girls from school: A case study of Temeke District, Dar es Salaam, Tanzania. Dissertation, Southern and Eastern African Regional Centre for Women's Law, University of Zimbabwe, Harare

AusAid (2012) *Adviser Remuneration Framework: Version 3*. Available at http://aid.dfat.gov.au/Publications/Documents/adviser-remuneration-framework.pdf [accessed 14 November 2013]

Australian Government (2013) *AusAID – Department of Foreign Affairs and Trade Integration. Latest News*. Available at http://aid.dfat.gov.au/LatestNews/Pages/dept-integration.aspx [accessed 6 January 2014]

Ayo, CK (2013) *Nigeria's education system is at the mercy of policy implementation*. Covenant University. Available http://covenantuniversity.edu.ng/News/Nigeria-s-Education-System-is-at-the-Mercy-of-Policy-Implementation#.VIbhN3vh2Sp [accessed 9 December 2014]

Aziz, R (2013) *Obama 2014 budget: Continued support for Global Fund, paired with PEPFAR cut leave: Blueprint goals in question*. Center for Global Health Policy: Science Speaks. Available at http://sciencespeaksblog.org/2013/04/10/cut-to-pepfar-support-for-global-fund-in-obama-2014-budget-leave-blueprint-goals-in-question/ [accessed 23 January 2014]

Badroodien, A & McGrath, S (2005) *International Influences on the Evolution of South Africa's National Skills Development Strategy, 1989–2004*. Eschborn: Deutsche Gesellschaft für Technische Zusammenarbeit

Baleta, A (1999) South Africa's AIDS care thrown into confusion. *The Lancet* 354(9191): 1711

Barber, J P (2004) *Mandela's World: The International Dimension of South Africa's Political Revolution 1990-99*. Oxford: James Currey

Barker, A & Peters, BG (eds) (1993) *The Politics of Expert Advice. Creating, Using and Manipulating Scientific Knowledge for Public Policy*. Pittsburgh: University of Pittsburgh Press

Barrett, AM, Chawla-Duggan, R, Lowe, J, Nikel, J & Ukpo, E (2006) The Concept of Quality in Education: A Review of the 'International' Literature on the Concept of Quality in Education. *EdQual Working Paper (3)*. Bristol, Bath: University of Bristol, University of Bath

Barron, P, Gouws, H, Loots, B et al. (2009) *Consolidated Report of the Integrated Support Team: Review of Health Overspending and Macro-assessment of the Public Health System in South Africa*. Pretoria: DFID

Barry, SML, Mpangile, G & Loughran, L (2003) *Recommendations for USAID/Tanzania's HIV/AIDS Strategy 2005–2014*. Washington DC: USAID, The Synergy Project

Basic Education Development Committee (2001) *Primary Education Development Plan (2002–2006)*. Education Sector Development Programme. Dar es Salaam: Basic Education Development Committee

——— (2006) *Primary Education Development Programme II (2007–2011)*. Education Sector Development Programme. Dar es Salaam: Basic Education Development Committee

Bass, S & Renard, Y (2009) *UNDP-UNEP Poverty-Environment Initiative (PEI): Evaluation of the Partnership with Norway 2004–2008*. London: International Institute for Environment and Development (IIED)

BBC News (2006) SA's Zuma 'showered to avoid HIV'. Available at http://news.bbc.co.uk/2/hi/africa/4879822.stm [accessed 28 July 2014]

BBC News (2012, 5 November) Malawi suspends laws against homosexual relationships. Available at http://www.bbc.co.uk/news/world-africa-20209802 [accessed 18 December 2013]

Becerra, M, Lunnan, R & Huemer, L (2008) Trustworthiness, risk, and the transfer of tacit and explicit knowledge between alliance partners. *Journal of Management Studies* 45(4): 691–713

Bechmann, GI (ed.) (2003) *Expertise and Its Interfaces. The Tense Relationship of Science and Politics*. Berlin: edition sigma

Benatar, SR (1997) An old health care system gives place to new. *The Lancet* 349(9064): 1537–1545

Berg, EJ (1993) *Rethinking Technical Cooperation: Reforms for Capacity Building in Africa*. New York: Development Alternatives Inc

Berger, PL & Luckmann, T (1966) *The Social Construction of Reality: A Treatise in the Sociology of Knowledge*. London: The Penguin Press

Bertelsmann Stiftung (2014a) *BTI 2014: South Africa Country Report*. Gütersloh: Bertelsmann Stiftung

——— (2014b) *BTI 2014: Codebook for Country Assessments*. Gütersloh: Bertelsmann Stiftung

——— (2014c) *BTI 2014: Tanzania Country Report*. Gütersloh: Bertelsmann Stiftung

Berthélemy, J-C (2006) Bilateral donors' interest vs. recipients' development motives in aid allocation: Do all donors behave the same? *Review of Development Economics* 10(2): 179–194

Berthélemy, J-C & Tichit, A (2004) Bilateral donors' aid allocation decisions – A three-dimensional panel analysis. *International Review of Economics & Finance* 13(3): 253–274

Besharati, NA (2013) The establishment of the South African Development Partnership Agency: Institutional complexities and political exigencies. *South African Journal of International Affairs* 20(3): 357–377

Best Jobs Tanzania Blog (2013) Health advisor jobs at DFID Tanzania. Available at http://bestjobstanzania.blogspot.de/2013/02/health-advisor-jobs-at-dfid-tanzania.html [accessed 8 November 2013]

Bevan, S (2006, 11 December) African minister ends decade of denial on Aids. *The Telegraph*. Available at http://www.telegraph.co.uk/health/healthnews/3346075/African-minister-ends-decade-of-denial-on-Aids.html [accessed 25 July 2014]

Bhalalusesa, E (2003) Education for all: Is Tanzania on track? *NORRAG News* (32): 49–53

Bickerton, CJ, Cunliffe, P & Gourevitch, A (eds) (2007) *Politics Without Sovereignty: A Critique of Contemporary International Relations*. Oxon, New York: University College London Press

Bierschenk, T (1988) *Entwicklungshilfeprojekte als Verhandlungsfelder Strategischer Gruppen oder Wieviele Tierhaltungsprojekte gibt es Eigentlich im Atakora (VR Benin)?* Berlin: FU Berlin Institut für Ethnologie Abteilung Sozialanthropologie

Biesma, RG, Brugha, R, Harmer, A, Walsh, A, Spicer, N & Walt, G (2009) The effects of global health initiatives on country health systems: A review of the evidence from HIV/AIDS control. *Health Policy and Planning* 24(4): 239–252

Bigsten, A & Danielson, A (2001) Tanzania: Is the Ugly Duckling Finally Growing Up? *NAI Research Reports (120)*. Uppsala: Nordic Africa Institute

Bird, A (2001) Knowledge capacity building in South Africa: Both global and local strategies. In: W Gmelin, K King & S McGrath (eds) *Development Knowledge: National Research and International Cooperation*. Edinburgh, Bonn, Geneva: CAS, DSE, NORRAG. pp. 265–276

Bird, A & Heitmann, W (2011) Policy transfer or policy learning: Interactions between international and national skills development approaches to policy making in South Africa. Paper prepared for the NORRAG Conference on Policy Transfer or Policy Learning, Geneva

Birdsall, N, Mahgoub, A, Savedoff, WD & Vyborny, K (2011) *Cash on Delivery: A New Approach to Foreign Aid*. Washington DC: Center for Global Development

Blomley, T & Iddi, S (2009) *Participatory Forest Management in Tanzania: 1993–2009: Lessons Learned and Experiences to Date*. Dar es Salaam: Ministry of Natural Resources and Tourism, United Republic of Tanzania

Blomley, T & Ramadhani, H (2006) Going to scale with participatory forest management: Early lessons from Tanzania. *International Forestry Review* 8(1): 93–100

Blomley, T, Pfliegner, KIJ, Zahabu, E, Ahrends, A & Burgess, ND (2008) Seeing the wood for the trees: An assessment of the impact of participatory forest management on forest conditions in Tanzania. *Oryx* 42(3): 380–391

BMZ (2011) Forms of Development Cooperation Involving the Private Sector. *Strategy Paper (5)*. Bonn, Berlin: Federal Ministry for Economic Cooperation and Development (BMZ)

Bodibe, K (2011) HCT campaign: The numbers so far. health-e: online. Available at http://www. health-e.org.za/2011/06/30/hct-campaign-the-numbers-so-far-living-with-aids-478/ [accessed 30 July 2014]

Bogner, A & Menz, W (2009) The theory-generating expert interview. In: A Bogner, B Littig & W Menz (eds) *Interviewing Experts*. Basingstoke: Palgrave Macmillan. pp. 43–80

Bogner, A, Littig, B & Menz, W (eds) (2009) *Interviewing Experts*. Basingstoke: Palgrave Macmillan

Bojö, J & Reddy, RC (2002) Mainstreaming Environment in Poverty Reduction Strategies. *Environment Strategy Note (4)*. Washington DC: World Bank

Bond, P (2001) Foreign aid and development debates in post-apartheid South Africa. *Transformation* (45): 25–36

Booth, D & Cammack, D (2013) *Governance for Development in Africa: Solving Collective Action Problems*. London: Zed Books

Boseley, S (2011, 23 November) Crisis looms as Global Fund forced to cut back on Aids, malaria and TB grants. *The Guardian*. Available at http://www.theguardian.com/society/sarah-boseley-global-health/2011/nov/23/aids-tuberculosis [accessed 23 January 2014]

Botha, M (2004) *Partnerships, Cooperative Management and Incentives to Secure Biodiversity Conservation in Priority Areas in the Cape Floristic Region: Final Project Completion Report*. Claremont, Cape Town: Botanical Society of South Africa

Bradshaw, D, Dorrington, R & Laubscher, R (2012) *Rapid Mortality Surveillance Report 2011*. Cape Town: Burden of Disease Research Unit, Medical Research Council

Bratton, M & Landsberg, C (2000) South Africa. In: S Forman & S Patrick (eds) *Good Intentions: Pledges of Aid for Postconflict Recovery*. Boulder, Colorado: Lynne Rienner Publishers. pp. 259–314

Bräutigam, D (1992) Governance, economy, and foreign aid. *Studies in Comparative International Development* 27(3): 3–25

——— (2000) *Aid Dependence and Governance*. Expert Group on Development Issues 2000(1). Stockholm: Almqvist & Wiksell International

Bräutigam, D & Botchwey, K (1999) The Institutional Impact of Aid Dependence on Recipients in Africa. *CMI Working Papers (1)*. Bergen: Chr. Michelsen Institute

Bräutigam, D & Knack, S (2004) Foreign aid, institutions and governance in sub-Saharan Africa. *Economic Development and Cultural Change* 52(2): 255–286

Brown, A (2000) *Current issues in sector-wide approaches for health development: Tanzania case study*. Geneva: Overseas Development Institute, World Health Organization

Brown, W (2013) Sovereignty matters: Africa, donors, and the aid relationship. *African Affairs* 112(447): 262–282

Browne, S (2006) *Aid and Influence: Do Donors Help or Hinder?* London, Sterling, VA: Earthscan

Buchert, L (1995) *Recent Trends in Education Aid: Towards a Classification of Policies*. A Report from the IWGE. Paris: UNESCO International Institute for Educational Planning

——— (1997) *Education Policy Formulation in Tanzania: Co-ordination between the Government and International Aid Agencies*. A Report from the IWGE. Paris: UNESCO International Institute for Educational Planning

——— (1999) Co-ordination of aid to education at the country level: Some experiences and lessons from the United Republic of Tanzania in the 1990s. In: K King & L Buchert (eds) *Changing International Aid to Education: Global Patterns and National Contexts*. Paris: UNESCO Publishing, NORRAG. pp. 222–238

Bulíř, rA & Hamann, A J (2008) Volatility of development aid: From the frying pan into the fire? *World Development* 36(10): 2048–2066

Burki, O (2001) *Sector-wide approach in Tanzania. The health sector example. Observations from a Bi-Lateral*. End of assignment report. Swiss Agency for Development and Co-operation

Buss, l, Lames, M, Hustädt, E & Klinge, B (2012) *Report on the procurement of goods and services and the conclusion of financing agreements*. Eschborn: GIZ

Butler, A (2005) South Africa's HIV/AIDS policy, 1994–2004: How can it be explained? *African Affairs* 104(417): 591–614

Cadman, M, Petersen, C, Driver, A, Sekhran, N, Maze, K & Munzhedzi, S (2010) *Biodiversity for Development: South Africa's Landscape Approach to Conserving Biodiversity and Promoting Ecosystem Resilience*. Pretoria: South African National Biodiversity Institute

Cape Action for People and the Environment (2011) *Our Partnership*. Available at http://www.capeaction.org.za/ index.php/our-partnership [accessed 8 May 2014]

Cape Action Plan for the Environment (2000) *Implementation Programme Report*. CSIR Report (ENV-S-C 99130 D)

Cape Nature Conservation (2003) *Conservation stewardship: Pilot projects in the Swartland and Overberg*. Cape Town

CAPE Project Team (2000) *Cape Action Plan for the environment: A biodiversity strategy and action plan for the Cape Floral Kingdom*. Summary Report.

Carlsson, G (2012) Clear goals to be set for development assistance. Debate article. Svd Brännpunkt. Stockholm: Government Offices of Sweden. Available at http://www.government.se/sb/d/7958/a/189214 [accessed 22 January 2014]

Carothers, T & De Gramont, D (2013) *Development Aid Confronts Politics: The Almost Revolution*. Washington DC: Carnegie Endowment for International Peace

Carton, M & King, K (2004) Transforming the Labour Skills Arena in South Africa: The International Dimension. *Notes et Travaux (74)*. Geneva: Institute Universitaire d'Ètudes du Dèveloppement

CDU, CSU & FDP (2009) *Growth, education, unity. The coalition agreement between the CDU, CSU and FDP for the 17th legislative period*. Berlin

Celasun, O & Walliser, J (2008) Predictability of aid: Do fickle donors undermine aid effectiveness? *Economic Policy* 23(55): 545–594

Chêne, M. (2009) *Low salaries, the culture of per diems and corruption*. U4 Expert Answer. U4 Anti-Corruption Resource Centre, Transparency International, Chr. Michelsen Institute

Cherlet, J (2014) Epistemic and technological determinism in development aid. *Science, Technology & Human Values* 39(6): 773–794

Chigwedere, P, Seage, GR, Gruskin, S, Lee, T-H & Essex, M (2008) Estimating the lost benefits of antiretroviral drug use in South Africa. *Journal of Acquired Immune Deficiency Syndromes* 49(4): 410–415

Child, B (2010) *Independent Terminal Evaluation of the 'UNDP-GEF CAPE Agulhas Biodiversity Initiative (ABI)'*. Project Number: SAF/03/G31/A/1G/99. GEF, UNDP

Chisholm, L (2003) The state of curriculum reform in South Africa: The issue of Curriculum 2005. In: J Daniel, A Habib & R Southall (eds) *State of the Nation: South Africa, 2003–2004*. Cape Town, South Africa: HSRC Press. pp. 268–289

——— (2005) The making of South Africa's National Curriculum Statement. *Journal of Curriculum Studies* 37(2): 193–208

Chorley, M (2013, 04 December) UK government gave £80,000 in taxpayers' money to Zimbabwe government in contravention of its own rules. *Daily Mail Online*. Available at http://www.dailymail.co.uk/news/article-2518131/UK-government-gave-80-000-taxpayers-money-Zimbabwe-government-contravention-rules.html [accessed 27 January 2014]

Christie, P (2006) Changing regimes: Governmentality and education policy in post-apartheid South Africa. *International Journal of Educational Development* (26): 373–381

Christie, P & Collins, C (1984) Bantu education: Apartheid ideology and labour reproduction. In: P Kallaway (ed.) *Apartheid and Education: The Education of Black South Africans*. Johannesburg: Ravan Press. pp. 160–183

Clay, EJ, Geddes, M & Natali, L (2009) *Untying Aid: Is it Working?: An Evaluation of the Implementation of the Paris Declaration and of the 2001 DAC Recommendation of Untying ODA to the LDCs*. Copenhagen: Danish Institute for International Studies

Collins, C (2013, 19 May) Zambia: Cutting Pepfar will erode gains made in HIV/Aids fight. *Times of Zambia*. Available at http://allafrica.com/stories/201305270392.html [accessed 23 January 2014]

Conservation International (2013) *The Biodiversity Hotspots*. Available at http://www.conservation.org/where/priority_areas/hotspots/africa/Pages/africa.aspx [accessed 15 April 2013]

Coordinating AIDS Technical Support Group (2009) *Study on technical assistance and technical support to Global Fund grant implementation at country level.* Summary Report

Coovadia, H, Jewkes, R, Barron, P, Sanders, D & McIntyre, D (2009) The health and health system of South Africa: Historical roots of current public health challenges. *The Lancet* 374(9692): 817–834

Crane, W, Sandwith, T, McGregor, E & Younge, A (2009) Where conservation and community coincide: A human rights approach to conservation and development in the Cape Floristic Region, South Africa. In: J Campese, T Sunderland, T Greiber & G Oviedo (eds) *Rights-based Approaches: Exploring issues and Opportunities for Conservation.* Bogor: CIFOR, IUCN. pp. 141–161

Crouch, C (2005) *Post-democracy.* Cambridge: Polity Press

Crown Management Consultants (2009) Tanzania public service situation analysis: Towards a revised public service pay policy. Draft report. Dar es Salaam: Public Service Management

Dahl, RA (1971) *Polyarchy: Participation and Opposition.* New Haven; London: Yale University Press

Dahl, RA & Levi, M (2009) A conversation with Robert A Dahl. *Annual Review of Political Science* 12(1):1–9

Dalal-Clayton, DB, Bass, S & Antonio, E (2009) *The Challenges of Environmental Mainstreaming: Experience of Integrating Environment into Development Institutions and Decisions.* London: International Institute for Environment and Development

Dale, NJ (2005) Integrating Environmental Issues into PRSPs in ECA Countries. *Environment Strategy Note (12).* Washington DC: World Bank

Danida, Vice-President's Office, Prime Minister's Office Regional Administration and Local Government & Ministry of Natural Resources and Tourism (2010) *Annual Sector Review: Tanzania-Denmark Environmental Sector Programme Support.* Review Aide Memoire, Dar es Salaam

Deacon, R, Osman, R & Buchler, M (2009) *Audit and Interpretative Analysis of Education Research in South Africa: What Have We Learnt?* A research report submitted to the National Research Foundation

Death, C (2012) Environmental mainstreaming and post-sovereign governance in Tanzania: Draft paper – for panel 'Governing and contesting African governance' BISA-ISA Joint International Conference, Edinburgh, 20-22 June 2012. Aberystwyth University

Department of Basic Education (2011) *Annual Report 2010/11.* Pretoria: DBE

—————— (2012) *Annual Report 2011/12.* Pretoria: DBE

—————— (2013) *Annual Report 2012/13.* Pretoria: DBE

—————— (2014a) DBE and researchers exchange views on the South African schooling system. Available at http://www.education.gov.za/Home/EducationResearchIndaba/tabid/843/Default.aspx [accessed 14 March 2014]

—————— (2014b) *Education Statistics in South Africa 2012.* Pretoria: DBE

—————— (2014c) Department of Basic Education hosts Discipline in Education Summit on 7 & 8 March 2014. Available at http://www.education.gov.za/Newsroom/MediaReleases/tabid/347/ctl/Details/mid/2929/ItemID/3896/Default.aspx [accessed 14 March 2014]

Department of Education (1995) *White Paper on Education and Training in a Democratic South Africa: First Steps to Develop a New System.* Pretoria: DBE

Department of Education & Department of Labour (2002) *Report of the Study Team on the Implementation of the National Qualifications Framework.* Pretoria: DBE & DoL

—————— (2003) *An Interdependent National Qualifications Framework System: Consultative Document.* Pretoria: DBE & DoL

Department of Environmental Affairs (2010a) *Environmental Sector Skills Plan for South Africa: A Systems Approach to Human Capacity Development and Sector Skills Planning.* Pretoria: DEA

—————— (2010b) *National Protected Area Expansion Strategy for South Africa 2008: Priorities for Expanding the Protected Area Network for Ecological Sustainability and Climate Change Adaptation.* Pretoria: DEA

—————— (2012a) *Annual Report 2011/2012.* Pretoria: DEA Chief Directorate: Communications

—————— (2012b) *Environment Sector Research, Development and Evidence Framework: An approach to enhance science-policy interface and evidence-based policy making.* Pretoria: DEA

Department of Environmental Affairs and Tourism (2005) *South Africa's National Biodiversity Strategy and Action Plan.* Pretoria: DEAT

———— (2006) *South Africa Environment Outlook*. A report on the state of the environment. Pretoria: DEAT

———— (2009a) *South Africa's Fourth National Report to the Convention on Biological Diversity*. Pretoria: DEAT

———— (2009b) *South Africa's National Biodiversity Framework 2008. Government Gazette* (32474). Pretoria

Department of Health (1997) *White Paper for the Transformation of the Health System in South Africa*. Notice 667 of 1997. Pretoria: DoH

———— (2000) *HIV/AIDS & STD Strategic Plan for South Africa 2000–2005*. Pretoria: DoH

———— (2010) *Delivery Agreement for Outcome 2: A Long and Healthy Life for All South Africans*. Pretoria: DoH

———— (2011a) *Annual Report 2010/11*. Pretoria: DoH

———— (2011b) *Human resources for a healthy South Africa: HRH strategy for the health sector 2012/13–2016/17*. Pretoria: DoH

———— (2011c) National Health Insurance conference: 'Lessons for South Africa': National Consultative Health Forum (NCHF). December 7th–8th, 2011. Johannesburg, Pretoria

———— (2011d) *National Health Insurance in South Africa*. Policy Paper. Pretoria: DoH

———— (2011e) *The Aid Effectiveness Framework for Health in South Africa: Working together to implement the Negotiated Service Delivery Agreement and to attain the Millennium Development Goals*. Pretoria: DoH

———— (2012) *Annual Report 2011/2012*. Pretoria: DoH

Department of Higher Education and Training (2011) *Annual Report 2010/2011*. Pretoria: DHET

———— (2012a) *Annual Report 2011/2012*. Pretoria: DHET

———— (2012b) *Green Paper for Post-Schooling Education and Training. Government Gazette* (No. 34935). Pretoria: DHET

———— (2013a) *Annual Report 2012/2013*. Pretoria: DHET

———— (2013b) Vacancies closing. Available at http://www.dhet.gov.za/ LinkClick.aspx?fileticket=Y0I xcQ0NHPI%3D&tabid=241 [accessed 8 November 2013]

———— (2013c) *White Paper for Post-School Education and Training: Building an Expanded, Effective and Integrated Post-School System*. Pretoria: DHET

Department of Labour (1997) *Green Paper on Skills Development Strategy for Economic and Employment Growth in South Africa*. Pretoria: DoL

———— (1998) Employment Equity Act No. 55 of 1998. Pretoria: DoL

Department of Labour & GTZ (2008) *Joint focal area skills development & labour market midterm progress report 2008*. Pretoria: GTZ Focal Area Secretariat

Department of State & USAID (2010) *Leading Through Civilian Power. The First Quadrennial Diplomacy and Development Review*. Washington DC

Development Partners Group on Health (2006) *Terms of Reference for the Development Partners Group on Health* (DPG Health). Dar es Salaam: Development Partners Group Tanzania

———— (2014) *The Health Basket Fund*. Dar es Salaam: Development Partners Group Tanzania. Available at http://www.tzdpg.or.tz/dpg-website/sector-groups/cluster-2/health/top-tabs/basket-fund.html [accessed 5 November 2014]

Development Partners Group on HIV/AIDS (2013) *Terms of Reference for Development Partners Group on HIV/AIDS* (DPG-AIDS). Dar es Salaam: Development Partners Group Tanzania

Development Partners Group Tanzania (n.d.) Welcome to the DPG-Health website. Available at http://www.tzdpg.or.tz/index.php?id=1037 [accessed 29 August 2014]

———— (2007) *Draft Terms of Reference for the Pharmaceuticals Working Group (PWG) of the SWAP Committee*. Dar es Salaam: Development Partners Group Tanzania

———— (2010a) *Draft Terms of Reference Human Resources for Health Technical Working Group (Tanzania Mainland)*. Dar es Salaam: Development Partners Group Tanzania

———— (2010b) *Revised Terms of Reference*. Dar es Salaam: Development Partners Group Tanzania

———— (2012) *Final Performance Assessment Framework 2013* (PAF 2013). Dar es Salaam: Development Partners Group Tanzania

———— (2014a) *About DPG AIDS*. Available at http://www.tzdpg.or.tz/index.php?id=38 [accessed 29 August 2014]

———— (2014b) *DPG Environment, Natural Resources and Climate Change*. Dar es Salaam: Development Partners Group Tanzania. Available at http://www.tzdpg.or.tz/index.php?id=37 [accessed 19 March 2014]

———— (2014c) *Strengthening Aid Effectiveness in Tanzania: Welcome to the Development Partners Group in Tanzania*. Dar es Salaam: Development Partners Group Tanzania. Available at http://www.tzdpg.or.tz/dpg-website/dpg-tanzania.html [accessed 5 December 2014]

DFID (2006) *Developing Capacity: An Evaluation of DFID-funded Technical Co-operation for Economic Management in Sub-Saharan Africa*. Synthesis Report (EV667).

———— (2007) *Development on the Record: DFID Annual Report 2007*. London: DFID

———— (2011) *The Engine of Development: The Private Sector and Prosperity for Poor People*. London: DFID

———— (2013, 30 April) UK to end direct financial support to South Africa. Press release, London. Available at https://www.gov.uk/government/news/uk-to-end-direct-financial-support-to-south-africa [accessed 8 December 2014]

DFID South Africa (2013) *SARRAH 2013 Annual Review*. Pretoria: DFID

DFID Tanzania (2011) *Operational Plan 2011–2015*. Dar es Salaam: DFID

Dietrich, JW (2007) The politics of PEPFAR: The President's Emergency Plan for AIDS Relief. *Ethics & International Affairs* 21(3): 277–292

Dietrich, S (2006) *Careers with the World Bank. A Study on Recruitment Strategies and Qualification Requirements at the World Bank*. Erfurt: Erfurt School of Public Policy

Dijkstra, G (2005) The PRSP approach and the illusion of improved aid effectiveness: Lessons from Bolivia, Honduras and Nicaragua. *Development Policy Review* 23(4): 443–464

DPG (2010) *Comments on MKUKUTA II Priority Results Areas*. Dar es Salaam: DPG

Dreher, A, Sturm, J-E & Vreeland, JR (2009) Development aid and international politics: Does membership on the UN Security Council influence World Bank decisions? *Journal of Development Economics* 88(1): 1–18

Driscoll, R, Christiansen, K & Booth, D (2005) *Progress Reviews and Performance Assessment in Poverty-reduction Strategies and Budget Support: A Survey of Current Thinking and Practice*. London: Overseas Development Institute; Japan International Cooperation Agency

Driver, A, Sink, KJ, Nel, J et al. (2012) *National Biodiversity Assessment 2011: An Assessment of South Africa's Biodiversity and Ecosystems*. Synthesis report. Pretoria: South African National Biodiversity Institute; Department of Environmental Affairs

Du Plessis, W (2008) Legal mechanisms for cooperative governance in South Africa: Successes and failures. *SA Publiekreg = SA Public Law* 23(1): 87–110

Ear, S (2013) *Aid Dependence in Cambodia: How Foreign Assistance Undermines Democracy*. New York: Columbia University Press

Easterly, W (2002) The Cartel of Good Intentions: Markets vs. Bureaucracy in Foreign Aid. *Working Paper (4)*. Washington DC: Center for Global Development, Institute for International Economics

———— (2013) *The Tyranny of Experts: Economists, Dictators, and the Forgotten Rights of the Poor*. New York: Basic Books

ECDPM & ACE Europe (2006) *Changing Minds and Attitudes: Towards Improved Belgian Technical Assistance*. Reflection and Discussion Paper. Brussels: BTC/CTB

Economic and Social Research Foundation (2010) *Assessment of Effectiveness of Development Cooperation/External Resources and Partnership Principles in Context of the MKUKUTA/MKUZA Review*. Final report May 2010. Dar Es Salaam: ESRF

ED-DPG (2012) Education Development Partners Group Meeting, Canadian Cooperation Office Conference Room, 17th October 2012. Dar es Salaam: ED-DPG

Education Development Partners Group in Tanzania (2013) *Appraisal of the Tanzania Mainland Education Sector Development Plans*. Dar es Salaam: EDPG

Education Sector Development Committee (2011) *Education Sector Performance Report 2010/11*. Dar es Salaam: ESDC

———— (2012) *Education Sector Performance Report 2011/2012*. Dar es Salaam: ESDC

Edwards, K, Lukumbuzya, K & Kajembe, G (2012) *Capacity Needs Assessment of Government Institutions at Central, Regional, District and Local Levels for the Establishment and Management of a REDD+ Scheme in Tanzania*. Final report and Capacity Development Plan prepared by LTS International for the Ministry of Natural Resources and Tourism (MNRT) and the UN-REDD National Programme in Tanzania. LTS International Ltd, Penicuik

Elliott-Teague, G (2007) NGOs in policymaking in Tanzania: The relationships of group characteristics, political participation and policy outcomes. Dissertation, School of Public and Environmental Affairs, Indiana University, Bloomington

———— (2011) 'Public' interests and the development of Tanzanian environmental policy. *Politics & Policy* 39(5): 835–861

Embassy of the United States Dar es Salaam (2012) American people sponsor 21st century education program in Zanzibar, Dar es Salaam. Available at http://tanzania.usembassy.gov/pr_02292012.html [accessed 8 July 2014]

Eriksson Baaz, M (2005) *The Paternalism of Partnership. A Postcolonial Reading of Identity in Development Aid*. London, New York: Zed Books

European Commission (2008) *Reforming Technical Cooperation and Project Implementation Units for External Aid provided by the European Commission: A Backbone Strategy*. Luxemburg: EC

———— (2014) *Eurostat: R&D Expenditure. Data from October 2012*. Available at http://epp.eurostat.ec.europa.eu/ statistics_explained/index.php/R_%26_D_expenditure [accessed 10 March 2014]

European Union (2012) Summaries of EU legislation: Public works contracts, public supply contracts and public service contracts. Available at http://europa.eu/legislation_summaries/internal_market/businesses/public_procurement/l22009_en.htm [accessed 31 October 2013]

Evers, H-D (2005) Wissen ist Macht: Experten als Strategische Gruppe. *ZEF Working Paper Series (8)*. Bonn: Universität Bonn, Zentrum für Entwicklungsforschung

Evers, H-D & Menkhoff, T (2002) Selling Expert Knowledge: The Role of Consultants in Singapore's New Economy. *ZEF Discussion Papers on Development Policy (55)*. Bonn: Universität Bonn, Zentrum für Entwicklungsforschung

Evers, H-D, Kaiser, M & Müller, C (2009) Knowledge in development: Epistemic machineries in a global context. *International Social Science Journal* 60(195): 55–68

Evers, H-D, Schiel, T & Korff, R (1988) *Strategische Gruppen: Vergleichende Studien zu Staat, Bürokratie und Klassenbildung in der Dritten Welt*. Berlin: D. Reimer

Executive Council of the African Union (2006) *Decision on the Report on the Conference of Ministers of Science and Technology Doc. EX.CL/224 (VIII)*. Khartoum: AU

Express (2013, 17 May) Overseas aid is being wasted through Government mismanagement, report says. Available at http://www.express.co.uk/news/uk/400392/Overseas-aid-is-being-wasted-through-Government-mismanagement-report-says [accessed 27 January 2014]

FAO (2010a) *Global Forest Resources Assessment 2010: Global Tables*. Rome: FAO

———— (2010b) *Global Forest Resources Assessment 2010*. Main report. Rome: FAO

———— (2012) *Participatory Forestry*. Available at http://www.fao.org/forestry/participatory/en/ [accessed 3 April 2014]

Faul, MV (2016) Networks and power: Why networks are hierarchical not flat and what can be done about it. *Global Policy* 7(2): 185–197

Federal Democratic Republic of Ethiopia (2002) *Foreign Affairs and National Security Policy and Strategy*. Addis Ababa

File, J, Van den Heever, A & Saunders, SJ (1989) Towards the day of hard choices. *Nature* (341): 96–98

Fiske, EB & Ladd, HF (2005) *Elusive Equity: Education Reform in Post-apartheid South Africa*. Cape Town: HSRC Press

Fleck, RK & Kilby, C (2010) Changing aid regimes? U.S. foreign aid from the Cold War to the War on Terror. *Journal of Development Economics* 91(2): 185–197

Fölscher, A, Smith, M & Davies, T (2010) *Development Cooperation Review III - Final Report*. Pretoria: National Treasury

Forss, K, Carlsen, J, Froyland, E, Sitari, T & Vilby, K (1988) *Evaluation of the Effectiveness of Technical Assistance Personell Financed by the Nordic Countries*. A study commissioned by Danida, Finnida, NORAD, Sida. Evaluation reports (5)

Foster, M (2000) New Approaches to Development Co-operation: What Can We Learn From Experience with Implementing Sector wide Approaches? *Working Paper (140)*. London: Overseas Development Institute

Foster, M & Mwinyimvua, H (2003) *Public Expenditure Review: HIV/AIDS Multi-Sectoral Update for 2004*. London: DFID Health Systems Resource Centre

Foster, M, Brown, A & Conway, T (2000) *Sector-wide Approaches for Health Development: A Review of Experience*. Geneva: World Health Organization

Fourie, P & Meyer, M (2010) *The Politics of AIDS Denialism. South Africa's Failure to Respond*. Farnham: Ashgate

Fourie, P, Perche, D & Schoeman, R (2010) Donor assistance for AIDS in South Africa: Many actors, multiple agendas. *Strategic Review for Southern Africa* 32(2)

Fourth High Level Forum on Aid Effectiveness (2011) *Busan Partnership for Effective Development Co-operation*. Busan: OECD, Busan

Fraser-Hurt, N, Zuma, K & Njuho, P et al. (2011) *The HIV Epidemic in South Africa: What Do We Know and How Has it Changed?* Report prepared for SANAC. World Bank; Human Sciences Research Council; Health and Development Africa; UNAIDS

Gaillard, J (2010) Measuring research and development in developing countries: Main characteristics and implications for the Frascati Manual. *Science Technology & Society* 15(1): 77–111

Galabawa, C J (1990) *Implementing Educational Policies in Tanzania*. Washington DC: World Bank

——— (2001) Developments and issues regarding universal primary education (UPE) in Tanzania. ADEA biennial meeting 2001, Arusha, Tanzania. Paris: Association for the Development of Education in Africa

Gibbon, T (2014) *Driving Change: The Story of the South Africa Norway Tertiary Education Development Programme*. Cape Town: African Minds

Gilbert, N & Cherry, M (2008) Incoming South African health minister raises hopes on HIV. *Nature*. Available at http://www.nature.com/news/2008/080926/full/news.2008.1138.html [accessed 28 July 2014]

Gilens, M (2005) Inequality and democratic responsiveness. *Public Opinion Quarterly* 69(5): 778–796

Girvan, N (2007) Power Imbalances and Development Knowledge. Theme Paper prepared for the project Southern Perspectives on Reform of the International Development Architecture. Ottawa: The North-South Institute

GIZ (n.d.) *Selection procedure for consulting firms and suppliers*. Eschborn: GIZ

——— (2007) *Partnering for Regional Cooperation and Development: South African-German Trilateral Cooperation Programme (TriCo)*. Available at http://www.giz.de/en/worldwide/17558.html [accessed 8 December 2014]

——— (2011) *National Personnel (NP) Policy*. Eschborn: GIZ

——— (2012a) *Company Report 2011*. Eschborn: GIZ

——— (2012b) *Investing in the Future – Vocational Training for Climate and Environment*. Available at http://www.giz.de/en/worldwide/17848.html [accessed 10 June 2014]

——— (2012c) *Vocational training in South Africa – Greener and more practice-oriented*. Available at http://www.giz.de/en/mediacenter/9158.html [accessed 10 June 2014]

——— (2013a) *Company Report 2012: Solutions That Work*. Eschborn: GIZ

——— (2013b) *Development Cooperation Trainee Programme*. Eschborn: GIZ. Available at http://www.giz.de/en/jobs/446.html [accessed 26 September 2013]

——— (2013c) *GIZ in South Africa. Programmes and Projects*. Pretoria: GIZ

GIZ Tanzanian German Programme to Support Health (2011) GIZ Professional Group Meeting, Documentation, White Sands, Dar es Salaam, 6–7 December 2011

Glaser, BG & Strauss, AL (1967) *The Discovery of Grounded Theory: Strategies for Qualitative Research*. Chicago: Aldine

Gläser, J & Laudel, G (2010) *Experteninterviews und qualitative Inhaltsanalyse als Instrumente rekonstruierender Untersuchungen*. 4 ed. VS Verlag für Sozialwissenschaften

——— (2013) Life with and without coding: Two methods for early-stage data analysis in qualitative research aiming at causal explanations. *Forum: Qualitative Social Research (Online Journal)* 14(2)

Glennie, J (2008) *The Trouble With Aid. Why Less Could Mean More for Africa*. London (et al.): Zed Books
———— (2011, 13 May) Is cash on delivery the future for aid? Results-based aid is a welcome innovation, but the problem about what to do when targets aren't met is profound. Poverty matters blog. *The Guardian*. Available at http://www.theguardian.com/global-development/poverty-matters/2011/may/13/cash-delivery-future-results-based-aid [accessed 21 January 2014]
Glennie, J & Prizzon, A (2012) *From high to low aid: A proposal to classify countries by aid receipt*. ODI Background Note. London: Overseas Development Institute
Global Campaign For Education (2013) *Education Aid Watch 2013*. Johannesburg: GCE
Global Environment Facility (2007) *National Grasslands Biodiversity Programme (NGBP): Request for CEO Endorsement/Approval*. Washington DC: GEF
———— (2010a) *Financing the Stewardship of Global Biodiversity*. Washington DC: GEF
———— (2010b) *System for Transparent Allocation of Resources* (STAR). Washington DC: GEF
———— (2012) *South Africa and the GEF: Fact Sheet*. Washington DC: GEF
Global Environment Facility Evaluation Office (2008) *GEF Country Portfolio Evaluation: South Africa (1994–2007)*. Evaluation reports (43). Washington DC: GEF
Gould, J (2005a) Conclusion: The politics of consultation. In: J Gould (ed.) *The New Conditionality: The Politics of Poverty Reduction Strategies*. London, New York: Zed Books. pp. 135–151
———— (2005b) Poverty, politics and states of partnership. In: J Gould (ed.) *The New Conditionality: The Politics of Poverty Reduction Strategies*. London, New York: Zed Books. pp. 1–16
Gould, J & Ojanen, J (2003) 'Merging in the Circle': The Politics of Tanzania's Poverty Reduction Strategy. *Policy Papers (2)*. University of Helsinki: Institute of Development Studies
———— (2005) Tanzania: Merging in the circle. In: J Gould (ed.) *The New Conditionality: The Politics of Poverty Reduction Strategies*. London, New York: Zed Books. pp. 17–65
Government of Tanzania (2002) Agreed Notes from the Workshop on the Report of the Group of Independent Advisors on Development Co-operation Issues Between Tanzania and its Aid Donors. In: SM Wangwe (ed.) *NEPAD at Country Level – Changing Aid Relationships in Tanzania*. Dar es Salaam: Mkuki na Nyota Publishers. pp. 125–129
———— (2011a) *Budget Books 2011–2012 Volume II: Recurrent Expenditures*. Dar es Salaam
———— (2011b) *Budget Books 2011–2012 Volume IV: Development Expenditures*. Dar es Salaam
———— (2012a) *Budget Books 2012–2013 Volume II: Recurrent Expenditure for CFS and Supply Votes*. Dar es Salaam
———— (2012b) *Budget Books 2012–2013 Volume IV: Development Expenditures for Supply Votes and Regions*. Dar es Salaam
———— (2013a) *Budget Books 2013–2014 Volume II: Public Expenditure Estimates Supply Votes as Passed by the National Assembly*. Dar es Salaam
———— (2013b) *Budget Books 2013–2014 Volume IV: Public Expenditure Estimates Development as Passed by the National Assembly*. Dar es Salaam
Government of Tanzania & Danida (2007) *Programme Document: Environmental Sector Programme Support*. Dar es Salaam
Government of Tanzania & Development Partners (2007) *Code of Conduct for the Tanzania Health Sector Wide Approach (SWAp) between the Ministry of Health and Social Welfare (MoHSW); Prime Minister's Office Regional Administration and Local Government (PMO-RALG); Ministry of Finance (MoF); and Development Partners in the Health Sector*. Dar es Salaam
Government of Tanzania & Health Basket Partners (2011) *Side Agreement between Health Basket Partners and The Government of Tanzania, Fiscal Year 2011/12*. Dar es Salaam
Government of the Netherlands (2013, 9 April) New agenda for aid, trade and investment. Available at http://www.government.nl/issues/development-cooperation/news/2013/04/09/new-agenda-for-aid-trade-and-investment.html [accessed 25 April 2013]
Greenhill, R (2006) *Real Aid 2: Making Technical Assistance Work*. Johannesburg: ActionAid International
Greenhill, R, Prizzon, A & Rogerson, A (2013) The Age of Choice: Developing Countries in the New Aid Landscape: A Synthesis Report. *ODI Working Paper (364)*. London: Overseas Development Institute

Grimwood, A, Crewe, M & Betteridge, D (2000) HIV/AIDS – Current issues. In: A Ntuli (ed.) *South African Health Review*. Durban: Health Systems Trust. pp. 287–299

GTZ (2007) *German Technical Co-operation with South Africa*. Pretoria: GTZ

Haan, A de & Everest-Phillips, M (2010) Can new aid modalities handle politics? In: G Mavrotas (ed.) *Foreign Aid for Development. Issues, Challenges, and the New Agenda*. New York: Oxford University Press. pp. 197–221

Haas, PM (1992) Introduction: Epistemic communities and international policy coordination. *International Organization* 46(1): 1–35

Hagmann, T (2012, 11 July) Supporting stability, abetting repression. *New York Times*. Available at http://www.nytimes.com/2012/07/12/opinion/abetting-repression-in-ethiopia.html?_r=0 [accessed 18 December 2013]

Hajidimitriou, YA, Sklavounos, NS & Rotsios, KP (2012) The impact of trust on knowledge transfer in international business systems. *Scientific Bulletin - Economic Sciences* 11(2): 39–49

HakiElimu (2011) Education sector budget 2011/2012: Is there any hope for improving education? *HakiElimu Brief (6E)*. Dar es Salaam: HakiElimu

Hamman, K (2009) *CapeNature: Building institutional capacity. M&E case study (15)*. Cape Town: Cape Action for People and the Environment

Hansen, MT (1999) The search-transfer problem: The role of weak ties in sharing knowledge across organization subunits. *Administrative Science Quarterly* 44(1): 82–111

Harrison, G (2004) *The World Bank and Africa. The Construction of Governance States*. London (et al.): Routledge

Harrison, G & Mulley, S (2009) Tanzania: A genuine case of recipient leadership in the aid system? In: L Whitfield (ed.) *The Politics of Aid: African Strategies for Dealing with Donors*. New York: Oxford University Press. pp. 271–298

Health Systems Trust (2010) *The 10 Point Plan*. Kwik Skwiz (Vol. 2 No. 1). Westville: HST

Heitmann, W (2010) Systems building and consulting through networking with social partners. In: W Zehender (ed.) *Networking with Partners*. Wiesbaden: Universum Verlagsanstalt. pp. 99–123

Helen Suzman Foundation (2011) *Submission to National Department of Health: National Health Insurance Green Paper*. Parktown: Helen Suzman Foundation

Helleiner, GK (2000) External conditionality, local ownership, and development. In: J Freedman (ed.) *Transforming Development: Foreign Aid for a Changing World*. Toronto, Buffalo, London: University of Toronto Press. pp. 82–97

Helleiner, GK, Killick, T, Lipumba, N, Ndulu, BJ & Svendsen, KE (1995) *Report of the Group of Independent Advisers on Development Cooperation Issues Between Tanzania and its Aid Donors*. Copenhagen: Royal Danish Ministry of Foreign Affairs

Hepworth, N (2009) Capacity building or capacity demolition? Rethinking donor support to unlock self-determined and sustainble water resource management in East Africa. mimeo, n.p.

Heywood, M (2003) Preventing mother-to-child HIV transmission in South Africa: Background, strategies and outcomes of the Treatment Action Campaign case against the Minister of Health. Current Developments. *South African Journal on Human Rights* 19(2): 278–315

Hingora, A (n.d.) *Developments of Health Sector Reforms in Tanzania*. Dar es Salaam: Ministry of Health

Hjelmåker, L (2013) Opening statement at the 2013 GBS Annual Review, Dar es Salaam

Hobbs, G (2001) *The Health Sector-Wide Approach and Health Sector Basket Fund*. Dar es Salaam: Economic and Social Research Foundation

Hoeffler, A & Outram, V (2008) Need, Merit or Self-Interest – What Determines the Allocation of Aid? *CSAE WPS (19)*. University of Oxford: Centre for the Study of African Economies

―――― (2011) Need, merit, or self-interest – What determines the allocation of aid? *Review of Development Economics* 15(2): 237–250

Holtom, D (2002) *Tanzania's Poverty Reduction Strategy Paper 'Everyone Wants a Success Story': Feedback Report for Interviewees*. Swansea: Centre For Development Studies

―――― (2007) The challenge of consensus building: Tanzania's PRSP 1998–2001. *The Journal of Modern African Studies* 45(02): 233–251

Hood, C (1991) A public management for all seasons? *Public Administration Review* 69(1): 3–19

Hood, C & Peters, G (2004) The middle aging of new public management: Into the age of paradox? *Journal of Public Administration Research and Theory* 14(3): 267–282

Hornidge, A (2012) 'Knowledge' in development discourse: A critical review. In: A Hornidge & C Antweiler (eds) *Environmental Uncertainty and Local Knowledge. South East Asia as a Laboratory of Global Ecological Change.* Bielefeld: Transcript. pp. 21–53

Howell, J & Lind, J (2009a) Changing donor policy and practice in civil society in the post-9/11 aid context. *Third World Quarterly* 30(7): 1279–1296

———— (2009b) *Counter-terrorism, Aid and Civil Society: Before and After the War on Terror.* Basingstoke: Palgrave MacMillan

Human Sciences Research Council (1995) *Ways of Seeing the National Qualifications Framework.* Pretoria: HSRC

———— (2011) *Highlights from TIMSS 2011: The South African Perspective.* Pretoria: HSRC

Hunsmann, M (2013) Depoliticising an epidemic – International AIDS control and the politics of health in Tanzania. Dissertation, Ecole des Hautes Etudes en Sciences Sociales, Paris

Huntley, BJ & Redford, KH (2014) Mainstreaming biodiversity in practice: A STAP advisory document. Washington DC: Global Environment Facility

Hüsken, T (2006) *Der Stamm der Experten. Rhetorik und Praxis des Interkulturellen Managements in der deutschen staatlichen Entwicklungszusammenarbeit.* Bielefeld: transcript Verlag

Hutton, G (2004) *Global Health Initiatives in HIV/AIDS in Tanzania: Situation Analysis and Review of Key Issues.* A briefing paper established in the frame of the SCD-STI SWAp Mandate 2003-4. Bern, Basel: Swiss Agency for Development and Co-operation, Swiss Tropical Institute

Hyden, G & Karlstrom, B (1993) Structural adjustment as a policy process: The case of Tanzania. *World Development* 21(9): 1395–1404

ICAI (2014) *DFID's Private Sector Development Work.* Report (35). London: Independent Commission for Aid Impact

Ifakara Health Institute (2014) *Frequently Asked Questions: Where does IHI get its funding from?* Available at http://www.ihi.or.tz/about/faq#q3 [accessed 12/03/2014]

Inka Consult (2008) *Final Report on Needs Assessment for Strengthening National Capacity to Adapt to the Adverse Impact of Climate Change.* August

Inkpen, AC & Tsang, EWK (2005) Social capital, networks, and knowledge transfer. *The Academy of Management Review* 30(1): 146–165

Institute for Health Metrics and Evaluation (2012a) *Financing Global Health 2012: Methods Annex.* Seattle: IHME

———— (2012b) *Financing Global Health 2012: The End of the Golden Age?* Seattle: IHME

International Bank for Reconstruction and Development (2013) *Voting Power of Executive Directors.* Corporate Secretariat. Washington DC: IBRD

International Bank for Reconstruction and Development, International Finance Corporation & International Development Association (2013) *Executive Directors and Alternates.* Corporate Secretariat, Washington DC: IBRD

International Civil Service Commission (2013) *United Nations Common System of Salaries, Allowances and Benefits.* New York: United Nations

International Development Cooperation Unit (2003) *Policy Framework and Procedural Guidelines for the Management of Official Development Assistance.* Pretoria: National Treasury

Irikefe, V, Vaidyanathan, G, Nordling, L, Twahirwa, A, Nakkazi, E & Monastersky, R (2011) Science in Africa: The view from the front line. *Nature* 474 (7353): 556–559

IRIN News (2002, 22 February) South Africa: Defiant province to give AIDS drugs to mothers. (Johannesburg) Available at http://www.irinnews.org/report/30414/south-africa-defiant-province-to-give-aids-drugs-to-mothers [accessed 25 July 2014]

———— (2006, 25 October) Tanzania: ARV roll-out slowly improving (Dar es Salaam). Available at http://www.irinnews.org/report/62627/tanzania-arv-rollout-slowly-improving [accessed 6 October 2014]

——— (2007a, 15 March) South Africa: Activists welcome ambitious new AIDS plan (Johannesburg). Available at http://www.irinnews.org/report/70725/south-africa-activists-welcome-ambitious-new-aids-plan [accessed 25 July 2014]

——— (2007b, 8 June) Tanzania: Concern over school drop-out rate (Dar es Salaam). Available at http://www.irinnews.org/report/72628/tanzania-concern-over-school-drop-out-rate [accessed 10 July 2014]

——— (2011a, 1 December) South Africa: Country launches new HIV, TB plan (East London). Available at http://www.irinnews.org/report/94365/south-africa-country-launches-new-hiv-tb-plan [accessed 31 July 2014]

——— (2011b, 24 November) HIV/AIDS: Global Fund cancels funding (Johannesburg). Available at http://www.irinnews.org/report/94293/hiv-aids-global-fund-cancels-funding [accessed 6 November 2014]

——— (2012, 12 December) Guinea-Bissau: HIV/AIDS fight hit by Global Fund cuts (Dakar/Bissau). Available at http://www.irinnews.org/report/97029/guinea-bissau-hiv-aids-fight-hit-by-global-fund-cuts [accessed 23 January 2014]

——— (2013a, 09 January) Concerns over HIV/AIDS funding cuts (Addis Ababa) Available at http://www.irinnews.org/report/97204/ethiopia-concerns-over-hiv-aids-funding-cuts [accessed 23 January 2014]

——— (2013b, 12 July) Vietnam concerned over HIV donor funding cuts (Bangkok). Available at http://www.irinnews.org/report/98402/vietnam-concerned-over-hiv-donor-funding-cuts [accessed 23 January 2014]

IUCN (2012a) *The IUCN Red List of Threatened Species*. Version 2012.2. Number of extinct, threatened and other species of animals in each Red List Category in each country. IUCN

——— (2012b) *The IUCN Red List of Threatened Species*. Version 2012.2. Number of extinct, threatened and other species of plants in each Red List Category in each country. IUCN

IUCN & UNEP-WCMC (2011) *The World Database on Protected Areas* (WDPA). Cambridge (UK): UNEP-WCMC. Available at http://www.wdpa.org/resources/statistics/2011MDG_National_Stats.xls [accessed 16 April 2013]

Jadoo, Y (2014) 'No delays' in roll-out of NHI. *The Citizen*. Available at http://citizen.co.za/166771/no-delays-in-roll-out-of-nhi/ [accessed 25 August 2014]

Jansen, EG (2009) Does aid work? Reflections on a natural resources programme in Tanzania. *U4 issue (2)*. Bergen: Chr. Michelsen Institute

Jaycox, EV (1993) Capacity building: The missing link in African development. Address to the African-American Institute, Reston, Virginia

Jepma, C (1991) *The Tying of Aid*. Paris: OECD Development Centre Studies

Jerve, AM (2006) Exploring the Research-Policy Linkage: The Case of Reforms in Financing Primary Education in Tanzania. *Working Paper (3)*. Bergen: Chr. Michelsen Institute

JICA (Japan International Cooperation Agency) (2008) *Effective Technical Cooperation for Capacity Development: Key Findings*. Tokyo: JICA

Johansson, LM & Pettersson, J (2005) Tied Aid, Trade-Facilitating Aid or Trade-Diverting Aid? *Working Paper (5)*. Uppsala: Uppsala University, Department of Economics

Johnson, RW & Schlemmer, L (1996) *Launching Democracy in South Africa: The First Open Election, April 1994*. New Haven: Yale University Press

Joint Assistance Strategy for Tanzania Working Group & Independent Monitoring Group (2010) *Joint Government and Development Partners Roadmap to Improve Development Cooperation in Tanzania*. Dar es Salaam: Development Partners Group Tanzania

Jolly, R (1989) A future for UN aid and technical assistance? *Development* (4): 21–26

Kagame, P (2007) Making Aid Work for Africa. *Brenthurst Paper (7)*. Johannesburg: The Brenthurst Foundation

Kahn, T (2012, 28 August) Anxious times for HIV patients as US cuts aid. *Business Day Live*. Available at http://www.bdlive.co.za/national/health/2012/08/28/anxious-times-for-hiv-patients-as-us-cuts-aid [accessed 23 January 2014]

———— (2014a, 30 January) Motsoaledi pledges NHI white paper is 'imminent'. *Business Day Live.* Available at http://www.bdlive.co.za/national/health/2014/01/30/motsoaledi-pledges-nhi-white-paper-is-imminent [accessed 8 August 2014]

———— (2014b, 23 October) NHI still a priority despite finance plan delays. *Business Day Live.* Available at http://www.bdlive.co.za/economy/2014/10/23/nhi-still-a-priority-despite-finance-plan delays [accessed 27 October 2014]

Kaijage, E & Kuhanwa, Z (2013) *Tanzania: Mapping REDD+ Finance Flows 2009–2012.* A Forest Trends REDDX report.

Kaijage, J (2013, 21 October) Tanzania: Poor performances worry education stakeholders. *Daily News.* Available at http://allafrica.com/stories/201310211838.html [accessed 30 June 2014]

Kapp, C (2009) Barbara Hogan: South Africa's Minister of Health. *The Lancet* 373(9660): 291

Karani, I (2010) *Evaluation: Finnish Support to Forestry and Biological Resources: Country Reports Part 3. Tanzania.* Evaluation report (5/II). Helsinki: Ministry for Foreign Affairs of Finland

Kassim, M (2014, 26 February) Govt for formation of Aids Trust Fund. IPP media news. Available at http://www.ippmedia.com/frontend/index.php/.itm.c/2.au/articles107818/javascript/page_home.js?l=65209 [accessed 6 November 2014]

Katila, M, Williams, PJ, Ishengoma, R & Juma, S (2003) *Three Decades of Swedish Support to the Tanzanian Forestry Sector: Evaluation of the Period 1969–2002.* Sida Evaluation (03/12). Stockholm: Department for Natural Resources and Environment

Katz, IT, Bassett, IV & Wright, AA (2013) PEPFAR in transition — Implications for HIV care in South Africa. *New England Journal of Medicine* 369(15): 1385–1387

Kavanagh, MM (2014) *The Politics of Transition & The Economics of HIV: AIDS and PEPFAR in South Africa.* Philadelphia: Health Global Access Project/UPenn

Keevy, J (2013) The National Qualifications Framework in South Africa: 1995–2013. *International Journal of Continuing Education and Lifelong Learning* 6(1): 19–35

Kelland, K (2011, 23 November) AIDS, TB, malaria fund forced to cut grants. Reuters, London. Available at http://www.reuters.com/article/2011/11/23/us-aids-malaria-tb-fund-idUSTRE7AM23F20111123 [accessed 23 January 2014]

Kenya Ministry of Education (2012) *Accelerating 21st Century Education.* Nairobi: Ministry of Education. Available at http://www.education.go.ke/News.aspx?nid=401 [accessed 9 July 2014]

Khumalo, G (2009, 11 May) Education stakeholders welcome department split. South African Government News Agency, Pretoria. Available at http://www.sanews.gov.za/south-africa/education-stakeholders-welcome-department-split [accessed 9 June 2014]

King, K (1999) Aid to South African education: A case of the reluctant recipient? In: K King & L Buchert (eds) *Changing International Aid to Education. Global Patterns and National Contexts.* Paris: UNESCO Publishing, NORRAG. pp. 257–279

———— (2004) *Development Knowledge and the Global Policy Agenda. Whose Knowledge? Whose Policy?* Geneva: United Nations Research Institute for Social Development

Kingdon, JW (1984) *Agendas, Alternatives and Public Policies.* Boston: Little, Brown & Co

Kisting, D (2012, 10 January) Namibia's language policy is 'poisoning' its children. *The Guardian.* Available at http://www.theguardian.com/education/2012/jan/10/namibia-english-crisis [accessed 9 December 2014]

Knack, S (2001) Aid dependence and the quality of governance: Cross-country empirical tests. *Southern Economic Journal* 68(2): 310–329

Knack, S & Rahman, A (2007) Donor fragmentation and bureaucratic quality in aid recipients. *Journal of Development Economics* 83(1): 176–197

Knorr-Cetina, K (1981) *The Manufacture of Knowledge: An Essay on the Constructivist and Contextual Nature of Science.* Oxford, New York: Pergamon Press

Knorr-Cetina, K (1984) *Die Fabrikation von Erkenntnis. Zur Anthropologie der Naturwissenschaft.* Frankfurt am Main: Suhrkamp

Knorr-Cetina, KD (2007) Culture in global knowledge societies: Knowledge cultures and epistemic cultures. *Interdisciplinary Science Reviews* 32(4): 351–375

Kötschau, K & Marauhn, T (2008) *Good Governance and Developing Countries: Interdisciplinary Perspectives.* Frankfurt am Main; New York: Lang

Kotze, LJ (2006) Improving unsustainable environmental governance in South Africa: The case for holistic governance. *PER* 9 (1): 75–118

Kraak, A (2004) The National Skills Development Strategy: A new institutional regime for skills formation in post-apartheid South Africa. In: SA McGrath (ed.) *Shifting Understandings of Skills in South Africa: Overcoming the Historical Imprint of a Low Regime.* Cape Town: Human Sciences Research Council. pp. 116–139

———— (2008) A critical review of the National Skills Development Strategy in South Africa. *Journal of Vocational Education & Training* 60(1): 1–18

Kulindwa, K, Lokina, R & Hepelwa, A (2010) *Poverty-Environment Policy Analysis.* Dar es Salaam: University of Dar es Salaam, Department of Economics

Kumaranayake, L, Lake, S, Mujinja, P, Hongoro, C & Mpembeni, R (2000) How do countries regulate the health sector? Evidence from Tanzania and Zimbabwe. *Health Policy and Planning* 15(4): 357–367

Kwesigabo, G, Mwangu, MA, Kakoko, DC et al. (2012) Tanzania's health system and workforce crisis. *Journal of Public Health Policy* 33: S35

Lamtey, G (2012, 18 February) Govt out to set up Aids Trust Fund. IPP media news. Available at http://www.ippmedia.com/frontend/index.php?l=38585 [accessed 23 January 2014]

Lancaster, C (2007) *Foreign Aid: Diplomacy, Development, Domestic Politics.* Chicago: University of Chicago Press

Land, T (2007) Joint Evaluation Study of Provision of Technical Assistance Personnel: What Can We Learn from Promising Experiences? Synthesis Report. *Discussion Paper (78).* Maastricht: The European Centre for Development Policy Management

Languille, S (2013) Managing quality education by numbers: The case of Tanzania. *NORRAG News* (49). Geneva

Lentsch, J & Weingart, P (2009a) Introduction: The quest for quality as a challenge to scientific policy advice: An overdue debate? In: J Lentsch & P Weingart (eds) *Scientific Advice to Policy Making. International Comparison.* Opladen, Farmington Hills: Barbara Budrich. pp. 3–18

———— (2009b) *Scientific Advice to Policy Making. International Comparison.* Opladen, Farmington Hills: Barbara Budrich

———— (2011) Introduction: The quest for quality as a challenge to scientific policy advice: An overdue debate? In: J Lentsch & P Weingart (eds) *The Politics of Scientific Advice: Institutional Design for Quality Assurance.* Cambridge, New York: Cambridge University Press. pp. 3–18

Lesink, R & White, H (1999) *Aid Dependence: Issues and Indicators.* Stockholm: Expert Group on Development Issues (2)

Levin, DZ & Cross, R (2004) The strength of weak ties you can trust: The mediating role of trust in effective knowledge transfer. *Management Science* 50(11): 1477–1490

Levin, DZ, Cross, R & Abrams, LC (2003) Why Should I Trust You? Predictors of Interpersonal Trust in a Knowledge Transfer Context. *Working Paper.* Denver: Academy of Management

Levine, A (2002) Convergence or convenience? International conservation NGOs and development assistance in Tanzania. *World Development* 30(6): 1043–1055

Littig, B (2008) Interviews mit Eliten - Interviews mit ExpertInnen: Gibt es Unterschiede? *Forum Qualitative Sozialforschung/ Forum: Qualitative Social Research (Online Journal)* 9(3)

Lochner, P, Weaver, A, Gelderblom, C, Peart, R, Sandwith, T & Fowkes, S (2003) Aligning the diverse: The development of a biodiversity conservation strategy for the Cape Floristic Region. *Biological Conservation* 112(1-2): 29–43

Lockheed, ME & Hanushek, E (1994) Concepts of Educational Efficiency and Effectiveness. *Human Resources Development and Operations Policy Working Papers (24).* Washington DC: World Bank

Loomis, RA (1968) Why overseas technical assistance Is ineffective. *American Journal of Agricultural Economics* 50(5): 1329–1341

Luttrell, C & Pantaleo, I (2008) *Budget support, aid instruments and the environment: The country context. Tanzania country case study*. Overseas Development Institute, Economic and Social Research Foundation

Magesa, SM, Mwape, B & Mboera (2011) Challenges and opportunities in building health research capacity in Tanzania: A case of the National Institute for Medical Research. *Tanzania Journal of Health Research* 13 (Suppl. 1)

Mandela, N (1993) South Africa's future foreign policy. *Foreign Affairs* 72(5): 86–94

Manyika, F, Kajembe, GC, Silayo, DSA & Vatn, A (2013) Strategic power and power struggles in the national REDD+ governance process in Tanzania: Any effect on its legitimacy? *Tanzania Journal of Forestry And Nature Conservation* 83(1)

Mapunda, M (2003) Towards partnership in health: Experiences in resource allocation in Tanzania, focusing on sector wide approach (SWAp) and health basket fund. *Bulletin of Medicus Mundi Switzerland* (91)

Martens, B (2008) Why do aid agencies exist? In: W Easterly (ed.) *Reinventing Foreign Aid*. Cambridge, Mass: MIT Press. pp. 285–311

Massero, L (2013, 27 May) Tanzania to cut malaria deaths by 2015. All Africa, Dar es Salaam. Available at http://allafrica.com/stories/201305281233.html [accessed 29 August 2014]

Mattheyse, M (2007) *Prevalence versus Incidence of HIV - What Do They Tell Us? South African Medical Research Council*. Available at http://www.mrc.ac.za/public/facts11.htm [accessed 28 January 2014]

Mayosi, BM, Lawn, JE, Van Niekerk, A, Bradshaw, D, Abdool Karim, SS & Coovadia, HM (2012) Health in South Africa: Changes and challenges since 2009. *The Lancet* 380(9858): 2029–2043

Mayosi, BM, Mekwa, NJ, Blackburn, J et al. (2011) 2011 *National Health Research Summit Report: Strengthening Research for Health, Development and Innovation in South Africa*. Pretoria: Department of Health

Mbengashe, T (2012) The national HIV counselling and testing campaign and treatment expansion in South Africa: A return on investments in combination prevention. XIX International AIDS Conference, 26 July 2012, Washington DC

Mbilinyi, M (2003) Equity, Justice and Transformation in Education: The Challenge of Mwalimu Julius Nyerere Today. *Working Paper Series (2003.5)*. Dar es Salaam: HakiElimu

McDonald, DA (2002) What is environmental justice? In: DA McDonald (ed.) *Environmental Justice in South Africa*. Athens; Cape Town: Ohio University Press; University of Cape Town Press. pp. 1–12

McIntyre, D (2010) National Health Insurance: Providing a vocabulary for public engagement. In: F Sharon & A Padarath (eds) *South African Health Review 2010*. Durban: Health Systems Trust. pp. 145–156

McIntyre, D, Garshong, B & Mtei, G et al. (2008) Beyond fragmentation and towards universal coverage: Insights from Ghana, South Africa and the United Republic of Tanzania. *Bulletin of the World Health Organization* 86(11): 871–876

Mendizabal, E, Jones, H & Clarke, J (2012) *Review of Emerging Models of Advisory Capacity in Health and Education Sectors: Final Report*. Overseas Development Institute

Meuser, M & Nagel, U (2009) The expert interview and changes in knowledge production. In: A Bogner, B Littig & W Menz (eds) *Interviewing Experts*. Basingstoke: Palgrave Machmillan. pp. 17–42

Mgaya, G (2013, 29 October) Tanzania: In education, quality is the catchword. *Tanzania Daily News*, Dar es Salaam. Available at http://allafrica.com/stories/201310290028.html [accessed 30 June 2014]

Mhonyiwa, JE, Ponera, G & Mrutu, AS (2011) *The SACMEQ III Project in Tanzania: A Study of the Conditions of Schooling and the Quality of Education*. Paris: The Southern and Eastern Africa Consortium for Monitoring Educational Quality

Microsoft News Center (2009, 23 September) Cisco, Intel, Microsoft, Government of Kenya and USAID launch joint project to enable 21st-century education in Kenya schools. Available at http://www.microsoft.com/en-us/news/press/2009/sep09/09-23cgikenyapr.aspx [accessed 9 July 2014]

Milledge, S, Gelvas, IK & Ahrends, A (2007) *Forestry, Governance and National Development: Lessons Learned from a Logging Boom in Southern Tanzania*. Dar es Salaam: TRAFFIC East/Southern Africa; Tanzania Development Partners Group; Ministry of Natural Resources and Tourism

Mills, A, Ally, M, Goudge, J, Gyapong, J & Mtei, G (2012) Progress towards universal coverage: The health systems of Ghana, South Africa and Tanzania. *Health Policy and Planning* 27(suppl 1): i4

Ministry for Foreign Affairs (2003) *Shared Responsibility: Sweden's Policy for Global Development.* Government Bill 2002/03:122. Stockholm: Ministry for Foreign Affairs

———— (2008a) *Global Challenges - Our Responsibility: Communication on Sweden's Policy for Global Development.* Government Communication 2007/08:89. Stockholm: Ministry for Foreign Affairs

———— (2008b) *Sweden and Africa – A Policy to Address Common Challenges and Opportunities.* Government Communication 2007/08: 67. Stockholm: Ministry for Foreign Affairs

Ministry of Education and Culture (1995) *Education and Training Policy.* Dar Es Salaam: Ministry of Education and Culture

———— (2004) *Secondary Education Development Plan (SEDP) 2004–2009.* Education Sector Development Programme. Dar es Salaam: Ministry of Education and Culture

Ministry of Education and Vocational Training (2007) *Information & Communication Technology (ICT). Policy for Basic Education. ICT for Improved Education.* Dar es Salaam: Ministry of Education and Vocational Training

———— (2008) *Evaluation of the Impact of the Primary Education Development Plan (PEDP) 2002–2006.* Dar es Salaam: Ministry of Education and Vocational Training

———— (2010a) *Higher Education Development Programme 2010–2015: Enhanced Relevance, Access and Quality in Higher Education.* Dar es Salaam: Ministry of Education and Vocational Training

———— (2010b) *Secondary Education Development Programme II (July 2010–June 2015).* Education Sector Development Programme. Dar es Salaam: Ministry of Education and Vocational Training

———— (2012a) *Evaluation of the Impact of the Primary Education Development Programme Phase Two (PEDP II) 2007–2011.* Dar es Salaam: Ministry of Education and Vocational Training

———— (2012b) *Primary Education Development Programme (PEDP) Phase III (2012–2016).* Education Sector Development Programme. Dar es Salaam: Ministry of Education and Vocational Training

———— (2014) *Introduction to MoEVT.* Available at http://www.moe.go.tz/index.php?option= com_cont ent&view=article&id=1577&Itemid=629 [accessed 11 July 2014]

Ministry of Finance (2012) *Government Budget for Financial Year 2012/2013: Citizens' Budget Edition.* Dar es Salaam: Ministry of Finance

Ministry of Foreign Affairs (2013) *International Relations: The Principles of Ethiopia's Foreign Policy.* Federal Democratic Republic of Ethiopia. Available at http://www.mfa.gov.et/internationalMore. php?pg=27 [accessed 10 December 2013]

Ministry of Foreign Affairs of Denmark (2009) *Guidelines for Technical Assistance.* Copenhagen: Ministry of Foreign Affairs

———— (2013) *Annual Report 2012.* Copenhagen: Ministry of Foreign Affairs

———— (2014) *About Danida.* Copenhagen: Ministry of Foreign Affairs. Available at http://um.dk/en/ danida-en/about-danida/ [accessed 10 January 2014]

Ministry of Foreign Affairs of Denmark & Government of Tanzania (2009) *United Republic of Tanzania Health Sector Programme Support HSPS IV (2009–2014).* Annex 1: Support to the Health Sector in Mainland.

Ministry of Health (1999) *Health Sector Reform Programme of Work 1999–2002.* Dar es Salaam: Ministry of Health

———— (2003) *Second Health Sector Strategic Plan (HSSP) (July 2003–June 2008): 'Reforms Towards Delivering Quality Health Services and Clients Satisfaction'.* Dar es Salaam: Ministry of Health

Ministry of Health and Social Welfare (2009) *Health Sector Strategic Plan III: July 2009–June 2015.* Dar es Salaam: Ministry of Health and Social Welfare

———— (2012) *Health Sector Public Expenditure Review 2010/2011.* Dar es Salaam: Ministry of Health and Social Welfare

Ministry of Health and Social Welfare, Prime Minister's Office for Regional Administration and Local Government & Development Partners (2009) Health basket fund generic document: Final draft. Dar es Salaam

Ministry of Natural Resources and Tourism (2006) *Participatory Forest Management in Tanzania: Facts and Figures.* Dar es Salaam: Extension and Publicity Unit, Forestry and Beekeeping Division

Ministry of Planning, Economy and Empowerment (2006) *MKUKUTA Monitoring Master Plan and Indicator Information.* Dar es Salaam: Ministry of Planning, Economy and Empowerment

Mkandawire, T (2010) Aid, accountability, and democracy in Africa. *Social Research* 77(4): 1149–1182

Mo Ibrahim Foundation (2013) *2013 Ibrahim Index of African Governance (IIAG).* Available at http://www.moibrahimfoundation.org/downloads/2013/2013-IIAG.xls [accessed 26 February 2014]

Moleke, P (2003) The state of the labour market in contemporary South Africa. In: J Daniel, A Habib & R Southall (eds) *State of the Nation: South Africa, 2003–2004.* Cape Town: HSRC Press. pp. 204–224

Moloi, K, Mkwanazi, T & Bojabotseha, T (2014) Higher education in South Africa at the crossroads. *Mediterranean Journal of Social Sciences* 5(2): 469–475

Moloi, MQ & Chetty, M (2010) *The SACMEQ III Project in South Africa: A Study of the Conditions of Schooling and the Quality of Education.* Pretoria: Department of Basic Education

Moodley, J & Vawda, S (2000) *Development Cooperation Report II for South Africa 1994–1999: Evaluation of ODA to the Skills Development Sector.* Pretoria: National Treasury

Morgan, P (2010) *AusAID's Approach to Technical Assistance: Getting Beyond 'Good Enough'.* Report prepared for AusAid Office of Development Effectiveness

Morss, ER (1984) Institutional destruction resulting from donor and project proliferation in sub-Saharan African countries. *World Development* 12(4): 465–470

Mosoba, T & Mugarula, F (2013, 24 November) Donors want Dar to hand back stolen aid millions. *The Citizen.* Available at http://www.thecitizen.co.tz/News/Donors-demand-Sh644m-from-govt/-/1840392/2086214/-/item/1/-/yiodra/-/index.html [accessed 9 December 2013]

Moss, T, Pettersson, G & Van de Walle, N (2008) An aid-institutions paradox? A review essay on aid dependency and state building in sub-Saharan Africa. In: W Easterly (ed.) *Reinventing Foreign Aid.* Cambridge, Mass: MIT Press. pp. 255–281

Moss, T, Roodman, D & Standley, S (2005) The Global War on Terror and U.S. Development Assistance: USAID Allocation by Country, 1998–2005. *Working Paper (62).* Center for Global Development

Mouton, J (2007) *Study on National Research Systems: A Meta-Review. Regional Report on Sub Saharan Africa.* UNESCO Forum on Higher Education, Research and Knowledge

——— (2008) *Mapping Research Systems in Developing Countries: Regional Report on Sub-Saharan Africa.* Paris: Centre for Research on Science and Technology, Institute for Research on Development, UNESCO

Mouton, J, Boshoff, N, De Waal, L et al. (2008) The state of public science in the SADC region. In: P Kotecha (ed.) *Towards a Common Future: Higher Education in the SADC Region. Research Findings from Four SARUA Studies.* Johannesburg: Southern African Regional Universities Association. pp. 199–302

Msila, V (2007) From apartheid education to the revised national curriculum statement: Pedagogy for identity formation and national building in South Africa. *Nordic Journal of African Studies* 16(2): 146–160

Müller, K & Fourie, A (2011) *Innovations for Biodiversity Conservation: The Case of the Conservation Stewardship Programme, Western Cape, South Africa.* Stellenbosch: Stellenbosch University, School of Public Management & Planning

Mummenthey, C (2008) *Implementing Efficient and Effective Learnerships in the Construction Industry: A Study on the Learnership System in the Building/Civil Sector of the Western Cape.* Pretoria: Department of Labour, German Technical Co-operation

Mummert, U (2013) Multiple Prinzipale, Agenten und Ziele: Konsequenzen für die Entwicklungspolitik. In: J Faust (ed.) *Politische Ökonomie der Entwicklungszusammenarbeit.* Baden-Baden: Nomos. pp. 51–87

Mushi, PAK (2009) *History and Development of Education in Tanzania.* Dar es Salaam: Dar es Salaam University Press

Mwalyosi, R & Sosovele, H (2001) *The integration of Bbiodiversity into national environmental assessment procedures: Case study Tanzania.* Produced for the Biodiversity Planning Support Programme. National Case Studies (12). UNDP, UNEP, GEF

Mwenda, A (2006) Foreign Aid and the Weakening of Democratic Accountability in Uganda. *Foreign Policy Briefing (88)*. Cato Institute, Washington

Nahapiet, J (2011) A social perspective: Exploring the links between human capital and social capital. In: A Burton-Jones & J Spender (eds.) *The Oxford Handbook of Human Capital*. Oxford (et al.): Oxford University Press

Nahapiet, J & Ghoshal, S (1998) Social capital, intellectual capital, and the organizational advantage. *The Academy of Management Review* 23(2): 242–266

NAM Aidsmap (2014) *CD4 cell counts*. London: NAM Publications

National AIDS Control Programme (2008) *National Guidelines for the Management of HIV and AIDS*. 3rd ed (revised February 2009). Dar es Salaam, Government of Tanzania

National Audit Office (2012) *Briefing to support the International Development Committee's inquiry into the Department for International Development's Annual Report and Accounts 2011-12*. London: National Audit Office

National Statistics System (N/A) *Statistical Reform in South Africa*. Republic of South Africa

National Training Board (1994) *A Discussion Document on a National Training Strategy Initiative: A Preliminary Report by the National Training Board*. Pretoria: National Training Board

Nattrass, N (2006a) Antiretroviral treatment and the problem of political will in South Africa. *The Southern African Journal of HIV Medicine* 7(2): 29–31

——— (2006b) South Africa's 'Rollout' of Highly Active Antiretroviral Therapy: A Critical Assessment. *CSSR Working Paper (158)*. Cape Town: University of Cape Town, Centre for Social Science Research

——— (2008) Aids and the scientific governance of medicine in post-apartheid South Africa. *African Affairs* 107(429): 157–176

Ndinda, L (2010, 17 February) Under international pressure, Uganda mulls amending anti-gay bill. *Deutsche Welle*. Available at http://www.dw.de/under-international-pressure-uganda-mulls-amending-anti-gay-bill/a-5242627-1 [accessed 18 December 2013]

Ndlovu, ME (2013, 21 May) Zimbabwe's educational legacy from the 1980s: Was it all so rosy? Sokwanele Civic Action Support. Available at http://www.sokwanele.com/zimbabwe%E2%80%99s-educational-legacy-1980s-was-it-all-so-rosy/21052013 [accessed 9 December 2014]

Ndlovu, N (2005) An Exploratory Analysis of HIV and AIDS Donor Funding in South Africa. *Budget Brief (155)*. IDASA Budget Information Service

NEPAD Planning and Coordinating Agency (2014) *African Innovation Outlook II*. Pretoria: NPCA

Netherlands Ministry of Foreign Affairs (2010) Letter to the House of Representatives outlining development cooperation policy. The Hague: Netherlands Ministry of Foreign Affairs

——— (2011) Letter to the House of Representatives presenting the spearheads of development cooperation policy. The Hague: Netherlands Ministry of Foreign Affairs

Neumayer, E (2003) What factors determine the allocation of aid by Arab countries and multilateral agencies? *Journal of Development Studies* 39(4): 134–147

Nevondwe, L & Odeku, KO (2013) Constitutional right to education in South Africa: A myth or a reality? *Mediterranean Journal of Social Sciences* 4(13): 847–860

Ngaga, YM, Treue, T, Meilby, H et al. (2014) Participatory forest management for more than a decade in Tanzania: Does it live up to its goals? *Tanzania Journal of Forestry and Nature Conservation* 83(1)

Ngeleza, B, Chabane, S & Dlamini, D (2000) *Development Cooporation Report II for South Africa 1994–1999. Section II: Evaluation of ODA to the Education Sector*. Johannesburg: International Organisation Development

Ngirwa, CC, Euwema, M, Babyegeya, E & Stouten, J (2013) Managing change in higher education institutions in Tanzania: A historical perspective. *Higher Education Management & Policy* 24(3): 127–144

Nielinger, O (2006) *Information and Communication Technologies (ICT) for Development in Africa: An Assessment of ICT Strategies and ICT Utilisation in Tanzania*. Frankfurt am Main; New York: Peter Lang

Nindi, SJ (2012) *Final Report on Institutional Capacity Needs and Entry Points for Mainstreaming Climate Change Adaptation into Development Planning in Tanzania*. Dar es Salaam

Niskanen, WA (1971, repr. 2007) *Bureaucracy and Representative Government*. New Brunswick, NJ: Aldine Transaction

Nissanke, M (2010) Reconstructing the aid effectiveness debate. In: G Mavrotas (ed.) *Foreign Aid for Development: Issues, Challenges, and the New Agenda*. New York: Oxford University Press. pp. 57–93

Nkosi, S (2012, 17 August) Tanzania's schools go backwards. *Mail & Guardian*. Available at http://mg.co.za/article/2012-08-17-00-tanzanias-schools-go-backwards [accessed 5 February 2013]

Nordeco & Arcacia (2013) *National REDD+ Strategy Development and Implementation Process in Tanzania*. Mid-term review final report

Norwegian Agency for Development Cooperation (2014) *Facts about Tanzania*. Available at http://www.norad.no/en/countries/africa/tanzania [accessed 5 November 2014]

Norwegian Ministry of Foreign Affairs (2009) *Climate, Conflict and Capital: Norwegian Development Policy Adapting to Change*. Report No. 13 (2008–2009) to the Storting. Recommendation from the Ministry of Foreign Affairs of 13 February 2009, approved in the Council of State on the same date. (Stoltenberg II Government). Oslo: Norwegian Ministry of Foreign Affairs

Nunnenkamp, P & Thiele, R (2006) Targeting aid to the needy and deserving: Nothing but promises? *The World Economy* 29(9): 1177–1201

Nuscheler, F (2005) *Entwicklungspolitik*. 5 ed. Bonn: Bundeszentrale für polit. Bildung

Nyerere, JK (1967) *Education for Self-reliance*. Dar es Salaam, United Republic of Tanzania

——— (1973) *Freedom and Development: Uhuru na Maendeleo. A Selection from Writings and Speeches 1968–1973*. Nairobi; New York: Oxford University Press

Ocheni, S & Nwankwo, BC (2012) Analysis of colonialism and its impact in Africa. *Cross-Cultural Communication* 8(3): 46–54

Odora Hoppers, Catherine A (ed.) (2002) *Indigenous Knowledge and the Integration of Knowledge Systems: Towards a Philosophy of Articulation*. Claremont, Cape Town: NAE

OECD (2005) *The Paris Declaration on Aid Effectiveness*. Paris: OECD Publishing

——— (2007) *OECD Reviews of Innovation Policy: South Africa*. Paris: OECD Publishing

——— (2008) The challenge of capacity development. *OECD Journal on Development* 8(3): 233–276

——— (2009a) *Managing Aid: Practices of DAC Member Countries*. Paris: OECD Publishing

——— (2009b) *Survey on the Levels of Decentralisation to the Field in DAC members' Development Co-operation Systems*. Report (DCD(2009)3/FINAL). Paris: OECD Development Co-operation Directorate

——— (2011a) *2011 DAC Report on Multilateral Aid*. Paris: OECD Publishing

——— (2011b) Busan Partnership for Effective Development Co-operation: Fourth High Level Forum on Aid Effectiveness, Busan, Republic of Korea, 29 November-1 December 2011, Busan

——— (2011c) *Denmark: Development Assistance Committee (DAC) Peer Review 2011*. Paris: OECD Publishing

——— (2011d) *The Netherlands: Development Assistance Committee (DAC) Peer Review 2011*. Paris: OECD Publishing

——— (2012a) *2012 DAC Report on Multilateral Aid*. 2012 DAC Report on Multilateral Aid

——— (2012b) *Development Co-operation Report 2012: Lessons in Linking Sustainability and Development*. 2012 DAC Report on Multilateral Aid

——— (2012c) *The list of CRS purpose codes, taking effect in 2012 reporting on 2011 flows*. Paris: OECD DAC Secretariat

——— (2013a) *OECD Development Co-operation Peer Review: Sweden 2013*. Paris: OECD Publishing

——— (2013b, 3 April) Aid to poor countries slips further as governments tighten budgets. Available at http://www.oecd.org/dac/stats/aidtopoorcountriesslipsfurtherasgovernmentstightenbudgets.htm [accessed 11 December 2013]

OECD.Stat (2014a) *Aid (ODA) by Sector and Donor*. Paris: OECD. Available at http://stats.oecd.org/ [accessed 16 January 2014]

——— (2014b) *Aid Activities Targeting Global Environmental Objectives*. Paris: OECD. Available at http://stats.oecd.org/Index.aspx?DataSetCode=RIOMARKERS [accessed 21 January 2014]

OECD/DAC Capacity Development Team (2009) *Inventory of Donor Approaches to Capacity Development: What We Are Learning?*. Paris: OECD

Olukoshi, AO (1998) *The Elusive Prince of Denmark: Structural Adjustment and the Crisis of Governance in Africa*. Uppsala: Nordiska Afrikaninstitutet

Omari, IM & Baser, H (2012) *Education Sector Human Resources Situation Analysis: A Consultancy Report for the Ministry of Education and Vocational Training*. Dar es Salaam: Ministry of Education and Vocational Training

Omari, IM, Mbise, A, Mahenge, ST, Malekela, G & Besha, M (1983) *Universal Primary Education in Tanzania*. IDRC-TS (42). Ottawa: International Development Research Centre

Pallangyo, DM (2011) Tanzania's framework environmental law and the balancing of interests. In: M Faure & W du Plessis (eds) *The Balancing of Interests in Environmental Law in Africa*. Pretoria: Pretoria University Law Press. pp. 485–518

Parliamentary Monitoring Group (2009) Budget Speech of Honourable Dr. A. Motsoaledi, MP, Minister of Health, Delivered to the National Assembly, Parliament of the Republic of South Africa on June 30 2009, Cape Town. Available at http://www.pmg.org.za/briefing/20090630-health-ministers-budget-speech [accessed 1 August 2014]

—— (2012) *Department of Environmental Affairs Annual Report 2011/12*. Available at http://www.pmg.org.za/report/20121016-department-environmental-affairs-their-annual-report-and-audited-fina [accessed 14 February 2014]

Parmanand, S (2013, 3 June) Top AusAID private sector partners: 2012 updates. Devex. Available at https://www.devex.com/en/news/top-ausaid-private-sector-partners-2012-updates/81112 [accessed 13 December 2013]

Pearson, M (2011) *Results Based Aid and Results Based Financing: What Are They? Have They Delivered Results?* London: HLSP Institute

Pender, J (2007) Country ownership: The evasion of donor accountability. In: CJ Bickerton, P Cunliffe & A Gourevitch (eds) *Politics Without Sovereignty: A Critique of Contemporary International Relations*. Oxon; New York: University College London Press. pp. 112–130

PER Macro Group (2013) Rapid Budget Analysis 2013: Draft Synoptic Note. Dar es Salaam

Peta, B (2006, 9 May) ANC's Zuma cleared of rape charge, but rebuked by judge. *The Independent*. Available at http://www.independent.co.uk/news/world/africa/ancs-zuma-cleared-of-rape-charge-but-rebuked-by-judge-477374.html [accessed 28 July 2014]

Petermann, J-H (2013) *Between Export Promotion and Poverty Reduction: The Foreign Economic Policy of Untying Official Development Assistance*. Wiesbaden: Springer

Petersen, C & Huntley, B (2005) Mainstreaming Biodiversity in Production Landscapes. *GEF Working Paper (20)*. Washington DC: Global Environment Facility

Piccio, L (2013, 10 June) Top USAID contract awardees: A primer. Devex. Available at https://www.devex.com/en/news/top-usaid-contract-awardees-a-primer/81198 [accessed 12 December 2013]

Pincin, JA (2012) *Foreign Aid and Political Influence of the Development Assistance Committee Countries*. MPRA Paper (39668). Munich: University Library of Munich

Plank, DN (1993) Aid, debt, and the end of sovereignty: Mozambique and its donors. *The Journal of Modern African Studies* 31(3): 407–430

Policy Forum (2009) Reforming Allowances: A Win-Win Approach to Improved Service Delivery, Higher Salaries for Civil Servants and Saving Money. *Policy Brief (9)*. Dar es Salaam: Policy Forum

—— (2010a) Are we Investing Enough on Education? Education Development Budget 2010/2011. *Policy Brief (3:10)*. Dar es Salaam: Policy Forum

—— (2010b) Dependency on Foreign Aid: How the Situation Could be Saved: An Analysis of Tanzania's Budget 2010/2011. *Policy Brief (3:10)*. Dar es Salaam: Policy Forum

Policy Forum & HakiElimu (2011) 2011/2012 Education Budget. Does It Lead to Quality Education? *Policy Brief (1)*. Dar es Salaam: Policy Forum

Polidano, C (2000) Measuring public sector capacity. *World Development* 28(5): 805–822

Preisendörfer, P (1995) Vertrauen als soziologische Kategorie: Möglichkeiten und Grenzen einer entscheidungstheoretischen Fundierung des Vertrauenskonzept. *Zeitschrift für Soziologie* 24(4): 263–272

President's Office Public Service Management (2011) *The Functions and Organisation Structure of the Prime Minister's Office, Regional Administration and Local Governance.* Approved by the President on 3rd June,2011. Dar es Salaam, United Republic of Tanzania

President's Office, PC (2012) *The Tanzania Five Year Development Plan 2011/12–2015–16: Unleashing Tanzania's Latent Growth Potentials.* Dar es Salaam, United Republic of Tanzania

Prime Minister's Office (2001) *National Policy on HIV/AIDS.* Dar es Salaam, United Republic of Tanzania

——— (2009) *National Multisectoral HIV Prevention Strategy 2009–2012: 'Towards Achieving Tanzania Without HIV'.* Dar es Salaam, United Republic of Tanzania

Provost, C (2013, 06 December) UK's trade development programme failed to prioritise poor – Aid watchdog. *The Guardian.* Available at http://www.theguardian.com/global-development/2013/dec/06/trade-development-failed-poor-trademark-southern-africa-aid [accessed 27 January 2014]

Provost, C & Hughes, N (2012, 21 September) Why is so much UK aid money still going to companies based in Britain?: 'Untied' aid is thought to benefit local firms in developing countries, but the lucrative DfID contracts end up in UK hands. *The Guardian.* Available at http://www.theguardian.com/global-development/datablog/2012/sep/21/why-is-uk-aid-going-to-uk-companies [accessed 13 December 2013]

Psacharopoulos, G (1994) Returns to investment in education: A global update. *World Development* 22(9): 1325–1343

Puren, A (2011) The HIV-1 epidemic in South Africa: The leading edge and the measurement of incidence. *Southern African Journal of Epidemiology and Infection* 46(4): 198–201

Radetzki, M (1973) *Aid and Development: A Handbook for Small Donors.* Foreword by Erik Lundberg. New York: Praeger

Ramkolowan, Y & Stern, M (2011) *The Developmental Effectiveness of Untied Aid: Evaluation of the Implementation of the Paris Declaration and of the 2001 DAC Recommendation on Untying ODA to the LDCs. South Africa Country Study.* Pretoria

Rasool, F & Botha, CJ (2011) The nature, extent and effect of skills shortages on skills migration in South Africa. *South African Journal of Human Resource Management* 9(1): 1–12

Republic of South Africa (1995) South African Qualifications Authority Act 58 of 1995. Pretoria

——— (1996) Constitution of the Republic of South Africa Act 108 of 1996. Pretoria

——— (1998a) National Environmental Management Act 107 of 1998. Pretoria

——— (1998b) Skills Development Act 97 of 1998. Pretoria

——— (1999) Skills Development Levies Act 1999. Pretoria

——— (2003) National Environmental Management: Protected Areas Act 57 of 2003. Pretoria

——— (2004a) National Environmental Management: Biodiversity Act 10 of 2004. Pretoria

——— (2004b) National Health Act 61 of 2003. *Government Gazette* 469(26595). Cape Town

——— (2008a) Higher Education Amendment Act 39 of 2008. *Government Gazette* 521(31651). Cape Town

——— (2008b) Skills Development Amendment Act 37 of 2008. *Government Gazette* 521(31666). Pretoria

——— (2009a) *Biodiversity Fiscal Incentives: A Framework on Fiscal Incentives for Biodiversity.* Pretoria

——— (2009b) General and Further Education and Training Quality Assurance Amendment Act 50 of 2008. *Government Gazette* 523(31785). Cape Town

——— (2009c) National Qualifications Framework Act 67 of 2008. *Government Gazette* 524(31909). Cape Town

——— (2012) *Global AIDS Response Progress Report 2012.* Pretoria

Ridde, V (2010) Per diems undermine health interventions, systems and research in Africa: Burying our heads in the sand. Editorial. *Tropical Medicine & International Health* (Early View, 28 June 2010: online version of record published before inclusion in an issue)

Riedel, D (2010, 26 July) Entwicklungspolitik darf auch interessengeleitet sein. *Handelsblatt online.* Available at http://www.handelsblatt.com/politik/deutschland/dirk-niebel-entwicklungspolitik-darf-auch-interessengeleitet-sein/v_detail_tab_print/3498804.html [accessed 22 January 2014]

Robi, A (2012, 16 December) Tanzania: 5,000 pregnant girls drop out of school. AllAfrica Global Media. Available at http://allafrica.com/stories/201211160227.html [accessed 11 July 2014]

Rottenburg, R (2000) Accountability for development aid. In: H Kalthoff, R Rottenburg & H-J Wagener (eds) *Facts and Figures: Economic Representations and Practices.* Marburg: Metropolis Verlag. pp. 143–173

——— (2009) *Far-fetched Facts: A Parable of Development Aid.* Cambridge, Mass: MIT Press

Royal Ministry of Foreign Affairs Norway & Asplan Analyse (1994) *Technical Cooperation in Transition. Review of Norwegian Policy in Light of DAC Principles on Technical Cooperation.* Oslo

Rubin, E (2012) *Assessment of DP Practices in Tanzania in Financing Allowances, Salary Top-ups, Civil Servant Salary Payments, and Parallel and/or Integrated PIUs.* Assessment report

Rugonzibwa, P (2012, 11 June) Tanzania: State wants NEMC to become financially independent. AllAfrica.com. http://allafrica.com/stories/201206111136.html [accessed 17 February 2014]

Rutasitara, L, Lokina, RB & Yona, F (2010) *Mainstreaming Environment into MKUKUTA II Process: Interim Report to Ministry of Finance and Economic Affairs.* Dar es Salaam: University of Dar es Salaam, Department of Economics

Rwamucyo, E (2012, 3 December) Rwanda: Implication of donor suspension of aid to Rwanda over DRC crisis. *The New Times.* Available at http://allafrica.com/stories/201212030223.html [accessed 18 December 2013]

Samoff, J (1992) The intellectual/financial complex of foreign aid. *Review of African Political Economy* (53): 60–75

——— (2009) *The Fast Track to Planned Dependence: Education Aid to Africa.* Stanford University

Samoff, J, with Bidemi Carrol (2003) Education for all in Africa: Still a distant dream. In: RF Arnove & CA Torres (eds) *Comparative Education: The Dialectic of the Global and the Local.* 2 ed. Lanham: Rowman & Littlefield. pp. 357–388

Samoff, J, with Suleman Sumra (1994) From planning to marketing: Making education and training policy in Tanzania. In: J Samoff (ed.) *Coping with Crisis: Austerity, Adjustment and Human Resources.* London (et al.): Cassell (et al.). pp. 134–172

SANAC (2007) *HIV & AIDS and STI Strategic Plan for South Africa 2007–2011.* Pretoria: SANAC

——— (2010) *National Strategic Plan 2007–2011 Mid Term Review 2010.* Pretoria: SANAC

——— (2011a) *Getting to Success: Improving HIV Prevention Efforts in South Africa.* Pretoria: SANAC

——— (2011b) *Know Your Epidemic, Know Your Reponse: Summary Report 2011. Simplified Version of the Analysis of South Africa's HIV and AIDS Epidemic and the Reponse.* Pretoria: SANAC

——— (2011c) *National Strategic Plan on HIV, STIs and TB 2012–2016.* Pretoria: SANAC

——— (2013) *South Africa's National Aids Spending Assessment Brief (2007/08–2009/10)* (Based on 1 July 2012 report). Pretoria: SANAC

SANAC Secretariat (2010) *The National HIV Counselling and Testing Campaign Strategy.* Pretoria: SANAC

SANBI (2013) *Final Strategic Plan 2013–2018.* Pretoria: SANBI

Santos, B de Sousa (ed.) (2007) *Another Knowledge is Possible: Beyond Northern Epistemologies.* London: Verso

Sapa & AFP (2007, 6 June) UN praises SA Aids plan. *Health 24.* Available at http://www.health24.com/Medical/HIV-AIDS/News/UN-praises-SA-Aids-plan-20120721 [accessed 25 July 2014]

SARRAH (2011a) Project brief: Project team for planning the implementation of the NHI

——— (2011b) *South African Minister of Health visit to UK, 15th & 16th September 2011.* Report & follow up actions

——— (2012a) *Minister and Deputy Minister's visits to London, July & August 2012.* Report

——— (2012b) *NHS Trust Hospitals: Visit by Director-General, National Department of Health, South Africa 9th & 10th October 2012.* Report

Scharpf, FW (2005) Legitimationskonzepte jenseits des Nationalstaats. In: GF Schuppert, I Pernice, UR Haltern & M Bach (eds) *Europawissenschaft.* Baden-Baden: Nomos. pp. 705–742

Schneider, CJ & Tobin, JL (2010) Tying the Hands of its Masters? Interest Coalitions and Multilateral Aid Allocations in the European Union. *Working Paper.* San Diego: University of California, Georgetown University

Schneider, H (2002) On the fault-line: The politics of AIDS policy in contemporary South Africa. *African Studies* 61(1): 145–167

Schneider, H & Gilson, L (1999) Small fish in a big pond?: External aid and the health sector in South Africa. *Health Policy and Planning* 14(3): 264–272

Schneider, H & Stein, J (2001) Implementing AIDS policy in post-apartheid South Africa. *Social Science & Medicine* (52): 723–731

School of Public Health and Allied Sciences (2009) *Analysis of the constraints in human resource availability (training, recruitment, deployment, and retention) especially in hard to reach areas.* Final report. Dar es Salaam: Muhimbili University of Health and Allied Sciences

Schütz, A (1953) Common-sense and scientific interpretation of human action. *Philosophy and Phenomenological Research* 14(1): 1–38

Section27 (2011) *An Assessment of the Draft NSP for HIV/AIDS (II).* Johannesburg: Section27

Semali, IAJ (2003) Understanding stakeholders' roles in health sector reform process in Tanzania: The case of decentralizing the immunization program. Dissertation, Universität Basel, Basel

Senkubuge, F & Mayosi, BM (2013) The state of the national health research system in South Africa. In: A Padarath & R English (eds) *South African Health Review 2012/13.* Durban: HST. pp. 141–150

Shija, AE, Msovela, J & Mboera, LE (2012) Maternal health in fifty years of Tanzania independence: Challenges and opportunities of reducing maternal mortality. *Tanzania Journal of Health Research* 13(5 Suppl 1)

Shikwati, J (2006) *The Future of Africa in the World.* Nairobi: Inter Region Economic Network

Sida (Swedish International Development Cooperation Agency) (2013a) *Our work in Tanzania.* Available at http://www.sida.se/English/Countries-and-regions/Africa/Tanzania/Our-work-in-Tanzania/ [accessed 29 January 2014]

——— (2013b) *Working at Sida: Are you interested in working with development cooperation?* Available at http://www.sida.se/English/About-us/Working-at-Sida/ [accessed 29 October 2013]

——— (2013c) *Working at Sida: Vacancies.* Available at http://www.sida.se/English/About-us/Working-at-Sida/Vacancies-/ [accessed 31 October 2013]

Sikika (2011) *2010/2011 Health Sector Budget Analysis.* Dar es Salaam: Sikika

Simmel, G (1950) *The Sociology of Georg Simme.* Glencoe, Illinois: Free Press

Smith, BC (2007) *Good Governance and Development.* Basingstoke: Palgrave MacMillan

Smith, D (2009, 10 May) South African health minister sacked as Jacob Zuma names first cabinet. *The Guardian.* Available at http://www.theguardian.com/world/2009/may/10/jacob-zuma-barbara-hogan [accessed 28 July 2014]

——— (2013, 30 April) South Africa warns aid cut means change in relationship with UK. *The Guardian.* Available at http://www.theguardian.com/global-development/2013/apr/30/south-africa-aid-cut-uk [accessed 8 December 2014]

Smith, DJ (2003) Patronage, per diems and the 'Workshop Mentality': The practice of family planning programs in Southeastern Nigeria. *World Development* 31(4): 703–715

Smith, MJ, Jennings, R & Solanki, G (2005) Perspectives on learnerships: A critique of South Africa's transformation of apprenticeships. *Journal of Vocational Education & Training* 57(4): 537–561

Sokoine University of Agriculture Directorate of Research & Postgraduate Studies (2014) *Funding of research.* Available at http://www.suanet.ac.tz/drpgs/index.php?option=com_content&view=category&layout= blog&id=98&Itemid=124 [accessed 12 March 2014]

Soni, R (2000) *Development Coorporation Report II for South Africa 1994–1999: DCR Synthesis Report.* Section I. Johannesburg: International Organisation Development

Søreide, T, Tostensen, A & Aagedal Skage, I (2012) *Hunting for per diem. The uses and abuses of travel compensation in three developing countries.* Oslo:Norad Evaluation Department

Soroka, SN & Wlezien, C (2010) *Degrees of Democracy: Politics, Public Opinion, and Policy.* Cambridge; New York: Cambridge University Press

Sosibo, K (2007, 24 August) Madlala-Routledge forced to pay for Spain trip. *Mail & Guardian.* Available at http://mg.co.za/article/2007-08-24-madlala-routledge-forced-to-pay-for-spain-trip [accessed 25 July 2014]

Sosovele, H (2011) Governance challenges in Tanzania's environmental impact assessment practice. *African Journal of Environmental Science and Technology* 5(2): 126–130

South African Private Practitioner Forum (2011) *SAPPF Submissions on the Green Paper on National Health Insurance*. Johannesburg: SAPPF

South African Qualifications Authority (2012) *Key Readings: The South African NQF 1995–2011: Special Edition in Recognition of the Contribution of Samuel BA Isaacs to the Development of the NQF in South Africa*. 12 ed. Waterkloof: SAQA

Southern African Development Community (2012) *SADC Member States*. Available at http://www.sadc.int/member-states/ [accessed 10 March 2014]

Spaull, N (2012) Poverty & Privilege: Primary School Inequality in South Africa. *Stellenbosch Economic Working Papers (13)*. Stellenbosch: Stellenbosch University

—— (2013) *South Africa's Education Crisis: The Quality of Education in South Africa 1994–2011*. Johannesburg: Centre for Development and Enterprise

Statistics South Africa (2004) *Primary Tables South Africa: Census 1996 and 2001 Compared*. Pretoria: Statistics South Africa

—— (2012) *Census 2011: Statistical Release*. Pretoria: Statistics South Africa

—— (2013) *Statistical Release: Mid-year Population Estimates 2013*. Pretoria: Statistics South Africa

Stehr, N (2010) Knowledge, democracy and power. *Central European Journal of Public Policy* 4(1): 14–35

Stickler, A & Barr, C (2011, 6 August) Revealed: Aid to Ethiopia increases despite serious human rights abuses. The Bureau of Investigative Journalism. Available at http://www.thebureauinvestigates.com/2011/08/06/revealed-britain-and-eu-increase-aid-to-ethiopia-despite-serious-human-rights-abuses/ [accessed 18 December 2013]

Stoppard, A (2002, 18 January) Health-South Africa: Doctors defy ban on anti-retroviral drugs. Inter Press Service News Agency, Johannesburg. Available at http://www.ipsnews.net/2002/01/health-south-africa-doctors-defy-ban-on-anti-retroviral-drugs/ [accessed 25 July 2014]

Stovel, K & Shaw, L (2012) Brokerage. *Annual Review of Sociology* 38(1): 139–158

Stuart, M (2014) The White Paper on Post School Education & Training. The Skills Handbook Blog, 16 January 2014. Available at http://www.skillshandbook.co.za/2014/01/the-white-paper-on-post-school.html [accessed 10 June 2014]

Stumm, M (2011) More responsibility for developing countries. *D+C* (3): 118–120

Sumra, S & Rajani, R (2006) Secondary Education in Tanzania: Key Policy Challenges. *Working Paper (4)*. Dar es Salaam: HakiElimu

Szulanski, G (2000) The process of knowledge transfer: A diachronic analysis of stickiness. *Organizational Behavior and Human Decision Processes* 82(1): 9–27

TACAIDS (2003) *National Multi-Sectoral Strategic Framework on HIV/AIDS 2003–2007*. Dar Es Salaam: Prime Minister's Office

—— (2007) *The Second National Multi-Sectoral Strategic Framework on HIV and AIDS (2008–2012)*. Dar Es Salaam: Prime Minister's Office

—— (2010) *Public Expenditure Review 2007–2009 HIV and AIDS. Tanzania Mainland*. Dar es Salaam: TACAIDS

—— (2011) *Medium Term Review of the Second National Multi Sectoral Strategic Framework 2008–2012: Programmatic Assessment*. Dar Es Salaam: Prime Minister's Office

—— (2012) *Public Expenditure Review 2011, HIV and AIDS: Tanzania Mainland*. Dar es Salaam: TACAIDS

—— (2014a) *Functions of TACAIDS*. Available at http://www.tacaids.go.tz/index.php?option=com_content& view=article&id=174:goals-objectives-functions&catid=24:what-we-do&Itemid=126 [accessed 29 August 2014]

—— (2014b) *Global Fund*. Available at http://www.tacaids.go.tz/index.php?option=com_content& view=article&id=97:global-fund&catid=39&Itemid=89 [accessed 29 August 2014]

—— (2014c) *Historical Background*. Available at http://www.tacaids.go.tz/index.php?option=com_content& amp;view=article&id=102&Itemid=53 [accessed 24 September 2014]

—— (2014d) *Treatment and Care*. Available at http://www.tacaids.go.tz/index.php?option=com_content& view=article&id=56:treatment-and-care&catid=31&Itemid=161 [accessed 20 October 2014]

TACAIDS, Zanzibar Aids Commission, National Bureau of Statistics, Office of the Chief Government Statistician & IFC International (2013) *Tanzania HIV/AIDS and Malaria Indicator Survey 2011-12*. Dar es Salaam

Tacconi, L (2012) Redefining payments for environmental services. *Ecological Economics* 73: 29–36

Tambwe, A (2013, 7 September) Time for a critical look at Tanzania's education system. *Daily News.* Available at http://www.dailynews.co.tz/index.php/features/21967-time-for-a-critical-look-at-tanzania-s-education-system [accessed 5 February 2014]

Tanzania Daily News (2012, 5 November) Tanzania: Legislators divided over readmitting 'mother' students. AllAfrica Global Media. Available at http://allafrica.com/stories/201211050157.html [accessed 11 July 2014]

——— (2013, 22 August) Tanzania: HIV/Aids fight in Tanzania under siege as donors pull out. All Africa. Available at http://allafrica.com/stories/201308220106.html [accessed 21 February 2014]

Tanzania Institute of Education (2014) *Research Information and Publications (RIP)*. Available at http://www.tie.go.tz/index.php/departments-and-sections/rip [accessed 13 March 2014]

Tanzania Ministry of Finance (2013) Speech by the Minister for Finance Hon. Dr. William Augustao Mgimwa (MP), introducing to the National Assembly the estimates of government revenue and expenditure for fiscal year 2013/2014, Dodoma

Taylor, N, Van der Berg, S & Mabogoane, T (2012) *What Makes Schools Effective? Report of South Africa's National School Effectiveness Study*. Cape Town: Pearson Education

TEEB (2011) *The Economics of Ecosystems and Biodiversity in National and International Policy Making*. Edited by Patrick ten Brink. London; Washington D.C.: Earthscan

Temba, P (2012, 12 February) Kilimanjaro RC prepares circular for priority of environmental conservation. *Daily News*. Available at http://www.dailynews.co.tz/index.php/local-news/1798-kilimanjaro-rc-prepares-circular-for-priority-of-environmental-conservation [accessed 29 May 2013]

Terzi, C (2012) *Review of Individual Consultancies in the United Nations System*. Geneva: United Nations, Joint Inspection Unit

The Lancet (2008) Can Zuma lead South Africa to a healthy future? *The Lancet* 371(9607): 90

——— (2011) HIV treatment as prevention-it works. *The Lancet* 377(9779): 1719

The Lancet South Africa Series Executive Summary Core Group (2009) Health in South Africa: Executive Summary for the Series. *The Lancet* (August 2009)

The Presidency (2009) Address by President Jacob Zuma on the occasion of World Aids Day. Pretoria Showgrounds. Available at http://www.thepresidency.gov.za/pebble.asp? relid=576 [accessed 28 July 2014]

Thede, N (2013) Policy coherence for development and securitisation: Competing paradigms or stabilising North–South hierarchies? *Third World Quarterly* 34(5): 784–799

Therkildsen, O (2002) Keeping the state accountable: Is aid no better than oil? *IDS Bulletin* 33(3): 1–17

Therkildsen, O & Tidemand, P (2007) *Staff Management and Organisational Performance in Tanzania and Uganda: Public Servant Perspectives*. Danish Institute for International Studies

Timberg, C (2006, 27 October) In South Africa, a dramatic shift on AIDS. *Washington Post Foreign Service*. Available at http://www.washingtonpost.com/wp-dyn/content/article/2006/10/26/AR2006102601874.html [accessed 25 July 2014]

Tjønneland, EN, Pillay, P, Slob, A, Willemsen, A & Jerve, AM (2008) *Managing Aid Exit and Transformation: South Africa Country Case Study*. Joint Donor Evaluation. Stockholm: Sida, Netherlands Ministry of Foreign Affairs, Danida, Norad

Torres, R-M (2001) 'Knowledge-based international aid': Do we want it, do we need it? In: W Gmelin, K King & S McGrath (eds) *Development Knowledge, National Research and International Cooperation*. Edinburgh, Bonn, Geneva: CAS, DSE, NORRAG. pp. 103–124

Tortell, P (2010) *C.A.P.E. Biodiversity Conservation and Sustainable Development Project: Terminal Evaluation Report*. Wellington, Western Cape: Cape Action for People and the Environment

——— (2011) *UNDP/GEF/SANBI National Grasslands Biodiversity Programme (PIMS 2929): Mid-Term Evaluation Report*. Wellington, Western Cape

Tran, M (2014, 8 January) UK MPs censure DfID over decision to end aid to India and South Africa: Department for International Development accused of political expediency and ignoring recommended review procedures. *The Guardian.* Available at http://www.theguardian.com/global-development/2014/jan/08/uk-mps-dfid-end-aid-india-south-africa [accessed 10 February 2014]

Treatment Action Campaign (2008) Health Minister Barbara Hogan delivers landmark speech at HIV Vaccine Conference. Available at http://www.tac.org.za/community/node/2421 [accessed 25 July 2014]

Treatment Action Campaign & Section27 (2011) *NSP Review: Engaging with South Africa's National Strategic Plan for HIV, STIs and TB.* NSP Review (1). Johannesburg: TAC; Section27

Treue, T, Ngaga, Y, Meilby, H et al. (2014) Does participatory forest management promote sustainable forest utilisation in Tanzania? *International Forestry Review* 16(1): 23–38

Truman, HS (1947) Special message to the Congress on Greece and Turkey: The Truman Doctrine. Published by The American Presidency Project. Available at http://www.presidency.ucsb.edu/ws/?pid=12846 [accessed 18 December 2013]

—— (1949) Inaugural address, Washington DC. Available at https://www.trumanlibrary.org/whistlestop/50yr_archive/inagural20jan1949.htm [accessed 14 July 2016]

Tsai, W & Ghoshal, S (1998) Social capital and value creation: The role of intrafirm networks. *The Academy of Management Journal* 41(4): 464–476

Turpie, JK, Marais, C & Blignaut, JN (2008) The working for water programme: Evolution of a payments for ecosystem services mechanism that addresses both poverty and ecosystem service delivery in South Africa. *Ecological Economics* 65(4): 788–798

Twaweza (2013) *Form Four examination results: Citizens report on the learning crisis in Tanzania.* Brief (2). Dar es Salaam: Twaweza

UN Inter-agency Group for Child Mortality Estimation (2013) *Under-five mortality rate: Estimates generated by the UN Inter-agency Group for Child Mortality Estimation (IGME) in 2013.* Available at http://www.childmortality.org/files_v16/download/U5MR.xlsx [accessed 28 August 2014]

UN Maternal Mortality Estimation Inter-agency Group (2010) *Maternal mortality in 1990–2010: United Republic of Tanzania.* Available at http://www.who.int/gho/maternal_health/countries/tza.xls [accessed 28 August 2014]

UN-REDD Programme (2011) *The UN-REDD Programme Strategy 2011–2015.* Geneva: FAO, UNDP, UNEP

UNAIDS (2010) *Getting to Zero: UNAIDS 2011–2015 Strategy.* Geneva: Joint United Nations Programme on HIV/AIDS

UNDP (United Nations Development Programme) (2012) *UNDP Jobs: Programme: Specialist, Energy and Climate Change.* Available at http://jobs.undp.org/cj_view_job.cfm?cur_job_id=33704 [accessed 22 October 2013]

—— (2013a) *Presentation of the JPO Programme.* Available at http://www.jposc.org/content/programme/presentation-en.html [accessed 25 September 2013]

—— (2013b) *Individual consultant Procurement Notice for individual consultants and individual consultants assigned by consulting firms/institutions.* Project 'Support the effective implementation of National Mine Action Programme'

UNDP & UNEP (2014) *Improved Monitoring of Poverty–Environment Objectives in Tanzania.* UNEP-UNDP Poverty Environment Initiative. Available at http://www.unpei.org/our-stories/improved-monitoring-of-poverty-environment-objectives-in-tanzania [accessed 26 March 2014]

UNEP (United Nations Environment Programme) (2013) *Green Economy Scoping Study: South African Green Economy Modelling Report (SAGEM): Focus on Natural Resource Management, Agriculture, Transport and Energy Sectors.* UNEP; Department of Environmental Affairs

UNEP – Convention on Biological Diversity (2014) *United Republic of Tanzania – Country Profile.* Available http://www.cbd.int/countries/profile/default.shtml?country=tz#status [accessed 19 March 2014]

UNESCO (1999) *Declaration on Science and the Use of Scientific Knowledge.* World Conference on Science, Budapest

UNESCO Institute for Statistics (2014) *United Republic of Tanzania*. Available at http://www.uis.unesco. org/DataCentre/Pages/country-profile.aspx?code=TZA&regioncode=40540 [accessed 11 July 2014]

UNESCO Office Dakar and Regional Bureau for Education in Africa; UNESCO Office Dar es Salaam & Ministry of Education and Vocational Training (2011) *Tanzania Education Sector Analysis: Beyond Primary Education, the Quest for Balanced and Efficient Policy Choices for Human Development and Economic Growth*. Dar es Salaam: UNESCO

UNFCCC Conference of the Parties (2008) *Report of the Conference of the Parties on its Thirteenth Session, held in Bali from 3 to 15 December 2007*. Addendum. Part Two: Action taken by the Conference of the Parties at its thirteenth session. FCCC/CP/2007/6/Add.1

UNICEF Tanzania (2010) *Children and Women in Tanzania: Volume I Mainland*. Dar es Salaam

———— (2014) *Children and AIDS - Overview*. Available at http://www.unicef.org/tanzania/6912_10620. html [accessed 29 August 2014]

United Nations (1945) *Charter of the United Nations and Statute of the International Court of Justice*. Available at http://www.un.org/en/sections/un-charter/un-charter-fulltext/index.html [accessed 14 July 2016]

———— (1997) *Kyoto Protocol to the United Nations Framework Convention on Climate Change*. UN Doc FCCC/CP/1997/7/Add.1, 10 Dec 1997; 37 ILM 22 (1998)

———— (2012) Dar-es-Salaam (Tanzania) *National Officer Category - Annual salaries and allowances*. Available at http://www.un.org/depts/OHRM/salaries_allowances/salaries/salaryscale/gs/daresale/ dare38n.xls [accessed 5 November 2013]

———— (2013a) *Pay and benefits*. Available at https://careers.un.org/lbw/home.aspx?viewtype=SAL [accessed 5 November 2013]

———— (2013b) *Pay and benefits: National Professional Officers*. Available at https://careers.un.org/lbw/ home.aspx?viewtype=SAL [accessed 31 October 2013]

———— (2015) *Transforming Our World: The 2030 Agenda for Sustainable Development*. A/RES/70/1. New York: United Nations

United Nations Economic and Social Council (1971) Science in underdeveloped countries: World plan of action for the application of science and technology to development. *Minerva* 9(1): 101–121

United Republic of Tanzania (1997) *National Environmental Policy*. Dar es Salaam: Vice-President's Office

———— (1998) *National Forest Policy*. Dar es Salaam

———— (2000) *Poverty Reduction Strategy Paper*. Dar es Salaam

———— (2001) The Education and Training Sector Development Programme Document. Final draft. Dar es Salaam

———— (2002) *The Forest Act*. Dar es Salaam

———— (2003) *HIV/AIDS Care and Treatment Plan 2003–2008*. Developed in collaboration with the William J Clinton Foundation. Dar es Salaam

———— (2004) The Environmental Management Act, 2004. Dar es Salaam

———— (2005) *National Strategy for Growth and Reduction of Poverty (NSGRP)*. Dar es Salaam: Vice-President's Office

———— (2006a) *Joint Assistance Strategy for Tanzania* (JAST). Dar es Salaam

———— (2006b) *Joint Assistance Strategy for Tanzania* (JAST). Dar es Salaam

———— (2008a) *Education Sector Development Programme (2008-17)*. Rev. ed. Dar es Salaam

———— (2008b) Memorandum of Understanding between the Partners (Government of Tanzania & Development Partners) participating in the pooled funding ('Basket') of the Health Sector: 1 July 2008 – 30 June 2015, Dar es Salaam

———— (2009) *Fourth National Report on Implementation of Convention on Biological Diversity (CBD)*. Dar es Salaam: Vice-President's Office-Division of Environment

———— (2010) *National Strategy for Growth and Reduction of Poverty II (NSGRP II)*. Dar es Salaam: Ministry of Finance and Economic Affairs, MKUKUTA Secretariat

———— (2011) *Partnership Framework Memorandum Governing General Budget Support (GBS) for Implementation of MKUKUTA II*. Dar es Salaam: Ministry of Finance

——— (2012a) *Country Progress Reporting. Part A: Tanzania Mainland*. Dar es Salaam: TACAIDS, Zanzibar AIDS Commission

——— (2012b) *Education Sector Development Programme: Joint Education Sector Review 2012: Aide Memoire*. Dar es Salaam.

——— (2012c) *National Report for the United Nations Conference on Sustainable Development, Rio+20*. Dar es Salaam: Vice-President's Office – Division of Environment

——— (2012d) *National Strategy for Reduced Emissions from Deforestation and Forest Degradation*: 2nd draft. Dar es Salaam: Vice-President's Office

United States of America, Department of State (2012) *PEPFAR Blueprint: Creating an AIDS-free Generation*. Washington DC: The Office of the Global Aids Coordinator

University of Cape Town (2007) *Public Participation in Environmental Decision-making in the New South Africa: A Research Project to Identify Practical Lessons Learned*. Final research project report. Geneva: UCT, UNITAR

USAID (2009) *USAID/Tanzania Education Strategy for Improving the Quality of Education FY 2009–2013*. Washington DC: USAID; Dar es Salaam

——— (2011) *USAID Education Strategy 2011–2015: Opportunity Through Learning*. Washington DC: USAID

——— (2013) *Tanzania: HIV/AIDS*. Available at http://www.usaid.gov/tanzania/hivaids [accessed 29 January 2014]

USAID & Creative Associates International (2014) *TZ21 – Community Engagement in Reading and ICT Installation Mtwara*. Available at http://crea-tz21.com/community-engagement-in-reading-and-ict-installation-mtwara/ [accessed 9 July 2014]

Uwezo (2013) *Are Our Children Learning? Annual Learning Assessment Report 2012*. Dar es Salaam: Uwezo Tanzania

Van Cranenburgh, O (1996) Tanzania's 1995 multi-party elections: The emerging party system. *Party Politics* 2(4): 535–547

Van den Heever, AM (2011) *Evaluation of the Green Paper on National Health Insurance*. Submission to national Department of Health

Van der Berg, S (2007) Apartheid's enduring legacy: Inequalities in education. *Journal of African Economies* 16(5): 849–880

Van der Berg, S, Taylor, S, Gustafsson, M, Spaull, N & Armstrong, P (2011) *Improving Education Quality in South Africa: Report for the National Planning Commission*. September 2011. Stellenbosch: University of Stellenbosch, Department of Economics

Van der Veen, AM (2011) *Ideas, Interests and Foreign Aid*. New York: Cambridge University Press

Venkatesh, KK, Mayer, KH & Carpenter, CCJ (2012) Low-cost generic drugs under the President's Emergency Plan for AIDS Relief drove down treatment cost; more are needed. *Health Affairs* 31(7): 1429–1438

Venter, F (2007) The South African national strategic plan: What does it mean for our health system? *Southern African Journal of HIV Medicine* 8(2)

——— (2013) HIV Treatment in South Africa: The challenges of an increasingly successful antiretroviral programme. In: A Padarath & R English (eds) *South African Health Review 2012/13*. Durban: HST. pp. 37–48

Vestergaard, J (2011) *The World Bank and the Emerging World Order. Adjusting to Multipolarity at the Second Decimal Point*. DIIS Report. Copenhagen: Danish Institute for International Studies

Vian, T, Miller, C, Themba, Z & Bukuluki, P (2013) Perceptions of per diems in the health sector: Evidence and implications. *Health Policy and Planning* 28(3): 237–246

Vice-President's Office (2004) *Public Expenditure Review of Environment Financial Year 2004*. Dar es Salaam: Vice-President's Office

——— (2005) *The Development of Indicators of Poverty-Environment Linkages*. Final report. Dar es Salaam: Vice-President's Office

——— (2007) *National Capacity Self Assessment Report and Action Plan for the Implementation of Post Rio Conventions*. Dar es Salaam: Vice-President's Office

Villarino, E (2011, 6 September) Top USAID private sector partners: A primer. Devex. Available at https://www.devex.com/en/news/top-usaid-private-sector-partners-a-primer/75832 [accessed 12 December 2013]

Wagner, D (2003) Aid and trade – An empirical study. *Journal of the Japanese and International Economies* 17(2): 153–173

Walt, G & Gilson, L (1994) Reforming the health sector in developing countries: The central role of policy analysis. *Health Policy and Planning* 9(4): 353–370

Wangwe, S (2004) The politics of autonomy and sovereignty: Tanzania's aid relationship. In: S Bromley, M Mackintosh, W Brown & M Wuyts (eds) *Making the International: Economic Interdependence and Political Order*. London: The Open University, Pluto Press. pp. 379–411

Wangwe, SM & Rweyemamu, DC (2001) The state of Tanzania's social sector in the development context. Paper presented at the CSSC Stakeholders Consultation in Bagamoyo, Tanzania. Dar es Salaam: Economic and Social Research Foundation

Warren, DM, Slikkerveer, LJ, Brokensha, D & Dechering, W (eds) (1995) *The Cultural Dimension of Development: Indigenous Knowledge Systems*. London: Intermediate Technology Publications

Wedgwood, R (2006) Education and Poverty Reduction in Tanzania. *Working Paper (9)*. Dar es Salaam: HakiElimu

Weingart, P (2002) African solutions for African problems: Science and political legitimacy. In: J Mouton, R Waast & F Ritchie (eds) *Science in Africa: Proceedings of a Symposium Held on 17 & 18 October 2001, Somerset West*. Centre for Interdisciplinary Studies, University of Stellenbosch . pp. 199–216

————— (2003) Paradox in scientific advising. In: GI Bechmann (ed.) *Expertise and Its Interfaces. The Tense Relationship of Science and Politics*. Berlin: edition sigma. pp. 53–89

————— (2006) Knowledge and inequality. In: G Therborn (ed.) *Inequalities of the World*. London; New York: Verso. pp. 163–190

Weissman, SR (1990) Structural adjustment in Africa: Insights from the experiences of Ghana and Senegal. *World Development* 18(12): 1621–1634

White House (2010) *Fact Sheet: US Global Development Policy*. Office of the Press Secretary, The White House, Washington

Whitfield, L (2009a) Aid and power: A comparative analysis of the country studies. In: L Whitfield (ed.) *The Politics of Aid: African Strategies for Dealing with Donors*. New York: Oxford University Press. pp. 329–360

————— (2009b) *The Politics of Aid: African Strategies for Dealing with Donors*. New York: Oxford University Press

Whitfield, L & Fraser, A (2009) Negotiating aid. In: L Whitfield (ed.) *The Politics of Aid: African Strategies for Dealing with Donors*. New York: Oxford University Press. pp. 27–44

————— (2010) Negotiating aid: The structural conditions shaping the negotiating strategies of African governments. *International Negotiation* 15(3): 341–366

WHO (2014) *Global health expenditure database: Table of key indicators, sources and methods by country and indicators: Tanzania*. Available at http://apps.who.int/nha/database/StandardReport.aspx?ID= REP_WEB_MINI_TEMPLATE_WEB_VERSION&COUNTRYKEY=84664 [accessed 20 February 2014]

Williams, G, Jones, S, Imber, V & Cox, A (2003) *A Vision for the Future of Technical Assistance in the International Development System*. Oxford Policy Management

Wines, M (2004, 10 February) South Africa: Minister defends garlic aids diet. *New York Times*. Available at http://www.nytimes.com/2004/02/10/world/world-briefing-africa-south-africa-minister-defends-garlic-aids-diet.html [accessed 23 July 2014]

Wood, B, Betts, J, Etta, F et al. (2011) *The Evaluation of the Paris Declaration*. Phase 2: Final report. Copenhagen: Danish Institute for International Studies

Woods, N (2005) The shifting politics of foreign aid. *International Affairs* 81(2): 393–409

World Bank (1988) *Education in Sub-Saharan Africa: Policies for Adjustment, Revitalization, and Expansion*. A World Bank policy study. Washington: DC World Bank

————— (1989) *Sub-Saharan Africa: From Crisis to Sustainable Growth. A Long-term Perspective Study*. 2 ed. Washington DC: World Bank

—— (1992) *Governance and Development*. Washington, DC World Bank

—— (1993) *World Development Report 1993: Investing in Health*. New York: Oxford University Press

—— (1995) *Priorities and Strategies for Education: A World Bank Review*. Development in Practice series. Washington DC: World Bank

—— (1996) *Toward Environmentally Sustainable Development in Sub-Saharan Africa: A World Bank Agenda*. Development in Practice series. Washington DC: World Bank

—— (1999a) *Education Sector Strategy*. Washington DC: World Bank

—— (1999b) *South Africa Country Assistance Strategy: Building a Knowledge Partnership*. Washington DC: World Bank

—— (1999c) *World Development Report 1998/99: Knowledge for Development*. Washington DC: Oxford University Press

—— (2001) *Making Sustainable Commitments: An Environment Strategy for the World Bank*. Washington DC: World Bank

—— (2003) *Tanzania – Multi-Sectoral AIDS Project*. Project appraisal document. Washington DC: World Bank

—— (2005a) *Capacity Enhancement through Knowledge Transfer. A Behavioral Framework for Reflection, Action and Results*. Washington DC: World Bank

—— (2005b) *Tanzania – Primary Education Development Program. Implementation Completion Report* (32071). Washington DC: World Bank

—— (2006) *South Africa – Cape Peninsula Biodiversity Conservation Project: Implementation Completion and Results Report*. Washington DC: World Bank

—— (2010a) *African Capacity Building Foundation (ACBF) Regional Capacity Building Project: Project Information Document*. Concept Stage. Washington DC: World Bank

—— (2010b) *Country Office Annual Salary Review 2010*. Washington DC: World Bank

—— (2010c) *Tanzania – Forest Conservation and Management Project, and Eastern Arc Forests Conservation and Management Project*. Washington DC: World Bank

—— (2011a) *Guidelines for the selection and employment of consultants under IBRD loans and IDA credits & grants by World Bank borrowers*. Washington DC: World Bank

—— (2011b) *South Africa - Biodiversity Conservation and Sustainable Development Project: Implementation Completion and Results Report*. Washington DC: World Bank

—— (2012a) *FAQs: about the World Bank*. Available at http://web.worldbank.org/WBSITE/ EXTERNAL/EXTSITETOOLS/0,,contentMDK:20147466~menuPK:344189~pagePK:98400~piPK:98 424~theSitePK:95474,00.html#8 [accessed 30 April 2013]

—— (2012b) *How the Project Cycle works*. Available at http://web.worldbank.org/ WBSITE/ EXTERNAL/COUNTRIES/AFRICAEXT/0,,menuPK:258677~pagePK:64087557~piPK:64087559~th eSitePK:258644,00.html#approval [accessed 21 August 2012]

—— (2012c) *IBRD Articles of Agreement* (as amended effective 27 June 2012): Article V. Available at http://web.worldbank.org/WBSITE/EXTERNAL/EXTABOUTUS/ORGANIZATION/BODEXT/0 ,,contentMDK:20049604~noSURL:Y~pagePK:64020054~piPK:64020408~theSitePK:278036~is CURL:Y~isCURL:Y,00.html#3 [accessed 29 April 2013]

—— (2012d) *Professional and technical opportunities*. Available at http://web.worldbank.org/WBSITE/ EXTERNAL/EXTJOBSNEW/0,,contentMDK:23123966~menuPK:8453473~pagePK:8453902~piPK: 8453359~theSitePK:8453353,00.html [accessed 25 September 2013]

—— (2012e) *Toward a Green, Clean, and Resilient World for All: A World Bank Group Environment Strategy 2012–2022*. Washington DC: World Bank

—— (2012f) YPP at a glance. Available at http://web.worldbank.org/WBSITE/EXTERNAL/EXTJO BSNEW/0,,contentMDK:23124011~menuPK:8526385~pagePK:8453902~piPK:8453359~theSite PK:8453353,00.html [accessed 26 September 2013]

—— (2012g) *Comprehensive Climate Change Planning in Tanzania: South-South Knowledge Exchange Hub*. Dar es Salaam: World Bank

—— (2013a) *Biodiversity Conservation and Sustainable Development Project*. Available at http://web. worldbank.org/WBSITE/EXTERNAL/NEWS/0,,contentMDK:23169150~menuPK:141310~pagePK: 34370~piPK:34424~theSitePK:4607,00.html [accessed 6 May 2014]

——— (2013b) *Tanzania Overview: Strategy*. Available at http://www.worldbank.org/en/country/tanzania/overview [accessed 8 January 2014]

——— (2013c) *The worldwide governance indicators, 2013 update: Aggregate indicators of governance 1996–2012*. Available at http://info.worldbank.org/governance/wgi/wgidataset.xlsx [accessed 26 February 2014]

——— (2014a) *World development indicators: Net ODA received (% of GNI)*. Available at http://data.worldbank.org/indicator/DT.ODA.ODAT.GN.ZS [accessed 12 February 2014]

——— (2014b) *World development indicators: Aid dependency*. Available at http://wdi.worldbank.org/table/6.11# [accessed 3 December 2014]

——— (2014c) *World development indicators: Life expectancy at birth, total (years)*. Available at http://api.worldbank.org/v2/en/indicator/sp.dyn.le00.in?downloadformat=excel [accessed 28 August 2014]

World Bank (2016a) Bank Guidance: Thresholds for procurement approaches and methods by country. Washington DC: World Bank.

——— (2016b) *World development indicators: Net official development assistance received (current USD)*. Available at http://api.worldbank.org/v2/en/indicator/dt.oda.odat.cd?downloadformat=excel [accessed 4 August 2016]

World Bank Independent Evaluation Group (2008) *Using Knowledge to Improve Development Effectiveness: An Evaluation of the World Bank Economic and Sector Work and Technical Assistance, 2000–2006*. Washington DC: World Bank

World Commission on Environment and Development (1987) *Our Common Future*. Oxford (et al.): Oxford University Press

World Conference on Education for All (1990) *Meeting Basic Learning Needs: A Vision for the 1990s: Background Document*. New York: Inter-Agency Commission (UNDO, UNESCO, UNICEF, World Bank) for the World Conference on Education for All

World Health Organization (1946) Constitution of the World Health Organization, as adopted by the International Health Conference, New York, 19 June – 22 July 1946; signed on 22 July 1946 by the representatives of 61 States (Official records of the WHO, No. 2, p. 100) and entered into force on 7 April 1948

——— (2006) *Engaging for Health: Eleventh General Programme of Work 2006–2015. A Global Health Agenda*. Geneva: WHO

——— (2008) *Medium-Term Strategic Plan 2008–2013 and Programme Budget 2008–2009*. Geneva: WHO

——— (2009a) Rapid advice: Antiretroviral therapy for HIV infection in adults and adolescents. Geneva: WHO Press

——— (2009b) *WHO Country Cooperation Strategy 2008–2013: South Africa*. Brazzaville: WHO Regional Office for Africa

——— (2009c) *WHO Country Cooperation Strategy 2010–2015: Tanzania*. Brazzaville: WHO Regional Office for Africa

——— (2010) *Achieving Sustainable Health Development in the African Region: Strategic Directions for WHO 2010–2015*. Brazzaville: WHO Regional Office for Africa

——— (2013) *Composition of the Executive Board*. Available at http://www.who.int/governance/eb/eb_composition/en/index.html [accessed 29 April 2013]

World Health Organization South Africa (2009) *2009 Annual Report*. Pretoria: WHO

World Health Organization, UNICEF & UNAIDS (2013) *Global Update on HIV Treatment 2013: Results, Impact and Opportunities*. WHO report in partnership with UNICEF and UNAIDS. Geneva: WHO

Wouters, E, Van Rensburg, HJ & Meulemans, H (2010) The National Strategic Plan of South Africa: What are the prospects of success after the repeated failure of previous AIDS policy? *Health Policy Plan* 25(3): 171–185

Wright, C (2012) *DFID South Africa: Review of the SARRAH Programme: November 2011 – January 2012*. Pretoria: DFID

Wright, S (ed.) (1999) *African Foreign Policies*. Boulder, Colorado: Westview Press

Wunder, S (2005) Payments for Environmental Services: Some Nuts and Bolts. *CIFOR Occasional Paper (42)*. Bogor, Indonesia: Center for International Forestry Research

WYG International Limited (2011) *Phase Two Evaluation of the Implementation of the Paris Declaration and Accra Agenda in South Africa: Final Country Evaluation Report*. Pretoria

Yamauchi, F (2005) Race, equity, and public schools in post-apartheid South Africa: Equal opportunity for all kids. *Economics of Education Review* 24(2): 213–233

—————— (2011) School quality, clustering and government subsidy in post-apartheid South Africa. *Economics of Education Review* 30(1): 146–156

Younas, J (2008) Motivation for bilateral aid allocation: Altruism or trade benefits. *European Journal of Political Economy* 24(3): 661–674

Younge, A & Fowkes, S (2003) The Cape Action Plan for the Environment: Overview of an ecoregional planning process. *Biological Conservation* 112(1-2): 15–28

Youssef, C (2005) World Bank priorities in education lending: An ever-changing endeavour. *Paterson Review – A Graduate Journal of International Affairs* 6: 1–29

Zaheer, A, McEvily, B & Perrone, V (1998) Does trust matter? Exploring the effects of interorganizational and interpersonal trust on performance. *Organization Science* 9(2): 141–159

Ziai, A (2010) Zur Kritik des Entwicklungsdiskurses. *Aus Politik und Zeitgeschichte* (10): 23–29

—————— (2011) Some Reflections on the Concept of 'Development'. *Working Paper Series (81)*. Bonn: University of Bonn, Center for Development Research

—————— (2014) Progressing towards incoherence: Development discourse since the 1980s. *Momentum Quarterly* 3(1)

Appendix

The following table provides a detailed list of interviews carried out in the context of this study. For reasons of anonymity, we do not provide names of informants but their official position, the organisation they were affiliated with at the time of the interview, and the sector they were engaged in. If more than one position is listed, the interview was carried out with two or three persons. The reference numbers on the right are the ones used for marking citations in the text.

Table 21: List of interviewees

Date	Organisation	Position	Sector	No.
		SOUTH AFRICA		
02.11.11	DFID	Senior Health Advisor	Health	1
31.10.11	GIZ	Programme Director Skills Development Programmes, Interview 1	Education	2
21.11.12	GIZ	Programme Director Skills Development Programmes, Interview 2	Education	3
02.11.11	GIZ	Programme Manager Multisectoral HIV/Aids Programme	Health	4
02.11.11	Swedish Embassy	Senior HIV/Aids Advisor & Programme Officer	Health	5
03.11.11	UNAIDS	Senior Policy & Programme Advisor	Health	6
02.11.11	UNDP	Principal Technical Advisor: Ecosystems and Environment	Environment	7
03.11.11	UNDP	Programme Manager Environment and Energy	Environment	8
04.11.11	US Embassy	Health Attaché	Health	9
19.11.12	World Bank	Regional Coordinator	General	10
01.11.11	WHO	Medical Officer HIV	Health	11
31.10.11	WHO	WHO Representative	Health	12
08.11.11	CapeNature	Executive Director: Environment Support Services	Environment	13
20.11.12	DEA	Chief Directorate – Environment Specialist	Environment	14
22.11.12	DEA	Head: Environment Planning	Environment	15
19.11.12	DEA	Director for Sustainable Development & Green Economy	Environment	16
23.11.12	DoH	Senior M&E and Research Specialist	Health	17
19.11.12	DoH	Director: Development Cooperation - International Relations	Health	18
19.11.12	DoH	Chief Director HIV and AIDS, STI	Health	19
21.11.12	DHET	DDG: Special Projects Unit	Education	20
21.11.12	DHET	Chief Director: International Relations	Education	21

Date	Organisation	Position	Sector	No.
20.11.12	DoL	DDG: Public Employment Services	Education	22
22.11.12	National Treasury	Chief Director International Development Cooperation	General	23
01.11.11	SANBI	Chief Executive Officer SANBI	Environment	24
09.11.11	SANBI	Director SANBI Fynbos Programme - CAPE Coordinator	Environment	25
04.11.11	SANBI	SANBI National Grasslands Programme Officer	Environment	26
01.11.11	Section27	Executive Director	Health	27
10.11.11	University of Western Cape	Professor, School of Public Health	Health	28
23.11.12	University of Witwatersrand	Professor, Wits Reproductive Health and HIV Institute	Health	29

		TANZANIA		
12.03.13	CIDA	First Secretary Development/Education Sector Team Leader	Education	30
09.05.12	CIDA	Education Advisor	Education	31
12.03.13	Consultant	Education expert	Education	32
07.05.12	Danida	Programme Officer Environment	Environment	33
06.03.13	Danida	Senior Advisor Health Policy, Planning and Management	Health	34
04.03.13	DFID	Education Advisor	Education	35
07.03.13	Finnish Embassy	Counsellor Natural Resources	Environment	36
10.05.12	GIZ	Programme Manager Health Coordination	Health	37
07.03.13	Netherlands Embassy	First Secretary Health & HIV/Aids	Health	38
04.05.12	Norway Embassy	Counsellor Environment and Climate Change	Environment	39
07.05.12	Swedish Embassy	First Secretary Education & Research	Education	40
08.05.12	UNDP	Practice Specialist Environment	Environment	41
08.05.12	USAID	Team Leader Education	Education	42
13.03.13	USAID	Health Office Director	Health	43
09.05.12	WHO	National Professional Officer Health Service Delivery National Professional Officer Managerial Processes for National Health Systems	Health	44
05.03.13	World Bank	Education Specialist	Education	45
03.05.12	World Bank	Senior Environmental Specialist	Environment	46
03.05.12	World Bank	Senior Health Specialist	Health	47
15.03.13	MoEVT	Officer Higher Education Department	Education	48

Date	Organisation	Position	Sector	No.
12.03.13	MoEVT	Director of Primary Education	Education	49
11.03.13	MoEVT	Assistant Director Monitoring & Evaluation Assistant Director Policy and Planning	Education	50
15.03.13	MoEVT	Assistant Director Teacher Education Department Officer Teacher Education Principal Education Officer	Education	51
10.05.12	MoHSW	prev. Chief Medical Officer	Health	52
01.05.12	MoHSW	prev. Chief Medical Officer	Health	53
04.03.13	MoHSW	Head of Health Care Financing	Health	54
13.03.13	MNRT	National Forest and Beekeeping Programme	Environment	55
05.03.13	MNRT	Assistant Director Policy and Planning	Environment	56
11.03.13	MNRT	Tanzania Forest Services, Publicity Officer	Environment	57
14.03.13	MNRT	prev. Director Forest and Beekeeping Division	Environment	58
07.03.13	NEMC	Senior Environment Management Officer	Environment	59
11.03.13	PMO-RALG	Permanent Secretary	Education	60
04.03.13	TACAIDS	Director of Finance and Administration	Health	61
08.03.13	TACAIDS	Director of Policy and Planning	Health	62
04.03.13	TACAIDS	Executive Chairman TACAIDS	Health	63
08.05.12	TACAIDS	prev. Executive Chairman TACAIDS	Health	64
05.03.13	TACAIDS	prev. Director of Policy and Planning TACAIDS	Health	65
09.05.12	VPO-DoE	prev. Director of Environment; Consultant	Environment	66
11.03.13	VPO-DoE	Director of Environment	Environment	67
07.03.13	Ifakara Health Institute	Lead Policy Translation Thematic Group	Health	68
06.03.13	University of Dar es Salaam	Professor, Institute for Resource Assessment	Environment	69
07.05.12	Twaweza	Head of Twaweza	Education	70
13.03.13	University of Bagamoyo	Professor, Educational Research and Psychology	Education	71
GERMANY				
17.01.12	GIZ	prev. Tanzania Portfolio Manager	General	72
06.02.12	GIZ	Public Health Consultant - prev. GIZ	Health	73